Science and Parascience

Also by Brian Inglis

THE FREEDOM OF THE PRESS IN IRELAND, 1784–1841
THE STORY OF IRELAND
REVOLUTION IN MEDICINE
WEST BRITON
FRINGE MEDICINE
A HISTORY OF MEDICINE
PRIVATE CONSCIENCE, PUBLIC MORALITY
DRUGS, DOCTORS AND DISEASE
ABDICATION
POVERTY AND THE INDUSTRIAL REVOLUTION
ROGER CASEMENT
THE FORBIDDEN GAME
THE OPIUM WAR
NATURAL AND SUPERNATURAL
THE BOOK OF THE BACK
NATURAL MEDICINE
THE DISEASES OF CIVILISATION
THE ALTERNATIVE HEALTH GUIDE (with Ruth West)

Science and Parascience

A history of the paranormal, 1914–1939

Brian Inglis

www.whitecrowbooks.com

Science and Parascience.

Copyright © 1984, 2022 by Brian Inglis. All rights reserved.

Published by White Crow Books: an imprint of White Crow Productions Ltd.

The right of Brian Inglis to be identified as the author of this work has been asserted in accordance with the Copyright, Design and Patents act 1988.

No part of this book may be reproduced, copied or used in any form or manner whatsoever without written permission, except in the case of brief quotations in reviews and critical articles.

For information, contact White Crow Books
by e-mail at info@whitecrowbooks.com.

Cover Design by Astrid@Astridpaints.com
Interior design by Velin Saramov

Paperback ISBN: 978-1-78677-189-6
eBook ISBN: 978-1-910121-02-3

Non Fiction / Body, Mind & Spirit / Parapsychology

www.whitecrowbooks.com

It is a stupid presumption to go about despising and condemning as false anything that seems to us improbable; this is a common fault among those who think they have more intelligence than the crowd. I used to be like that once, and if I heard talk of ghosts walking or prognostications of future events, of enchantments or sorceries, or some other tale I could not swallow, I would pity the poor people who were taken in by such nonsense. And now I find that I was at least as much to be pitied myself. Not that experience has since shown me anything that transcends my former beliefs, though this has not been for lack of curiosity; but reason has taught me to condemn anything so positively as false and impossible is to claim that our own brains have the privilege of knowing the bounds and limits of God's will, and of mother nature's power. I have learned too, that there is no more patent folly in the world than to reduce these things to the measure of our own power and capacity.

Montaigne: *Essays* (tr. J. M. Cohen)

Contents

	Introduction	11
1	The Forerunners	17
2	The First World War	46
3	Post-War Britain	67
4	The Continental Mediums 1918–24	95
5	The USA	141
6	The SPR in Decline	197
7	Mind over Matter	237
8	Extra-sensory Perception	260
9	Backlash	290
10	Balance Sheet	302
	Postscript	338
	Acknowledgments	343
	Sources	345
	Source References	356
	Index	371

Illustrations

	page
'Eva' during seances	30
'Eva's' parody portraits	31
Stanislawa Tomczyk	35
Raymond	51
Kathleen Goligher	79
'Freddy Jackson'	86
The Cottingley 'magnetic bath'	91
'Eva'	105
Kluski hands	122
Ossowiecki's drawing	137
'Margery' in the Houdini cage	167
'Margery' extruding an ectoplasmic hand	186
Mirabelli	224
A Mirabelli materialisation	225
The compote glass	262
'Some sort of grinning monster'	269
The 'Zener Cards'	272
The Ossowiecki experiments	286
Eleanor Sidgwick	303
Gladys Osborne Leonard	303
Sir Oliver Lodge	303
Sir William Barrett	303
Camille Flammarion	303
Dr W. J. Crawford	303

Introduction

In *Natural and Supernatural* I presented the historical evidence for psychic – or, as they are now more commonly described – paranormal phenomena. It was not my intention to 'sell' the paranormal: some reviewers, in fact, observed that I gave no indication of my own views about it. But those sceptics – using that term as it is generally used in this context, to describe people who cannot accept the paranormal's existence – who reviewed the book were in no doubt. Anybody who gave the evidence straight, without indicating that the sources must be tainted either by delusion or deception, must be a believer. C. P. Snow went further. The author of *Natural and Supernatural*, he asserted in his *Financial Times* review, clearly had a longing to believe, and 'not only such a longing, but a superlative capacity. He can believe in almost anything.'

Not so. To declare my preconceptions: I am an unreconstructed agnostic in these matters, with no 'beliefs', in the sense of believing in spirits, survival after death and the like; but I accept the evidence for the paranormal on precisely the same basis as I accept the evidence for, say, meteorites, or lightning, both of which were once in the supernatural category, but were taken out of it because the quantity of the evidence for them, and the quality of the sources, made continued scepticism impossible.

Lord Snow was confusing different kinds of belief, as his list showed: 'gods, spirits, reincarnation, immortality, various kinds of heaven, various kinds of hell, all kinds of after-life, divination, including divination via the entrails of birds or alternatively of playing cards, the influence of the stars, Velikovsky, flying saucers, perceiving the future – all the rest.' Only one of these is (or may be) paranormal: perceiving the future. Another is a device to try to exploit psychic powers: divination. The rest are all beliefs either in hypotheses – Velikovsky, astrology, flying saucers – or in religious teachings. As such they are of no concern to me, except where they impinge upon psychical research. And as it happens, the only belief of this kind which did have a significant impact between the wars was *dis*belief, of the kind Snow exemplified; the hostile scepticism of the scientific Establishment.

This is consequently the only form of belief which features most prominently in any survey of the evidence from this period for paranormal phenomena: extra-sensory perception (ESP) – telepathy, clairvoyance, precognition, retrocognition; telekinesis (now more commonly described as psychokinesis, or PK) – the action of mind or unaccounted for forces on matter; and hauntings of various kinds. Inevitably this involves dealing with diviners, mediums, psychics and sensitives, but it does not involve accepting their beliefs, or their interpretations of the phenomena. Indeed it does not necessitate accepting any interpretation, let alone any belief.

I want to stress this point, because too casual a use of the term 'belief' in this context has caused only confusion. We can accept reports, where the sources are reliable, of actual experiences without feeling the need to attach beliefs to them: for example, reports of 'seeing a ghost'. 'The tea-party question, "Do you believe in ghosts?", is one of the most ambiguous that can be asked,' Henry Habberley Price, Wykeham Professor of Logic at Oxford, pointed out some thirty years ago; 'but if we take it to mean "Do you believe that people sometimes experience apparitions?", the answer is that they certainly do.' No one who examined the evidence, he claimed, could possibly doubt that hundreds of people in their right minds have seen or heard somebody, often somebody they knew, who was not there. 'Instead of disputing the facts,' Price argued, 'we must try to explain them.'

Needless to say – or it should be needless to say – the experience of seeing an apparition is not necessarily paranormal. It may on investigation be attributed to illusion, or to a practical joke. My own view, however, is that there is now far too much evidence for paranormal experiences to account for all of them in such terms. And if I am told that I am indulging in a quibble, because this amounts to a *belief*, I can only cite Henri Bergson, who claimed he believed in telepathy for the same reason that he believed in the defeat of the Spanish Armada in 1588: 'My belief is not the mathematical certainty that the demonstration of Pythagoras's theorem gives me,' he explained; 'it is not the physical certainty that I have of the law of the fall of bodies; but it is at least all the certainty that we can obtain in a historical or judicial matter.'

I would go further, and echo the Swiss psychologist, Théodor Flournoy, when he had to admit that his scepticism about the

Introduction

existence of telekinetic forces emanating from mediums had been eroded by what he had witnessed. 'There is no question here of conviction, in the moral, religious or philosophical sense of the term,' he was careful to insist. 'This belief is for me devoid of all vital importance; it does not move any essential fibre of my being and I would not feel the least inclination to submit to the slightest martyrdom in my defence.'

As it happens, the period covered in *Science and Parascience* makes it easier to disclaim any 'longing to believe'. I had thought 1914 was a convenient stopping-off point for *Natural and Supernatural* because the First World War brought the initial phase of psychical research to a close, and the second phase did not begin until twenty years later, with the publication of J. B. Rhine's *Extra-sensory Perception*. But though the war did cause some disruption of research, it was far less than I had thought; and the 1920s were a period of intense research activity, some of it of a high quality, and productive of positive results. If they have since been ridiculed by sceptics, and brushed under the carpet by psychical researchers, the main reason, I am sure, is not merely that they are hard to credit, but also that they are so often embarrassing, and sometimes repulsive.

In my experience, what most psychical researchers would like to obtain would be simple but clear-cut proofs of the reality of extra-sensory perception, or the ability of mind to influence matter (some, but by no means all, also hope for evidence pointing to survival after death). But the last thing they want is what they so often, particularly in this inter-war period, have obtained from, say, exhibitions of mediumship, with trumpets flying around darkened rooms, or ectoplasm erupting into grotesque forms.

I cited Maeterlinck's comment in *The Unknown Guest*, in 1914, and it is equally relevant to the era that followed: the 'unknown guest' being the disembodied manipulator of the paranormal forces involved – for what is particularly disconcerting about them is that so often they appear to *be* manipulated, as if by some entity, 'facetious, teasing, arch, or simply sleepy, bewildered, inconsistent, absent-minded'. The 'guest' 'readily performs the most glamorous feats of sleight-of-hand, provided that we can derive no profit from them,' Maeterlinck complained. 'It lifts up tables, moves the heaviest articles, produces flowers and hair, sets strings vibrating, gives life to inanimate objects and passes through solid matter, conjures up ghosts, subjugates time and space, creates light; but all, it seems, on one condition, that its performances should be without rhyme or reason, and keep to the provinces of supernaturally vain and puerile recreations.'

'Puerile' is often the appropriate word. Yet as many an eminent scientist has pointed out, it is anomalies, and often the most irritatingly trivial-looking anomalies, which compel reassessments and sometimes lead to revolutionary changes. The story of Newton's apple may be a myth, but it is an appropriate myth: and if an apple actually materialised out of the air or levitated to a height of six inches, the event would surely be significant. I have no 'longing to believe' in materialisations (or levitations) of apples, or tables – let alone of people; but the range and quality of the evidence for phenomena of this kind deserves to be better known.

There is one other problem which I have found even more difficult to deal with here than in *Natural and Supernatural*: the fact that the phenomena, when they are not trivial, can be literally incredible, and an affront to common sense. The difficulty here is that the more recent in time the reports, the more difficult they are to stomach. All of us have what Renée Haynes, the author of a recent history of the Society for Psychical Research, has engagingly called a 'boggle-threshold'; and although public opinion polls in Western countries have been showing that readiness to accept some psychic phenomena is increasing – the great majority of people in Britain, for example, from 70 to 80 per cent, now accept ESP – boggle-thresholds for others remain low. Far fewer people, I suspect, would now accept ectoplasmic materialisations than would have accepted them half a century ago.

The temptation has been to leave out some of the more grotesque manifestations of the period, and to concentrate upon the research into, say, telepathy, or precognition. It is a temptation which I have felt bound to resist, for the reason I gave in *Natural and Supernatural*, citing the words of the eminent mathematician, Augustus de Morgan, when he was confronted with the same problem in the 1850s. People like himself, he said, who had observed certain happenings, were sometimes reproached for their failure to accommodate their reports 'to the swallow of their hearers'. But he felt bound to follow the legal principle which calls upon judges, if they hear counsel say to a witness 'do you expect the jury to believe . . . ?', to intervene: 'The witness is to mind his *truth*; the jury will take care of the credibility.'

I have tried to summarise the evidence for supernormal phenomena (as they were usually called in this period) without distorting it; but in fairness to those who provided it, I should add that

Introduction

their work ought not to be criticised on the strength, or weakness, of my version. Nobody who reads the accounts of their investigations could fail to be struck by the patient, painstaking way in which the leading psychical researchers sought to overcome the difficulties that confronted them, and it is impossible adequately to sum up in a few sentences a series of tests whose records fill a book. Where sceptics have too often erred in the past is in criticising the evidence second-hand, as it were, often on the basis of earlier, and also second-hand, criticism, without going back to the original source material. It is still there, in abundance. It should first be studied, if it is to be seriously attacked.

1 The Forerunners

Until the eighteenth century it had been taken for granted by the great majority of philosophers and scientists that there were phenomena which could only be explained in terms of the existence of a spirit world. The motive force behind them might be neutral, like magnetism; but it could be wielded for good by God and his angels, and for evil by the devil and his demons. A few individuals, too, could wield it: witches, sorcerers, alchemists. It enabled some people to report what was happening at a distance – clairvoyance; to read people's minds – thought-transference; to see into the past and the future; to move objects without using physical force; to heal the sick; to put a hex on healthy men and women. When exploited by a saintly individual, the use of the force was deemed miraculous; otherwise it was usually regarded as diabolic, except where it occurred too frequently and too casually, as in glimpses of the future in dreams.

The force itself had been taken to be natural: 'miracles' occurred when God was using it, or when he granted the power to his chosen few to exploit it. But after the Renaissance the term 'supernatural' came in, along with the idea that the force operated *outside* nature's laws according to the will, or the whim, of God. And with the development of mechanist theories, belief in the existence of the force came to be regarded as an occultist illusion, and the phenomena as superstitions. There were no miracles, David Hume argued. Miracles were contrary to the uniform experience of mankind, 'and as a uniform experience amounts to a proof, there is here a direct and full proof, from the nature of the fact, against the existence of any miracle.'

In ordinary circumstances, the fallacy should have been obvious. Miraculous happenings might not have been common, but they had happened often enough, and been sufficiently well-attested, to show that experience had *not* been uniform. But by this time scientists were longing for mechanist certainties; miracles did not fit into the new pattern of science. The assumption grew that there were natural laws, which could not be broken. They were supposed

Science and Parascience

to be derived from mathematical calculations, and up to a point they were; but the interpretations often were not. Thus the law of gravity became Newton's monument; but the fact that it revealed that matter could act on matter at a distance was not taken into consideration when dismissing as supernatural, and consequently as spurious, the unaccountable movements of material objects so often reported in, say, accounts of hauntings. Clairvoyance, thought-transference, prevision, spiritual healing and many more were also bundled unceremoniously into superstition's lumber room.

How unwise this was ought to have become obvious from a humiliation which the new orthodoxy suffered for rejecting meteorites as a superstition lingering on from the time when Jove was thought to punish erring mortals by hurling his thunderbolts. But when the evidence for their reality had eventually to be conceded, early in the nineteenth century, scientists did not learn humility: they simply congratulated themselves upon having corrected the errors of their predecessors. And from this time on the great majority of them declined to accept even the possibility that those phenomena which had been classified as superstitions ought to be regarded as natural, but as yet unexplained.

In the course of the century, however, the new orthodoxy was subjected to a series of shocks. Disciples of Mesmer, exploring the trance state, found that some mesmerised subjects were capable of producing what came to be known as the 'higher phenomena', the commonest of which was a form of second sight: 'travelling clairvoyance'. Asked what was happening somewhere at a distance, they would 'visit' the place and give a description whose accuracy could be subsequently verified. Some of the most distinguished scientists of the era, confronted with the evidence, found themselves reluctantly compelled to accept it as genuine, and in 1831 a commission of enquiry set up by the French Academy of the Sciences confirmed that clairvoyance had been satisfactorily demonstrated. But by this time scepticism on the Hume model was established; its report was set aside.

The second of the shocks was felt in the 1850s, with the craze for table-turning. All over America and Europe families and groups of friends sat around tables in darkness or near-darkness, waiting for raps, tilts, and unaccountable movements. Even the most diehard of sceptics could not seriously claim that the movements did not happen, or were faked; but Faraday saved their faces by reporting an experiment which, he claimed, revealed that the effects were

The Forerunners

the result of unconscious muscular pressure. The experiment was bogus, in that it only showed how unconscious muscular pressure could move loose table *tops* – not the tables themselves; but it served its purpose, and gradually the table-turning craze died away.

Connected with table-turning, however, were other phenomena which appeared to suggest that the evidence for the belief in spirits had not been invalidated, after all, by the march of science. Spiritualist mediums began to make their reputations by producing a variety of manifestations, some of which were very similar to those which the Church for centuries had claimed as miracles. And the career of one of the mediums in the Victorian era, Daniel Dunglas Home, was so well documented by contemporaries that it still remains the most difficult to explain away of all the evidence for what, in this period, came to be called psychical phenomena.

Daniel Dunglas Home

For twenty years, with only occasional gaps when his powers deserted him, Home gave seances to friends and acquaintances, two or three times a week. The effects varied, and sometimes nothing happened; but usually rapping noises could be heard from around the room, and in due course the seance table could be felt by the sitters to shudder, before starting to move around, rear up on two legs, and rise in the air while the sitters' fingertips were on top, touching it lightly (or not at all). Musical instruments, brought by visitors and left in a corner of the room, would begin to play, often soulfully. Disembodied hands appeared and circled round the table; sitters could inspect them, touch them, shake them (they felt like real hands, but if anybody tried to cling on to them they melted away). If pen and paper were on an adjacent table, the pen might write messages, purporting to come from deceased persons, and apparently in their handwriting. On a few occasions, Home himself levitated, floating over the sitters' heads; or he would literally play with fire, stirring up the hot coals with his hands, carrying them around, even bathing his face in them.

It was not simply these effects, many of which were the commonplace of seances, that were striking; so, also, were the circumstances in which they were produced. There could be no question of conjuring tricks; not merely were the seances often held in houses Home had never been to before, in rooms he had never entered until the seance began; they were held in daylight, or gaslight, or by the light of a fire – good enough light, almost always, for the eight or nine people present to watch Home, and satisfy themselves that he was not using hands or feet or gadgetry of any kind. And he had no assistant to play the tricks while he himself was being watched.

Neither were the sitters credulous believers. Many of them admitted they had been sceptical, even derisive; and they represented a fair cross section of the ruling classes, including royalty – the Tsar Alexander II, the Emperor Napoleon III, and Queen Sophie of the Netherlands; members of the aristocracies of several European countries; literary lions, among them Elizabeth Barrett Browning, Thomas Augustus Trollope, Thackeray, Lytton, Ruskin; eminent scientists, Alfred Russel Wallace, William Crookes, and Francis Galton – along with many other men and women whose names were familiar, even household words, in their own time. Famous conjurors, too, came to his seances hoping to be able to catch him out; but they all went away disappointed. And as he refused to take any payment for his seances, those who hoped to accuse him of cupidity could point only to a venial willingness to accept the hospitality of the rich and famous. Home's private life, too, was by all accounts impeccable. It could hardly have been otherwise without detection, as he was just about the best-known international figure, bar a few crowned heads and famous statesmen, of his era.

When, towards the end of his career, Home was asked to demonstrate his powers in laboratory trials, he willingly consented. In tests by Alexander von Boutlerow in Russia, and William Crookes in England, Home showed that he was able to produce telekinetic effects at a distance which could be recorded and measured on weighing machines. And when illness terminated his career as a medium in 1874, although he had often been denounced as a trickster, nobody had ever detected him in any attempt at trickery during a seance.

The Society for Psychical Research

Fortunately for the peace of mind of sceptics, however, mediumship had by this time taken a course which brought it into disrepute. One of the other mediums whom Crookes tested, Florence Cook, produced 'full form' materialisations – to all appearances living human beings; and other mediums followed. Naturally sceptics assumed that these 'materialisations' were the mediums themselves, or accomplices smuggled into the seance; and sometimes trickery was exposed. What was needed, some of the more responsible spiritualists (as they had come to call themselves: with a capital 'S' where they looked upon their belief as a religion) realised, was a more systematic investigation of the phenomena.

This happened also to be the view of a young scientist, William Barrett, Professor of Physics in the Royal College of Science in Dublin, who had been impressed by demonstrations of the 'higher phenomena' of mesmerism. In 1876 he read a paper on thought-transference at the annual meeting of the British Association for the Advancement of Science – to the fury of some of its members, one of whom wrote to *The Times* to say its proceedings had been 'degraded'; and six years later Barrett took up a suggestion made to him by a leading spiritualist, Dawson Rogers, and convened the meeting which gave birth to the Society for Psychical Research (SPR), with the Cambridge philosopher, Henry Sidgwick, one of the most respected figures in the British academic world at the time, as President, and his friends Frederic Myers and Edmund Gurney as Joint Honorary Secretaries.

They shared a conviction that, as Myers put it, 'The deep questions thus at issue must be fought out in a way more thorough than the champions either of religion or of materialism had yet suggested'; they must be resolved by experiment and observation, 'by the application to phenomena within us and around us of precisely the same methods of deliberate, dispassionate exact enquiry which have built up our actual knowledge of the world which we can touch and see.' Five investigating committees were set up: one to deal with 'the extent of any influence which may be exerted by one mind upon another', other than through the normal sensory channels; one with 'hypnotism and the forms of so-called mesmeric trance, with its alleged immunity to pain'; one with 'sensitives' to find whether they 'possess any power of perception beyond a highly exalted sensibility of the recognised sensory organs'; one with apparitions and 'disturbances in houses reputed to be haunted'; and one with 'the various physical phenomena commonly called Spiritualistic, with an attempt to discover their causes and general laws'.

For a time, all went well. It was not easy for sceptics to dismiss out of hand the work of an organisation whose members included scientists of the calibre of Crookes, Wallace, Lord Rayleigh, Oliver Lodge, Balfour Stewart and J. J. Thomson, along with eminences in other fields: Arthur Balfour, and his brother Gerald; Gladstone, Tennyson, Ruskin, and Lewis Carroll. On a visit to Boston, too, Barrett brought together a group of distinguished academic figures to form an American Society; among them William James, who was shortly to be appointed Professor of Philosophy at Harvard.

James had been impressed by what he had heard in England from the Cambridge trio, Myers in particular; and when the opportunity came to investigate a medium who was making a reputation for herself in Boston, Mrs Leonora Piper, he decided to take it, sceptical though he was about her powers. The outcome was significant. James was gradually forced to the conclusion that she was genuine; she could not have collected the information which she gave him and others, even by an elaborate intelligence network. Yet the mechanics of the process by which it was transmitted were distinctly dubious, in that the purported source of the information, her spirit 'control', was not what he claimed to be.

Most mediums received and relayed their information while in a trance state through 'communicators', assumed to be the spirits of the dead: and usually there was a 'control', a spirit who, as it were, lined up and introduced the appropriate 'communicators' to individual sitters who wanted to reassure themselves that their loved ones lived on in the spirit. These 'controls' were often American Indians, or improbable-sounding small children, which was not calculated to inspire confidence in doubters (one of the most often encountered in Europe, 'John King', actually claimed to have been a pirate in his lifetime). Mrs Piper's control, 'Dr Phinuit', was to show that doubts were justified; his account of his life as a doctor in France was checked and found to be false, and he faded out, to be replaced by other 'controls'. But these, too, could also easily be taken in by sitters pretending to have a dead relative, who would promptly be paraded as a 'communicator'.

To James, this made Mrs Piper's mediumship of even greater psychological interest and concern. The processes by which she received her information might be hopelessly confused; yet he felt 'as absolutely certain as of any personal fact in the world that she knows things in her trances which she cannot possibly have heard in her waking state'; a verdict which Oliver Lodge, in Britain, also reached after testing her. Lodge even found that she knew things relating to his family which he did not know, and which she could not possibly have known, but which when he checked them proved to be correct.

Eusapia Palladino

One of the implications ought to have been obvious: that deception practised by an entranced medium should not be taken as evidence of conscious fraud. But on this issue, Sidgwick was confused. He had already laid down that the results obtained with mediums or 'psychics' would be retrospectively set aside if they were later caught cheating, and that they would not again be investigated on the society's behalf. The rule had originally been applied when two sisters who had demonstrated telepathic abilities were caught signalling to each other, though in earlier trials they had not been in a position to cheat, which was harsh enough; but the consequences of enforcing the rule were to be even more unfortunate when, in the 1890s, a medium emerged whose capacity to produce what were commonly described as the physical phenomena of spiritualism was second only to that of D. D. Home: Eusapia Palladino.

Of peasant stock, Eusapia had none of Home's *savoir faire*, but she had almost as extensive a repertoire. Her powers were displayed in what by this time were becoming familiar ways. The seance-room table would shift around, rising up on one leg and often leaving the floor altogether, though her feet and hands were being held; objects at a distance from the sitters would move, and fly around over their heads; musical instruments would sound (though they did not play as well as they had for Home). And there was one element which had only rarely been a feature of Home's seances: mischief. The sitters would feel themselves being prodded or pinched; their spectacles were taken off their noses; their cravats and their shoelaces were untied.

In the matter of illumination, Eusapia's seances were less impressive than Home's. Her 'control' – the ubiquitous 'John King' – dictated how much light would be permitted. But this was not quite the problem that it might have been because, by a fortunate dispensation, the more confident the entranced Eusapia felt in her powers, the more light 'John King' was prepared to allow, as if he liked to bask in reflected credit. And in one respect, Eusapia's career was to be even more impressive than Home's. Her mediumship was carefully investigated by several of the most eminent scientists in Europe, in Italy, Poland, Germany and France. Most of them were reluctantly forced to the conclusion that it was genuine; and even those who refused to accept the possibility of telekinetic phenomena were unable to account for the effects which she produced.

In her trance states, however, her investigators had soon found that Eusapia was not to be trusted: she would stealthily free a hand or a foot from control, if she were permitted to, and use it, say, to assist the movement of the table. She did not deny this; she was not accountable for her behaviour, she claimed, when entranced, and it was up to her investigators to take suitable precautions, which usually they did. But when in 1895 she was invited to Cambridge to demonstrate her powers, although in some seances she did so very effectively (impressing, among others, Lord Rayleigh and J. J. Thomson), Sidgwick's protégé Richard Hodgson let her cheat in a test. When she did, he claimed to have exposed her; a claim which Sidgwick upheld, ruling that as fraud must have been used 'from first to last', she could not be tested further on the SPR's behalf.

The result was that the society was cut off from participation in trials of the most promising subject to have appeared since Home's retirement. Over the next years Eusapia was subjected to a series of tests by European scientists, in which strict precautions were taken to ensure she could not supplement her psychic powers with physical force; and she came through them all successfully, including a protracted series from 1905 to 1908 conducted by Professor Jules Courtier of the Sorbonne, with such colleagues as Henri Bergson, Jean-Baptiste Perrin, Jacques-Arsène d'Arsonval and the Curies. Only then did Eleanor Sidgwick, who after her husband's death had become effectively the director of the SPR, sanction a further investigation on its behalf to be undertaken by three deeply sceptical men, all with experience of sleight-of-hand and of exposing bogus mediums: Hereward Carrington, an American who had written a book largely devoted to descriptions of the tricks mediums played; Wortley Baggally, an accomplished conjuror whose boast it was that he had investigated most of the best-known mediums in Britain without finding one who was genuine; and the Hon. Everard Feilding, assistant Hon. Secretary of the SPR and, by his own admission, a sceptic about physical mediumship.

Their report, written by Feilding, remains a classic exposition of the pains of conversion. The ordinary reaction to a bizarre fact from a balanced mind, he observed in his summing up, is to reject it. 'Tables, we knew, or thought we knew, do not go into the air by themselves; curtains do not bulge out without some mechanical agency; and although we saw them do so, we still refused to believe that they did.' They had preferred to assume at the start that she must be deceiving, or hallucinating, them. Painfully, they had been forced to realise that they were being guided not by their observation but by their emotions – the very guide which, in their arrogance, they had assumed they would be able to set aside in the course of carrying out their appointed task.

At this point, telekinesis was nearer to acceptance than it has ever been, before or since; but scientists in the United States remained to be converted, and Carrington arranged for her to cross the Atlantic in 1910. Unluckily he did not have the backing of the American SPR, run at the time by James Hervey Hyslop, who had been Professor of Logic at Columbia University until he had given up his Chair in order to devote the remainder of his life to psychical research, at his own expense. He was a man of manifest integrity, and he succeeded in reanimating the American SPR; but he was not in sympathy with Carrington, and found the physical phenomena of mediumship repulsive. His assumption was that Eusapia must be fraudulent; but he regarded her as a hysteric (hysterics, as Charcot had demonstrated, were capable of superhuman feats, such as bending their bodies backwards into the shape of a rainbow; and this, Hyslop realised, could be confused with supernormal feats). She ought to be investigated as a victim of a mental disorder, he argued, rather than as a medium; and he refused to have anything to do with her.

Carrington, however, hoped he could enlist William James as a supporter. James had earlier expressed his distaste for what he had described as 'this particularly crass and low type of supernatural phenomenon', and like the Sidgwicks had resisted accepting it. But at a seance in 1908 he had himself observed the movement of objects in good light, 'the phenomena being slow enough, and often enough repeated, to leave my own mind in no doubt at the time as to what was witnessed'; and although he remained uncertain whether to accept the evidence of his own eyes, he noted in an article in *The American Magazine* the following year that Eusapia was still making converts of some of the most eminent scientists in Europe, 'and of our own psychical researcher, Carrington, whose book on *The Physical Phenomena of Spiritualism* (against them, rather!) makes his conquest strategically important'. But this turned out to be the last report James was ever to make on psychical research. He managed to attend one seance with Eusapia (noting 'queer twisting of my chair'), but news of his brother Henry's serious illness caused him to leave for England, so that he was not available to exercise his authority when the crisis broke. And when he returned that summer he was mortally ill, barely surviving the journey; he died a few days after he had reached home.

In the meantime, there had been a repetition of the Cambridge fiasco fifteen years before. The two most vocal opponents of psychical research in the United States at the time were Hugo Muensterberg, James's successor at Harvard, and Joseph Jastrow, Professor of Psychology at the University of Wisconsin. Muensterberg had asserted that what were claimed to be psychic facts 'do not exist, and never will exist'; Jastrow thought they 'could only be attributed to fraud, hallucination and mental disorder'. They followed the course set by Hodgson. In a trial, when Eusapia was in her trance she was allowed to extricate a foot from control; it was caught by a conjuror who had been smuggled in for that purpose; and, as Muensterberg described the episode in the *Metropolitan Magazine*, 'she responded with the wild scream which indicated that she knew at last that she was trapped, and her glory was shattered'.

Eusapia had warned her investigators in advance that in her trance state, she would free a foot or a hand if she was allowed to; and afterwards she protested that her cry when her foot was seized was the natural reaction to her trance being broken, not an admission of guilt. Yet the best testimonial that her powers were genuine came, paradoxically, from Muensterberg himself. So gratified was he by the success of his coup that in his report he wrote that her achievement before she had actually been caught had been 'splendid'; she had managed while her hands were securely held to insert her loosened foot under her chair and up behind the curtain at their backs, 'without changing in the least the position of her body', to enable her to 'play thumb and fingers' with his hip, arm and neck. 'I felt perfectly the hand and the fingers, which was far from agreeable.'

Ironically it was another sceptic, Stanley L. Krebs, who pointed out that for Muensterberg's recollection to be a correct description, 'it would be necessary for Eusapia's leg to be articulated at the knee, upon a motionless hip, making a rotation of about 135°, as well as an elongation of almost double its length', and 'a transformation of a foot into a hand which grasped him between the thumb and fingers'. It was consequently necessary, Krebs argued, to reject Muensterberg's explanation, and find a better one. Years later Hyslop, too, was to admit that at the time, he had received some telling evidence in Eusapia's favour, which he had not reported because of his conviction that she ought to be given treatment for her hysteria, rather than exploited for psychical research. One of the sitters who had been involved in the exposure had told him that some of the phenomena witnessed earlier had been inexplicable; another sitter, a distinguished scientist (Hyslop did not disclose his identity) 'had stated privately his personal conviction that some of the phenomena were genuine'; and another, who at the time had put his name to Muensterberg's report, had later claimed that he had done so only under protest. But these revelations were not published until 1919; and by then, Eusapia was dead. She had continued on occasions to produce phenomena; but the reports from her investigators were no longer taken seriously. It was generally assumed that her exposure had been devastating and final.

'Eva C.'

How, then, were the finger-and-thumb pinches administered which Muensterberg – and many earlier investigators – delivered? In the course of the Cambridge tests Mrs Myers, who had been brought in to keep control of Eusapia's feet, had been able from her position on the floor to see in the dim light the medium's back outlined against the ceiling; and in her notes she had described seeing what looked to her like 'prolongations', each 'like the neck of a swan' emerging from Eusapia's body. Her sister-in-law Mrs Stanley, wife of the explorer, also saw what looked like a human hand growing out of Eusapia's back. Visible or invisible, these additional limbs were so commonly encountered at seances that they had acquired the name of 'pseudopods'; and it was in the years leading up to the First World War that for the first time they could be systematically investigated, owing to the availability of a young medium who could produce them and other manifestations, and who was prepared to give her full time to working with psychical researchers.

As a young girl, growing up in Algiers, Marthe Béraud had been found to be a powerful physical medium; and hearing of her feats, Charles Richet had gone to Algiers in 1905 to investigate. Richet had made his name both as a physiologist and as a psychologist – specialisation had not then erected its barriers; he had been one of the researchers who helped to legitimise hypnosis, in the course of which he had encountered the 'higher phenomena'; and after protracted tests of Eusapia he had reluctantly come to the conclusion that the physical phenomena were genuine, too. Marthe's effects were even harder to accept: she could produce 'full form' materialisations. Most mediums who had produced them before had been able to do so only when hidden in a 'cabinet' – normally a curtained-off recess, or corner of a room; Richet to his astonishment saw the whole process.

'A kind of liquid jelly' – for which he coined the term 'ectoplasm' – emerged from her, Richet reported, organising itself into 'the shape of a face or a limb'. Sometimes the forms were imperfect; sometimes two-dimensional, 'so that in spite of oneself, one is inclined to imagine some fraud'. But even if the medium had been able to secrete muslin, or some such substance, on or in her person, how – he asked himself – could she make it gradually take on a succession of different shapes, whether two-dimensional or complete? And once, Richet saw a 'full form' materialisation of the kind Crookes had reported with 'Katie King'; but whereas 'Katie' had emerged from behind curtains, Richet watched the ectoplasm gradually take shape, and then disappear, from start to finish.

Richet was able to observe Marthe in unusually satisfactory conditions. 'The light was ample for perfect visibility; the proximity very close indeed; the time often very long, enabling me to observe closely every detail.' Even if she had had an accomplice in the house, he insisted that it would have been impossible to generate, under his eyes, 'those clouds which developed into bony and mobile masses just in front of me'. From his observation, he felt he could describe the stages in the formation of ectoplasm. Initially 'a whitish steam, perhaps luminous, taking the shape of gauze or muslin, in which there develops a hand or an arm that gradually gains consistency', it would then begin to make what he described as *personal* movements; 'it creeps, rises from the ground, and puts forth tentacles like an amoeba'. It was not necessarily connected with the medium, but it usually was; and it emanated from her.

Inevitably there had been accusations of trickery. A coachman who had been with the family, but had been sacked, put it about that it was he who had 'materialised'; but as there had been 'full form' materialisations into which he could not have fitted, and as

The Forerunners

he had not been present at the seances, how could he, and the other performers of Marthe's varied materialised roles, have gained access? A lawyer who was a friend of the family eventually came up with an explanation. He, too, had not been at the seances, but he claimed that when he had taxed Marthe with cheating she had broken down and confessed that there had been a trapdoor in the angle of the room curtained off as the 'cabinet' through which, 'when the room had been darkened, a young girl was introduced'. Marthe's part had been secondary, as she only had to pretend to be asleep while the other girl played the 'materialisations'. 'She was very repentant at having set her hand to trickery', the lawyer complacently recalled; but she put forward, 'as her constant excuse, the compulsory role of medium which she had been obliged to play and the existence of the trapdoor'.

Richet's reply was characteristically blunt: 'Well! Nothing is easier than to ascertain the existence of a trapdoor.' There was no trapdoor. The lawyer lamely excused himself by saying that he had not himself been responsible for the trapdoor hypothesis – he had heard about it from Marthe. Either his story of the confession was an invention, or, more probably, Marthe had been pulling his leg – understandably, as he had told her he knew she must be a cheat.

Still, stories of such confessions tend to come into common currency and stay there, after the denials are forgotten. Marthe had decided, or was persuaded, that her talents as a physical medium ought to be more systematically investigated, under conditions which would rule out any possibility of trickery. In 1910 she had put herself into the hands of a well-off and shrewd Parisian woman of the world, Juliette Bisson, with whom she took up residence. Mme Bisson enlisted the help first of Richet, and later of Baron Schrenck-Notzing, one of the most dedicated and experienced of the investigators of physical mediums; and Marthe was subjected to a series of carefully controlled trials.

The results were published in two works, Mme Bisson's in French and Schrenck's in German, in the winter of 1913–14. Taken at their face value, they constituted easily the most striking evidence for the reality of the physical phenomena of mediumship which had so far appeared in book form. Not merely did the investigators reproduce the actual notes taken at the sessions; they provided scores of photographs illustrating what they, along with other investigators, scientists, academics and doctors, had seen.

Striking evidence, however, is not necessarily convincing evi-

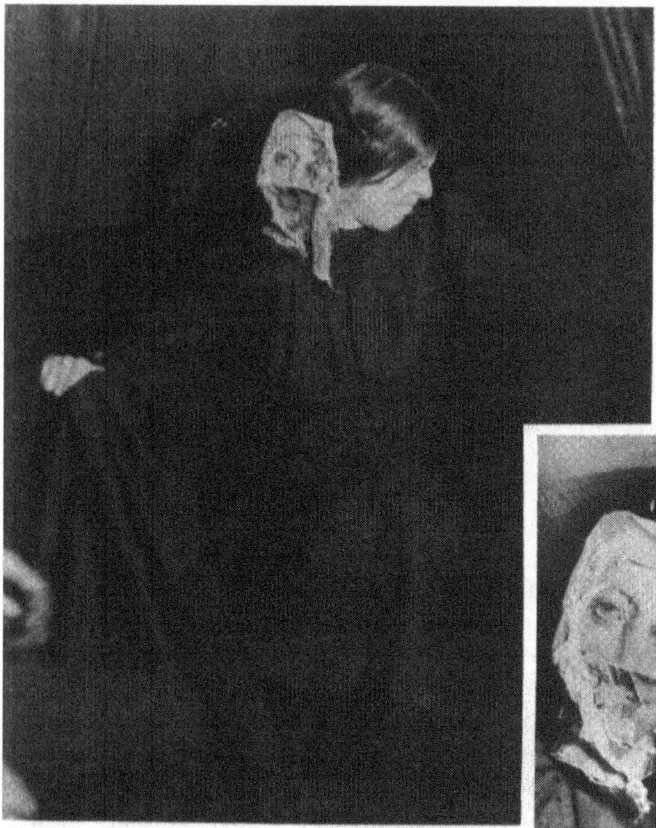

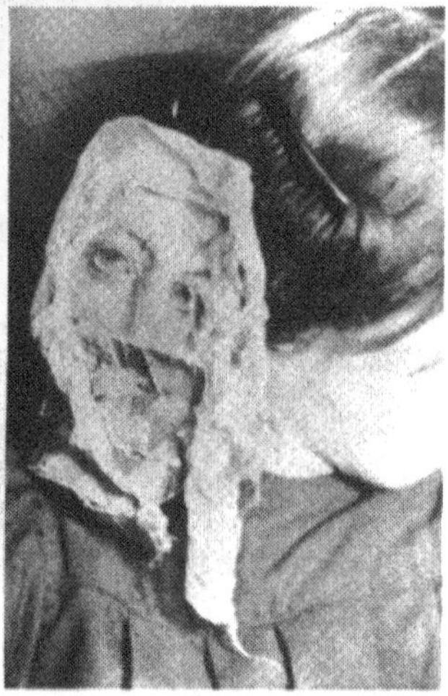

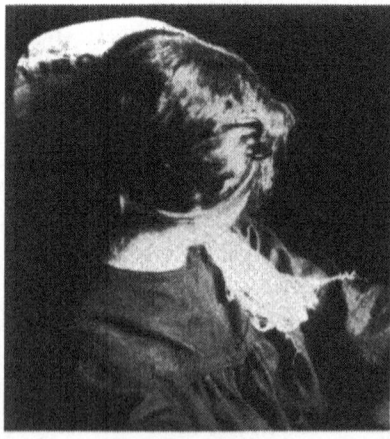

One of 'Eva's' early productions (8 May, 1912) was of a type that became familiar to her investigators: flawed portraits, looking like pictures on pie-crust.

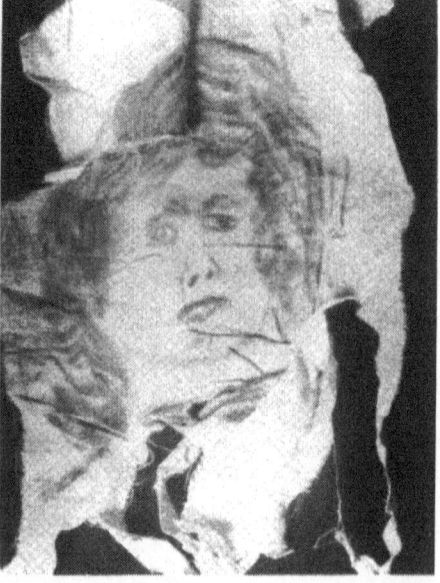

One of 'Eva's' chiffon-like productions.

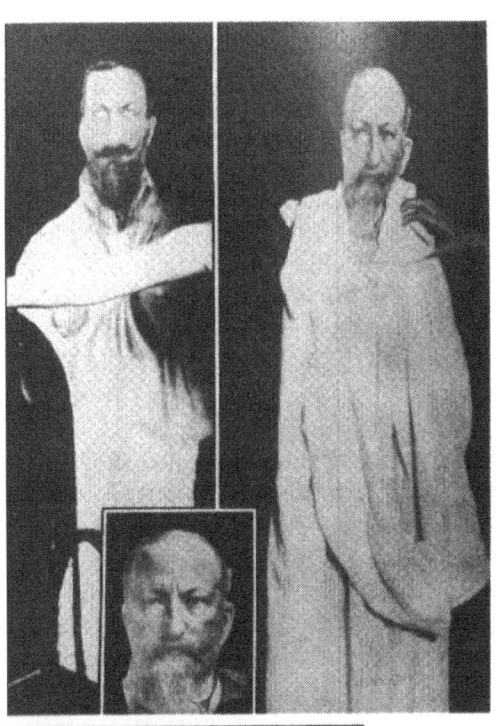

'Eva' produced a string of parody portraits derived from what she had seen in periodicals, ranging from President Wilson to Paris models. This trio, with the originals, were among those which Schrenk included in his *Phenomena of Materialisation*: the King of Bulgaria (left), Monna Dilze (below right) and President Poincaré (below left).

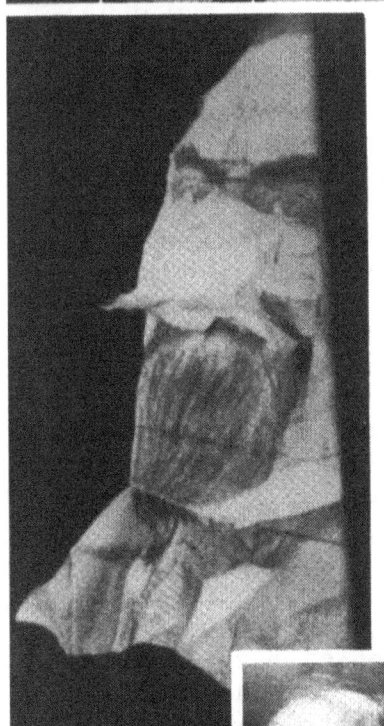

dence; and paradoxically the photographs actually cast doubt upon the validity of the trials, by straining credibility even for people who accepted physical phenomena. As Richet had occasionally noticed in the Algiers seances, some of the most remarkable of the materialisations looked like cut-outs made of paper, or of some flimsy material such as chiffon. Sometimes they even had a creased or crumpled look, as if they had been tightly folded and then spread out, needing to be ironed.

This in itself would have sufficed to arouse suspicion; but there was an even more dubious aspect, which was pounced upon by a writer in a Paris magazine (characteristically it was a magazine devoted to occult subjects: only later was it picked up and splashed in *Le Matin* and other leading newspapers in Europe). In one of the photographs 'Eva C.' (as it had been decided to call Marthe, to try to preserve her anonymity) appeared to have a paper cut-out attached behind her head, on which were the letters MIRO. This, the writer of the article pointed out, was in fact part of the masthead of the Paris journal *Le Miroir*, and some of the other 'materialisations' of the two-dimensional kind were blown-up cut-outs from that journal.

At first sight this looked damning, and inevitably it was cited, then and later, as proof of fraud. But a study of the evidence about 'MIRO' in the transcript made at the time of the seance showed that it was noted by Schrenck, who recognised it as the masthead: 'I can not form any opinion,' she had observed, 'of this curious result.' At the next seance, 'Eva' herself explained while in her trance (hypnotically-induced, as usual, by Mme Bisson) that she had wanted to send Madame Bisson the written thought that she was 'Eva's' mirror; and this was how the 'thought' had emerged. On examination, too, it was found that the faces which had appeared at the seances, and had been photographed, although they did indeed resemble some which had appeared in *Le Miroir*, were not copies. They looked more like parodies.

This did not, of course, prove that 'Eva' had not cheated. She could have prepared the parodies herself, and smuggled them in. But how? Before each session she was stripped and searched, and brought into the seance room either dressed in a close-fitting garment or naked. The cut-outs were often life-size; how could she have expected to bring them in, time after time, without being detected? Experienced researchers such as Richet and Schrenck could not have allowed themselves to be tricked in so elementary a fashion; and the stock explanation which sceptics commonly adopted in such cases, that psychical researchers' minds became enfeebled, could hardly be applied in Richet's case, as in 1913 he was awarded the Nobel Prize for his work in neuro-physiology.

Two German sceptics who had attended seances with Schrenck in Munich, Dr Walter von Gulat-Wellenburg and Dr Mathilde von Kemnitz (who was later to marry the odious General Ludendorff) had to admit that the only way in which 'Eva' could have passed their scrutiny was by carrying in her 'props' where they could not be seen: within her body. She must be swallowing them, they argued, before the seance, then regurgitating them; and they cited a magician whose stock in trade was playing the same trick with, among other things, live frogs.

The transcripts describing what happened at seances, and the photographs accompanying them, reveal that this was nonsense. Even if 'Eva' had trained herself in the art of 'rumination', as it was sometimes described from the analogy of cattle, she could not have regurgitated the life-size forms which the photographs showed. It was not as if she enjoyed privacy in the 'cabinet'; cameras were positioned to take pictures of her even when she was not visible to onlookers. As her hands were ordinarily in sight, being held, she could not have regurgitated paper or chiffon and hung it up, in the way the 'portraits' appeared to hang. In any case, though the photographs could not show it, witnesses testified that the forms did not simply appear and disappear; sometimes they gradually evolved, changing their contours in the process.

To no avail. Had Mme Bisson and Schrenck been able to employ film, their evidence would have had to be taken more seriously; but film could not be used in the seance room where there was only just enough light for witnesses to follow the action. The investigators realised their labours were not complete. During 1914 they embarked upon a new series of tests, with more outside witnesses at each seance, ranging from Professor Courtier of the Sorbonne, who had organised the Paris trials of Eusapia, to W. B. Yeats.

Yeats attended five seances with 'Eva', and left an account of them. The first three were almost total failures, 'although a small luminous spot over the left breast appeared in one'. During the fourth, luminous threads were seen, and 'a luminous mass about the size of a breakfast plate, but irregular in shape, on the left breast'. Little happened in the fifth, except for a vague light, fluctuating in intensity, on the medium's lap, 'like a fragment of the Milky Way'. To Yeats, deeply involved as he had been in occultism, the series must have been a disappointment; but it can be credited to 'Eva', on much the same principle as Sherlock Holmes stressed the significance of the dog that did not bark in the night. Mme Bisson, a woman of culture, would presumably have been anxious that the poet should not be disappointed. If she were in collusion with 'Eva' to provide phenomena by sleight of hand – and from Yeats's description of the preliminary precautions, there would have had to be such collusion, for the medium to be able to fake the 'threads' and luminosities – surely she would have laid on something more spectacular for his benefit?

Stanislawa Tomczyk

Although the 'MIRO' episode was a setback, in that the presumed 'exposure' of the medium obtained far more publicity than the painstaking research described by Schrenck and Mme Bisson in their books, there was some compensation for psychical researchers in the achievements of another medium, a young Polish girl, Stanislawa Tomczyk.

An account of her mediumship had appeared in 1909, in the *Annales des Sciences Psychiques.* Julian Ochorowicz, the leading psychical researcher in Poland, described how under hypnosis she could move objects on a table in front of her without touching them, and sometimes raise them into the air. At first, watching her, he had assumed she was using fine threads, as her hands moved like a puppet manipulator's, and photographs taken during seances sometimes showed what appeared to be threads connecting her hands to the objects. They were also tangible, he found – but they were not ordinary thread. 'I have felt this thread in my hand, on my face, on my hair,' Ochorowicz explained. 'When the medium draws her hands apart, the thread thins and finally vanishes; it feels, to the touch, like a spider's web. If it is cut through, it immediately reconstitutes itself; it appears to be formed by a succession of points.' He added that when photographed, it could be seen to be 'much thinner' than ordinary thread. Mediums, he surmised, could form a kind of vitalised matter outside themselves which might or might not be visible and tangible, but which could operate in a similar fashion to forces which *were* visible and tangible.

Stanislawa had then been formally tested by scientists in Warsaw. Their report confirmed that she was able to move a celluloid ball, placed on a dynamometer designed to detect any physical

The Forerunners

force which she might use; she could move it even when a screen was interposed between her hands and the ball. Cagily, the committee adopted the precedent set by the members of the Sorbonne committee with Eusapia, who had described in detail what she had been able to show them, but had declined to commit themselves further. The facts were as stated, the Warsaw report asserted, but were 'incomprehensible'.

Tested by Schrenck and a number of other scientists, Stanislawa did even better. With movements of her hands, but without physical contact, she was able to exert a pressure of fifty grams on a letter-weighing machine; and a teaspoon in a glass was thrown out of the glass. Everard Feilding, who had come as an observer on behalf of the SPR, was impressed. There were times when she could not produce any psychic phenomena; but even these were full of interest because while they lasted, it was as if a poltergeist took over in her vicinity, with raps, movements of furniture and translocation of objects, sometimes to another room. These manifestations ceased when her power returned, enabling her to move objects on the table top, as Ochorowicz had described. Feilding had seen a cigarette lift up on one end; and on occasion, small objects would levitate to a height of from six to eighteen inches.

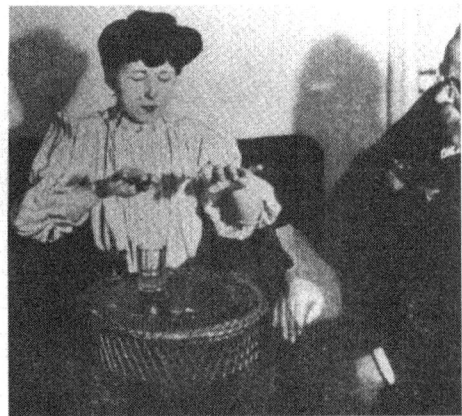

Stanislawa Tomczyk levitating small objects (the one on the right was a lit cigarette). The proximity of her investigator underlines E. J. Dingwall's comment.

These findings were particularly welcome to psychical researchers, as 'threads' had often been reported before with D. D. Home and with Eusapia, and had been one of the counts used in attempts to discredit mediums. Ochorowicz, too, was a researcher of long experience and manifest integrity; his *Mental Suggestion*, published in 1887, had been a deeply felt and often moving account of his gradual realisation, in the course of projects which he had begun in the expectation of discrediting the findings of the psychical researchers, that it was his own materialist preconceptions that were being undermined. And as Eric Dingwall was to point out, the type of effects which Stanislawa could produce were relatively easy to monitor, as her investigators could sit close to her and observe every move of her hands. 'Can we indeed suppose that her investigators were so amazingly incompetent that they all failed to detect her methods of gaining possession of her threads and attaching, detaching and getting rid of them?' Dingwall asked. 'Certainly if this be the case, then human testimony is worthless in this branch of psychical research.'

To the relief of some members of the SPR, too, Stanislawa was not a spiritualist. As with 'Eva', the effects occurred while she was under hypnosis. She was not aware of what she had been doing, when she came out of her trance, and displayed little interest in her powers. In 1914 Stanislawa came to London for tests. The results were not striking: according to Feilding the poltergeist effects, when she was not being formally tested, were more remarkable. But although there were several blank sittings, on one occasion 'a small celluloid ball was levitated to a height of about nine inches above the table', untouched by the medium's hands. It was enough to confirm for Feilding that a supernormal force was involved, 'in the nature of a discharge of energy from her own organism'; and if this were the case, he surmised, 'it may be that we have here a basis for the explanation of a great part, if not the whole, of the so-called physical phenomena of spiritualism'.

Henri Bergson

As it happened, an explanation was also presented at this time for psychic powers in general, with particular reference to their elusive nature. Henri Bergson's *Creative Evolution*, published in 1907, had established his reputation; and although he had not undertaken psychical research himself, he had been one of the observers at Eusapia's Sorbonne trials. Having heard and read enough to convince him of the reality of psychic phenomena he had been casting around for a way to fuse them in with his 'life force' philosophy, and he expounded it in his Presidential Address to the SPR in 1913.

One of the problems confronting psychical researchers from the start had been to find an explanation for the fact that the phenomena they were investigating were so elusive; twenty years earlier Arthur Balfour, in his Presidential Address (it was typical of him that he should have accepted the Presidency at a time when he was leading the Tory party in the Commons; few politicians, then or later, would have cared to risk the ridicule of their colleagues by such a step), had tentatively offered a hypothesis. Many rudimentary physical organs have never developed; may there not also be senses, Balfour surmised, never developed by natural selection, 'mere by-products of the great evolutionary machine?' And if so – he was only, he insisted, hazarding a guess – might not some individuals be abnormally endowed with faculties which, 'had they been of any value or purpose in the struggle for existence, might have been normally developed and thus become the common possession of the whole race?'

This tentative explanation for the existence of psychic faculties, intriguing though it was, invited a counter-question: why had potentially so valuable – indeed invaluable – an evolutionary development been blocked? Bergson provided an answer. The function of the brain, he argued, is to select. For evolutionary purposes the need is to select what is immediately useful; to choose which perceptions should be 'actualised', and which should be kept out. Inevitably, communications directly through the five senses – especially when the senses become more efficient, as they did with vision – had priority. Nevertheless, just as useless memories occasionally slip into consciousness, 'may there not be, around our normal perception, a fringe of perceptions – most often unconscious, but all ready to enter consciousness, and in fact entering it in certain exceptional cases, or in certain predisposed subjects?'

Our bodies, Bergson continued, are external to each other in space; as are our minds, insofar as they are attached to our bodies. But if they are attached to the body only by a part of themselves, 'we may conjecture that for the remainder of them there is not also this sharp separation'. The promptings of the detached remainder – 'urges' which, he suggested, were 'analogous to the phenomena of endosmosis' – could be an embarrassment if they clashed with the demands of the attached part of the mind: 'If such endosmosis exists, we can forsee that nature will have taken every precaution to neutralise its effect, and that certain mechanisms must be specially charged with the duty of throwing back into the unconscious the presentations so provoked, for they would be very embarrassing in everyday life.'

Here, there was a link with the work of Eugene Marais, the South African zoologist whose articles on termites had just been published. Marais had drawn attention to the fact that the activities of all the termites in a colony appeared to be directed by what, for want of a better term, he felt reluctantly compelled to describe as a soul. At any given moment they might be switched by the soul's instructions from their various tasks to other, also various, tasks; and although individual termites could not see even what they were doing – they could not see at all – the soul nevertheless created sophisticated structures, like arches of a kind that the human race had taken millennia to learn how to construct.

Bergson's proposition was that man, with his developing individual mind, would have been hampered by such exterior interruptions; evolution had consequently done its best to get rid of the soul's promptings. 'One or other of these presentations might yet, however, at times pass through as contraband, especially if the inhibiting mechanism were functioning badly; and these again would be facts with which psychical research would be concerned.'

The Sceptics: Scientists

With a workable hypothesis on which to build a theory to account for psychical phenomena, and with mediums of the calibre of Mrs Piper, Marthe Béraud and Stanislawa Tomczyk as demonstrators, it might have seemed that psychical research was poised in 1914 for another advance, in spite of the American setback. But two apparently insoluble problems remained – the first being that the phenomena did not lend themselves to the process which had brought magnetism, meteorites and even hypnosis out of the supernatural and into the natural camp. In the abstract, telepathy and telekinesis might have been presented as suitable candidates for admission. But they did not manifest themselves, as a rule, in the abstract. They often manifested themselves in embarrassing, ridiculous and occasionally repellent ways.

In *The Unknown Guest*, published in 1914, Maeterlinck addressed himself to this problem. The 'guest' – was it Bergson's 'endosmosis', seeking admission? Marais' 'soul'? The spirit world? –

has not the stage to itself; and its voice is not the voice that sounds in our ears, which were never made to catch the echoes of a world that is not like ours. If it could speak to us itself and tell us what it knows, we should probably at that instant cease to be on this earth. But we are immured in our bodies, entombed prisoners with whom it cannot communicate at will. It roams around the walls, it utters warning cries, it knocks at every door, but all that reaches us is a vague disquiet, an indistinct murmur that is sometimes translated to us by a half-awakened gaoler who, like ourselves, is a lifelong captive.

The 'gaoler' – whether the shaman of a tribal community, an Old Testament prophet or a spiritualist medium – naturally attributed the source of the communications to whatever source his beliefs pointed to; 'if he has a favourite spirit, angel, demon or god, he will express himself in its name'. As for the unknown guest, it 'seems to care but little as to the garments in which it is rigged out, having indeed no choice in the matter; for, either because it is unable to manifest itself or because we are incapable of understanding it, it has to be content with whatever comes to hand'.

Such speculations, however, were unlikely to commend themselves to scientists. This happened to be the period when orthodox science reached the furthest point in its climb towards what most of its practitioners and theorists regarded as its ultimate destination: total objectivity. Materialism had all but taken over. Human beings, it was assumed, would eventually be shown to work on the same mechanistic principle as machines, even if on a more sophisticated level. On the strength of this assumption, a body of dogma had been built up asserting that there were certain natural laws – much as divine laws had been enshrined in the dogmas of the Catholic Church. As these laws of nature were presumed to be unchanging and immutable, psychic phenomena not merely did not happen; they *could* not happen.

The Establishment – in the sense of men and women of influence in government and affairs in general – tended to accept the academic verdict. Half a century earlier W. E. H. Lecky had observed in his *History of Rationalism* that nearly all educated men, even if they could not give a satisfactory explanation of reported phenomena, 'never on that account dream of ascribing them to supernatural agency'; they shared 'an absolute and even derisive incredulity which dispenses with all examination of the evidence'. This was true even of Protestants. God being omnipotent, Protestants could not dispute that he *might* intervene; they even prayed for his intervention to scatter enemies in wartime and to heal the sick, or end droughts, in time of peace. But they discounted the possibility of discarnate spirits having any earthly role.

Most scientists of the time were implacably hostile. To Wilhem Wundt, clairvoyance and telepathy were superstitious 'absurdities'. While on a visit to Ireland, von Helmholtz told Barrett that neither the testimony of all the Fellows of the Royal Society nor the evidence of his own senses would lead him 'to believe in the transmission of thought from one person to another, independently of the recognised channels of sensation'. And this was not surprising. Even the possibility of communication at a distance between two people, other than through the known sensory channels, would 'indicate the presence of a crack in the very foundations of nature', Alfred Jodl laid down in his *Textbook of Psychology* in 1903; if proven, such communication would necessitate 'a complete revision of fundamental principles'.

If this were the orthodox attitude to telepathy, what scientists felt about mediumship, ectoplasm, materialisation, apports and the rest can be imagined. It was widely assumed that those scientists who had accepted them must be suffering from some mental disorder. F. C. S. Schiller, a Fellow of Corpus Christi College, Oxford and subsequently Professor of Philosophy at the University of California, was to recall that when he became an undergraduate in 1882, the year the SPR was founded, anybody who engaged in psychical research was regarded as crazy: 'I remember, for example, that the first thing I ever heard about Sir William Crookes was that he *had* been a brilliant scientist, but that recently he had unfortunately gone off his head, and lapsed into spiritualism.' It was not until many years later, when Schiller met Crookes, that he realised 'how grotesquely false this calumny had been'. And similar tales were circulated, 'no doubt from the highest scientific motives, about Sidgwick, William James and the rest'.

The most charitable interpretation that academics could put on the decision of a colleague to undertake psychical research was that he must have been afflicted by a 'longing to believe'. Schiller had accepted this explanation himself, as a young man; but eventually it had dawned upon him that there existed in some a will to *dis*believe, every bit as strong and 'much craftier and more difficult to discount, because it concealed itself under such specious disguises and assumed an air of scientific rectitude'. For some scientists, rationalism had become a religion. When Oliver Lodge described Tyndall as the Royal Institution's 'officiating priest' he

The Forerunners

was close to the mark, as Tyndall preached materialism with much the same zeal as nonconformists preached their brand of Christianity – and in much the same language; he denounced Spiritualism as 'intellectual whoredom'.

His disciples kept up the tradition, notably Horatio Bryan Donkin and Ray Lankester. In the 1870s they had been instrumental in obtaining the prosecution of the American medium Henry Slade under the Vagrancy Acts (Slade was convicted and given a prison sentence, the judge's verdict being that his mediumship must be fraudulent, as the phenomena were contrary to 'the well-known course of nature'); but Slade escaped on a technicality. In 1913 they were still vigorously carrying on the campaign, both by this time having acquired knighthoods. In a short-lived quarterly, *Bedrock*, Lankester cited ten reasons why the psychical researchers' evidence ought to be rejected, each of them, in his opinion, stronger than the evidence itself: lying, deception, defective memory, fancy, mental disorder, poor observation, misinterpretation (or a combination of the two), lack of experience, and coincidence.

Yet the picture of psychical researchers as gullible incompetents was in fact very far from the reality. If one thing stands out in the reports of their research, it is the enormous pains that were taken from the start to try to make it, and keep it, scientific. 'To point to a scientific journal where hard-headedness and never-sleeping suspicion of sources of error might be seen in their full bloom,' William James had felt justified in claiming, 'I think I should have to fall back on the *Proceedings* of the Society for Psychical Research.'

Almost without exception, too, the leading psychical researchers were men and women whose integrity has never been seriously impugned. That Crookes had been accused of being, as he put it, a 'Don Juan' by the mother of one of the mediums he had been testing was to provide the excuse for smear stories about him; but he would hardly have been awarded the Order of Merit, as he was in 1910, nor would the members of the Royal Society have elected him their President, as they did in 1913, if there had been any doubts about his integrity. So far from traducing the psychical researchers, in fact, Donkin had felt compelled to fall back on the argument that arguments derived from their integrity were irrelevant.

'In all scientific enquiries the good faith of individuals concerned should form no part of the data on which the conclusion is to rest,' he had claimed; the results of tests should be shown to stand in their own right, regardless of who performed them. Nevertheless when the results were impressive, sceptics switched to a different line: that there might have been collusion. 'We have done all that we can when the critic has nothing left but to allege that the investigator is in the trick,' as Sidgwick put it. 'But when he has nothing else left to allege, he will allege that.'

The likes of Donkin and Lankester were a minority, but they had one considerable advantage. Posing as they did as hard-headed rationalists, what they wrote carried conviction to those who, in this context, could be described as agnostics rather than as atheists, and who were comforted when reassured that they did not need to bother about psychical research. 'The mistake of agnosticism has been that it has said not merely "I do not know", but "I will not consider",' Lowes Dickinson perceptively noted in his *Religion and Criticism* in 1906. 'Such a position is hampering not merely to life but to truth.'

As a result, psychical research stood little chance of acceptance as an academic discipline, or even as a field of research. When funds were made available for that purpose, the universities managed to ignore or subvert the donor's wishes. The University of Pennsylvania had accepted a legacy which had been offered to found a Chair of Philosophy on condition that an investigation was conducted into spiritualism; the investigation was duly held, but it was rigged to ensure a dismissive verdict. Harvard accepted a bequest to set up research as a memorial to Hodgson, whose last years had been spent in Boston, where his innate scepticism had finally been conquered by Mrs Piper; it had not been used. And although the Stanford University authorities had felt compelled to appoint a Fellow to undertake research into telepathy, as the donor of $50,000 for that purpose was a brother of the founder, the post was given to John E. Coover, a forty-year-old psychologist who had shown no previous interest in the subject, and who was to make no secret of his scepticism.

Sceptics: The SPR

Damaging though the influence of materialism and rationalism was, for the prospects of psychical research in this period, it is possible that it did less harm than the scepticism of the psychical researchers themselves. Although most of them were prepared to accept in theory the existence of psychic powers, two inhibiting forces continually impeded acceptance in practice: fear of being caught out by fraudulent mediums, and made to look ridiculous; and 'thus far and no farther' preconceptions which permitted the acceptance of, say, mental mediumship, but not of physical mediumship.

At first sight it seemed odd that Sidgwick, Myers and Gurney, who in the early years had directed the society's work, should then have given it that negative direction. But Sidgwick's heart was not in psychical research so much as in the clues it might provide about the mysteries of life, and perhaps of after-life. His 'liberal heart', William James recalled, worked alongside an intellect 'which acted destructively on almost every particular object of belief that was offered to his acceptance', and one of those objects was the evidence for the physical phenomena of mediumship; in particular, the spiritualist element. 'The natural drift of my mind,' he had admitted in 1886, 'is now towards total incredulity in respect to extra-human intelligences.' His wife Eleanor shared his incredulity.

Gurney had died in 1888; Sidgwick in 1900; Myers in 1901. But the Cambridge nucleus which they had formed survived, remaining in control of the society. Eleanor Sidgwick in particular became, and for over thirty years remained, the dominant influence; with her brother, Gerald Balfour, her Newnham colleague, Mrs A. W. Verrall, and her close associates, J. G. Piddington, Treasurer, and Alice Johnson, Secretary, forming an unassailable autocracy.

The social standing of the nucleus reinforced their intellectual attitudes. These were sometimes put down to snobbery: to a feeling that mediums were not in their class. In her history of the SPR Renée Haynes has argued persuasively that this was a mistaken view: 'They shared certain ideas, notably that of what they would have called a "sense of honour", and these ideas inspired certain codes of behaviour.' They were aware that people who had not had what they would have called their advantages in life did not necessarily share their code, 'and were therefore cautious in their dealings with those who did not necessarily hold to it, and might be tempted to cheat for money, or for power, or for self-inflation'.

The mistrust was understandable, in view of the critics waiting to pounce. What were unsatisfactory were the expedients the nucleus used to try to avoid being deceived. Mediums who charged for their services were ruled out for purposes of investigation. Yet why should mediums have been expected to give their services free, while doctors exacted fees? Most damaging of all was the willingness of the nucleus to allow the society's publications to be exploited by men who, like Frank Podmore, had no scruples about using the tactics of its sceptical enemies to discredit mediums and psychical researchers with whom they were out of sympathy.

In Podmore's case this was particularly harmful, as he was a prolific author, and as such became the unofficial spokesman for the society through his books (officially the society had no corporate opinions, but the reading public naturally assumed that, as he had the blessing of Sidgwick, he was expressing the society's point of view). Podmore was an industrious researcher, who did a great deal to open up the early history of psychical research to inspection. But when he came across accounts of phenomena which he could not accept, such as telekinesis, he would take elaborate pains to show how they could have been faked; and where the evidence suggested that the medium could not have faked, he did not hesitate to disparage the investigator – just as Sidgwick, ironically, had warned that sceptics would do.

Nor was Podmore unrepresentative. The majority of the society's active members, Alfred Russel Wallace told an acquaintance who contemplated joining, were 'absurdly and illogically sceptical'; it had become a society 'for the suppression of facts, for the wholesale imputation of imposture, for the discouragement of the sensitive, and the repudiation of every revelation of the kind which was said to be pressing itself upon humanity from the regions of light and knowledge'. Intemperate though the criticism was, there was plenty of justification for Wallace's annoyance.

Sarajevo

Before the First World War broke out, there had been countless portents of a coming Armageddon from mediums in trances, in automatic writing, in dreams and in visions – as in Jung's 'terrible visions of tides of blood'. Most were in similarly vague general terms; but a few contained more specific prophetic glimpses. Before the international situation became really serious, a member of the SPR referred in her automatic writing to 'Lusitania' with the cryptic comment, 'Foam and fire – mest [sic] the funnel'. And most striking of all was the nightmare which Richet was to recount in his *Thirty Years of Psychical Research*, from the story which had appeared in *Psychische Studien* in 1918. The facts, it was claimed, had been checked.

The Forerunners

Monsignor Joseph de Lanyi, Bishop of Grosswardin, dreamed on the morning of June 28th, at 4 a.m. that he saw on his study table a black-edged letter bearing the arms of the Archduke. M. de Lanyi had been professor of the Hungarian language to the Archduke. In his dream he opened the letter and at its head saw a street into which an alley opened. The Archduke was seated in a motorcar with his wife; facing him was a general, and another officer by the side of the chauffeur. There was a crowd about the car and from the crowd two young men stepped forward and fired on the royal couple. The text of the letter ran, 'Your Eminence, dear Dr Lanyi, my wife and I have been victims of a political crime at Sarajevo. We commend ourselves to your prayers. Sarajevo, June 28, 1914, 4 a.m.'

'Then,' says Mgr de Lanyi, 'I woke up trembling; I saw that the time was 4.30 a.m., and I wrote down my dream, reproducing the characters that had appeared to me in the Archduke's letter. At six, when my servant came, he found me seated at my table, much shaken and telling my rosary. I said at once to him, "Call my mother and my host, that I may tell them the dreadful dream I have had."'

During the day, a telegram arrived with the news of the assassination. The dream had been almost entirely accurate.

2 The First World War

Ordinarily the war might have been expected to push psychical research into the background, at least in the countries involved. But throughout its duration the main adversaries, Germany on the one hand and France and Britain on the other, faced each other from trenches; and as to gain ground through them proved immensely costly in lives, at all times there were thousands of parents with a son who had just been reported killed or missing. Many would hear of some medium who might be able to obtain information about him – perhaps even bring him back as a 'communicator'.

Had the war broken out a few years earlier, the Cambridge nucleus would have been horrified at this development; but their attitude had been profoundly modified by the discovery of what appeared to be a systematic attempt on the part of the deceased to communicate with the living world, through members of the society who were practising automatists.

The 'Cross-correspondences'

In their research into the trance state the mesmerists had discovered that entranced subjects, though not fully aware of what they were doing, could seem as if they were – like sleepwalkers. And with the emergence of spiritualism, mediums began to exploit this 'automatism' as a way to communicate with the spirits. At first, seance-room tables supplied the answers, responding to sitters' questions by tilting – one for 'yes', two for 'no' – or by raps. Then the ouija board was invented, with the letters of the alphabet and numbers round its perimeter; by putting their fingers on an upturned glass, or on a planchette – a pencil mounted on casters – sitters could obtain messages at speed, glass or planchette darting from letter to letter. But the commonest and simplest method of establishing this form of communication, as Lodge described it, was 'writing performed through the agency of subconscious intelligence, the writer leaving his or her hand at liberty to write whatever comes, without attempting to control it, and without necessarily attending at the time to what is being written'. The mentality involved was usually a dream-like state, and the content often of no more value than a dream – as it also was with the ouija board and planchette as an aid. But sometimes the message could appear to show that 'this subliminal portion of the person is in touch, either telepathically or in some other way, with intelligences not ordinarily accessible – with living people at a distance perhaps, or more often with the apparently more accessible people who have passed on'.

The handwriting might be very different from the medium's normal hand, a characteristic which was usually attributed to the 'control' or 'communicator' having taken over. But with few exceptions – Stainton Moses' *Spirit Teachings* was one – the material, though often couched in flowing (and high-flown) prose, had been of little interest to psychical researchers. A few members of the SPR, however, indulged in automatic writing when the fancy took them – or, as some believed, literally when the spirit moved them; and a few began to receive messages purporting to come from Gurney, Sidgwick and Myers. Often these messages were of a kind which people who had known the three men agreed were in character: the style, the references, the tone were often reminiscent of the living individuals. But this, it was realised, could not be regarded as proof that they were communicating from the spirit world; it might simply be that the automatist was unconsciously imposing her own image of them.

Nevertheless the automatists were asked to send the scripts to the society's offices, where they could be studied and filed; and eventually Alice Johnson realised that there were sometimes links between the scripts of automatists who were not, and could not have been, in communication with each other. Mrs Verrall was in Cambridge; Mrs Piper in Boston; Mrs Fleming (Rudyard Kipling's sister) in India. Taken separately, the scripts read like the ramblings of classical scholars; put alongside each other, they sometimes inter-related, much as the pieces of a jigsaw, when fitted together, produce a picture. It was as if the three men had evolved an ingenious way of demonstrating their survival; and these 'cross-correspondences' were to become the society's chief preoccupation.

A typical example of a cross-correspondence was given by Eleanor Sidgwick in the course of a lecture in Cambridge. On 6

January 1909 one of the automatists – Mrs Verrall – had produced some verses apparently relating to the experiences of St Paul on the road to Damascus, along with a note signed 'F.W.H.M.' – Frederic Myers' initials – saying that there should also have been an allusion to the *Chemin de Damas*: 'Remember what Renan wrote about it.' Two days later another of the automatists, 'Mrs Willett' – a pseudonym for Mrs Winifred Coombe-Tennant – was told by 'Myers' in her script to write to Mrs Verrall and say the words, 'Eikon Renam. Eikon Renam.' The cross-correspondence, in this case, appeared to be 'Renan' (slips were common in automatic writing). Mrs Verrall accordingly looked up Renan's book on the apostles, which neither she nor Mrs Coombe-Tennant had read; and she found that Renan had described St Paul as having seen Jesus, the Eikon (or icon), on the road to Damascus, though no such encounter is described in the Acts version.

As an example, this cross-correspondence was typical not merely because it suggested a single intelligence was putting the same idea to both automatists, but also because it was an idea of the kind which might have been expected to appeal to 'Myers', if he retained his worldly interests. The cross-correspondences seemed to represent the most significant evidence for survival after bodily death that had yet been discovered, ruling out the possibility of simple thought-transference between medium and sitters. If there was telepathic communication – sometimes between India, the United States and Britain – it must be on a different level from any which had been found before.

Raymond

One of the first of the leading members of the society openly to avow that the evidence for survival had convinced him had been Oliver Lodge. He had been appointed Principal of the new University of Birmingham in 1900, and knighted two years later. Although still in his fifties, he had already won the reputation of a sage: the friend and adviser of a remarkable range of men and women, particularly those of a radical, inquiring cast of mind, whatever their political affiliations: among them Balfour, Bryce, Joseph Chamberlain, Keir Hardie and the Webbs. Bernard Shaw brought the draft of *Major Barbara* to him, to get his opinion on how to improve the last act; and he was the confidant of many other literary figures.

The First World War

Only among scientists did Lodge have his detractors. This was not because his research in the field of, among other things, wireless telegraphy was considered inadequate; on the contrary, the feeling was that his achievements in this field made it all the more disgraceful that he should have let the side down not merely by dabbling in the occult, but by claiming that such lunacies as the physical phenomena of mediumship were genuine – a betrayal which led Sir James Dewar, to whom posterity is grateful as the inventor of the vacuum flask, to denounce Lodge as 'that arrant humbug who is doing so much harm to English science'.

The materialists had fresh cause for wrath when Lodge's *The Survival of Man* was published in 1909, revealing that his experience with mediums had led him to accept the evidence for life after death. Not that, to most materialists, survival in the accepted decorous tradition of the Church of England posed any serious threat. Most regarded it as a superstition, but a relatively harmless one. A scientist could be a Christian – could even, as in Faraday's case, be a member of an extreme Presbyterian sect – so long as he did not ask fellow scientists to believe that his God interfered with life on earth. But spiritualism – even if, as in Lodge's case, it was not a religion – was a different matter; for Lodge to have embraced it struck them as intolerable. His reputation as a sage only made matters worse; it gave him unique opportunities to undermine the campaign launched by Tyndall to replace other forms of religion with the new materialist faith.

Lodge insisted that a distinction must be made between acceptance of the evidence, and religious belief based on it. He was 'convinced of human survival and the persistence of personality', he told J. Arthur Hill, his unofficial assistant in psychic matters, in 1912; but 'without accepting all the tenets of the people who call themselves Spiritualists'. This was not a distinction calculated to impress sceptics, and he was under no illusions about the adverse effects his identification with psychical research had on many of his colleagues: 'That my occasional psychic utterances do harm to my scientific reputation – even so far as causing some of them to think me more or less cracked – is manifest.'

So convinced had he become of the reality of the phenomena he had investigated, however, that he felt in honour bound not to allow fears for his reputation to prevent him from continuing to explore mediumship, with particular reference to the evidence for survival after death which the cross-correspondences were providing. In 1914 Eleanor Sidgwick and her brother Gerald Balfour also 'burnt their boats', according to Lodge, at a meeting of the society – its meetings were private – 'by expressing themselves as completely satisfied that telepathic communication with the dead was possible' – though, with characteristic caution, accepting the reality of the 'communicators' but *not* of the spirit 'controls'. As they had been a long time doubtful, and had been very critical, their conversion, he felt, was all the more valuable.

Lodge was now to be the recipient of information from a different type of cross-correspondence: obtained originally from one of the automatists, but then supplemented by mediums. On 8 August 1915 Mrs Piper, who was still contributing her share from Boston, reported that she had received a message for him through automatic writing:

> 'Myers says, you take the part of the poet and he will act as faunus. – adding 'ask Verrall'.

On receiving the message Lodge wrote to Mrs Verrall; she explained that the reference was to a passage in the *Carmen Saeculare*, in which Horace thanked Faunus for protecting him from serious injury when he was felled by a tree which had been struck by lightning. Lodge took this to be a warning that some blow was going to fall on him, but that he could count on help from 'Myers'.

On 14 September Lodge's youngest son, Raymond, to whom he was very close, was killed in the course of the Ypres campaign. By this time there were a number of mediums with whom Lodge and his wife were acquainted, and some of them claimed that 'Raymond' had become a 'communicator', and was passing messages through them to his parents; but as they were of the 'tell them not to worry' type, all too familiarly vague, the Lodges were not impressed, until one came from an unexpected source.

On 25 September a Frenchwoman living in London, who had lost sons in the trenches, asked Lady Lodge to come with her to a professional medium, Mrs Osborne Leonard, whom the Lodges did not know. Suddenly the medium broke off from passing messages in French to say that she had one from 'Raymond'. 'Tell father I have met some friends of his.' When asked if he could name any of the friends, 'Raymond' replied 'Yes. Myers.' And when Lodge went himself to sit with Mrs Leonard, 'Raymond' again communicated through her 'control', 'Feda'.

Although Lodge had not disclosed his identity, it was none the less possible that Mrs Leonard had recognised him; but it seemed inconceivable that she should have recognised Lady Lodge, who

The First World War

had not been introduced when she came with her friend. In any case, if the Lodges had any doubts – and by this time Lodge was experienced in the wiles, conscious and unconscious, of mediums – they were soon dispelled. Other mediums were continuing to provide messages from 'Raymond' and one of them (a man, which was unusual: Vout Peters) told Lady Lodge that some photographs had been taken of him, in one of which he was in a group, holding a walking stick. The Lodges, who had no knowledge of it, were naturally anxious to see it, but inquiries elicited no information. Then, two months later, the mother of a fellow-officer wrote to say she had been sent a group photograph which included Raymond; would they like a copy?

Before it arrived, Lodge had a sitting with Mrs Leonard, and he asked 'Raymond', through 'Feda', whether he recollected the occasion. 'Raymond' did, describing how he had been sitting down while the photograph was taken, with others sitting and standing behind him. Somebody, he remembered, had wanted to lean on him. The photograph had been taken out of doors; and according to 'Feda' it would show what appeared to be a black background with vertical lines. Four days later, when the copy arrived, the description proved reasonably accurate – in one respect, strikingly so, as the arm of another officer was indeed leaning on Raymond's shoulder; Raymond, as his father noted, appearing 'rather annoyed'.

The group photograph. Raymond, leaned upon, is second from the right in the front row.

This was not the only evidence which Lodge provided in his book *Raymond*; he emphasised this example because it contained a simple cross-correspondence, the information coming through two mediums. The hypothesis of telepathy on Mrs Leonard's part was consequently hard to sustain, as he had not seen the photograph before she described it; and this, he thought, made it 'a first-class case'. But he reiterated that the proofs were cumulative, 'and though it is legitimate to emphasise anything like a crucial instance, it always needs supplementing by many others, lest there may have been some oversight'. As time went on, he and his wife and other members of his family found the accumulation of proof became overwhelming; it was as if 'Raymond' was with them, enjoying the conversation.

They became more concerned with the enjoyment, in fact, than with testing the mediums; but on occasion 'Raymond' passed tests they themselves devised. Once some of the family who were staying in their family home near Birmingham, knowing that others were having a sitting with Mrs Leonard, held one themselves, their aim being to try to get 'Feda' to say the word 'Honolulu'. 'Feda', in London, duly passed on a message from 'Raymond' including the word, and reported that he was 'rolling with laughter' – a good test, Lodge thought, excluding as it did anything in the nature of conscious or unconscious collusion. It did not, he admitted, rule out the possibility of telepathy. But telepathy, he pointed out, was itself not a 'normal' explanation; 'and I venture to say that there is no normal explanation, since in my judgment chance is out of the question'. And as between telepathy and survival, for him 'the hypothesis of surviving intelligence and personality – not only surviving but anxious and able with difficulty to communicate – is the simplest and most straightforward, and the only one which fits all the facts'.

If Lodge had been unpopular with the predominantly materialist science establishment before, he was now execrated. One of his critics, Charles A. Mercier, even devoted an entire book to denouncing him. Significantly, Mercier was a psychiatrist; by this time psychiatry had sustained the fissure – now being laboriously bridged – between the analysts and the behaviourists, and the behaviourists were trying to establish themselves as respectable scientists in the strictest mechanist tradition. This was the standpoint from which Mercier attacked Lodge; characteristically, Lodge refused to be roused. Mercier seemed to be 'a well-known, energetic and amusingly able man', Lodge wrote to Hill. 'I think that the best plan with a man of this kind is not to take him too seriously.'

But *Raymond* also made Lodge unpopular with another Establishment; the Church of England. The Church felt threatened by spiritualism – as well it might, for it had trimmed to the materialists, rather than do battle with them; possibly because Huxley's demolition of Bishop 'Soapy Sam' Wilberforce in the 'apes or angels' contest was too painful a memory. The Church accepted angels – but only in their place, in heaven. Spirits were frowned upon, and mediumship denounced as potentially destructive of Christian values. In addition there was a feeling shared by many people who were neither materialists nor, in any active sense, Christians: that mediumship was basically fraudulent, its practitioners trading upon the gullible. The fact that the gullible, in this case, were so often the bereaved made it all the more shocking.

Mrs Osborne Leonard

In 1917 Eleanor Sidgwick formally acknowledged her acceptance of survival in one of her characteristic cool, lucid surveys for the society's *Proceedings*. The cross-correspondences, she pointed out, were the equivalent of the pieces of a mosaic, which could when rearranged indicate a purposefulness, an intelligent design.

> We have to seek the designer. It cannot be the supraliminal intelligence of either automatist, since *ex-hypothesi*, neither of them is aware of the design until it is completed. Nor, for a similar reason, can it be attributed to some other living person since, so far as can be ascertained, no other living person had any knowledge of what was going on. It is extremely difficult to suppose that the design is an elaborate plot of the subliminal intelligence of either or both automatists acting independently and without any knowledge on the part of the supraliminal consciousness; and the only remaining hypothesis seems to be that the designer is an external intelligence, not in the body.

In addition, there was the way in which the scripts showed literary knowledge, or propounded literary puzzles beyond the automatists' knowledge; 'I must admit,' she concluded, 'that the general effect of the evidence on my own mind is that there is co-operation with us by friends and former fellow-workers no longer in the body.'

In her commentary, Eleanor Sidgwick warned that just as

nobody should 'let his reason abdicate in favour of the untrustworthy and ill-regulated mental stratum that the subliminal, left to itself, is liable to be', nobody should 'treat his own automatic writing, and still less communications through other mediums, whether private or professional, as oracles'. Even if contact really was made with a 'communicator', this could not guarantee that his message came through correctly: 'Our evidence, indeed, goes to show that it is often, if not always, adulterated by the automatist's own mind.'

This was a salutary warning, as the tendency had been for spiritualists to assume, once they had convinced themselves that the 'communicator' really was the deceased individual he purported to be, that his 'communications' were automatically trustworthy; and sceptics, just as irrationally, had cited errors as evidence that the 'communicator' could not be genuine. The mediumship of Mrs Piper had shown that in a flow of material which the sitter could testify was 'veridical' – the term which psychical researchers had adopted to describe information provided by mediums, or by people in dreams or in trance states, which turned out to be correct – there were often elementary mistakes of a kind which the presumed 'communicator' would certainly not have made. And they occasionally crept in during sittings with Mrs Osborne Leonard, who now established herself as the foremost medium in Britain.

Mrs Leonard was in her early thirties. As a child, she was to recall in her autobiography, she had had visions, but she had not dared to confide in her well-to-do parents, as soon as she realised how disapproving they were, such visions being then, as sometimes they still are, widely regarded as indicating incipient insanity.

During her adolescence the family fortunes collapsed; she earned her living for a while by acting and singing, and married an actor, Frederick Leonard. Whiling away some off-stage time with some friends and a ouija board, she received a message from a 'communicator' with an unpronounceable name, beginning with 'F'; to simplify matters, she asked if she might use the name 'Feda'; and 'Feda', agreeing, announced that she was henceforth to take over as Mrs Leonard's spirit 'control'.

In her conscious state, Mrs Leonard had no desire to be 'controlled'; and a curious relationship developed between the two, not unlike a marriage where the partners, though fond of each other, are also a little ashamed, and inclined to speak disparagingly of, one another. Unlike a marriage, however, they could not constant-

The First World War

ly get on each other's nerves, as they were not in direct communication. 'Feda' emerged only when Mrs Leonard was in a trance.

'Feda' sounded like a young and unsophisticated girl; but she was tough. By leaving messages for Mrs Leonard, she gave what amounted to a course of apprenticeship, until she considered Mrs Leonard sufficiently competent to give professional public sittings, as for a while she did. But with the outbreak of war, the crowds of distraught relations of men killed or missing in the trenches became too much for her – or, rather, for 'Feda'; 'Feda' gave instructions that henceforth Mrs Leonard must give sittings only to individuals, and in private. She obeyed, and she might have continued to give them in obscurity, as scores of mediums were doing, had it not been for that chance encounter with the Lodges and the blaze of publicity which followed the publication of *Raymond*.

As Eleanor Sidgwick had warned, the material was not always reliable. 'Feda' occasionally slipped up on details; as when, at a sitting in 1917, she gave Helen Verrall a broadly accurate picture of her recently deceased mother, but claimed, incorrectly, that she wore 'widow's bands' around her wrists. The inference, Helen thought, was that 'a certain amount of veridical information about my mother was woven by 'Feda' into an imaginary picture of an elderly widow based on preconceived ideas of the appearance that a widow was likely to have'. The most likely explanation, Helen came to think, was that 'Feda', when she described somebody, was not really 'seeing' anything; she was 'receiving a series of mental impressions which she translated into visual terms'.

'Feda's' errors and inconsistencies, however, appeared trivial when set against the mass of veridical material in the detailed transcripts of sittings with Mrs Leonard – for by this time, it had become common practice for sitters to bring along a note-taker. And any lingering suspicion that she might be using her wits to extract and play back information dissolved in the repeated examples of the way in which 'Feda' provided information which the sitter could not have given her – even, in some cases, telepathically.

A typical example was furnished by Mrs Hugh Talbot, who had a sitting with Mrs Leonard in 1917. She had never been to a medium before, and had not given either her name or her address; yet not merely did 'Feda' give a good description of her dead husband, relating incidents which Mrs Talbot was certain could be known only to him and to herself, she also described personal effects of his which his widow had kept, including some leatherbound books, in one of which 'he' – the 'communicator' who had presented himself to 'Feda' as the former Hugh Talbot – thought she would find something to interest her, on page twelve, or thirteen. Although Mrs Talbot vaguely recalled some scrapbooks of her husband's, she was not sure whether they were still in her possession; but after she had returned home, a search revealed them lying at the back of the top shelf of a book-case. On page thirteen of the one to which the 'communicator' had drawn her attention was an unnervingly apposite account of a man supposedly describing what had happened when he was dying. 'From certain glances of curiosity or commiseration which it was supposed I was unable to see' he had found out that he was dying; and when he encountered members of his family and friends who had pre-deceased him, who did not smile with any compassion, or speak to him 'yet communicated to me their unaltered and unalterable affection', he had realised that he must be dead.

It was obvious that a medium had at last been found who might be of inestimable value to the society for research purposes, particularly as she was very willing to co-operate. To prevent her from becoming spoiled by adulation, or corrupted by the payments which rich bereaved parents might be expected to offer to obtain her services, the society – in a variant of the traditional 'if you can't lick 'em, join 'em' notion – decided that Mrs Leonard should be put on the payroll, initially for a trial period, with a weekly salary paid to her on condition that she would give sittings only to people nominated by the society, and with a note-taker present on the society's behalf.

From the start, it proved a fruitful venture. Of the scores of reports which flowed from it, one in particular was impressively documented: from Radclyffe Hall, who was to achieve instant notoriety, and later, posterity's apologies, as the author of *The Well of Loneliness*.

Hall had no interest in psychical research; but when a dear friend of hers, 'A.V.B.', died, she let herself be persuaded to go to a sitting with Mrs Leonard. She did not disclose her identity; but 'Feda' provided a description of 'A.V.B.', 'brief but unmistakable; except my friend, whom it fitted exactly, I had lost no one to whom it corresponded in the very least'. At a second sitting 'A.V.B.' reminded her of a place which they had visited together, Watergate Bay – the last outing they had made before her death. Subsequently Hall and her friend, Una, Lady Troubridge, had a succession of sittings during which 'Feda' produced a mass of detailed information about 'A.V.B.', her looks and her quirks, the great bulk of it being correct.

So veridical was it, in fact, that Radclyffe Hall and Lady Troubridge began to suspect that Mrs Leonard might have checked up on 'A.V.B.' Initially they had been careful to try to preserve their anonymity; but 'A.V.B.' had actually given her own name at one of the sessions. They realised, however, that in order to obtain the details which 'Feda' had provided, it would not have helped Mrs Leonard (or an agent) merely to have visited the remote country village, and looked around: she (or the agent) would have had to ask people living there many probing questions. Radclyffe Hall had some inquiries made on her own behalf; and these satisfied her that neither Mrs Leonard nor an agent had been down to collect the information 'Feda' had provided. In any case, Radclyffe Hall insisted, 'Feda' provided many details of a kind which no inquiry would have elicited, as they concerned events far from the cottage, and known only to herself and Lady Troubridge.

Sometimes, too, 'A.V.B.' began to come through in different and even more affecting ways. Radclyffe Hall described how she had complained she could not make Mrs Leonard laugh, while in her trance.

> One day, however, she suddenly succeeded in doing so, and what ensued was extraordinarily reminiscent of 'A.V.B.'s own laugh, and this laugh has, since then, often occurred. On several occasions the timbre of Mrs Leonard's voice has changed, and has become very like 'A.V.B.'s voice; startlingly so, once or twice. 'A.V.B.' has herself remarked upon this, which appears only to be possible during the earlier part of the personal controls. On one occasion 'A.V.B.' said discontentedly 'Oh! now the power is going, can't you hear my voice getting "Mrs Leonards" again?', which statement was correct.

A 'Traveller' in Dublin

In Ireland, too – still a part of the United Kingdom – wartime demand grew for the services of mediums; at least from the 'Protestant Ascendancy', the Anglo-Irish; Catholics were warned off by their priests.

The Irish, like the Scots, had a long tradition of belief in the occult. 'Fairies' – in the sense of entities which had psychic powers to help or to harm, and sometimes manifested themselves in human shape as 'the little people' – were a living part of folklore, so much so that it was rare for a farmer to dare to cut down a thorn bush, thorn bushes being under their protection. To Yeats, to 'A.E.', and to James Stephens (*The Crock of Gold* was published in 1912) fairy lore was far from being either a silly relic of old superstition or an excuse for Peter-Pan-style sentiment. They knew there were Powers; sometimes of Darkness.

Yeats occasionally straddled the crevasse which increasingly separated 'Golden Dawn' occultists and mystics such as A.E. from psychical researchers of the SPR type. And one of Yeats's protégés, Lennox Robinson, made a contribution to experiments of a kind which the society could approve – though research conducted in Ireland was unlikely to meet with any warm response from Eleanor Sidgwick, even when it was vouched for by William Barrett, by this time Sir William, F.R.S.

Like his fellow-physicists, Crookes and Lodge, Barrett's initial scepticism about mediumship and spiritualism had gradually been eroded until he had come to accept survival after death. To obtain further proof, he had come to the conclusion that the simplest way was with the help of an ouija board and a 'traveller' (as the planchette had come to be called). This entailed finding by trial and error individuals, singly or in small groups, for whom the 'traveller' would provide information from 'communicators' direct, as it were, without the need for a professional medium.

Barrett was under no illusion that the evidence produced in this way would be trustworthy. He assumed that it would be 'scrappy, disjointed and confused', not to be wholly relied upon even when some of the material turned out to be veridical. Nevertheless he hoped that the messages might provide some clues about their source. In particular, he was looking for indications which might determine whether the source was telepathy between the sitters, or whether it could only be accounted for by postulating the existence of discarnate entities – spirits. He was not himself psychic, but he had two friends with mediumistic gifts: Lennox Robinson, who in his early twenties had been appointed by Yeats to be a director and manager of the Abbey Theatre; and the level-headed Mrs Travers Smith, daughter of Edward Dowden – Professor of English Literature at Trinity College, Dublin, one of the most respected critics of the late Victorian era – and wife of a fashionable Dublin doctor. And as note-taker there was the Rev. E. Savell Hicks, who for many years was to be Dublin's leading Presbyterian minister, admired and trusted by his Catholic counterparts even in those pre-ecumenical times.

The First World War

Any hope that the sessions would provide direct access to 'communicators' was quickly dashed. From the start, a number of rival 'controls' competed for mastery, and to make matters worse, the victor was 'Peter Rooney', a self-confessed Irish-American layabout and jailbird who informed them that he had committed suicide by throwing himself under a tram. Had his story been confirmed, it would at least have provided some evidence for the spiritist hypothesis; but when Barrett checked on it, he found that there was indeed a Peter Rooney in Boston, but he did not have a police record; although he had been involved in an accident, it had been a scalp wound resulting from a fall from the elevated railway, which he had survived; and he was still alive.

Taxed with the deception, 'Peter Rooney' remained unabashed. His real identity, he informed the sitters through the 'traveller', was no concern of theirs. All he wanted to do was help them in their investigation; and, disconcertingly, he showed himself to be extremely helpful, in spite of being 'a rather primitive creature', according to Mrs Travers Smith, with 'very strong likes and dislikes'. But the fact that he was 'very vain, and fond of a display of his powers' admirably suited the group's purpose. It was actually 'Peter' who urged the group to demonstrate to doubters that they were not using physical force to push the 'traveller', consciously or unconsciously, towards specific letters, and suggested how they could do it. Sometimes Robinson and Mrs Smith wore blindfolds; sometimes an opaque screen was placed between them and the ouija board. Yet even in these conditions, 'Peter' continued to pass messages; the 'traveller' darting so quickly from letter to letter round the perimeter of the board that Savell Hicks was thankful he had learned shorthand – particularly as, whenever he had to ask for a pause for clarification, 'Peter' would be exasperated, and begin his reply with 'FOOL . . .'

Among the many visitors who attended sessions was the young Eric Dodds, later to succeed Gilbert Murray as Regius Professor of Greek at Oxford, and to be President of the SPR. Dodds was sceptical, but his suspicion that the sitters, even when blindfolded, might come to know how the letters were distributed round the board was removed when he found that the letters were periodically shuffled. Yet he could not bring himself to accept the spiritist hypothesis: 'The least unlikely explanation,' he decided after attending on several occasions, 'appeared to be some sort of gradual telepathic leakage from the watching sitters to the blinded sensitives.'

Science and Parascience

'Telepathic leakage' certainly provided the obvious explanation for some of the information. Once, when a friend of Mrs Travers Smith's had come to watch and listen to the proceedings, the 'traveller' embarked on a rambling tale about a romantic haunted castle belonging to the visitor. Knowing he had no castles, and becoming bored with the story, Mrs Travers Smith asked whether he was interested: 'very much', he replied – the 'traveller' was describing the plot of a play which he had just begun to write. On another occasion a message came through from a friend of hers, indicating he was sitting half-asleep in his drawing room, and describing what had happened to him over Christmas – correctly, as he was to verify when they met.

Still, there were many occasions when telepathic leakage did not provide a plausible explanation of the 'traveller's' tales – as 'Peter' sometimes took pleasure in pointing out. Asked to find something to 'read', and to spell it out, for example, 'Peter' said he would read a passage from a calendar; it was quite a long passage, but when the sitters found the calendar and looked it up, he had got it right.

The most striking rebuttal of the telepathic leakage theory came one evening when a 'communicator' came through claiming to be Sir Hugh Lane – a close friend of both Mrs Travers Smith and Robinson – to say that he had been on board the *Lusitania*, which had just been reported sunk off the Irish coast, and that he had been drowned. They had known that Lane was in the United States; but he was not expected back for several weeks. Hardly had the message been passed when they heard a newspaper boy out in the street shouting 'Stop Press'. Robinson went out to buy a copy; and there was Lane's name in the passenger list.

So little knowledge had Robinson and Mrs Travers Smith had of the message the 'traveller' was spelling out, Savell Hicks wrote to tell Barrett, that they had been laughing and talking while the 'traveller' spelled out the message; as soon as he read it to them, both broke down and wept – 'such a piece of heartless play-acting, as one must assume if they were cognisant of what was coming through, is, as no doubt you will agree, knowing them both, quite unthinkable'.

But did 'Lane's' communication constitute positive evidence in favour of the spiritist case? Mrs Travers Smith remained doubtful – in spite of the fact that 'Lane' had added some veridical material; as if anxious to impress her, he had reminded her of the effect her piano-playing had made on him not long before, and she recalled that Lane had indeed, on that occasion, 'kept me at the piano for a long time and made me play things I hadn't looked at for years'. Nevertheless as a 'communicator' he had not been able to tell her things she did not know, like the number of his *Lusitania* cabin. More impressive, to her mind, were those occasions when the 'communicator' was somebody whom no one present at the session had ever heard of, and when the information passed was not of a kind that would have been published, so that one of them might have read it and forgotten; and when a London woman came through to say she had just died, and gave some trivial details about herself which Barrett, when he checked, found were correct.

The case which most impressed the group came when, in 1915, the 'traveller' answered the sitters' question 'who is there?' by giving the name of a young officer killed in France, the cousin of one of the members of the group; he asked her to tell his mother to give his pearl tie-pin to the girl he was going to marry, and gave the girl's name and address. The cousin, though aware the officer had been killed, said she did not know he had been engaged; and she had never heard of the fiancée. Nor, Barrett found, had the officer's parents; and when a letter sent to the girl at the address the 'communicator' had given was returned by the Post Office, he assumed it must be just another case of the message being misleading. However,

> Six months later it was discovered that the officer had been engaged, shortly before he left for the front, to the very lady whose name was given; he had, however, told no one. Neither his cousin nor any of his own family in Ireland were aware of the fact, and had never seen the lady nor heard her name, until the War Office sent over the deceased officer's effects. Then they found that he had put this lady's name in his will as his next of kin, both Christian and surname being precisely the same as given through the automatist; and what is equally remarkable, *a pearl tie-pin was found in his effects*.

Here, Barrett pointed out, there could be no question of explaining the fact by subliminal memory, or telepathy between the living, or collusion; it had the appearance of being 'an unexpected psychical invasion of the sitters by some personality of whom they were not thinking'.

Messages like these, in Mrs Travers Smith's view, could be explained in only one way: 'an ardent desire on the part of some external influence to communicate with this world'. It was irrational, she felt, to think that they could have come from any other source: 'Something more improbable may be suggested by way of explanation. I am inclined to believe what is obvious.'

By the standards later demanded of – and by – parapsychologists the work Barrett's group did could be described as amateurish; yet in a sense this lends it an authority which more elaborately organised trials rarely carry. They were exploring, rather than trying to prove something. 'I would not make any effort to speak to the beloved dead through automatic writing or the ouija board,' Mrs Travers Smith insisted. 'The evidence they offer of their identity is too ephemeral and unsatisfactory.' Ephemeral and unsatisfactory though it may have been, she none the less felt bound to accept that on occasion it inclined her to believe that the person who communicated was the person she had known – not an impersonation, though it was only after 'Lane' had on several occasions been a 'communicator' that she became 'almost convinced it was he who spoke to us'. Her descriptions of the sessions do not sound like the work of somebody with a package to sell. Nor, for that matter, do Barrett's; and as the messages were all recorded at the time, and often attested by a range of witnesses, there was little room for the kind of exaggeration that the passage of time is apt to encourage. Tentative though Barrett's project was, the reports provided a useful addition to the growing store of knowledge about the uses of automatism in psychical research.

The Goligher Circle

Barrett was also involved, though only briefly, with a series of experiments which were being conducted during the war in Belfast. They represented the first attempt systematically to study the physical phenomena of mediumship with the help of engineering techniques and apparatus; the investigator being W. J. Crawford, a young lecturer in mechanical engineering in Queens University. It is not known how Crawford's interest in the subject was aroused, but it seems likely that he was the Crawford (unidentified by any initial) who had attended one of the seances with 'Eva C' in 1914.

Finding a Belfast family, the Golighers, who held seances, he won their confidence and was allowed to join the circle; and eventually they let him introduce a variety of gadgets to see if he could cast any light on the nature of the forces involved in the rappings and telekinetic phenomena.

He soon ruled out deception. The Golighers had held their

seances as a Spiritualist observance, comparable to family prayers; as they had been held in private, there had been no incentive to deceive others, and he could think of no reason why they should have perpetuated a fraudulent rigmarole merely for their own benefit. The seances, too, were held in light good enough to see that none of the circle was using hands or feet to make the sounds, or move the objects in the centre of the circle. They would even hold their linked hands above their heads while Crawford moved into the circle, to examine the seance table and the objects on or around it, while the seance was in progress.

In an attempt to trace the source of the rappings, Crawford used a phonograph. Years before, though he was unlikely to have known, a similar method had been adopted by the Russian anthropologist, Waldemar Bogoraz, investigating a Siberian shaman who had produced voices from various parts of his hut. Suspecting that he might be creating the illusion by ventriloquism, Bogoraz had tested him with a phonograph and found that the voices apparently came from independent sources (as the term 'ventriloquism' had originally implied, before being taken over, like conjuring and magic, to describe a trick).

Crawford found that although the phonograph was placed several feet away from the medium – Kathleen, one of the Goligher daughters – the spirit control 'sang' into the horn in a way which caused 'blasting' of the kind which would ordinarily have indicated that the voice must have been very close to, if not actually in, the instrument's horn.

Crawford's most elaborate set of experiments were along similar lines to those which had been held with Eusapia at the Sorbonne, but with refinements which he introduced in the course of the series. The medium's chair was placed on a weighing machine, and an instrument designed to measure the elasticity of gases was used to detect the directions taken by the telekinetic forces unleashed by her during the seances. They showed that when the table in front of her levitated, the force involved appeared to be operating on the cantilever principle, fixed at one end – the medium, supported to some extent by the combined psychic assistance of her family; firm, yet flexible, at the other end, so that the force was deflected upwards off the floor to lever up the table. The raps, too, appeared to be caused by psychic 'rods' emanating from her to different parts of the room. A Belfast woman, with the reputation of herself being psychic, who was brought to one of the seances, claimed she could see the 'rods', which looked to her like thin ribbons; and sometimes they appeared in photographs which Crawford took. They tended, however, not to show up in good light – which also seemed to disrupt the linkage, so that the medium could not use the 'rod'. When it was operating, he could put his hand in the way of the 'rod' without feeling anything, or stopping it from working; and it could discharge an electroscope. The 'rod' would also obey his instructions.

As Barrett lived in Ireland, he was the obvious man to investigate Crawford's work with the Golighers on the SPR's behalf. He had cautiously committed himself to acceptance of telekinesis nearly thirty years before: 'So far as the evidence is trustworthy,' he had written, 'I, for one, believe it points to the conclusion that, under conditions which are so restricted that we are not put to intellectual confusion by frequent interruptions of the regular course of material laws, *mind, occasionally and unconsciously, can exert a direct influence upon lifeless matter.*' But the physical phenomena of mediumship still repelled him. He had grudgingly admitted that Eusapia appeared to have supernormal powers, but described her as 'a medium of an unreliable type, who has been convicted of imposture both in England and America, and with whom therefore I should not care to have any sittings'. Certainly he was not predisposed in the Golighers' favour when, during the Christmas holidays in 1915, he went to Belfast at Crawford's invitation to attend a seance; and he took the precaution of bringing with him a sceptical friend, a doctor.

At the start of the proceedings they sat outside the family circle; Barrett was agreeably surprised to find that the light was good enough for them to see what was happening. The initial manifestations, as usual, were raps, or knocks, sometimes sounding as if from the table in the middle of the circle, sometimes as if from outside the circle. The knocks answered questions (three for yes, two for doubtful, one for no); when the doctor asked for a louder knock 'a tremendous bang' came, 'which shook the room', and which Barrett realised could not have been produced by the slipper-shod feet of the family. Next, there were sounds as if somebody was using a saw, and of a ball bouncing. When a trumpet which had been placed below the table (musical instruments had originally been included at seances by mediums who hoped to emulate Home; they also served as objects which could be made to move at a distance from the medium) began to float around, Barrett and his friend were encouraged to try to catch it; 'but in spite of all our endeavours it eluded us, darting in and out and changing its position as we tried to seize it'.

> Then the table began to rise from the floor, until it reached a height of some twelve or eighteen inches, and remained thus suspended and quite level. We were allowed, first myself and then Dr W., to go beneath the clasped hands of the sitters into the circle and try to force the table down. This both of us found it impossible to do; though we laid hold of the sides of the table it resisted our strongest efforts to push it down. I then sat on the table when it was about a foot off the floor, and it swayed me about, finally tipping me off.

Later the table turned upside down, and floated with its legs in the air; yet when they went back into the circle to try to lift it, they found it immovable.

Impressed, they came back the following evening to watch some trials with Crawford's weighing machine. The knocks, however, informed them that there would be no demonstrations, because of some material cause which, they were led to infer, related to the medium. When the doctor examined her, he confirmed that she was suffering from what Barrett discreetly referred to as 'a feminine disorder'; and they had had to return to Dublin before she could resume the seances.

Barrett described what he had seen in a paper read at a meeting of the SPR in January 1916; and later in the year, Crawford gave an account of his researches in *The Reality of Psychic Phenomena*. It was a remarkable work, not just for its demonstration of how the physical phenomena of mediumship could be tested with the help of engineering techniques and equipment, but for its revelation of the importance of incorporating the subjective, or human, element into the procedure. Here was an account by a man who was not primarily concerned to prove or disprove the reality of the physical phenomena of mediumship; having accepted their reality, he had concentrated upon finding out how they worked. As the seances were family affairs, he had taken care to behave, so far as was practicable, as one of the family; he had not, as had so often been the policy of investigators, even asked Kathleen to submit to being treated by him as if she were an object of suspicion, on the ground that this would be essential if other psychical researchers were to be convinced. Crawford had been content to win the family's confidence, assuming that he would later be able to bring in witnesses without disrupting the seances; and Barrett's visit had shown that this policy had worked.

Science and Parascience

From the point of view of psychical research in Britain, Crawford's findings were obviously of extreme importance. Here was the opportunity to catch up with the researchers on the Continent, in the field where the SPR had so conspicuously lagged behind. Lodge would have been the obvious person to review the book for the *Journal*, but he could have been expected to give it a favourable notice. Eleanor Sidgwick therefore decided to review it herself; and she dismissed Crawford's evidence with a contemptuous 'the more rationalistic hypothesis is that the cantilever in question is the leg and foot of the medium'.

Her antipathy to the physical phenomena may not have been her only reason for this verdict. Crawford had committed the heinous sin of submitting reports of his work to the editor of *Light*, a journal which leaned too far to spiritualism, and paid too little attention to scientific method, for her taste. And perhaps it was no coincidence that shortly after Mrs Sidgwick's review appeared in the SPR *Journal*, a letter from Lodge was published in *Light* warmly congratulating Crawford on his investigation and putting a number of questions to him, which Crawford was naturally delighted to answer. The editor of *Light*, David Gow, thereafter had the benefit of Crawford's interim reports; and also had the satisfaction of citing any praise for what Crawford was doing from other sources – the *Westminster Gazette*, for one, still influential. 'If ever Dr Crawford's theory of the rods can be maintained,' its reviewer observed, 'surely the mechanists will be discredited for ever.'

3   Post-War Britain

The SPR could not look back over the war years with any sense of achievement: the value of the discovery of Mrs Osborne Leonard, important though it was for the purpose of serious investigation of mediumship, had been offset by the adverse effect which the publication of *Raymond* had on scientists, making the orthodox feel even more certain that they had been right to shun psychical research. None the less the society had one useful trump card in reserve, to remind the orthodox how wrong they and their predecessors had often been in the past: Lord Rayleigh, brother-in-law of Eleanor Sidgwick. He had been a member of the society from the start, and he took on the Presidency in 1919.

In his Presidential Address Rayleigh recalled that while he had been at Cambridge in the 1860s he had witnessed an exhibition of hypnosis, at that time 'dismissed as impossible and absurd'; after the experience he had realised that 'what was, or at any rate had recently been, orthodox opinion might be quite wrong' and this had led him to become interested in the research Crookes was doing with Home and other mediums. Although he had not himself seen any spectacular manifestations, what he had seen was enough to convince him that mediumship could not be accounted for by fraud. He therefore begged his fellow scientists to recognise the importance of research into phenomena which lay just outside that pale – globe lightning, for one (in which he had a particular interest), and telepathy.

Before the year was out, however, Rayleigh had died. He had been 'one of the great physical experimenters of all time', Philip Callahan has recently recalled in his *Tuning in to Nature*. 'He contributed considerably to our knowledge of both sound and light waves, and is the father of the mathematics of resonance as applied to the physics of sound and light. His work on the resolving power of the optical lens is classical.' And although Rayleigh had not been directly involved in psychical research since the foundation of the society, the continued support of a man who had been successively Cavendish Professor of Physics at Cambridge, President of the

Science and Parascience

British Association and of the Royal Society, and Chancellor of Cambridge University, as well as being the recipient of an O.M. and a Nobel Prize, was an asset the society could ill afford to lose.

Sir William Crookes, too, died in 1919. Like Rayleigh, he was a former President of both the British Association and the Royal Society, and an O.M. His contribution to psychical research had been all-important: it had been his decision to investigate mediums, and his reports had encouraged the Cambridge nucleus to investigate on their own account in the 1870s. And although Crookes's experiences with mediums, and still more with their backers, had frightened him off formal psychical research, he had made it clear in his Presidential Address to the British Association in 1898 that he stood by what he had reported.

Because Crookes had ceased to identify himself publicly with psychical research, the rumour periodically resurfaced that he had at last realised he had been duped; and in 1916 he wrote restating his position to the editor of *Light*, repeating what he had told the British Association eighteen years before: 'I adhere to my published statements and have nothing to retract.' He added that although he had not committed himself to any generalisations from the facts, this must not be held to invalidate his testimony about the facts themselves: 'In my opinion they substantiate the claims which have been made for them by several of my colleagues and friends in the Society for Psychical Research, *viz*, that they point to the existence of another order of human life continuous with this, and demonstrate the possibility in certain circumstances of communication between this world and the next.'

The implication was that Crookes had not personally obtained evidence which had convinced him of the reality of an after-life. He was to get it a few months later. In *Survival*, published in New York in 1924, Miss F. R. Scatcherd described a seance she had attended with Crookes in 1917, where his deceased wife had 'communicated', telling her husband that although he could not see her, 'I am here beside you, Willie dear' and demonstrating her presence by causing a musical-box to float around the room. The light had just been good enough, Miss Scatcherd claimed, for her to see ectoplasm forming itself 'into a rough gripping apparatus' which groped for the musical-box; and also to see it as it was whirled 'round and round Sir William's head'. More impressively, although the box had been so constructed that it could not be stopped or started by any of the assembled company, it was stopped or started at their request by 'the unseen intelligence'.

Post-War Britain

It was difficult then, and it has been difficult since, for sceptics to reconcile Crookes's contributions to conventional science with his interest in psychical research. Some have settled this to their own satisfaction by the time-dishonoured technique of suggesting that he seduced, or was seduced by, the medium Florence Cook, and collaborated with her in fraud. The grotesque implausibility of this smear has recently provoked a writer in the *New Scientist* to offer an alternative proposition: that Crookes's mind was temporarily unhinged by thallium poisoning.

The poison must have been remarkably selective. Crookes's work with vacuum tubes arose out of, and in the course of, his investigation of mediums, to find what they could do telekinetically. As Francis Galton described in a letter to his cousin, Charles Darwin, in 1872, Crookes was experimenting to find whether mediums could influence needles suspended in a vacuum, and he found that 'different people had different power over the needles, and that the same person might have different power at a different time'. Crookes, Galton commented, 'believes he has hold of quite a grand discovery'. He had, indeed; though it was to take a very different course from what he had originally envisaged.

Of the Old Guard, Barrett was still active, but chiefly in Ireland; and Lodge, though he remained a contributor to the Society's publications, was mainly concerned with the Survival issue. No scientists of comparable stature had come into the SPR from the succeeding generations; and orthodoxy's hostility remained unabated. The sceptics were now backed by the formidable talents of Bertrand Russell.

> That man is the product of causes which had no prevision of the end they were achieving; that his origin, his growth, his hopes and fears, his loves and his beliefs, are but the outcome of accidental collocations of atoms; that no fire, no heroism, no intensity of thought and feeling, can preserve individual life beyond the grave; that all the labours of the ages, all the devotion, all the inspiration, all the noonday brightness of human genius, are destined to extinction in the vast death of the solar system, and that the whole temple of man's achievement must inevitably be buried beneath the debris of a universe in ruins – all these things, if not quite beyond dispute, are yet so nearly certain that no philosophy which rejects them can hope to stand.

Churchmen, too, far from being heartened by the evidence which psychical research was providing for Survival, were for the most part hostile. A few individuals were involved with the society – William Boyd-Carpenter, Bishop of Ripon, had been President in 1912; but the view of the majority was probably best expressed by W. R. Inge, the Dean of St Pauls, who throughout the years between the wars was to be the most widely read and quoted of churchmen (unable, as some Fleet Street wit put it, to decide whether he wished to be a pillar of the Church or two columns in the *Evening Standard*). In one of his columns in 1922 he denounced Spiritualism as 'an outburst of puerile superstition which carries us back to the mentality of barbarians'. As Edwyn Bevan was to observe in his *Seers and Sybils*, by the 1920s liberal Protestants – Protestants, that is, of the type who made up the bulk of the Established Church's congregations – in general accepted life in the spirit after death but refused to accept that there could be 'any interference with the sequence of material mechanical processes in the world except from conscious beings in the flesh', and certainly not from discarnate human spirits. Mrs Stobart was to make a valiant effort in her books to remind her co-religionists that the Bible, upon which they based their faith, was packed with psychical phenomena and spirit interventions; but to no purpose.

'Feda'

The only field of research in which the SPR could claim success in this period was with Mrs Osborne Leonard. 'Feda' had not matured, but she had developed, becoming a character in her own right. 'Feda', Lady Troubridge explained,

> has not a high opinion of Mrs Leonard. And although she will conscientiously, if rather obviously against the grain, do her any kindness in her power, she never, in my experience conveys any impression that she *likes* her. She frequently indeed, expresses open scorn of Mrs Leonard's opinions, likes or dislikes and speaks of her as a not very satisfactory and distinctly inferior instrument, who must be protected and humoured merely because, such as she is, there is none better to hand. Her instinctive antagonism to Mrs Leonard is repressed, tempered by a certain recognition of Mrs Leonard's good qualities which her honesty will not let her deny; but the antagonism is unmistakably there.

Mrs Leonard, for her part, bestowed upon 'Feda' only 'a rather patronising liking, often obscured by distinct irritation'. She resented the suggestion sometimes made that 'Feda' was her 'higher self', pointing out that she did not share 'Feda's' childish weaknesses (which included giving away Mrs Leonard's wedding ring to casual sitters and, on one occasion, throwing it in the fire, 'from which a distressed sitter rescued it').

In one sense, Mrs Leonard had the last word: she could prevent 'Feda' from taking over. In another, 'Feda' was mistress: she could refuse to co-operate, and thereby cut off Mrs Leonard's source of income. As a result, Mrs Leonard had to put up with what Lady Troubridge described as 'Feda's' 'infantilism and obstinacy'.

'Feda' also appeared conscientiously to wish to prove the reality of survival; she had come up with some ingenious ways of demonstrating to sitters, and to still unconvinced members of the SPR, that she really was obtaining her information from the 'communicators', and not from telepathic or other links with the sitter. In the SPR *Journal* for May 1921 the Rev. C. Drayton Thomas gave details of sittings – there had been fifty-three in all – he had had with Mrs Leonard; the 'communicator' claimed to be Thomas's father and, in addition to other information, told him about items which he would find in the newspapers the following day. For example, on 10 October 1919 his 'father' told him: 'In *The Times* for tomorrow, 2nd column of front page, half way down or nearly so, will be your name and your father's, your own coming first.'

About a quarter down the column, the next day, Thomas found the name 'Charles John Workman'. Thomas's name was Charles: his father's, John. Or on 27 February 1920, his 'father' said there would be a reference in the first column of the paper the next day to a place his mother had been very fond of in her childhood, and 'quite close is a name suggesting music'. In the first column Thomas found 'I. of W.' – his mother had grown up in the Isle of Wight – and just below, the name 'Harper'.

The references, Thomas pointed out, contained information not merely about what was going to appear in the next day's papers, but also about members of his family, some revealing intimate acquaintanceship. Nor could they be explained away by chance. He had compared some of the information given with other issues of *The Times*; there were a few coincidences, but nothing like the number of correct forecasts. As a check, Barrett wrote to the manager of *The Times* on behalf of the SPR to find out whether the Births, Deaths and Marriages columns would have been set up in type at the times of the sittings. From his reply it was clear that some of them would have been; but their position on the page would ordinarily not have been established until later.

Science and Parascience

The method which 'Feda' most often adopted came to be known as 'book tests' – devised, 'Feda' claimed, by the 'communicators' themselves to establish themselves in their own right, by proving that the information could not possibly come from the living. In his *Some New Evidence for Human Survival* Drayton Thomas described how he and a 'communicator' had discussed the possibility of direct communication in his home, by the established spiritualist method of 'raps'. For a time he obtained no convincing evidence, but eventually one night he three times distinctly heard a loud double knock. Three days later 'Feda' greeted him when he came for a sitting with the claim 'that *she* had succeeded in coming to our house and giving raps there'; and to prove it, she gave a book test. In the fifth book from the left on the second shelf behind his study door, 'near the top of page 17 you will see words which will serve to indicate what "Feda" was attempting to do when knocking in your room'. The book, Thomas found on his return, was a collection of Shakespeare's plays, beginning with *King Henry VI*. The third line of the page 'Feda' had indicated read 'I will not answer thee with words, but blows'.

Pamela Glenconner provided an even more striking example of a book test in *The Earthen Vessel*. 'Bim' – Edward Wyndham Tennant, who had been killed on the Somme in 1916 – was the 'communicator'; his father, Lord Glenconner, and his brother, David, the sitters. The message, 'Feda' said, was particularly for 'Bim's' father. The book was the ninth 'on the third shelf, counting from left to right in the bookcase on the right of the door in the drawing room'; he was to note the title, and read page thirty-seven. Glenconner's major interest was forestry; the book's title was *Trees*. Glenconner's worry had been that young trees were so often ruined by 'the beetle', so that 'Bim' had been known to whisper to his mother at the start of family walks 'see if we can get through the wood without hearing about the beetle'. The sentence at the bottom of page thirty-six, leading on into page thirty-seven, ran: 'Sometimes you will see curious marks in the wood; these are caused by a tunnelling beetle, very injurious to the trees.'

'Feda' was far from consistently successful in her book tests. Combing through the reports put in to the SPR Eleanor Sidgwick calculated in 1921 that in the course of 532 tests, 92 were successful and 100 approximately successful (for example, the appropriate term or idea was found on the page opposite to the one with the number which 'Feda' had given). Only in one third of the tests, therefore, could she claim some success; and a possible objection was that a similar success rate could be obtained by chance. This was tested in 1923 by nearly two thousand trials which followed the same lines as 'Feda's' but in which the place, the book and the page were selected at random. The outcome was a success rate of less than one in twenty.

'On the whole,' Eleanor Sidgwick cautiously commented, 'I think that the evidence before us does constitute a reasonable *prima facie* case for belief' – not, indeed, for belief in Survival, though she would not have ruled that out, but for belief in clairvoyance, as distinct from telepathy; the ability of the human mind to tune in, or to be tuned in, to objects, rather than to thoughts. It had taken forty years for her to break the habit of thinking in terms only of communication between minds; the book tests had finally accomplished it.

'Phantasms' revisited

In 1922 Eleanor Sidgwick – Mrs Henry Sidgwick, as she sometimes still continued to sign herself – performed a further useful service in the role she had taken up of sorter-out and assessor of the mass of material which came in to the society's office: a survey of the cases of telepathy between living persons which had come in since the publication of *Phantasms of the Living*, the initial survey, in 1886. Cases which had already appeared in the *Proceedings* were not included; this, she admitted, somewhat reduced the collection's value. She did, however, include some which had been in the *Journal*, as it was then, unlike the *Proceedings*, published for private circulation to members only.

Thirty of the cases were in the category of experiments; 170 were of spontaneous experiences, a third of them relating to dreams. They ranged from apparitions 'to purely ideational and emotional impressions and motor impulses'. Many of them were of a relatively trivial kind, interesting chiefly because they illustrated how telepathic communication operated on different everyday levels.

One such was contributed by Lowes Dickinson, long a member of the society. Hearing the doorbell ring in her London home, one day in 1917, his sister Janet had suddenly had the impression that it was her cousin Harry, 'come to tell me his mother was ill', as he had once done a year before. It turned out to be a telegram, on another matter; but she mentioned what she had thought it was to her maid. Later that morning she went out; when she returned the maid told her that her cousin had come round, in her absence, to ask her to go to see his mother. 'I had not been thinking of my aunt,' Janet wrote in her account of the episode, five days later, 'nor do I often see her.' The maid confirmed the account; and cousin Harry recalled in a letter to Janet that at the time she thought that he was at the door, he had been 'in great anxiety of mind', because he had some work to finish but felt he could not go out and leave his mother, and he was 'considering calling round and asking you to sit with her.'

A few cases were more dramatic. One, contributed by Lodge, concerned the proprietor of a large slate quarry. On his way home from the quarry he had what he described as 'a sort of message' in which he 'seemed to see a certain portion of the quarry', and the men working there, in great danger. So strong was the feeling that he wired the manager to tell him to take the men off work. 'It was very fortunate that you did wire,' the manager wrote to him the next day, 'because about an hour later the whole of the place where they were working upon went down.' Nothing could have saved the men, had they been working at the time.

As in many cases of this kind, it was possible to present a 'natural' explanation, in terms of intuition; an experienced quarry proprietor might have unconsciously noted some fault. Yet this would not explain why the feeling that something was amiss came on him later, in the way it did. And in a few of the dramatic cases, no such explanation could be offered.

The one which attracted most interest had been brought to Lodge's attention by the father of David McConnel, a pilot in the Royal Flying Corps, who was killed shortly after the end of the First World War when his aircraft crashed in fog on a routine flight. McConnel had been detailed to take an aeroplane to Tadcaster; and before he left, he had looked in on a fellow officer, James Larkin, to say he expected to be back in time for tea. Larkin spent that afternoon in his room writing letters and reading until – as he described the episode in a letter to David's father –

> I heard someone walking up the passage; the door opened with the usual noise and clatter which David always made; I heard his 'Hello boy', and I turned half round in my chair and saw him standing in the doorway, half in and half out of the room, holding the door knob in his hand. He was dressed in his full flying clothes but wearing his naval cap, there being nothing unusual in his appearance. His cap was pushed back on his head and he was smiling, as he always was when he came into the rooms and greeted us. In reply to his 'Hello

boy' I remarked 'Hello! back already?' He replied, 'Yes. Got them all right, had a good trip.' I am not positively sure of the exact words he used, but he said 'Had a good trip' or 'Had a fine trip' or words to that effect. I was looking at him the whole time he was speaking. He said 'Well, cheerio!' closed the door noisily and went out.

The time must have been between a quarter and half past three, Larkin knew; another officer had come in a few minutes later, at a quarter to four, to say he hoped David would be back in good time, as they had planned to go into Lincoln that evening. Larkin had replied that David *was* back, as he had been in the room a few minutes before. When, that evening in Lincoln, he heard that David had crashed and was dead, he at first assumed that he must have returned, but then taken off again, and been killed on the second flight. Later that evening, he learned the truth:

> As you can understand, Mr McConnel, I was at a loss to solve the problem. There was no disputing that he *had* been killed whilst flying to Tadcaster, presumably at 3.25, as we ascertained that his watch had stopped at that time. I tried to persuade myself that I had not seen him or spoken to him in this room, but I could not make myself believe otherwise, as I was undeniably awake and his appearance, voice, manner had all been so natural. I am of such a sceptical nature regarding things of this kind that even now I wish to think otherwise, that I did not see him, but I am unable to do so.

To emphasise the point about his sceptical nature, Larkin added that although he had heard of similar happenings, he had always totally disbelieved in them, imagining that the persons to whom they happened were nervous and highly strung: he had always been among the incredulous ones, 'only too ready to pooh-pooh the idea'. And he was sure he had been wide awake at the time. Nor, he insisted, could it have been a case of mistaken identity; to an inquiry from Eleanor Sidgwick, when she came to compile an account of the episode for the society's *Proceedings*, he replied that the light in his room had been good, and the only other two officers who, like David, wore naval caps, bore no resemblance to him.

The Goligher Circle revisited

In one area of psychical research, however, the SPR was out of touch; and in this period it happened to be the main area. In Belfast, Crawford was continuing his work with the Golighers; but his periodic reports were published in *Light*. As if to show his contempt for Eleanor Sidgwick's review of *The Reality of Psychic Phenomena*, Crawford ignored it in his next book, *Experiments in Psychical Science*, published in 1919, and primarily designed to answer questions such as those which Lodge had posed, which he had not fully answered before. For example: if his 'cantilever' theory were correct, would not adding weights to the table, and therefore necessitating the use of more psychic power by the medium, 'at length reach such magnitude that, the medium would topple over in her chair?' And what were the medium's sensations, during sessions?

When the table was being levitated, Crawford had found, almost all of its weight was added to the weight of the medium. 'For all practical purposes of calculation, the effect is the same as though the table was resting upon her head, or as though she was holding it up with her hands.' In his early experiments, the medium's muscles had reacted, as she sat in her chair, as if she *were* applying physical force – as it might be to her chair, holding herself down. But gradually this muscular effort had diminished; she told him that 'she experiences now no sensation whatever during the occurrence of phenomena' – though the phenomena themselves had not changed.

The explanation, Crawford thought, was that Kathleen Goligher supplied the cantilever material – the ectoplasm; but that energy was also coming from outside her. It was supplied, he surmised, by the members of her family, but channeled through the medium's body which was 'either directly or indirectly the focus of all the mechanical actions which result in phenomena', so that raps, say, outside the circle were sometimes accompanied by spasmodic body movements. This was important, Crawford argued, in connection with allegations of fraud, so often made in the past about mediums, because 'not only is it the focus, but it also seems to supply a kind of duplicate of portions of her body which can be temporarily detached and projected into the space in front of her'. As a result things happened in seances 'which, from the very nature of the case, sometimes bear a superficial appearance of fraud'; and it was this, he feared, which had led to many mediums being wrongfully accused.

The Golighers' seances, he reiterated, were 'above suspicion'; but the elements in the SPR that rejected the physical phenomena were unlikely to take Crawford's word for it – or even Barrett's, as Eleanor Sidgwick's review, which had blandly ignored his evidence, has shown. Another investigator, however, had subsequently attended a seance; a newcomer to psychical research who was destined to play an important role in the years ahead.

At Eton and at Cambridge, Whately Smith had aspired to become an orthodox scientist. The war had intervened; he had joined the Royal Flying Corps and flown as a pilot until a forced landing grounded him, and severely damaged his health. Hearing about Mrs Leonard's mediumship, he had had some sittings with her; and he had attended a seance with Crawford and the Goligher circle.

Describing what he had witnessed in the SPR's *Proceedings*, Whately Smith feared that as the history of the investigation of the physical phenomena formed 'an almost unbroken record of fraud and malobservation, of initial plausibility and subsequent exposure', it was asking for trouble to express an opinion in favour of them; but his scrutiny of Crawford's work had compelled him to accept that in the case of the Belfast circle, they were genuine. In light sufficient to see every object in the seance room, he had watched the movements of the table, heard the raps, and so on; and he had himself been allowed to make tests – for example, to try to discover the force involved in moving the large metal trumpet which featured in the seances.

The trumpet had begun by moving from outside the circle into the circle, and under the table, where it 'separated into its two component parts'. The two parts then rose into the air and came towards where he was sitting, outside the circle. He took hold of them, and found he could move them to and fro; what he could *not* do was twist either of them. 'So great was the resistance to torque that I can only describe it by saying that it felt as if the lower ends of the two parts were embedded in a large mass of solid concrete, freely suspended so as to allow of transverse and longitudinal movement, but so heavy as to preclude twisting.'

Eventually the two parts of the trumpet fell to the floor, and the table began to move, first rotating and then, after some tilts, rising clear from the floor to the height of about twelve inches. Invited to enter the circle, and test the table for himself, Whately Smith grasped it with both hands and tried to stop it from moving. 'By dint of great exertion I could prevent it from moving in any one direction and could keep it steady for a second or so, but it instantly moved in some other direction, the force changing with great rapidity.' When he tried to lift the table off the floor he could not move it; when he relaxed his grip, it levitated beside him, and then, although it would move sideways when he pushed or pulled it, he could not force it back down on to the floor.

Could he have been the victim of an illusion? A professional magician, Whately Smith admitted, could easily make observers think they had seen something they expected to see, or by distracting them, stop them seeing what he did not wish them to see; but this would not account for his experiences while wrestling with the table; still less for the times when its movements were being 'recorded by mechanical apparatus'. Fraud, then? What would be the purpose? These were private seances. They could bring neither fame nor financial reward to the Golighers; in fact the family refused to admit visitors, except those who were helping Crawford investigate the phenomena, and he had found the family 'eminently upright, honourable and likeable people of the best type – quite incapable of practising a mean and objectless trickery'.

In any case, Whately Smith concluded, those who attributed the phenomena to fraud would have a job explaining how the fraud was perpetrated. Like other previous witnesses he had seen the phenomena in good light; like them, he had been allowed to inspect what was happening inside as well as outside the circle; like them, he had wrestled with table and trumpet, feeling them twisting and turning. How could such effects be achieved by a family sitting around in a circle, holding hands?

Still, he admitted that psychical researchers had a problem. Some orthodox scientists might be convinced, as he had been, by what they had seen. But others, who had not witnessed the phenomena, would dismiss them because the medium could not always produce them to order; and because if they were real, 'there can be no doubt, in this case at least, that they are directed by an intelligence of some kind or other'.

By the time Whately Smith's commentary, along with Barrett's earlier paper, was published in the *Proceedings* in 1919, Crawford was turning his attention to a different aspect of the phenomena: the processes by which the ectoplasm, emerging from Kathleen's body, formed itself into the psychic 'rods' which levitated the table. The 'rods', he found, could flatten out at the end farthest from her so that they could either push or pull – the pulling power being provided by 'a difference of air pressure' – suction, in other words, as if they resembled the tentacles of an octopus. They were adjustable: sometimes hard, sometimes soft. And when they left impressions in a bowl of clay (as Eusapia's pseudopods had often done), 'the working end of the psychic structure is often covered

Post-War Britain

At the end of his *Psychic Structures* Crawford had photographs which he had been able to take when the ectoplasm from Kathleen Goligher's body – commonly from her navel or her vagina – became visible, showing how it looked like a scarf, drooping floorwards, but then lifted to provide the cantilever effect.

with marks which are very similar to the fabric of the medium's stockings'; at the end of seances, 'various marks are left by the clay on the medium's stockings and shoes'.

In other words, the 'rods' were behaving as if they *were* the medium's feet. The discovery of fabric impressions on clay, and still more of clay on the medium's person, would have been regarded, even by many of those who accepted materialisations, as proof of fraud. But fraud, Crawford insisted, was out of the question. Kathleen's feet were sometimes tied to her chair, sometimes actually enclosed in a box: it made no difference. He could see that they were not responsible for the impressions in the clay: he could even walk between her and the clay without interrupting the 'rods' at their work. In any case, the impressions in the clay were often of a kind that could not have been made by a human foot. What was happening, he assumed, was that as the ectoplasm emerged from her it occasionally took on the appearance of whatever fabric she was wearing, and then carried bits of it, along with fluff, to the clay; and brought back traces of the clay to the point at which the ectoplasm re-entered her body.

To sceptics – and this would have included Eleanor Sidgwick and those of like mind in the SPR – Crawford's findings would have been simply another indication of the capacity of mediums for deception, and of investigators for self-deception. But to anybody who accepted the possibility of ectoplasmic materialisations these findings were of great significance. One of the problems which had bedevilled research into physical mediums had been the discovery that when they moved objects at a distance the force involved was not just an abstraction, telekinesis, which could be regarded as an indication of the medium's power to influence matter at a distance. That the movements were performed by pseudopods, arms and hands or legs and feet sprouting from the medium's body, was harder to swallow. Even harder to take was the possibility that these ectoplasmic limbs could so successfully mimic or counterfeit the human form that they looked real, felt real and smelled real. Hardest of all was acceptance of the fact that the descriptions of materialisations were to be relied upon: the ectoplasm could not merely create hands which, when shaken, seemed to be human hands: it could create clothes which to sight and touch appeared to be real clothes. And, understandably but ironically, the more closely they resembled real clothes the greater the risk the medium would run of being accused of fraud. Witnesses who would have been ready to accept a 'full-form' materialisation appearing in a robe would be likely to assume fraud if they happened to see on it a laundry mark.

Crawford's new findings, if he had been able to have them confirmed, as his earlier studies had been, by members of the SPR, would have compelled a radical revision of ideas about, and attitudes to, physical mediumship in the society. But Crawford, trying to catch up with his university commitments, had a nervous breakdown; and in the summer of 1920 he committed suicide. In a letter to Gow, the editor of *Light*, he explained that his collapse was due to overwork, and had nothing to do with the Goligher circle. 'My psychic work was all done before the collapse, and is the most perfect work I have done in my life,' he claimed; everything to do with it would bear every scrutiny, as it was done when his brain was working perfectly, 'and it could not be responsible for what has occurred.'

Crawford left his description of the research into the ectoplasmic processes to Gow, to prepare for posthumous publication; and *The Psychic Structures of the Goligher Circle* came out in 1921. Inevitably, the fact that Crawford had committed suicide fuelled suspicion, in spite of his disclaimers, that he realised he had been the Golighers' dupe. And since his later research had not been vetted, it was possible for sceptical SPR members to ignore it; in a review, Dingwall dismissed Crawford's methods as not calculated to appeal 'to many of the more critical students of psychical phenomena'. In 1921 the SPR despatched an investigator to Belfast; but he proved an unfortunate choice. Although Fournier d'Albe had been an admirer of Crookes, and was engaged on his biography, he was unsympathetic to much of Crookes's work in the psychic field (and seriously misleading about it, as Lodge was to complain in his review); and he had either not read Crawford's books carefully, or had singularly failed to take note of the advice Crawford had given.

From the start Crawford had emphasised the absolute necessity, if the phenomena were to be studied, of the investigator winning the Goligher family's confidence. After it was won, controls could be introduced with Kathleen's willing consent, but it was no use regarding the seances simply as laboratory-fodder. This was what Fournier proceeded to do. He observed and reported levitations, and admitted that the table resisted his attempts to shift it; but his ambition was to devise experiments whose results would be 'independent of anyone's testimony' — understandably, as he must have known that his testimony, even if supported by witnesses, would be rejected if it were favourable. And when he found he could make no progress to this objective, he became disgruntled. Although he could not account for some of the effects he witnessed, he wrote to tell Kathleen Goligher that as he had been unable to obtain conclusive evidence of their psychic origin they were of 'no scientific value,' and he had decided to terminate the investigation.

He did not disclose to her that he had begun to suspect that she was cheating. He kept that for his report to the SPR. Photographs he had taken of her ectoplasm, he explained, showed that it bore a resemblance to chiffon; and when a footstool was 'levitating' against the dark background he thought he had seen what might have been Kathleen's foot supplying the motive force. Yet he must have known that the 'chiffon' element had been observed and photographed by Schrenck, with whom he corresponded, with 'Eva'. He must also have known about pseudopods; yet he had neither bothered to prevent Kathleen from using her feet, nor had satisfied himself that it really was a foot, and not a pseudopod, which he saw. And ironically, when he published his findings in pamphlet form, an appendix contributed by Gow in his capacity as Crawford's literary executor not only went some way to demolishing Fournier's case, but showed that the evidence Crawford had provided had been better attested by outside witnesses than had been realised.

Crawford, the appendix revealed, had watched and photographed Kathleen's ectoplasm developing, noting how it appeared 'just as though it had been manufactured like cloth'. He had also been careful to ensure that in her trances, Kathleen could not use her feet. And he had obtained statements from a number of men and women who had attended seances, presumably intending to use them when he came to sum up the results of his investigation. One of them was the President of the Glasgow Society of Conjurors; like Barrett, he had been chiefly impressed by the invitation to wrestle with the levitated table, inside the circle: 'I could not pull it down for the life of me.' Another witness, noting that Fournier had complained of the poor light in which the seances were conducted, replied that he had been 'exceedingly surprised' at the seance he attended 'to find so much happening in so bright a light'. It had been good enough for him to read by; yet in these conditions he had seen the table levitate: 'I can solemnly assure you that not only did it leave the floor without contact, but remained in space, well over the heads of the sitters,' floating there for a couple of minutes, and resisting attempts to pull it down.

Perhaps for personal reasons – he may have been bored in

Belfast; evidently he never felt at ease with the Golighers, nor they with him – Fournier wanted to abandon the inquiry, and used the allegations of cheating as his excuse, knowing they would be likely to satisfy the SPR Council, as it was then composed, the more so in that Crawford had given his allegiance to Gow, and *Light*. Whatever the reasons, his decision effectively blocked the chance of a systematic follow-up of Crawford's work on the society's behalf; and in any case, Kathleen was about to marry, and terminate her career as a medium.

Neither Fournier nor anybody else had seriously suggested that if there were cheating, Crawford was involved. But this makes it very hard indeed to show how he could have been duped by the Golighers. He could *see* what was happening; and even if he were periodically busy with, say, camera angles and gadgets of various kinds, his descriptions are of what he saw when the gadgetry was set up, and they do not admit of the possibility that he could have been deceived day after day, month after month. Besides, if the Golighers were cheats – contrary to the view not just of Crawford, but of Barrett and Whately Smith – why would they have cheated to such little purpose, refusing to give public seances? The idea of the entire family giving seances night after night just to fool the unfortunate Crawford and the occasional witness he brought in, makes no sense. They might have played tricks for a week or two, as a family game; but that they should have played it for five years is surely inconceivable.

So long as physical mediumship remained an unfashionable area of psychical research, the full value of Crawford's work was unlikely to be appreciated. But now that psychokinesis is coming back into fashion, there are signs that it is being taken seriously again, as the record of research of a kind which had never before been undertaken, by a man with unusual qualifications, and with the integrity that must have been required to persuade the Golighers to accept so protracted, and doubtless frequently boring, a series of trials.

Psychic Photography

In 1919 a fresh effort was made to study one of the more contentious of the phenomena associated with spiritualism, with the setting up of a Society for the Study of Supernormal Pictures.

They were contentious because most of the photographs had

been of deceased persons, their faces apparently floating in the air above the sitters, who would often identify them as loved ones. The ability of the photographers to produce them by psychic means, either through being psychic themselves or by employing a medium to attend sessions, had endlessly been challenged; charges of fraud had been common, occasionally leading to prosecutions and prison sentences. And if it were accepted that such photographs could be genuine, the mechanics of the process by which the faces appeared remained baffling.

An interesting attempt had been made to solve it in the early 1890s by J. Traill Taylor, one of the leading photographers of the time. Taylor had come to the conclusion that it was no use continuing to refuse to investigate spirit photography on the ground that it was demonstrably fraudulent; as it had survived years of such criticism, and continued to flourish, it would be wise to subject it to formal tests. The method he devised was to use his own camera, and plates fresh from the makers, which the medium would not be allowed to touch; the sessions would be conducted in the presence of two witnesses (to ensure that neither the medium nor he himself cheated); and – an innovation – 'I would set a watch upon my own camera: in other words, I would use a binocular stereoscopic camera.' By this means Taylor hoped to discover whether the faces, if they appeared, really were looming over the sitters, as they seemed to be on prints; and whether they were two- or three-dimensional. The faces appeared; they were 'absolutely flat', he found. But even more remarkable, to him, was that the spirit faces were not captured, as the sitters themselves were, by the camera's lenses. The psychic component was impressed directly upon the plates – as a thumbprint might be. The psychic image, in other words, might be produced without a camera.

'But still the question obtrudes,' Traill Taylor observed,

> How came these figures there? I again assert that the plates were not tampered with by either myself or anyone present. Are they crystallisations of thought? Have lens and light really nothing to do with their formation? The whole subject was mysterious enough on the hypothesis of an invisible spirit, whether a thought projection or an actual spirit, being really in the vicinity of the sitter; but it is now a thousand times more so.

Taylor's question had remained unanswered. Few believers worried about how the features of a loved one came to be reproduced, so long as the reproduction could be construed as further evidence of the spirit's survival after death; and sceptics continued to assume that the 'spirits' could only be imposed on plates by fraud.

That fraud should have been common was not surprising, in view of the profit which could be made from providing such photographs; but there were some indications, apart from Traill Taylor's evidence, that mind or spirit could impinge on photographic plates. In the welter of dubious evidence about psychic photography, there were a few case histories where effective precautions appeared to have been taken to prevent fraud; and others where the characters of the witnesses made it improbable that they were engaged in deception.

Hyslop, for example, was sufficiently impressed by the evidence he received from the Rev. Charles Hall Cook, who had had to retire from the ministry through ill-health, to give it space in the *Journal* of the American Society for Psychical Research (ASPR). For Cook, psychic photography had become a hobby; and he combined his own experiments with the investigation of other photographers. Some of them, he decided, could not seriously be suspected of fraud: among them Mrs Margarite du Pont Lee, a wealthy woman who ran a charity. Her Kodak, she had found, kept on taking pictures of objects which were not in shot, or were in another room. Of course the same result could be obtained by a double exposure; but Cook could not think of any reason why Mrs Lee would want to cheat – 'her humanitarian work as well as intelligence make it difficult to impeach her veracity or honesty'.

There were cases, too, where the psychic element could not be attributed to the guile of the photographers. In his *Flight Towards Reality* Air Vice-Marshal Sir Victor Goddard has described one example, in connection with a photograph which, at the time he was writing –1915 – was still on his desk: an official picture, taken by Bassano's shortly after the end of the First World War, of Goddard's squadron. After the group photograph was pinned up, while the members of the squadron were identifying friends 'they saw – or they were prompted then to see, the face of Freddy Jackson, air mechanic, in the topmost row' – his expression seeming to indicate that he had only just arrived in time:

> Well, there he was, and no mistake, although a little fainter than the rest. Indeed he looked as though he was not altogether there; not really with that group, for he alone was capless, smiling; all the rest were serious and set, and wearing service caps. Most had not long

Science and Parascience

'There he was, and no mistake!' 'Freddy Jackson' can just be seen peeking out behind the fourth man from the left in the top row: more clearly in the blown-up version.

returned from Church Parade and marching in a military funeral. For Freddy Jackson had, upon that very spot – the Squadron tarmac – three days before, walked heedlessly into the whirling propeller of an aeroplane. He had been killed stone dead instantly. He, evidently, was quite unaware of it.

Inevitably, however, the believers in the possibility of psychic intervention of this kind and the sceptics who took for granted it was all fraudulent both tended to concentrate their attention on the professional spirit photographers, of whom the best known in Britain was William Hope.

A mass of evidence accumulated to vouch for Hope's ability to produce likenesses of the deceased on portraits of the living, some of it from individuals who knew what tricks to watch out for. Crookes had a seance with Hope in 1916, obtaining a spirit photograph of his 'dear departed'. In a letter to Lodge, he claimed it was very like what she had been ten years before, but it was not taken from any portrait of her. 'There could not possibly be any trickery as the plate never left my possession and I did all the manipulation and developing myself'; and he was glad to have what he regarded as 'this definite proof of survival'. Lodge, whom he might have expected also to be pleased, was uneasy: 'I confess I have been extremely sceptical about that man Hope,' he wrote back: 'I am impressed by your evidence, of course, but cannot say I am convinced.' Crookes replied that he had been an acknowledged expert on photography, in his youth, editing the *Journal of the London Photographic Society*, and writing many papers on the subject. He was 'acquainted with all the dodges, and had taken care to see that Hope had no access to the plate, except to put it into and take it out of the camera'.

Although Crookes had marked the plates to prevent substitution, Hope might have been up to some new dodge to dupe him – or so, at least, sceptics could claim. The founders of the Society for the Study of Supernormal Pictures were determined to introduce tests which would confound scepticism; and the most determined of them, as his great reputation would be at stake, was their Vice President, Sir Arthur Conan Doyle.

'When I had finished my medical education in 1882 I found myself, like many young medical men, a convinced materialist as regards our personal destiny,' Doyle recalled in his *The New Revelation*, published in 1918. He had accepted that there was a creator – or, rather 'an intelligent force behind all the operations of Nature'. But 'when it came to a question of our little personalities surviving death, it seemed to me that the whole analogy of Nature was against it. When the candle burns out, the light disappears . . . When the body dissolves, there is an end of the matter.' As for spiritualism, 'I had always regarded the subject as the greatest nonsense upon earth, and I had read of the conviction of fraudulent mediums and wondered how any sane man could believe such things.' Even when table-turning sessions with friends produced coherent messages, he assumed that somebody was cheating.

Nevertheless Doyle had been struck by the quality of some of the men who had accepted the evidence as genuine: Judge Edmonds in the United States, William Crookes and Alfred Russel Wallace in Britain; Camille Flammarion in France; and in 1891 he had joined the SPR. Reading Myers's *Human Personality*, with its examples of telepathy, finally banished his materialist doubts. 'I had said that the flame could not exist when the candle was gone. But here was the flame, a long way off the candle.'

Doyle claimed no psychic gifts himself; he would have remained a dilettante investigator, he admitted, had it not been for the Great War.

> In the presence of an agonised world, hearing every day of the deaths of the flower of our race in the first promise of their unfulfilled youth, seeing around one the wives and mothers who had no clear conception whither their loved one had gone, I seemed suddenly to see that this subject, with which I had so long dallied, was not merely a study of a force outside the rules of science, but that it was really something tremendous, a breaking down of the walls between two worlds, a direct undeniable message from beyond, a call of hope and of guidance to the human race at the time of its deepest affliction.

The Cottingley Fairies

As things turned out, however, the case which was to launch Doyle as the protagonist of psychic photography, at least for the general public, was not of a spirit photograph; not, at least, of the kind which had been most commonly encountered. Interest had been aroused a few years earlier by Andrew Lang and others in folklore, promoting speculation over whether fairies, elves, gnomes and other members of the species might conceivably have a real existence, remaining invisible to most people but visible to anybody with the appropriate psychic faculties. And a couple of photographs of fairies taken in a woodland beck, or glen, precipitated controversy which has not been settled to this day.

Doyle presented the pictures and gave an account of them in the *Strand* magazine; but the real work on the case had been done by Edward L. Gardner, one of the leading Theosophists of the time, and his son Leslie. In *Fairies*, Gardner was to recall that in May 1920 a friend sent him a couple of prints, asking him for his opinion; one of a group of fairy-like figures dancing in front of a girl, the other of 'a winged gnome-like creature near a girl's beckoning hand'. A woman had given his friend the prints after hearing him lecture; what he had said about fairies had caused her to wonder, she told him, whether they 'might be true after all'. Gardner took the pictures to be fakes, but asked to see the negatives, and passed them to an expert. To the surprise of both men the expert, following a careful examination, said that they were certainly not double exposures; that the fairies were not made out of paper or any fabric; that they were not painted on a photographed background; and – what most astonished him – they appeared to have moved during exposure.

Post-War Britain

Hearing of the photographs, Conan Doyle asked to see them, and it was agreed to ask for a second opinion from the Kodak company. It confirmed the first expert's view, but speculated about the possibility they might have been faked by some clever operation: 'After all,' as one of the men who had examined them put it, 'as fairies couldn't be true, the photographs must have been faked somehow.' If they were faked, however, it would have had to be cleverly done, which would have taken time.

Gardner decided to pursue the investigation himself, and set off for Cottingley, where the woman – Mrs Wright – who had sent him the prints lived. Three years before, she explained, a young cousin from South Africa, Frances Griffiths, had come to stay. She was ten years old, and used to go with Mrs Wright's thirteen-year-old daughter Elsie to play in the nearby glen where, they claimed, they were joined by fairies. Their parents had paid little attention, and merely chaffed the children; but when their father bought a small camera, they begged to be allowed to photograph the fairies, and to humour them he gave way. Developing the print for them 'in the scullery cupboard', he found to his astonishment that they had indeed taken a picture of fairies; and another, of a gnome-like creature, was taken a month later.

Gardner was impressed by the Wrights. Frances had returned to South Africa, but Elsie showed him the glen and answered his questions sensibly. Her father's testimony also carried conviction. He and his wife had thought the children must be fooling them, and had searched the glen and their bedroom for possible evidence, without finding anything suspicious; having decided to give them the benefit of the doubt, he had put the camera and the prints away.

There could be no question, Gardner decided, of the family being involved in the deception; and he did not see how the children could have contrived it on their own. To make sure they were not substituting their own film, when Frances came back to England for a holiday he arranged for the two girls to have cameras, with marked plates; they took three more fairy pictures, and the makers assured him that the plates had not been tampered with.

This left three questions. Had the girls found some way to rig up and photograph the 'fairies', ingenious enough to defy detection? If not, were the figures which appeared on the photographs the fairies which the children claimed to see regularly in the glen; or were they thought-forms? And if they were real, what *were* they; in other words, what do fairies consist of?

Science and Parascience

Needless to say, in the ensuing controversy (periodically revived since in articles and television programmes) these issues became confused, with all concerned tending to take sides, assuming that the photographs must either be wholly genuine, or faked. Lodge, however, was an exception. To explain the photographs rationally, he suggested, 'without accusation of fraud, the simplest hypothesis would seem to be that an imaginative child, playing the game of make-believe, might sometimes innocently assist the imagination of her playmates by figures designed by herself, if she had the skill, and that these figures might subsequently get photographed'. His mind was not closed on the issue, he concluded; but that was his impression.

If a recent article 'Cottingley: at last the truth' is indeed the truth, Lodge had come close to the mark. Frances Way and Elsie Hill, as they had become by marriage, had always maintained that the photographs were genuine: now, they admitted to Joe Cooper in an interview that four of them had been faked. But they had been faked because the children, and Frances in particular, had become accustomed to seeing fairies, down the glen. Irritated by the grown-ups jeering at the notion, they had made cut-outs, taking as models some illustrations in *Princess Mary's Gift Book*; and once launched into the deception, they had felt bound to keep it up.

It is always risky to rely upon testimonies half a century after the event; especially when, as in this case, they do not entirely coincide. Still, the new version goes some way to solving the mystery of the Cottingley Fairies – up to a point. Frances continues to insist that they did see fairies: 'They were real fairies,' she reiterated in the interview, 'sometimes they came up, only inches away.' And in one of the photographs, she maintains (Elsie disagrees), the fairy was genuine: one showing a sheath, or cocoon, in the grass, and a figure beside it. When Gardner questioned them, the girls had no idea what the cocoon was; they had never seen one before. Folklore experts, however, recognised it as an esoteric feature known as a 'magnetic bath', which fairies were thought to take for restorative purposes. This was not something which the girls were likely to have known from their *Gift Book* range of reading; and Frances still insists that they came upon it unawares: 'It was a wet Saturday afternoon and we were just mooching about with our cameras and Elsie had nothing prepared,' she recalls. 'I saw these fairies building up in the grasses and just aimed the camera and took a photograph.'

Post-War Britain

The Cottingley 'magnetic bath'.

Whatever the truth about the photographs, Doyle was left in no doubt that there were many people of standing who believed in fairies, and who claimed often to have seen them. There was general agreement, however, that they could not be real in quite the same sense as a blackbird was real: some individuals could see them, while their friends could see nothing. To Doyle, the evidence pointed to the existence of a population 'which may be as numerous as the human race, which pursues its own strange life in its own strange way, and which is only separated from ourselves by some difference of vibrations'. One possibility was 'that there is a dividing line, like the water edge, this line depending upon what we vaguely call a higher rate of vibrations', he suggested. 'Taking the vibration theory as a working hypothesis, one could conceive that by raising or lowering the rate the creatures could move from one side to the other of this line of material visibility, as the reptile scuttles back to the surf.' This was, he admitted, supposition; but 'intelligent supposition based on the available evidence is in the pioneer of science, and it may be that the actual solution will be found in this direction'.

Gardner, who had made a study of fairy lore, surmised that fairies of whatever species did not have bodies, human or otherwise; they had nuclei which might take different forms, and as such they could not be defined in terms of form, 'any more than one can so describe a tongue of flame'. When they took human form it might be grotesque or graceful, dense or ethereal.

Elsie had her own hypothesis, which she put tentatively to Lodge when he wrote to her to ask for more information. She described them as shimmering 'like a butterfly's wing', and said they were always associated in her mind with music: 'I am very ignorant,' she wrote, 'but could they possibly be "musical vibrations" which I see and which my mind gives form to? I really do not know what I am talking about when I suggest this, but I am sure there is something there with movement, colour and sound, which gives happiness.' Elsie added that she had also had quite a few other psychic experiences, such as 'seeing' her playmate arrive at her house with a new coat on, and hearing the latch click on the gate, some time before Frances actually did arrive – wearing the new coat, which Elsie had not seen before.

The Advent of Harry Price

However fascinating the subject of the composition of fairies might be to believers, the Cottingley photographs only served to confirm sceptics in the assumption that they were just another proof that psychic photography, in any of its forms, was fraudulent. The leading members of the SPR, Lodge and Barrett excepted, tended to share this view; and before the Cottingley echoes had died away they were given the chance to show that members of the society must not be identified with the gullible Conan Doyle.

It had been all too easy for photographers to take advantage of the demand for spirit pictures of sitters' loved ones, as Edward Bush showed in 1920 in his *Spirit Photography Exposed*, with its revealing descriptions of how 'extras', as the spirit portraits had come to be described, could be faked. But Hope had not yet been trapped in any deception; and in 1921 he managed to introduce an 'extra' into a photograph of James Douglas, the truculent columnist of the *Sunday Express*. Douglas issued a challenge to any photographer to duplicate the process without using psychic powers. It was accepted by William Marriott; and the experiment was carried with Conan Doyle and Everard Feilding, among others, in attendance. Marriott experienced no difficulty in producing an 'extra' – one photograph had a young woman with upcast eyes between Douglas and Doyle; 'another, of Doyle alone, showed fairies dancing round him'. Nothing could be inferred about the authenticity of spirit photography, Feilding pointed out; but the experiment at least revealed the helplessness of an ordinary observer in the hands of a skilled operator; and consequently also of the valuelessness of most reports of successes in 'what *appear* to be test conditions'.

Supporters of Hope promptly themselves challenged the findings: Douglas, they claimed, had bungled the arrangements (as indeed he had had to admit); and Marriott had not explained how he had done the trick. Marriott thereupon explained how he had done it, adding a list of other ways in which he might have done it, and offering to produce a set of fool-proof conditions under which, if any 'extras' appeared, he would admit that the case needed further investigation.

The test had been carried out at the new British College of Psychic Science, founded in 1920 by a shrewd and successful businessman, Hewat McKenzie, who had become interested in mediumship, and felt that the SPR was not doing enough in this field; he was more concerned to encourage mediums to develop their talents than to test them in order to make sure they were not cheating. Hope had naturally gravitated into the college's orbit; but in 1921 he agreed to have a formal test by a new member of the SPR, who was destined to become the most celebrated, or notorious, psychical researcher in Britain, Harry Price. Price was a smooth operator; he had great energy; as a skilled conjuror, he would be quick to detect trickery; and he had collected a fine library of works on conjuring and psychical research which he had offered to leave to the SPR on permanent loan. Who better could be found to expose Hope? And he did.

Or so it was assumed. In the light of Price's subsequent career, the exposure cannot be relied upon; but in any case, his report to the SPR was a slimy affair. Relations between the society and the college were not good; his report traded on this, boasting how he had fooled members of the college when he arrived with his fellow investigator. He had 'ingratiated himself with them in every way', and when Hope arrived 'I made myself extremely affable to him' – the tone making it clear that he was concerned less with putting the members of the college and Hope at their ease than with putting them off their guard. Price's account of Hope's substitution of the plates is unconvincing – knowing Price was so experienced in the ways of conjurors, Hope would have been unlikely to play so obvious a trick; and when members of the college who examined the sealed plates after the experiment found that they had been tampered with, the possibility was that Price, rather than Hope, had been responsible.

In any case, as Barrett pointed out, Hope should not have been condemned on the strength of this exposure; by this time the society had appointed a research officer, Eric Dingwall, who should have run the investigation, rather than leave it to Price. A fresh investigation, Barrett urged, should be mounted. But the Sidgwick-dominated SPR Council was in no mood to open up the case again; nor, in all probability, would Hope have consented to a further trial.

4 The Continental Mediums 1918-24

Despite the wartime divisions of Europe, psychical research was remarkably quick to recover after the Armistice, thanks largely to the generosity of a rich French industrialist, Jean Meyer. In 1919 he founded and funded the Institut Métapsychique International, with Richet as President and Gustave Geley as Director; and it was Geley who was to dominate the psychical research scene for the next few years. Meyer's support enabled him to investigate mediums all over Europe; and the Institute's journal, the *Revue Métapsychique*, began publishing a mass of varied and well-attested reports of investigations of a kind that had become rare in the publications of the SPR.

Born in 1868, Geley had had a brilliant career as a medical student, and started to practise as a doctor at Annecy; but he had become involved in the struggle to liberate science, and in particular biology, from neo-Darwinism, and in 1899 had written a book, *Les Preuves du Transformisme*, presenting a new version of Vitalism, akin in some respects to Bergson's and McDougall's. Like them, he realised that psychic phenomena fitted in well enough with Vitalist theory; but unlike McDougall, he was particularly attracted by the physical phenomena of mediumship, because it struck him as strikingly illustrating the psyche's ability to influence matter. Ectoplasmic materialisations, he believed, were analogous to the process by which a chrysalis, after dematerialising, rematerialised into a butterfly.

Towards the end of the war Geley had arranged with Mme Bisson to attend seances with Martha Béraud – 'Eva C.'. Initially they had been held at Mme Bisson's home, twice weekly for a year and a half; then, for a further three months, he and some colleagues had held them in his own laboratory. He presented his findings at a meeting in the Collège de France in 1918 in a paper entitled 'Supernormal Physiology', and two years later his *From the Unconscious to the Conscious* summarised them and showed how they could be incorporated into his Vitalist theory.

'Eva': Geley's investigations

Physical mediumship was sufficiently well known by 1920 for Geley to be able to claim 'no one nowadays is ignorant of what is meant by so-called supernormal physiology', manifested through mediums in the form of 'dynamic and material effects inexplicable by the regular play of their organs and transcending the field of organic action'; and he went on to describe the transcending process, as best he could, from his personal experience, chiefly with 'Eva'.

As a precaution Geley had permitted nobody else to have access to the seance room before a sitting. When Marthe arrived with Mme Bisson she was undressed in his presence, and that of any other doctor who was attending – convention permitting members of the medical profession to see her unclothed; and then, 'dressed in a tight garment, sewn up at the back and at the wrists', after Mme Bisson had put her in a hypnotic trance 'Eva' would be taken to the curtained-off recess – the curtains being there chiefly to shield her from the effects of sudden light. The rest of the seance room was kept light enough for all present to see what was happening; during seances 'Eva' would part the curtains so that she and the materialisations would both be visible.

Usually they were not long in coming. 'A substance at first amorphous or polymorphous', as Geley described it, exuded from 'the natural orifices'; sometimes from the top of her head, from her nipples or from the tips of her fingers, but most often from her mouth. The colour varied: it might be black, white or grey. To the touch, the substance was 'soft, and somewhat elastic, while spreading; hard, knotty or fibrous when it forms cords'. And it was mobile: sometimes evolving slowly, moving over the medium with 'a crawling reptilian movement'; sometimes appearing and disappearing in a flash.

Crookes and Richet, Geley recalled, had witnessed 'full-form' materialisations; he himself had not been so fortunate, but he had frequently seen complete fingers and hands, and 'a living head, whose bones I could feel under a thick mass of hair'. But the point which he was most concerned to emphasise was that there could be no question of the medium or anybody else smuggling complete heads or hands into the seance room, because the investigators could watch them evolve – as extracts from his notes described. He included one of them, in which he had recorded the evolutionary process as it was happening. From 'Eva's' mouth

The Continental Mediums

there descends to her knees a cord of white substance of the thickness of two fingers. This ribbon takes under our eyes varying forms; that of a large perforated membrane with swellings and vacant spaces; it gathers itself together, retracts, swells and narrows again. Here and there from the mass appear temporary protrusions, and these for a few seconds assume the form of fingers, the outline of hands, and then re-enter the mass. Finally the cord retracts on itself, lengthens to the knees; its end rises, detaches itself from the medium, and moves towards me. I can see then the extremity thicken like a swelling, and this terminal swelling expands into a perfectly modelled hand. I touch it; it gives a normal sensation. I feel the bones, and the fingers with their nails. Then the hand contracts, diminishes and disappears in the end of the cord. The cord makes a few movements, retracts, and returns to the medium's mouth.

The materialisations did not always remain in visible contact with the medium; sometimes heads would appear at a distance from her. And whereas in the earlier tests with Schrenck, they had so often been two-dimensional, in those which Geley had conducted in his laboratory – witnessed by, among many others, the bacteriologist Albert Calmette and Jules Courtier of the Sorbonne – they were usually three-dimensional (though not necessarily life-size: some were miniatures).

These three-dimensional forms, Geley pointed out, could be *simulacra*: *simulacra* 'of fingers, having the general form but without warmth, flexibility or joints; *simulacra* of faces, like masks, or as if cut out of paper'; and he cited M. de Fontenay's remark, 'one would think that some kind of malicious sprite was mocking the observers'. For Geley, however, this could be explained readily enough on his Vitalist theory. 'They are the products of a force whose metapsychic output is weak and whose means of execution is weaker still. It does what it can. It rarely succeeds, precisely because its activity, directed outside normal lines, has no longer the certainty which the normal biologic impulse gives to physiological activity.' And he cited, as a parallel, nature's failure always to produce perfect specimens at birth, resulting in the occasional monstrosity.

So confident was Geley that he had accumulated not merely the evidence required to convince scientists of the reality of materialisations, but also a credible explanation for them, that he rounded on the sceptics. 'I do not say "There was no trickery,"' he claimed; 'I say "There was no possibility of trickery,"' a boast which was lent support by the publication the same year of a revised and updated version of Schrenck's *Phenomena of Materialisation*, describing his work with 'Eva' and Stanislawa Tomczyk, and with other young mediums who had come to his attention while Germany had been cut off during the war. It contained scores of photographs designed to show materialisations in various stages, from the initial dribble of ectoplasm to full forms; and although a book could not show it, Schrenck pointed out that when a series of photographs taken simultaneously were analysed under a stereoscope, they showed a 'flowing transition from the flat to the plastic', refuting the rumination/regurgitation hypothesis.

In addition, the investigators had been able to grasp the materialised hands, and to hold them. Clutching them could hurt the medium; but the materialisations would then simply dissolve in their grasp, as if by evaporation, sometimes leaving faint traces behind, but never solid material of the kind which could have been swallowed and extruded – and which of course would also have been retained in an investigator's grasp.

Sometimes 'Eva' used her hands – though her wrists would as usual be held by sitters, one on each side of her – as if to mould the ectoplasm; and this, along with his experience of the ectoplasmic 'threads' which Stanislawa used in levitating objects, suggested to Schrenck that 'the lively wish of lifting an object from a distance leads to the associated idea of a thread, with which the experiment might be performed: thereupon the objective phantom of a thread is brought into being by a hallucination that realises itself in matter'.

'Eva': The SPR Trials

Although Geley's research findings had been ridiculed by sceptics, they had not been able to find any flaw, not even those of the kind which had been alleged in connection with the earlier work of Richet and Schrenck; and an impressive list was accumulating of scientists and savants who had attended seances and been convinced that the phenomena were genuine. There still remained, however, a formidable obstacle to their acceptance: the hostility of the Society for Psychical Research. Although it continued to maintain that it held no corporate views, so rigidly was it still controlled by Eleanor Sidgwick – as, in effect, general manager – that its publications tended to express her opinions and prejudices; and her antipathy to physical mediumship had remained unabated.

The Continental Mediums

The two substantial surveys of the pre-war research of 'Eva' by Mme Bisson and Schrenck, for example, had been given for review to the young Helen Verrall, whose father and mother had been in the Cambridge nucleus, and who was herself cast in the Sidgwick mould (as was her husband-to-be, another Trinity graduate, W. H. Salter). She did not allow the fact that she had had no experience of investigating physical mediumship to deter her from making clear her presumption that it was faked. When Hyslop argued that a distinction ought to be preserved between conscious fraud – as when a medium swallowed objects before a seance, intending to regurgitate them – and the kind of cheating which Eusapia admitted to, when she was in her trance, Helen Verrall magisterially rebuked him, arguing that if a solicitor misappropriated funds he could not successfully plead that he was in a state of dissociation of consciousness at the time. In this she was in fact in error; a solicitor could then have made such a plea successfully, if his counsel had been able to convince a jury that he had not been in his right mind at the time. But in any case the analogy was silly. Solicitors were not expected to go into trances in the course of their work; mediums were, and the consequences of possible alterations in their personality structure needed to be allowed for, and if necessary prevented.

Helen Verrall's review of the books by Bisson and Schrenck, along with sundry articles on 'Eva', some dating from the Algerian sittings, was in the Podmore tradition, concentrating upon the accusations of fraud. She devoted no fewer than five pages to the 'grave suspicion' arising from the lawyer's claim that he knew how Marthe Béraud had faked the manifestations, in spite of Richet's demonstration that the claim was false, as the alleged trapdoor did not exist. The speculations of Mathilde von Kemnitz and Dr von Gulat-Wellenburg, attributing the materialisations to 'Eva's' ability to swallow and regurgitate objects, and the 'MIRO' accusation, also received more attention in the review than the weight of evidence in 'Eva's' favour.

The extent of the continuing prejudice within the SPR against physical mediums was further revealed in Schiller's review of the English translation of Schrenck's *Phenomena of Materialisation*. Ordinarily Schiller was one of the more open-minded of the society's influential members, and he had to admit that if the facts really were as Schrenck and others claimed they had witnessed, science would have to accept that there must be some explanation for them, however absurd they seemed. But he could not help ridiculing Geley's concept of 'ideoplasty'. 'We are literally required to believe that "wishes become horses", and mediums can ride them,' he remarked. 'But what, pray, is an "objective phantom"? And how can a hallucination convert itself into reality, even for an instant?' Such notions suggested a confusion of thought and reality 'worthy of the maddest idealism'.

The SPR committee appointed to investigate 'Eva' consisted of Feilding, Whately Smith, Helen Verrall (by this time Mrs W. H. Salter) and V. J. Woolley, who was later for a time to become the society's research officer, and who in that role was to show a distinct reluctance to investigate physical mediumship. Still, Feilding and Whately Smith did not share the Cambridge nucleus's prejudice, and even Mrs Salter and Woolley had to admit that 'Eva' was helpful and co-operative in submitting to their precautions – which in fact were no more stringent than those to which she had been submitted on the Continent. Her conduct throughout, the committee's report was to emphasise, had been 'worthy of the highest approbation; patient under every control, she appeared to do all in her power to assist the observers in an investigation which at times, owing to the frequency of the sittings and the extreme heat which prevailed, could not fail to be wearisome both to the sitters and to her'.

How wearisome they must have been emerged clearly from the report. On arrival for a seance, Marthe was stripped and examined for possible concealed objects by a doctor, who 'examined the oral cavity, ears, and hair' (a gynaecological examination was considered, but thought unnecessary because of the impossibility of the medium being able to extrude objects hidden in her rectum or her vagina, fitted as she was into a stockinette costume and then sewn into it, so that nothing could emerge without being found in, or breaking through, the material). Sometimes she also had to wear a veil, so if she regurgitated anything she had swallowed it would immediately be detected. During the seances, investigators sat on either side of her, each holding a wrist – a task which presented no difficulty because unlike Eusapia, 'Eva' made no attempt to withdraw her hands from control, though she might move them around while her wrists were still held. The seances were conducted in a faint electric light, but with two flash-light cameras prepared for action at any moment, and a torch which could be used whenever there were signs of a materialisation.

If 'Eva' had had no previous reputation to live up to, the manifestations would have been considered quite striking. On a number of occasions what appeared to be saliva oozed from her mouth, solidifying into ectoplasm and taking curious shapes. A photograph showed what looked like a bony hand placed on her shoulder; another revealed what looked like a locket under her chin, on which there was a portrait. And although compared with what Richet, Schrenck and Geley had witnessed, this was unimpressive, it sufficed to convince Baggally, whom the committee had invited to attend in his capacity as a conjuror.

Baggally had taken for granted, he explained in his own report, that 'Eva' was employing rumination and regurgitation. But watching her from close range during the seances, he realised this was impossible, because some of the objects which he saw could not have been concealed in her gullet. Besides, if they had been they would have been wet to the touch, whereas when he felt them they were dry ('like a crumpled up, stiff veil').

During one seance, too, when she had asked for her hands to be freed, though her wrists were still held, Baggally – sitting beside her – saw her pull a grey substance of irregular shape from her mouth which under his eyes began to stretch out in various directions, until it 'suddenly vanished while I was intently watching it'. The manner in which objects suddenly disappeared in this way at seances, Baggally thought, was most perplexing; but he was certain that it could not be accounted for by the use of her hands, because the control 'by Mr Dingwall and myself was most rigid'.

Dingwall was the second conjuror present. A Cambridge graduate, he had recently joined the SPR; and he was co-opted on to the investigating committee after the ninth session. In his report he struck a new note. He was present not as a psychical researcher, but *'simply from the point of view of a practical "magician" or illusionist'*, whose task would be to 'show exactly how far these effects might be produced through normal agency'. In other words, he saw himself as the society's devil's advocate. His function would not be to decide whether phenomena were genuinely psychic, but merely to provide the evidence which would help investigators to make up their minds whether they were genuine or not, by showing them all the possible ways in which they could have been faked.

Much as Podmore would have done, Dingwall began by indicating where the earlier investigators had been lax; but the measure of his difficulty in finding serious laxity was revealed in his criticism of Schrenck for not noticing, until a sceptic had discovered them, some pin-holes in the curtains which provided 'Eva's' cabinet. The implication – that the medium might have used the curtains to pin up her two-dimensional forms and figures – was typical of the kind of speculation to which sceptics, confronted with Schrenck's and Mme Bisson's photographic evidence, had been reduced. Dingwall could find no fault in Geley's tests; but he was able to set them aside on the ground that Geley had yet to make a full report. From the available evidence, and from his observation during the London seance, Dingwall felt that one thing was clear. He could confidently state that if there had been fraud, it could only be accounted for if '(a) the medium possesses the power of regurgitation or rumination' and '(b) she secretes a particularly thick, white saliva'. Clearly (a) and (b) alone would not account for the phenomena witnessed; Dingwall was merely claiming that they were the essential prerequisites. But this, in effect, was acquitting the medium of fraud, because the precautions had ensured that her saliva, if regurgitated, could not have been white – as another magician bore witness, the most famous of them all: Harry Houdini.

Houdini had arrived in Europe on a tour in 1920, and in the course of it had fulfilled a long-standing ambition to meet Conan Doyle, whose work he greatly admired. The two men had taken an instant liking to each other, and Houdini had allowed himself to be persuaded that physical mediums were at least worth investigating, to see for himself whether they could do anything he could not do. On 22 June he attended one of the seances with 'Eva', and sent an account of it to Conan Doyle the next morning. 'Eva' had been made to drink coffee and eat cake, to make regurgitation of concealed materials impossible, and had been sewn into tights, with a net over her face. Yet she had manifested 'a froth-like substance, some five inches long'; then, 'a white, plaster-looking affair over her right eye'; and then, something that looked 'like a small face, say four inches in circumference'. Later she produced 'what appeared to be a rubberish substance, which she disengaged, showed us plainly, we held the electric torch, all saw it plainly, when, Presto! it vanished. It was a surprise effect indeed!'

Dingwall could offer nothing which would account for such effects. Fournier d'Albe, who along with a few other members of the society had been invited to attend some sittings, wrote to Schrenck to describe them, giving an account of what he considered the best of the sittings, towards the end of June. For the first time the investigators had felt the cold breeze which had previously been a characteristic of sittings with 'Eva' (as with many other mediums), as well as seeing 'a mass which hung from the mouth

The Continental Mediums

like a stalactite'; and he added that 'Mr Dingwell [sic], the amateur conjuror of the committee, assures me that the phenomena could not have been produced by trickery'. But this was for private consumption. Publicly Dingwall in his report adhered to his devil's advocate role. To explain the 'very remarkable phenomenon of a pointed waxy object' for example, which had been observed first inside, and then outside, the veil which covered the medium's face, he suggested that some substance might have been used which could be pushed through the veil in its liquid state, but would then harden. Supposing, he surmised, that the medium

> had a piece of wax which would easily melt if held in the mouth but would soon solidify if brought into contact with the air, it seems possible that such a phenomenon might be produced. The wax might be contained in some insoluble receptacle and then swallowed. If it were brought up by regurgitation and the veil were drawn into the mouth, the container might be broken, the wax melted and thus got through the meshes of the veil. By drawing quick respirations through the mouth the wax would be cooled and then forced slowly through the lips, assuming the pointed shape that was observed.

Far-fetched? Grotesque? Dingwall readily admitted as much. But he indignantly repudiated the other, simpler explanation which, he knew, would be advanced by sceptics; that he and Feilding had both been hallucinated. Both of them had seen the object, outside and free from the veil, *'and its bare point scraped over the back of my hand'*. Such theories, he argued, 'are conducive neither to the cause of honesty nor to that of truth, and the sooner they are discarded the better'. But he went on to recommend that trials should be made to test the wax hypothesis, and in retrospect it is not hard to see why. To accept the reality, even the possibility, of hallucination would in effect have been to disqualify him from maintaining that he was a reliable detector of conjuring tricks; if he could be hallucinated he would be no more trustworthy than anybody else. The 'wax' hypothesis gave him the let-out he would need if it were subsequently to be discovered that the medium had successfully tricked the investigators. Admittedly he might not have guessed precisely how she had done it, but at least he would be able to say he sensed there must have been *some* trick.

It was almost as if Dingwall hypnotised the committee with his surmise, far-fetched though it certainly was. Even when the medium produced her materialisations after tea and cake, Fournier told Schrenck, thereby effectively disposing of the regurgitation hypothesis, its members still could not bring themselves to accept that they were genuine. They were worried, too, by the quite frequent blank sittings. At two of them, Fournier observed, Feilding's wife Stanislawa was present: 'she seems to hinder the phenomena by her too critical attitude'. Perhaps she was jealous; whatever the reason, Stanislawa had reacted against mediumship, as her husband was to admit years later in a letter to W. B. Yeats – 'she hates spiritualism'. Feilding himself was disappointed. The results had been very interesting, he wrote to tell Schrenck, but 'unhappily not as impressive as previous reports had led us to hope for', and 'inasmuch as the regurgitation theory is the only theory that can hold the field in opposition to that of supernormal ideoplasm, it is a pity that we never got phenomena big enough to warrant us in declaring, as a matter of scientific certainty, that this theory is insufficient, however great its improbability may be'.

On these grounds, the committee declined to pronounce in 'Eva's' favour; a decision which not unnaturally irritated her continental investigators. The committee had conceded that the only way the phenomena might have been faked was by regurgitation, and however feeble the manifestations had been by 'Eva's' previous standards, they had effectively ruled out regurgitation, as it was impossible to take Dingwall's hypothesis seriously. Besides, tests had shown that professional regurgitators displayed 'several marked peculiarities of stomach and gullet', whereas two Paris specialists had pronounced 'Eva's' organs normal. Even if they had not been normal, Richet reiterated, no physiologist – and as one of the most eminent of the species, he could speak with authority – would accept that a regurgitator would have the power to do what 'Eva' did. And even if she had the power, how could she have passed the regurgitated matter through the veil, when her hands were held? Every experimenter had a right to be very exacting as to proof; 'but it is impossible not to be astonished at the glaring contradiction between the reports of these seances and the inferences drawn from them'.

There was to be a postscript to the London trials of 'Eva' which, though it attracted no attention, served to tie it in with the parallel investigations of psychic photography. During her tests two cameras had been positioned to take photographs stereoscopically. With the perversity which was to become so notorious a feature of attempts to record the phenomena objectively, many of the pictures had been spoiled; but it happened that the two which had been taken of the mask-like human face held like a locket under 'Eva's' chin had come out.

What had surprised the sitters was that the face on the locket was better-defined than the one they recalled seeing; and it was this which had attracted attention. But examining the pictures stereoscopically later, H. Dennis Taylor, a member of the society, realised that there was another curious feature which had been missed. Close inspection revealed that the mask was not being 'nipped' under her chin: it was semi-transparent, 'so that her chin could be seen through it'. And this, Taylor thought, raised the possibility 'that the mask was not really there at the time, and that the two images were impressed directly upon the plates as psychic photographs, the intelligence responsible having very crude conceptions of the appropriate relative perspectives of the two views that would be required' – a curious echo of the comments of his namesake, Traill Taylor, thirty years before.

'Eva': the face on the locket.

Willy Schneider

Disappointing though the SPR tests with 'Eva' were, the fact that a medium's powers might wane with advancing age was so well established that it caused no surprise; and by this time Schrenck had found another medium whose phenomena, even if less striking, were better suited to scientific investigation: Willy Schneider.

Science and Parascience

Schrenck was understandably annoyed by Dingwall's insinuation that he had been lax in his precautions with 'Eva'; he disposed of the mysterious 'pin-holes' in a letter to the SPR with a note from the photographer who had been responsible for setting up the cameras before seances began, explaining that he had pinned up bits of paper on the curtains, the better to line up the cameras. Schrenck realised, however, that it would be better to have so knowledgeable a young man as an ally than as a foe: and he invited Dingwall to come to Munich to watch tests with Schneider. Dingwall accepted the invitation, arriving in May 1922, along with Harry Price.

A few weeks before, Price had offered what the SPR *Journal* was to describe as his 'magnificent collection of books on magic and witchcraft' to the society on permanent loan, 'and so through his generosity Mr Price has given the officers of the Society the benefit of being able to consult what is generally considered to be the most complete library of magical literature in Great Britain, if not in Europe'. Events were soon to show that 'generosity' was not the appropriate term; he was using his library, and his photographic equipment, which he also handed over, to establish himself as a force to be reckoned with in the society. For the moment, however, he was content to stay in the background, leaving Dingwall in charge.

Willy was an eighteen-year-old Austrian, Dingwall wrote in his report to the SPR; 'One of a large family, he was born in a small frontier town near Simbach and is of humble origin' (his father was in fact a compositor; and his home village, Braunau, was soon to outstrip Simbach in fame, as the birthplace of Adolf Hitler). Hearing of his mediumistic powers Schrenck had invited him to Munich and there, during the winter of 1921, while working as a dental apprentice, he had given two seances a week in Schrenck's laboratory.

Some of the elaborate precautions required with 'Eva', Dingwall found, were for various reasons unnecessary. Willy did not need to sit in the 'cabinet' – the usual curtained-off corner of the seance room – or even with his back to it; he was out in the room. And as his speciality was the movement of objects at a distance, rather than the production of materialisations, regurgitation was not a risk. He was undressed, searched and dressed in a gown with luminous facings, so that he could be watched; and two controllers were appointed from among the sitters to ensure that he could not stretch out arms or feet. And though Dingwall found that the 'red

The Continental Mediums

light' in which the seances were held was 'rather poor', it was good enough to ensure that the sitters would instantly detect any successful attempt on Willy's part to escape from control.

The sitters, usually eight or ten of them, sat in a shallow semi-circle outside and facing the 'cabinet' – a curtain; Willy sitting at one end, with the two controllers (who were periodically changed); Schrenck at the other. Between the sitters and the curtain was a cage made of gauze mounted on a wooden frame, a yard away from the medium, into which the objects to be moved were put through a hinged flap. As the opening in the gauze was at the side away from the sitters and sideways-on both to Schrenck and the medium, objects inside the cage could not be moved by physical force unless somebody got up, walked round and opened the flap; and the light was good enough to ensure that any such move would be detected.

The first object put in the cage was a small four-legged oblong oaken table, weighing approximately thirty-three pounds and with a luminous triangle of paper attached at the end nearest the sitters, to enable them to observe its movements more easily. The first sitting was a blank; but during the second, 'some raps were heard on the table and it began to creak and move slightly, finally rising once or twice on what were presumably the two back legs, and then coming down with a loud thud on the carpet'. Schrenck then put a wound-up musical box into the cage (Dingwall had examined it, and found it to be 'of ordinary construction and apparently quite unprepared') and invited his guests to start it and stop it; 'several of the sitters, including ourselves, tried the experiment,' the result being that 'the box in every case obeyed'.

After an interval for 'general conversation', the gauze cage was removed and a table set with a heavily-shaded lamp on it, strong enough to illuminate any intrusive human hand stretching to move a bracelet which had been placed underneath the lamp. The medium was four feet away, but

> the table soon began to tilt and was then completely levitated to the height of about a foot, finally falling to the floor. This being again placed in position, the bracelet was suddenly twisted to the ground and then rose in the air and floated about, at the height of anything from one to three feet.

During these levitations, Dingwall noted, 'a part or parts of the bracelet was obscured' as if something had hold of it; and when a handkerchief was placed on the floor, it rose up as if supported by two fingers, remaining suspended for a few seconds, directly behind the lamp and clearly visible. In other words, the telekinetic effects appeared to be the work of an invisible hand – at one point, Dingwall actually saw 'an arm-like shape with a tapering point', and some sitters thought they saw fingers. But when the seance was over, they agreed 'that the medium could not possibly have produced normally the effects we had observed'. If they were fraudulent, Dingwall realised, 'a confederate must be assumed to be responsible'.

Could there be a false wall? Or a trapdoor? The next morning Dingwall asked if he could make a thorough search, and Schrenck 'immediately gave permission, though with some amusement'. There was no way, Dingwall found, in which a confederate could have been introduced, except through the door, and for the second seance he arranged that the door would be not merely locked, but sealed.

The phenomena at the second seance were much the same as those at the first, and Dingwall took the opportunity to engage in some trials of strength. He tried, unsuccessfully, to hold down the table when it began to levitate. And with another sitter, he held up a board to await developments: 'Within a few seconds I felt sharp thumps and blows against the surface nearest the medium. It was as if a small hand within a boxing glove were delivering the blows, the board being almost knocked out of our hands.' As the seals on the door remained unbroken, any idea that Willy had been able to smuggle in a confederate had to be ruled out.

The phenomena were indeed caused by unexplained supernormal agencies, Dingwall concluded; and 'however monstrous these phenomena may appear to those persons who are not acquainted with the mass of evidence now adduced in support of their reality, to ignore them is impossible for the scientific man'. If 'the scientific man' continued to insist that there must be fraud, it could only be fraud of a kind which would involve all those present at the seances. Could it seriously be suggested that all those who had attended – at a third seance, two nights later, there were three professors, two doctors and a general – were parties to a gigantic hoax? This was a hypothesis, Dingwall claimed, 'that we can scarcely entertain with patience'. In all, there had been

> twenty-seven German university professors, eighteen doctors and sixteen other savants. Some of these savants have attended sixteen to thirty sittings, and in sixty seances only three have been negative.

The Continental Mediums

Not one of these ninety persons hitherto invited has put forward the supposition that the medium is in any way normally responsible for the phenomena.

Dingwall might find it difficult to entertain the hypothesis with patience; and anybody who knew him would have smiled at the notion that he might be in collusion with a medium. Nevertheless he was a member of the Society for Psychical Research, which to some sceptics would have been sufficient ground for suspicion. As it happened, though, there was supporting testimony, from a very different source. Six months after their visit to Munich, Thomas Mann attended the seance which he was to describe in an essay, and in a letter to Schrenck which was not published for over half a century, when it appeared in *Encounter*. Mann was already an internationally established author, after *Buddenbrooks*, *Tonio Kröger* and *Death in Venice*; at the time he was writing *The Magic Mountain*, which was to win him a Nobel Prize. The account he sent to Schrenck was a model of detachment, simply relating what he had witnessed; in the essay, he vividly described his preconceptions and his reactions. Together they constitute one of the most engaging of all accounts of 'an experience in the occult', as the essay was entitled.

Full though the world was of weighty problems, the treatment of which would redound to a writer's credit, the essay began, 'I here venture to approach you with a theme which even myself cannot do otherwise than regard as preposterous and, indeed, suspect. Surprise and contempt, I know, will be my portion.' For himself, Mann felt embarrassed to have been led astray from his lawful concerns, like a man tempted from good wine by the heady fumes of wood alcohol. Nevertheless he felt bound to admit that in areas such as the study of mediumship, the pursuit of truth involved dealing with 'a great deal of filth and foolishness', because here 'nature takes the field, and nature is an equivocal element: impure, obscene, spiteful, demonic'.

Mann owed his invitation to the seance to chance: a conversation with a cartoonist who had come to draw him, and who told him about Willy Schneider's manifestations. Curious, Mann went with the cartoonist one evening to the baron's 'palatial residence', where he was introduced to his host and the other sitters, including two professors of zoology, and two doctors (one with a gadget to measure the medium's blood pressure).

The account Mann sent to Schrenck, written the following day, described how he had then exchanged a few words with Willy, 'partly to show him that I was not an enemy or malicious snooper, partly to form an impression of his personality'. Willy, Mann had found, was clearly of 'rather humble origin', friendly but not effusive; and Mann had watched while the medium changed, satisfying himself 'that the black tights Willy put on, and the black silk-quilted dressing gown with luminous stripes that he put over the tights, contained no device that might have served to delude the onlookers'. As an additional precaution, Willy's mouth was examined.

In the seance room, Willy was controlled by two of the witnesses, taking turns: one holding the medium's feet, the other, the medium's thumbs – though this was hardly necessary, Mann felt, as a dim red light and the luminous dressing gown enabled him to observe Willy throughout the seance. The sitters formed a three-quarter circle, linking hands when the seance began – again, not as a precaution to prevent anybody from assisting the manifestations, but because Schrenck thought that the linkage might, as with the Golighers, help to increase the medium's power.

Soon, Willy went into a trance and two of his 'controls', 'Erwin' and 'Mina', contested for supremacy while Willy was in convulsions, 'thrusting, jerking, whispering, panting and moaning', rather like somebody in orgasm: 'the sexual was so unmistakable that I was not surprised to hear later on that the young man's activity is often accompanied by erections and ejaculations, sometimes actively induced'. But there had been no manifestations before Willy came out of his trance, nor were there any when the seance was resumed after an interval; and at around 11.30 p.m. Schrenck decided to bring the seance to an end. However,

> this last attempt to stimulate the medium proved effective. Before the eyes of all those present, a handkerchief which had been lying on the floor beside the little table was lifted, rose with a quick sure movement into the relatively bright beam of the lamp-light, remained there for two or three seconds, during which time it changed shape as though being squeezed and shaken, and fell back on the floor.

The levitation, Mann remarked, was not 'spontaneous', in the sense that 'it did not rise empty and fluttering, of its own accord, but was lifted by a support inside it. It hung down in folds from the support and was violently manipulated from within.' And in a second levitation, soon after the first, 'the support was clearly marked by two knuckle-shaped protuberances'. Naturally the onlookers' excitement was intense: 'We leaned forward, cried out, and called each other's attention to what was happening.' And it happened once more; the third levitation being the most remarkable 'because at three different times the surface of the handkerchief clearly disclosed the working of an apparently claw-like organ considerably smaller than a human hand'.

> Further phenomena then followed in quick succession. The medium asked for the handkerchief to be removed. When this had been done, an indefinable something, which had not been among the objects on the floor, arose from the same place as the handkerchief. More or less shapeless, it seemed to be some twenty inches long and might have been taken for part of a forearm with the prehensile organ belonging to it (the suggestion of a closed hand).

Later, a bell which had been standing on the floor 'began to ring violently and was flung under the chair of one of the participants'; and 'a luminous ring with a luminous cord attached rose up to the table, moved back and forth along the edge of the table with a scratching sound, and was then laid down on the table top'. After that there were fewer effects, apart from luminosities appearing around the room, until Willy came out of his trance – by this time, resembling a deep sleep.

Thanking Schrenck for the opportunity to attend the seance, Mann concluded:

> Any thought of a swindle in the sense of a conjuring trick is absurd. There was simply no one there who could have rung the bell. Willy could not have done it, because his extremities were being held, and besides, he was five feet away, sunk in magnetic sleep. Who, or what, lifted the handkerchief and squeezed it from inside? I don't know, but like all the others I saw it with my un-prejudiced eyes, which were quite prepared to see nothing if there was nothing to be seen.

What, then, was the explanation? In his essay, which described the phenomena in considerably more detail, he admitted that 'all reasoned thinking and talking in this highly speculative field of facts is today premature, and can only seem to clarify without doing so'; but he presented the hypothesis then currently favoured by those psychical researchers who, like Schrenck, rejected spiritism. They assumed the existence of a teleplastic process – calling into existence shapes which possess all the properties and functions of normal, physiological, biologically-living organs. These teleplastic end-organs move apparently freely in space, but so far as can be observed have a close physiological and psychological relation with the medium, in such a way that any impression received through the teleplasm has its effect upon the medial organism, and vice versa . . . A fluid, in varying degrees of density, leaves the body of the medium as an amorphous, unorganised mass: takes form in various teleplastic organs, hands, feet, heads and so on; and after a brief existence in this form – during which, however, it displays all the attributes of living substance – dissolves and is reabsorbed into the medial organism. And this fluid, this substance, this substratum of the various organic formations, is uniform, undifferentiated; there is not such a thing as a bone substance, different from a muscular or visceral or nervous one; there is only the one substance, the basis and substratum of organic life.

To illustrate this thesis, Mann offered 'one single but striking example'. While Willy was under his usual careful control, what appeared to be a forearm and a hand would sometimes materialise to carry out a task which Eusapia had often been set, and accomplished; her pseudopods had implanted the impression of a palm or fingertips on some clay in a bowl. Impressions were duly found, after a test sitting; but on Willy's fingers *there were traces of clay.* Now I ask of nature and spirit, I inquire of reason and of logic on her throne; how, when and from where came the clay on Willy's fingers?'

The phenomena, Mann concluded in his account to Schrenck, might be aesthetically repellent, but their unquestionable reality 'must needs arouse the passionate curiosity of the scientist'. With Willy, Schrenck did in fact come closer to arousing scientists' curiosity, and convincing them of the reality of telekinetic forces, than any psychical researcher had previously managed to do. Although as always there was speculation about trickery, none of the scientists, academics, members of the professions and writers who attended seances detected Willy in any attempt at deception; no fewer than ninety-four of them signed declarations affirming that they had been convinced of his telekinetic powers.

Such attempts as were made to cast doubt on the genuineness of Willy's mediumship were laughable, as Dingwall was able to show in 1924 in a review of Schrenck's research, demolishing the hypotheses presented by some of Schrenck's critics and stressing the importance of the distinction between the research Schrenck had done with 'Eva' and his investigation of Willy. 'Eva' had produced materialisations – teleplasm; Willy had moved objects at a distance, and enclosed in a gauze cage – telekinesis. Teleplasmic effects, Dingwall insisted, might be faked; Willy's telekinetic effects could not be faked. A teleplastic medium could conceivably find some way to smuggle in the means to make her materialisations: 'but the important point is not what the mediums can bring in, but what use they can make of what they do bring in. Willy no doubt *can* bring in a teleplastic rod, but of what use is it to him? None whatever.'

The distinction was far from being as clear-cut as Dingwall sought to make it. The chief difference between Willy's mediumship and 'Eva's' was that his pseudopods for the most part did what they were required to do, moving objects in the cage, rather than making forms and faces; but the same process was at work – as might have been found if 'Eva' had been able to produce her forms and faces in a cage; she did, after all, often produce them through a veil.

Nevertheless from the point of view of a researcher who wanted to convince witnesses, Willy's telekinetic feats were certainly better designed to carry conviction; Dingwall rated Schrenck's findings 'by far the most important work on telekinesis since the SPR Report on Palladino or Dr Ochorowicz's observations on Mlle. T.' – Stanislawa Tomczyk. And Dingwall's irritation with sceptics, inside the SPR as well as outside, prompted him to lament their failure to recognise just how important Schrenck's work had been.

> The scientific mind is, unfortunately, only too often divided into watertight compartments, and presents the strange spectacle of the true and the false, the sublime and the ridiculous, all flourishing under the same mask of a united personality. In the ordinary sciences of today, religion has but little influence. The biologist does not fear that by presenting his work he is encroaching upon the domain of the Almighty, neither does the geologist regret that his results do not appear to tally with the statements in the Book. Facts concerning natural phenomena are now only condemned for these reasons in such places as Kentucky or the Kingsway Hall, whilst serious minded people smile quietly and pass on. But in psychical research the scientist joins the priest, and the philosopher the journalist, in deriding phenomena just as real and objective as the meteor or the eclipse.

The 1921 Congress

Scientific man was perfectly capable, then as in other eras, of ignoring evidence which he could not rebut. Yet in this period it was becoming increasingly difficult to ignore the kind of evidence which was presented at the first International Congress for Psychical Research, held in Copenhagen in 1921. Among those who read papers were Geley and Mme Bisson from France, Schrenck from Germany, Mrs Salter and Drayton Thomas from Britain, Carrington and Walter Prince from the United States; and the subjects ranged from 'Feda' to the 'higher phenomena' of hypnosis, from a controlled trial of a telepathic subject to a report of a poltergeist haunting.

The poltergeist case history was contributed by Schrenck, concerning the experience of the Sauerbrey family who lived near Weimar. Ernst Sauerbrey, a clockmaker, had been widowed and had married again. In 1919 his son by his first marriage, who had come on a visit, gave a demonstration of hypnotism with his stepmother as the subject. The experience shattered her. After he left, she became virtually paralysed, and for a year she lay helpless on a couch in the kitchen. Yet though she could not move, it was as if her trauma was causing movement all around her: cups, chairs, the kitchen table shifted about, the rappings were heard, night after night, around the kitchen. The kitchen clock refused to go, though Sauerbrey insisted there was nothing the matter with it; 'a dog, which at other times was unusually bold, was unusually oppressed by the onset of the phenomena'.

The case was unusually well-documented because the stepson had been charged with practising hypnotism, which was illegal. Sauerbrey, members of the family and a neighbour gave evidence, and their testimony received support from the police, who had been called in; no fewer than ten policemen had, at different times, witnessed the manifestations 'either through the open kitchen door, or through the key-hole'. One of them described how he had seen a jug of water, placed near the door, move towards Frau Sauerbrey as she lay in bed. At times the kitchen table had shaken so violently that anybody who wished to write on it had to grip the table leg between his knees. The manifestations continued for night after night until a nerve specialist was called in who managed to employ counter-suggestion successfully, freeing Frau Sauerbrey from her obsession. Shortly after, she died.

In Schrenck's view, the case pointed to 'an unregularised exteriorisation of vital forces in a person suffering from a severe illness; which forces, as a result of a peculiar and temporary psychic condition, broke out in unruly fashion'. Commenting in the SPR *Journal* on the abstract of his paper, an editorial note remarked that the case was unusual in that ordinarily poltergeist hauntings were hard to pin down – 'the phenomena may occur in a number of different places, so that the observer does not know where to watch'; but in this case they occurred only in the room where Frau Sauerbrey lay, and had been seen and heard by observers without difficulty. 'Under these circumstances it seems to be extremely improbable that a considerable number of witnesses, some of whom had very good opportunities for observation, extending over a period of more than two weeks, should in no case have detected Frau Sauerbrey's actions, had she been producing the phenomena by normal means.'

Telepathy

Perhaps because of the realisation that Coover's experiments at Stanford could be re-interpreted as giving positive results, there had been a number of experiments on the Continent designed to put the evidence for telepathy on a more scientific basis. In Paris, Geley had persuaded 'Mme B.', a well-known medium, to co-operate in trials to meet the challenge so often thrown down by sceptics, that mediums made their reputations because sitters remembered their lucky (or contrived) 'hits', and forgot the far greater number of 'misses'.

Geley invited twenty-four leading scientists and doctors to have a sitting with her, and to register the number of 'hits' and 'misses'. Remarkably, only two failed to keep their appointments; three replacements brought the total up to twenty-five. All possible precautions were taken to ensure that 'Mme B.' could not find out the identity of the sitters. One of them, Stanley de Brath – he was to be Geley's translator – went to see her the day after he arrived in Paris, without revealing his identity; she gave him information which he was sure she could not have obtained from any other source except himself. Seventeen of the sitters reported favourably; the most striking result of the inquiry, de Brath was to recall, was not just the large number of 'hits' which 'Mme B.' obtained, 'averaging two out of three', but also the precision of some of the details she provided, more than sufficient 'to eliminate the hypothesis of mere coincidence'.

Science and Parascience

In Germany a young doctor, Rudolf Tischner, who worked with Schrenck in Munich, had been experimenting on different lines; and his *Telepathy and Clairvoyance*, published in 1920, broke fresh ground, describing tests for extra-sensory perception – the term he coined – with a view to separating out transmission of thoughts from pure clairvoyance.

The search for suitable subjects with whom to undertake tests, Tischner explained, had provided him with 'plenty of opportunity of sorting the chaff from the grain' in order to eliminate the cheats and the illusionists. Scientists were too ready to think that only they could detect deception; 'it might be as well here, too, to credit the experienced worker with a little judgment on the subject, and not to think, as is often the case, that the investigator in occult matters is possessed of less intelligence and a weaker critical faculty than the average man'. And as it happened, the precautions he had had to take were bound up with those which he needed to distinguish telepathy from clairvoyance.

In the past, telepathy had often been explained away as hyperacuity of hearing, or 'Cumberlandism', called after the music-hall performer whose speciality was mind-reading by picking up tiny clues from the actions and behaviour of whoever was 'sending' the information. To investigate clairvoyance, Tischner realised, he must eliminate not only these possibilities, but also that of genuine telepathic communication; so neither he nor anybody else involved in the trials could be permitted to know what the subject was going to try to guess. For this purpose he used slips of paper, or postcards, with names, pictures or numbers on them, wrapped in black paper and sealed in envelopes. The medium they were testing, 'Miss von B.', was then left alone with the envelopes in a room, in which she could be watched by her investigators without her being able to see them. She was frequently able to draw the rough outline of the picture on the cards, and to write down some of the words scattered through what had been written on them, including on one occasion the signature of the writer, Lina Lüder, correct except for the omission of the umlaut.

The experiment as described did not wholly rule out the possibility of telepathic communication between the medium and whoever put the card into the envelope; but what it certainly did was to demonstrate extra-sensory perception on her part, as neither hyperacuity of hearing nor Cumberlandism would apply. Aware that he and his colleagues might be dismissed as her dupes, however, or accused of being in collusion with her, Tischner had brought in professors from the university as witnesses; and some of the trials were conducted under the supervision of a committee of fellow-members of a medical society.

Unable though he was to 'present an official certificate proving the scientific integrity of each of the members of the commission', Tischner felt justified in assuring readers that the society was unlikely to have nominated people of doubtful capacity as observers; and his work impressed Dingwall, who made the point in his introduction to the translation of *Telepathy and Clairvoyance* that it should not be considered in isolation; 'similar occurrences have been, and are still being, reported from all parts of the world. Although the value of these reports must necessarily vary, the general tenor of the content is invariably the same' – that 'under suitable conditions, certain persons display faculties described by Dr Tischner'. But the sceptics in Germany reacted no differently from scientists elsewhere. Even to contemplate the possibility of the existence of an exception to, or contradiction of, the laws of nature was unthinkable, Robert Meyer argued. 'We cannot afford to drop this principle, and the man who does not accept it is guilty of being illogical, or of believing in a superstition, or both.' It was Meyer who was being illogical, Tischner replied: 'The attraction of a piece of iron by a magnet, if regarded as an isolated fact, is a contradiction of the law of gravity, but if we presuppose a new kind of energy we can explain it easily.' Doubtless some similar source of as yet undiscovered energy would be found, and the laws of nature revised to meet them, as had been the case with X-rays and radium.

At the Copenhagen conference, however, the report of a telepathy experiment which excited most interest, as both original in its concept and, in terms of results, gratifyingly successful, had been set up by H. I. Brugmans and some colleagues in the psychological laboratory at Groningen in Holland, with a physics student, A. van Dam, as the chief subject. He was blindfolded, and put in a cubicle with a screen between him and a table, in front of him, on which was a checker-board, its horizontal bottom row lettered from A to H, its vertical rows numbered from 2 to 6. In turn, three agents tried to influence him telepathically to select with his hand a certain square – as it might be 'A3' or 'C5'. Sometimes the agents were in the room with him; sometimes in a different room, watching him through a glass screen. One of the agents, who was short-sighted, had poorer results when he was not in the same room; otherwise there was no difference between them – and the results were remarkable: 60 'hits' out of a total of 187 attempts, where chance expectation would have given only 4. All the sessions were successful, those undertaken after the subject had been given thirty grams of alcohol particularly so: he had then scored three hits out of each four attempts. 'If we have not committed some error,' Brugmans told his audience, begging them to tell him if they detected any flaws, 'the existence of telepathy is established . . .' And the consensus among later commentators – those, that is, who accept the possibility of telepathic communication – has been that its results rank among the most impressive ever to be obtained using laboratory methods.

It was of even more importance in re-establishing those methods, as J. B. Rhine was to testify: a double step forward, he recalled in his *Extrasensory Perception,* not merely striking in its value as proof, but also pointing to the need to 'go beyond the first problem of proof and to try to find facts of natural relationships in the direction mainly of physiological measurements correlated with success in telepathy'. But no single experiment could establish telepathy's existence. Even if there were no detectable flaws, sceptics could always fall back, as they did, on possible alternative explanations, ranging from Van Dam having hyperacuity of hearing, to collusion between him and one or more of the investigators.

Madame Przybylska

The most striking fact to emerge from the Copenhagen conference, was that Poland was proving to be the most prolific breeding ground for mediums. Stanislawa Tomczyck was in wedded retirement, and Ochorowicz had died; but they had started something.

The first intimation of psychic influences at work in Poland had been during the summer of 1920, when the Polish Government had rashly decided to liberate their compatriots in the Ukraine from the Bolsheviks. Madame Przybylska was not a professional medium, but she gave sittings to friends and, like Mrs Osborne Leonard, allowed them to take down the messages which she picked up by clairaudience; and in the summer of 1920 she had begun to provide them with forecasts of what was going to happen next in the war. These forecasts had been passed to the Polish Psychical Society at the time they were given, so that it had been possible to keep a record of what the medium had predicted, and compare it with the course which the campaign actually took.

The Continental Mediums

Her forecasts were notable not just for their general accuracy – on 10 June 1920, at a time when the Bolsheviks appeared to be routed, after the fall of Kiev, she forecast disasters, and the Bolshevik offensive at the end of the month took the Russian armies to Warsaw – she also gave some precise dates. On 12 July, for example, when the Poles were in full retreat, she named 15 August as the day on which victory would again go to them – as it did. And on 21 July she gave details:

> A visitant from Paris brings you an unexpected change. Your patriotism and heroism make a great impression on him.
>
> Great changes in August. Your strength is in the victories of Kowel and Kovno. Discord between the Bolshevist leaders and a great and unexpected change.
>
> You will re-take lost ground more quickly than you lost it, and many guns and prisoners. A great victory towards Vilna and Lida.

Events followed the course she had predicted. The 'visitant from Paris' was General Weygand; the victories were at the places she had named.

Mme Przybylska's predictions, attested by the signatures of twelve members of the Polish Psychical Research Society, were published in the *Revue Métapsychique*. Eugène Osty, who was working with Geley and was to succeed him as Director of the Institute, was to assert that he knew of no other precognitive series comparable to hers in the precision with which she had named people, places and dates; the reader would, in fact, be entitled to be utterly sceptical, but for the fact that the record had been attested by so many honourable witnesses.

Franek Kluski

At the Copenhagen conference Geley reported his research with another Pole, Franek Kluski; a 'universal medium', as Geley was later to describe him, 'a king among contemporaries'. A fifty-year-old writer who lived in Warsaw, Kluski needed darkness, but did not need a 'cabinet'; like Willy Schneider he could sit in the open with Geley and other investigators, Richet and Flammarion among them, controlling his hands and feet. While in his trance he would produce ectoplasm of a kind which Geley described as phosphorescent vapour. Sometimes it congealed into faces, or hands which appeared to move away from the medium and could make raps, and touch or stroke the sitters present. The phosphorescence made it possible for sitters to see what was happening, and to realise that it could not have been produced by sleight of hand, even had lax control permitted: 'The distance of the lights, the multiplicity of the phenomena, the variations of luminosity, the forms and faces,' Geley claimed, 'could never have been imitated by a single liberated hand.'

In his *Treatise on Parapsychology* René Sudre, who combined encyclopedic knowledge of the development of psychical research with a critical cast of mind, accepted that Kluski had been detected in what he described as 'venial tricks'; meaning that while in his trance he had sometimes, like Eusapia, managed to liberate a hand. But even when this was detected his accusers had had to accept the genuineness of his psychic faculties; as at the seances at the Paris Institute, carried out under particularly strict conditions for the benefit of French and foreign observers – thirty-five in all. Kluski and the sitters were actually chained together; yet they still witnessed materialisations.

Sudre had himself had twenty-five seances with Kluski. In one in Warsaw, a pair of lights hovering around the room 'stopped in front of me and became two eyes. Around the eyes the luminous shape of a face began to form and soon the head was clearly visible.' In the same seance, 'I saw a small light settle on a locked piano and at my request, three or four notes were struck.' At the Paris seances, the sitters were several times 'kissed by luminous and rather cold lips'.

One of Kluski's phenomena could not have been imitated, in the way he produced them, by any number of liberated hands. Geley and Richet knew that several mediums in the past seventy years had managed to make impressions on flour, plaster or paraffin wax at a distance, the explanation being that a pseudopod had impressed itself, leaving its shape on the mould when it dematerialised. They were not wholly convinced, however, by the evidence – good though it had been in Eusapia's case; and they took the opportunity in 1921 to test Kluski at the *Institut Métapsychique*, using paraffin wax. The 'materialised' entity, Geley explained, was

> asked to plunge a hand, a foot or even part of a face into the paraffin several times. A closely-fitting envelope is thus formed, which sets at once in air or by being dipped into another bowl of cold water. The envelope or 'glove' is then freed by dematerialisation of the member. Plaster can be poured at leisure into the glove, thus giving a perfect cast of the hand.

The Continental Mediums

While this was going on, the investigators were on either side of Kluski, holding his hands and periodically calling out that they retained their hold. They could actually hear the splashing in the bowls at a distance from them; and when the experiment was over, there were the 'gloves'. Although Kluski's hands were held by Geley on one side, and Richet on the other, 'a first mould was obtained of a child's hand, then a second of both hands, right and left; a third time of a child's foot' – creases in the skin and veins being visible on the plaster casts taken afterwards from the moulds. The child's hand was so small that it could not have been obtained from a living adult's hand, 'for the whole hand would have to be withdrawn through the narrow opening at the wrist'; the mould could not have been made, they decided on inspecting it, except by materialisation followed by dematerialisation, because only if the object dematerialised could it have been withdrawn from the neck of the paraffin wax 'glove' without ripping it open.

Some of the moulds obtained in this way were defective but, as Geley reiterated, 'to build up in a few seconds an organ or an organism biologically complete – to create life – is a metapsychic fact which can but rarely produce a perfect result'. He also found, and realised that it tied in with what Crawford had reported, that there were traces of wax on Kluski's hands and clothes – though he could not have left his chair – as if he had been dabbling in the wax. There were also splashes of it around the tank, as could be expected if the ectoplasm was stretching out from the medium in the form of a pseudopod, to perform the moulding feat.

Not long afterwards Houdini, who was beginning to demonstrate that he could do by his magic everything which mediums claimed to be able to do by psychic means, began to demonstrate how Kluski produced the moulds. According to Houdini's friend and fellow-magician, Joseph Rinn, Houdini had been baffled until Rinn showed him how simple it was to do the trick with the help of a glove in which some soluble substance could be put, which could be withdrawn when the mould had set. Fingerprints and other such corroborative details could be added afterwards.

Geley and Richet, therefore, could have been fooled, unless they had taken precautions to prevent Kluski from substituting hands made in this way. But they *had* taken the precautions. Unknown to Kluski or to anybody else, they had put a small amount of a soluble substance in the melted wax, invisible while in the wax, but detectable after the seance. They had consequently been able to satisfy themselves that the wax in which the hands

Science and Parascience

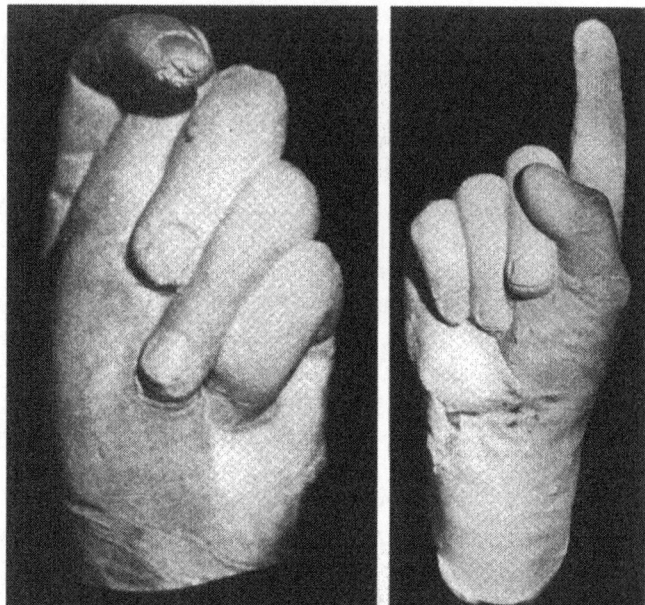

Two Kluski 'hands'.

appeared was the wax they had brought with them, so they knew there could not have been any substitution of previously prepared moulds. Even if Kluski could have escaped unnoticed from his controllers, too, he could not have done the trick Rinn's way: as many as nine moulds were obtained in a single sitting, and they were all different. An expert moulder working in Paris gave it as his opinion that the moulds could only have been made from living hands: the details were too delicate to have been imposed later in the way the conjurors were doing. The expert could not conceive how the moulds could have been obtained, in view of the fact that living hands could not have been withdrawn through the smaller wrist apertures: 'It is completely mysterious.'

Stefan Ossowiecki

The best-known of the Polish psychics in this period, however, was Stefan Ossowiecki, a clairvoyant. Born in 1877 of a family of whom several were regarded as psychic, Ossowiecki for a time during his childhood had been the centre of poltergeist-type disturbances, until he found that he could direct the forces himself, causing objects to move at a distance; but in the process, his clairvoyance disappeared. His father, worried at the way he was using telekinesis, had begged him to stop, and eventually he had allowed himself to be persuaded; thereupon his clairvoyant faculty was restored. He refused payment for his services, even when they were being requested for financial purposes, such as the discovery of lost property; and he was willing to submit to formal tests, the results of which, Richet thought, were 'the most positive in the whole history of mental metapsychics'.

The method commonly used was to pass sealed opaque envelopes to Ossowiecki, with written messages or drawings inside. He would take them one by one, hold them in his hand and usually after five to fifteen minutes, describe what the envelopes contained. Complete failures were rare. Occasionally he made minor mistakes with words; but as a rule he was right – sometimes even when he did not touch the envelope.

After the war Ossowiecki's gifts led to his becoming a social lion in the Polish capital, sought after by fashionable hostesses much as D. D Home had been half a century earlier. The list of those who tested his clairvoyant powers read like pages from *Who's Who*, including members of the Government, Marshal Josef Pilsudski, the President, among them. Pilsudski's contribution was a message in an opaque envelope, sealed with the seal of the Minister of War who, accompanied by the Marshal's ADC, brought it to Ossowiecki. Perhaps due to the presence of several intrigued witnesses, Ossowiecki took longer than usual – twenty-five minutes – before he could describe the contents: a chess formula, 'C2–4: C5–7'. Pilsudski confirmed by telephone that his solution was correct. To be on the safe side, the ADC brought the unopened envelope back to enable Pilsudski to reassure himself that the seals had not been tampered with; satisfied, he gave Geley permission to publish the tale.

Geley and Richet arrived in Warsaw to investigate Ossowiecki in the spring of 1921. 'Very energetic, he conducts much business with marked success,' Geley noted; 'Much loved by his friends, and always ready to serve and help them, he is a man of charming and unforgettable personality.' At a series of experiments, followed by a further series that autumn, he was able to produce evidence which left no doubt in their minds of his clairvoyant powers.

Ossowiecki did not merely 'see' what was in the opaque envelopes which they handed to him: he could provide information about the writers. Typical was an occasion that autumn when Geley gave him a missive from René Sudre in France. All that Geley knew was that the message referred to some unpublished experiment. Ossowiecki said he was unable to read the contents, because they were in print; but he could tell it was from someone who wanted to make his acquaintance, and that it had been prepared at six or seven in the evening by a man with a woman beside him in a room on a second floor:

> He is clean-shaven except for a small moustache. He is a man of thirty-eight to forty, slender, very acute. He is not bald, has a parting in his hair. She is stout but not tall; not blonde. She suggested this test. They have two children, a son and a daughter. I say this is all true but only one child is born; the lady appears stout because she is close on her confinement . . . it is a boy, I'm certain, you can write so to them.

A son was born to Mme Sudre three days later: the only error which Geley picked up subsequently was that she had not suggested the test.

On another occasion, Ossowiecki was consulted by the wife of one of the judges in the Polish Supreme Court about a lost brooch. He described the brooch, and also the man who, he told her, had picked it up in the street. The following day he happened to see, and recognise, the man he had described, taxed him with picking it up, and got it back – as the grateful recipient confirmed in a written account.

In general Ossowiecki was so consistently successful that Geley, after listing the precautions which were taken to ensure that his investigators could not know the contents of the envelopes in advance, felt justified in claiming not merely that 'the reality of the clairvoyance is absolutely certain' but also that as the experiments were repeatable at will and almost always successful, 'the inept objection continually repeated that metapsychic experiments are not scientific because they are not repeatable at will does not apply to Ossowiecki's gift'.

How did Ossowiecki pick up the messages? He appeared actually to 'see' what was written, or drawn, in his mind's eye; so that if a message was written in English, which he did not understand, he could give the appearance of the words in a sentence. Geley thought he was using a kind of psychometry; and Richet agreed that psychic 'touch' was commonly, though not always, involved, as he would gently knead the envelopes in his fingers. Ossowiecki himself thought that in certain states of mind he was tuning in to 'the spiritual unity of all humanity' which enabled him to perceive not only the contents of envelopes but the histories of some of the writers, because 'I see and hear outside time and space'.

Of all the psychics of this period, Ossowiecki provided the most convincing evidence for clairvoyance. His record had a consistency unmatched in the history of psychical research, and he was never detected in anything which could arouse suspicion. Doubtless he enjoyed the fame his gift brought him; but he steadfastly refused to accept any money from sitters. The 'extraordinary faculty of this great clairvoyant who was in private life an engineer and an accomplished gentleman' – Sudre's phrase – has remained one of the very few historical examples which parapsychologists cite freely, confident that nobody has yet found any evidence to show that the faculty was other than genuine.

Flammarion and Richet

In addition to the reports of the research of Geley and others, in the early 1920s, there were also two massive contributions from the elder statesmen of psychical research in France: Flammarion and Richet.

More than anybody else, Flammarion had been responsible for the popularisation of astronomy in France, and ultimately throughout Europe. With twelve others he had founded the Société Astronomique in 1887; that by the 1920s its membership was numbered in thousands was largely his achievement, as he had made technicalities readable in countless articles and books, opening up the subject to the general reader. But he had also always been fascinated by the supernormal. In 1861, at the age of sixteen, he had become what he lightly described as a card-carrying member of Alain Kardec's spiritist society; and in 1866 he had written *Des Forces Naturelles Inconnues* – forces for which he had coined the term 'psychic', soon to be in general use.

Impressed by the way in which Gurney had collected the material for his *Phantasms*, Flammarion had made a similar appeal to the French public in 1899, receiving over four thousand replies, which he sorted out and published with an analysis the following year. And in 1922 (as Mrs Sidgwick was also doing) he went back over the same ground, examining the case histories which had accumulated, and presenting them with commentaries in the three volumes, *Death and its Mystery*.

As evidence for supernormal phenomena, Flammarion's cases could not match Gurney's; he had made few attempts to follow them up, to check if they were genuine, part genuine or spurious. He also included a handful of cases derived from hearsay, at least one of which was later shown to be a myth: the once-familiar tale of Lord Dufferin's premonitory vision which had saved him from death when a lift which he had been going to take in a Paris hotel crashed to the ground. Unluckily for the story, there was no record of any such crash. Nevertheless most of the cases Flammarion included had been sent to him by men and women of standing – magistrates, academics, doctors – with their names and addresses, some with attestations. They were very similar, in general, to those which Gurney and Mrs Sidgwick had received, providing a mass of testimony for supernormal experiences, ranging from apparitions to clocks stopping at or near the time of a death.

It was not Flammarion's last contribution to psychical research; he was to provide an address for the SPR when, in recognition of his long services – longer than anybody else's, even Barrett's – he was elected President of the SPR in 1923. 'He was regarded with real affection by immense numbers of readers both in France and in England,' *The Times* obituary noted when he died two years later. 'He was indeed aptly named "the poet of the heavens".' The writer clearly had his popular works on astronomy in mind, but the designation was not inappropriate for what had been his other ambition: to marshal the evidence which pointed to the survival of the human spirit after death.

Richet's *Traité de Métapsychique* – the English translation appeared the following year as *Thirty Years of Psychical Research* – covered a wider range of phenomena than Flammarion's; and it had the advantage of a pre-publication puff from the author, on 13 February 1922, at the Academy of the Sciences, Richet's standing in orthodox circles being sufficient to break the long-established barrier to the subject being aired there.

Unlike Flammarion, throughout his career Richet had remained a convinced materialist, in spite of periodic shocks. 'In my servile respect for the classical tradition I mocked what was called spiritism,' he had told the SPR at a meeting in 1899; reading of Crookes's materialised spirit forms 'I allowed myself – here do I publicly beg his pardon for it – to laugh at them as heartily as almost everyone else was doing.' But he had gone to investigate Eusapia; and eventually he had been compelled to accept that the phenomena he had mocked were genuine, though he continued to reject the spiritualist interpretation. Like Crookes he had continued to conduct orthodox research while attending seances with mediums, until he confounded his critics, who thought he must have gone soft in the head to accept that the likes of Eusapia and 'Eva' could be genuine, by coming up with the discoveries about anaphylaxis that had won him his Nobel Prize.

Thirty Years of Psychical Research – dedicated to Crookes and Myers 'who, equally distinguished by their courage and by their insight, were the first to trace the outlines of this science', gave the evidence for what Richet thought were the three fundamentals, 'crypthesthesia' (telepathy and clairvoyance), telekinesis, and materialisations. It presented case histories, and considered their implications from his rationalist standpoint. Metapsychics, he insisted, was a branch of mechanist science. The facts

> do not contradict any accepted scientific truths. They are new; they are unusual; they are difficult to classify; but they do not demolish anything of what has been so laboriously built up in our classic edifice. If people dispute them *a priori*, it is because they have not sufficiently reflected on the profound difference which separates the unusual from the contradictory.

Telekinesis, Richet felt certain, would be found to be related to 'unrecognised latent powers in the human organism'. He even rejected the dualism of Bergson and McDougall. 'Everything seems to prove that intelligence is a function of the brain,' he insisted; he could not conceive of 'the persistence of the function (mind) without the organ (brain)'.

Poltergeists presented Richet with a problem. It would have been easy for him to rationalise them out of the psychic category into simple mischief and trickery, as Podmore had done; but Richet was too intellectually honest. The testimonies, he felt, were too precise and detailed 'for it to be possible to deny *everything*'; had there been only one such case, hallucination could have been invoked 'but that is a childish explanation. People say "hallucination" to dismiss a disquieting fact by a convenient word; this is much too simple.'

Richet's explanation was that hauntings were not the work of spirits, but were dependent upon somebody 'who, perhaps without knowing it, plays the part of medium'. Just as a medium at a seance could cause displacements of objects, so mediums who did not know themselves to be such could cause stones to fall and blows to be struck on walls. It was understandable that such hauntings should often be thought to be linked to some former tragedy. 'This, however, is probably a narrowly anthropomorphic notion; and rather than suppose the problematical survival of a human consciousness and vague symbolism of human intentions, I prefer to say without false shame that *I do not understand.*'

Most cases of haunting, in Richet's opinion, were cases of spontaneous telekinesis. 'Telekinesis is really one of the most important facts in metapsychic science,' he asserted. 'It is not to be despised because it is elementary, any more than a chemist should despise the law of combination of oxygen with hydrogen because it is an elementary phenomenon.' Similarly, the evidence for ectoplasm and materialisations was far too strong, Richet argued, to reject out of hand. The stock objection, that they could be produced by conjuring tricks, simply did not fit the known facts. In his experience, many of the most famous mediums had initially 'experienced some strange phenomena and, almost in spite of themselves, followed the path opening before them', without having had any opportunity to learn legerdemain. 'Only in order to discredit the facts has extraordinary skill been attributed to them – a skill greater than that of expert conjurors', as no conjuror had been able to perform some of their feats in the same conditions as the mediums had performed them. The reality of these materialisations, he claimed, 'must be conceded'.

Needless to say, it was not conceded. Sceptics could hardly ignore the book, as Richet had been able to bring it to their attention under the auspices of the Academy; but they could dismiss it on the ground that it did not provide scientific proof of supernormal phenomena. 'How can we call a collection a scientific treatise,' the psychologist Henri Pieron asked, 'in which not one actually demonstrated fact appears?' – a measure of the distance which psychology had moved from accepting eye-witness accounts of events as 'facts'. Pierre Janet might have been expected to be more sympathetic, as he had witnessed and reported striking examples of the 'higher phenomena' of hypnotism forty years earlier; but he had never been able to bring himself to accept that they were supernormal, and although he claimed to have read the book with sympathy, it had left him, 'without quite knowing why', rather more sceptical than he had been before. But his review in fact clearly showed why. Janet had wanted hard evidence, provid-

The Continental Mediums

ing irrefutable proof, rather than an abundance of cases, none of which in isolation could be held to be free from some possible weakness.

Richet's challenge was also taken up by some scientists at the Sorbonne, who offered to give 'Eva' a further series of tests. She had already, during the London trials, intimated that she did not want to continue her career as a medium; but she consented to one last attempt to convince the sceptics – her investigators having made no secret of their assumption that her phenomena had been faked. She was able to produce them in only two out of fifteen seances; and they were feeble even compared to what had been witnessed in London.

In his report Paul Henze, who had set up the committee, did not conceal his mocking delight; and another member of the committee had the gall to put his name to the report though he had attended only one sitting, and stayed only a quarter of an hour. 'Can it really be supposed,' Dingwall resignedly asked, 'that the meaning of mediumship, which had eluded tireless investigators for forty years, will be elucidated by a physiologist in fifteen minutes?' Nothing which 'Eva' had done had been regarded by the committee as in any way suspicious; but the story of her discomfiture was taken up in the newspapers and presented as if the precautions – which had been if anything less stringent than she had had to submit to before – had been too well designed for her to elude them: in short, that she had been exposed.

Jean Guzik

Geley refused to be discouraged by the Sorbonne verdict; another Polish medium, Jean Guzik, had been showing for years that he was capable of producing a range of psychic phenomena, and in the winter of 1922 he came to Paris for a series of test seances. In one respect they were unsatisfactory: Guzik needed darkness. The manifestations in general followed the familiar pattern, with objects moving, including heavy furniture, at a distance from the medium, luminosities, and materialisations. Sitters frequently felt touches, and kisses. The only unusual feature was the frequency with which sitters said that they were being touched or nudged by what they took to be an animal: a dog, or perhaps a monkey.

Materialised animal forms, Geley realised, were not likely to impress the kind of people he wanted to impress, if the animals could only be felt, not seen. With Guzik, he contented himself with the limited objective of persuading sitters that the movements of objects and the touches were supernormal. The medium's wrists were taped to the wrists of his controllers; and during seances, when the witnesses' hands formed a chain, they were in addition actually chained together, so that no individual could move from his seat, or even stretch, without involving the sitters on either side of him.

Eighty 'highly placed persons' as Geley described them, attended seances; all except three or four who happened to attend blank seances expressed themselves convinced; and thirty-four of them signed an agreed statement covering the phenomena they had witnessed. It described the precautions, and the way the medium was controlled by hands as well as wrist-tapes; Guzik, they agreed, always remained passive, though occasionally he would raise a hand (and the controlling hand along with it) over his head to enable the controller to feel something behind him. At the seances – held in different rooms, each inspected for trapdoors and such, and then locked and sealed – they witnessed a variety of phenomena, two classes of which they all vouched for:

> 1. Displacements, sometimes very considerable, of diverse objects without contact of the medium and, moreover, out of his reach (as far as 1½ metres). In order to be certain of no mal-observation, or error of memory, the position of these objects was minutely measured, and they were very often affixed to the floor or the table by gummed paper.
> 2. Contacts and touches were very frequent and very diverse as to the sensations produced, perceived on the arms, the backs or the heads of the controllers.

When the medium raised an arm, the controller whose hand went with it 'perceived material contacts several times'. The signatories concluded that although they could not be more specific they would affirm their conviction 'that the phenomena are not explicable by individual or collective illusion or hallucination, nor by any trickery'.

The thirty-four signatories were indeed 'highly placed'. They included twelve doctors of medicine: Professor Santoliquido of the Red Cross and the League of Nations; the editor of the *Petit Parisien*; the chief of the Identification Service at the Préfecture of Police; Count de Gramont and Professor Leclainche of the Institut de France; Marcel Prévost, author of *Cousin Laura*, playwright, novelist and member of the Academy; Professor Valée, Director of the National Laboratory of Sanitary Research; and three veterans of psychical research, Lodge, Richet and Flammarion. Nevertheless their testimony went for nothing, because Guzik was unwise enough to submit to further investigation by another Sorbonne team, one of whom had been involved in the 'Eva' tests.

The report of the investigators had curious echoes of its equivalent about Eusapia in the United States. There were ten seances, at some of which the customary phenomena were reported; when the lights were turned on at the third seance, for example, after one of the sitters had felt a blow, it was found that a chair which had been out of the medium's reach had moved by over a metre and a half. On the investigators' own reckoning, Geley was to point out, for the medium to have moved it by physical force he would have had to extricate himself from his controllers, get up, walk round behind one of the controllers' chairs, push it, and then return to his seat, and to control, undetected.

A comparable feat would have been required in the sixth seance, where a basket placed out of his reach had moved. But when the investigators found they could not detect how he was moving the objects, they decided to settle for the allegation that on some occasions he had been observed acting as if he were trying to free a leg; and they brought the trials to a close. 'The phenomena of touches, displacements and projections of objects,' they asserted in their report, 'are always produced within reach of the medium' – a claim which their own records showed was untrue. 'Their conviction is complete and without reserve' they concluded; adding that the phenomena presented to them involved no mystery. 'The medium produces them – by using his elbow to produce certain touches on the shoulders; by liberating one of his legs from control, he makes displacements, contacts and projection of objects by this liberated limb.'

It was an extraordinary document for them to put their names to, demonstrating as it did only that, by their own admission, they had been totally incompetent. Obviously if the reality of the phenomena were to be proved or disproved, the first task should have been to ensure that the medium was controlled in such a way as to make it impossible for him to use elbows or legs or any kind of physical force. Yet this was precisely what the controllers had failed to do – as the notes taken during the seances confirmed. After the second seance, which had produced manifestations, one of the controllers had admitted he was unable to recall whether at any time he had lost contact with the leg he was supposed to be controlling; and he could not even be sure, when he was in contact, whether it was Guzik's right leg or left leg he was supposed to be controlling. This, Geley protested,

> is really inconceivable. What! The controller, even before the beginning of the experiment, does not know if he is in control of the right or the left leg, and does not verify this? What a witness! In fine, whether the controllers 'have the impression' or 'have not the impression' they are sure of nothing. Unaccustomed to metapsychic experimentation, they avow their uncertainty, and rightly so. But what a contrast between these uncertainties and their conclusion: 'The undersigned declare that their conviction is complete and unreserved.'

Eugène Osty

Frustrating though such setbacks might be, so much was happening at the time that Geley could still hope gradually to wean the savants and scientists from their scepticism; and in this he had an ally in Eugène Osty, one of the thirty-four signatories, who had earlier been chiefly concerned with the investigation of clairvoyance and psychometry. Osty's *Supernormal Faculties in Man*, an expanded and updated version of a work which had appeared before the war, was published in 1923, and it gave a detailed account of experiments he had undertaken with sensitives, designed less to demonstrate the reality of their faculties than to explore the ways in which the information surfaced.

Some of his most impressive results had been obtained with Mme Morel, who, when in a hypnotic trance and given an object to hold, could provide a mass of information for the object's owner. In 1920, for example, a 'Mme R.' had found that a platinum brooch which belonged to her was missing. Her lady's maid accused the housemaid; the housemaid counter-accused the lady's maid. A friend took a coat belonging to 'Mme R.' to Mme Morel, and asked her what she could say about the missing jewel. It had been stolen, Mme Morel told her, but it was still in the house; 'a woman has taken it; she is not very tall, young, chestnut hair' and she was 'the youngest woman in the house, not the other'. But the thief was worried: 'I see her wrapping the jewel in an old newspaper and throwing it under a table in a long room like a hall.' If nothing were said, the jewel would be brought to 'Mme R.' in a few hours. It was; another servant came to her to say, 'Madame, here is your brooch. I have just found it in the hall in an old newspaper.'

The Continental Mediums

So accurate had Mme Morel's description been that when the local magistrate heard the story, and had the housemaid arrested, he assumed that Mme Morel must have been an accomplice, and threatened her with punishment too. 'In the middle ages,' Osty remarked, 'she would have been put to the torture and perhaps sent to the stake.' But when the housemaid confessed, the magistrate 'declared himself convinced of the existence of transcendental faculties'.

Osty was aware that Mme Morel might be picking up stray clues from her clients, and their emissaries; in the case of 'Mme R.', from the friend who had brought along her coat. But this could not account for what had happened on an occasion in 1914 when he had been asked by an estate agent whether he could help in tracing a missing man. Osty placed a neckerchief from the missing man's possessions in the hands of Mme Morel, while she was under hypnosis. She described the man as 'very old and wrinkled', with a long nose, white-haired, with one finger which had been hurt.

> I see a country house . . . he leaves that . . . he walks . . . he is ill, his breathing is difficult . . . and his brain is confused . . . he leaves the path . . . goes into a thicket, a wood . . . he sees much water near by . . . he falls on the damp ground . . . then after a little while, he breathes no more.

The man was lying, she claimed, not far from the house 'on his right side, one leg bent under him'; and she gave a direction for the path to be followed from the house to find his body, which would be by some blocks of stone, tall trees, and water.

All that Osty himself knew about the missing man was that he was over eighty and walked with a stoop, so the information could not have come from him, telepathically. So detailed was it, he assumed that if it were correct the body would quickly be found; but it was not found. Hypnotised afresh, Mme Morel repeated her story but in greater detail, with a reference to a woodman's hut containing tools. After a further search, the body was at last discovered just as she had described it, lying by a pool near large trees. Her only inaccuracy was that there were no 'blocks of stone' – yet even this was, in a sense, correct. One of the men on the search party, following the route she had prescribed, had called out, 'There is the stone she saw', just before he came upon the body. When the 'stone' was examined it turned out to be a large stump from a fallen tree, so covered with moss that it had been easy to mistake for a rock.

Science and Parascience

Occasionally the visions would turn out to relate to the future: Osty cited a case which he had used in his earlier work, 'very representative of similar incidents'. Another medium, Mme Fraya, had a dream in which she was exercising her faculty, and told one of her clients, whom she did not know, that her worry was over her son, who was being treated in an asylum, but all would be well because although he had been pronounced incurable, he would soon be returned to her entirely cured. In one respect the dream was unusual, in that it was broken into in the middle – Mme Fraya's maid had woken her to sign a registered letter being delivered by the postman – but had been resumed at the point it was broken off, so vividly that when she woke up again, she felt she could repeat what she had said word for word. About a week later, a new client appeared who turned out to be the lady in her dream. Without the need to go into a trance to exercise her mediumistic faculty, Mme Fraya repeated from memory what she had said in the dream, to the stupefaction of the woman.

With these and similar cases, Osty claimed, he could have filled several volumes; but he had been mainly concerned to explore the many different methods which sensitives adopted to obtain their information. Some needed to be hypnotised; others could perform in (apparently) a waking state. Some needed the client's presence; some, an object belonging to the client; for some, 'it is enough that the experimenter should be thinking of the person'. Others used a variety of devices: 'playing cards, a crystal ball, a glass of water, a candle-flame, coffee-grounds spilt on a plate, a heap of pins thrown on the carpet, etc etc.'

Osty was under no illusion about the reliability of this information. In the case of the missing man, when the neckerchief was put into Mme Morel's hands she had first described 'a person whom I recognised as myself'; then, another man whom he took to be the estate agent; then, a woman who, Osty thought, might have been the dead man's daughter-in-law – all these before she eventually got round to describing the man himself. But though she could make such mistakes, she never muddled up the characters of the different people; 'every feeling, act, scene and event were ascribed to the individual to whom they pertained'.

The mental images, Osty had decided, did not reflect reality; they were 'representations building up a fanciful interior language intended to bring the supernormal cognition into consciousness by all kinds of imaginative means'. In all his research he had never come across exact representations of what was actually happening:

The Continental Mediums

'The visual images have always seemed to be reconstructions of ideas, of notions, and of cognitions.' It was consequently desirable, Osty concluded, to help sensitives along, rather than to think in terms of catching them out, which it was only too easy to do; and he gave, as an example, an occasion when he had brought back a piece of string which had been in a cupboard from which money had been stolen, his idea being that this might assist the sensitive to identify the thief through psychometry. What she picked up was a strangling; and if Osty had not known what he was looking for, he might have let her develop the theme. Instead, he told her of the circumstances of the theft, asking her to 'see' it, which she then did, describing two men concerned in it so accurately that the police were able to identify them; and at their trial it became clear that her account of the theft was correct. 'Here, then, is a seance which began with imaginary matter,' Osty concluded, 'and ended with exact cognizance of the event, because I was able to give a slight indication enabling the subject to perceive the facts.'

As Schiller was to point out in his review of Osty's book for the SPR, and as Alan Gauld has recently echoed in his *Mediumship and Survival*, Osty's case histories from one point of view were unsatisfactory: he selected them and edited them in a way which made it impossible to tell what proportion of 'hits' there were to misinformation. Nevertheless 'It would take an immense mass of erroneous material to outweigh Osty's more remarkable cases,' Gauld feels, 'and a great deal of misrecording and misverification to undermine them.'

The Death of Geley

The second international psychical research congress was held in Warsaw in the summer of 1923; and although it lacked the sparkle of the first, it appeared to consolidate past gains. There were papers from Barrett and Mrs Sidgwick; from Mme Bisson, Geley and Sudre; from Brugmans; and from Schrenck – along with one from a new recruit, Traugott Oesterreich, Professor of Philosophy at Tübingen and author of *Occultism and Modern Science*, a critical but sympathetic survey of contemporary research.

Dingwall too presented a paper; and he took the opportunity of the visit to test Ossowiecki on the SPR's behalf, bringing with him a piece of paper with the message '*Les Vignobles du Rhin, de la Moselle et de la Bourgogne donnent un vin excellent*', and below it, a rough sketch of a bottle. The paper was dated, folded, and enclosed in an opaque red envelope, which was itself placed in an opaque black envelope, which was in turn placed in an opaque brown envelope. On his arrival in Warsaw Dingwall handed the brown envelope to Schrenck, as it had been agreed that it would be unwise for Dingwall himself to be present during the guessing, in case he should inadvertently give something away; and later that day, Schrenck handed Ossowiecki the packet. Geley, who was present, wrote down what he said:

> It is not you, Schrenck-Notzing, who have written. It is another man that I might be able to describe . . . The letter that I am holding has several envelopes . . . It is a letter and yet it is not a letter . . .

After switching to discuss other envelopes which Schrenck had given him, Ossowiecki came back to Dingwall's:

> There is a drawing by a man who is not an artist . . . something red with this bottle . . . There is without doubt a second red envelope . . . There is a square drawn at the corner of the paper. The bottle is very badly drawn. I see it! I see it.

He then drew what he 'saw', adding that there was also something written. After a pause, when Schrenck asked what language it was written in, Ossowiecki replied 'In French'; and went on:

> The bottle is a little inclined to one side. It has no cork. It is made up of several fine lines. There is first a brown envelope outside; then a greenish envelope, and then a red envelope. Inside a piece of white paper folded in two with the drawing inside. It is written on a single sheet.

The following day the packet was returned to Dingwall, who had taken the additional precaution of punching minute pinholes through the envelopes, so that he would be able to detect if there had been any attempt to open them up to get at the contents. When he had satisfied himself that they had not been tampered with, and opened them up himself in the presence of the others, Ossowiecki 'received an ovation, and fell on the necks of the observers with tears in his eyes' – not so surprising as it might sound, in view of Dingwall's already formidable reputation as a critical investigator.

Coincidence, Dingwall pointed out in his report to the SPR, could be excluded; and as there was no way in which Ossowiecki could have obtained prior knowledge of what was in the packet, this 'leaves us but little choice as to the proper interpretation to be

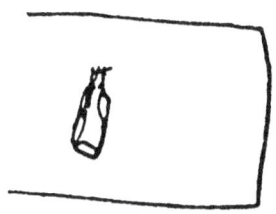

Drawing by Dr Dingwall.

Drawing by Monsieur Ossowiecki.

put upon the experiment. The supernormal character of the incident seems to me quite clear and decisive.'

With so many mediums available for research in and around Warsaw, Geley was tempted to concentrate his research effort there, in the coming months; but before he could complete his next series of trials the aircraft which was to bring him back to Paris from Warsaw crashed on take-off, and he was killed.

It was a shattering blow for psychical research, as Geley had emerged as the outstanding figure of the post-war period. 'This great idealist,' Sudre – a man not given to superlatives – described him, 'this vigorous thinker, is the glorious pioneer of a science which will hold his memory immortal.' To Lodge, Geley was 'a philosophic thinker of no small magnitude'; and Lodge endorsed another tribute which had emphasised, as well as Geley's dedication and conscientiousness, 'his exemplary simplicity, his rare faculty of reconciling the enthusiasm of the investigator with the reflective wisdom of the savant'; above all, his charity 'which extended itself unmeasured to his most sceptical adversaries'.

Scientists in Britain had been accused 'of a kind of insanity, over-credulity, mal-observation and the like', Lodge recalled; but in France, where hostility to psychical research was even more rampant, Geley had been accused, 'not so much of those things, or not only of those, but of downright fraud and deceitful co-operation; in other words, he was accused of being an accomplice and a liar'. Yet so convinced had he been that he could convert his critics simply by submitting to their demands for additional controls, to their specifications, that not merely had he allowed his premises to be examined for secret doors, but had submitted to being chained up with the medium and the other investigators. Innumerable demonstrations for scientists, doctors and journalists had proved that however exacting the precautions, the phenomena ordinarily occurred; and in none had any of the witnesses found any reason to suspect fraud. As a result, Geley had felt confident that eventually, 'the barriers would yield, one by one, to persuasive pressure before the evidence of facts, without any necessity for using violence' – in spite of the violence employed against him 'by adversaries who doubtless felt that their ground was beginning to shake under them'.

Geley himself did not doubt that his adversaries were indeed shaken. 'The heroic stage of metapsychics would seem to be nearing its end,' he wrote shortly before his death; the reality of mediumistic phenomena might not yet be accepted, but it was no longer so systematically denied. And in his *Clairvoyance and Materialisation*, published in 1924, he explained why he thought victory was almost won.

It was really two books, the first dealing with the mental, the second with the physical phenomena, going into much greater detail about his work with 'Eva' than its predecessor, which had been criticised for its lack of full descriptions of the seances. These he now provided – in such detail that, like Schrenck's book on physical mediumship, Geley's made it very clear that if there had been fraud it could not conceivably have been the unaided work of the mediums. Geley himself and many others must have been involved in collaborating with 'Eva', Kluski, Guzik and the rest. And that so many well-known respected scientists, academics and men and women in the professions who had come to the seances should have lent themselves to the deceit was becoming, on the evidence, increasingly implausible.

Geley recognised, however, that it might take time before his evidence was accepted. Many scientists he knew had refused even to examine it; for a reason which Auguste Lumière, the great innovator in photography (who had himself had trouble with sceptics) had recently advanced. The chief cause of their hatred of new ideas which were incompatible with their preconceptions, Lumière had written, 'lay in their failure to realise that science was in a state of continuous evolution'. And there was another, 'perhaps even more important', cause:

> Learned men only reach positions of authority in advanced age; they have therefore lived for many years under the dominion of ideas from which it is extremely difficult for them to free themselves. How hard to have to abandon principles that have been in lifelong use to buttress learned works. The inevitable result of these facts is the prevalence of routine thought. Very often the effort required from a man who ought to be able to escape from the old rut is beyond his powers; and, moreover, human nature is so constituted that it always tends to accept the solutions that demand least effort.

Geley went on to cite Paul Broca, the nineteenth-century surgeon and anthropologist; a tag which has often since been cited and paraphrased, but not always attributed to Broca:

> A new truth contrary to the prejudices of our teachers has no means wherewith to overcome their hostility, for they are open neither to facts nor to reasoning; it is necessary to wait for their death. Innovators must resign themselves patiently to wait for their death, as the Russians of 1812 awaited 'General February'.

Geley also had one important piece of advice as a legacy for his colleagues. From his own experience, he had realised that psychical researchers would have to abandon the hope, dear to those who wanted to satisfy the demands of orthodox scientists, that the subject to be investigated – the medium – should be testable by anybody – believer, agnostic or sceptic. Investigations must be treated as 'collective experiments', Geley emphasised, *'for the phenomena are the results of subconscious psycho-physiological collaboration between the medium and the experimenters'*. It was 'absurd and useless to expect any result from competitions, challenges or offers of prizes to mediums', because it was not only the mediums' but also the experimenters' latent powers which would have to be called upon. In such circumstances the hostility of an experimenter would be prejudicial – but so also would be an experimenter's strong desire for success.

5 The USA

The early years of the First World War, when the United States was still neutral, were an unproductive period for psychical research. Coover was thought to have killed off telepathy; Jastrow and Muensterberg to have discredited the physical phenomena of mediumship. But one practitioner of what might have been described as the psychophysiological phenomena of mediumship did succeed in making a reputation for herself: Mrs Pearl Curran, though her 'control', 'Patience Worth'.

'Patience Worth'

Mrs Curran had had only a perfunctory education, and had never been outside the Middle West when, at the age of thirty-one, she was invited to a ouija session. She was not a spiritualist – both she and her husband were hostile to spiritualism; but occasionally she joined in the pastime, without enthusiasm, largely because a friend of hers was interested. For some months nothing of particular importance was registered; then a 'communicator' emerged: 'Patience Worth', who claimed to be a British girl who had lived in the seventeenth century, and had emigrated to America, where she had been killed by Indians.

'Patience' proved unusual in that not only was she a forceful personality, taking over as 'control'; she also displayed remarkable literary talents. Her prose and her poetry could, and can, be praised or derided according to taste; but what could not, and cannot, seriously be disputed is that they revealed capabilities of a kind far beyond those of Mrs Curran. In certain respects, in fact, they are unique in the history of literature. In a matter of seconds, 'Patience' could turn out long, passable passages of verse on any subject given to her.

Unlike Mrs Leonard, Mrs Curran did not go into a trance; simply into a state of mild abstraction. Conversation took place between her and 'Patience' through the planchette, 'Patience' being a little contemptuous of her other self. When Mrs Curran tried to put in a word for herself, as deserving some credit for what 'Patience' wrote, 'Patience's' reply was 'so doth the piggie who scratcheth upon an oak deem his fleas the falling acorn's cause' – typical of her earthy sense of humour. Even the most captious critics have had to concede that she had an engaging ability to throw off apposite aphorisms in this way. Schiller, for one, was inclined to think her work had been overpraised; 'but no writer need be ashamed of bits of proverbial philosophy like "beat the hound and lose the hare", "it taketh a wise man to be a good fool", "a basting but toughens an old goose", "wisdom patches the seat of learning" and "give me not wisdom enough to understand the universe but folly enough to tolerate it".'

'Patience' was investigated in 1914 by Casper Yost, editor of the Sunday *St Louis Globe-Democrat*, and one of the most respected of American journalists; the founder of the Society of Newspaper Editors, he was to be its President for four years in the 1920s. Convinced that 'Patience' was genuine, and that she had real literary ability, Yost wrote about her in his paper, and overnight she became a celebrity.

That summer, 'Patience' wrote a book: 60,000 words long, *Telka* was about a girl living in the country in Anglo-Saxon Britain; and although the style ('soft-footed strideth Telka, bare toes a-sunk in soft earth, and bits o' green a-cling, bedamped, unto her snowy limbs. Smocked brown and aproned blue, she seemeth a bit o' earth and sky alight amid the field') is to a later generation all too painfully reminiscent of *Cold Comfort Farm*, it came over at the time as unusual and fresh. More significant, however, was the fact that over 90 per cent of the words used were Anglo-Saxon, a staggering proportion considering that as early as the fifteenth century, Anglo-Saxon accounted for only half the words in written English. To maintain the 90 per cent would have required a specialist's knowledge of the language, coupled with the considerable labour of fusing the words into sentences. Yet *Telka* emerged from the planchette in about thirty-six hours' writing time, interspersed with snatches of conversation on various subjects.

Here, then, was a notable opportunity for psychical researchers to carry on their study of multiple personality, particularly as 'Patience' occasionally displayed clairvoyant abilities. Asked what Christmas present was on its way to one of the sitters, 'Patience' replied 'fifteen pieces and one cracked'; when the set of jars arrived the next morning, one was cracked.

The USA

The obvious choice as investigator was Morton Prince, whose study of 'Sally Beauchamp' had led to the acceptance by psychologists of multiple personality; and arrangements were made for the Currans to visit him in Boston. The outcome was farcical. Morton Prince adopted the role of an inquisitor: 'Patience' refused to be bullied:

> Prince: What year were you born in, and where?
> 'Patience': 'Tis apry you be. I be atrothed unto the Puller.
> Prince: Answer my question! You said you would co-operate.
> 'Patience': Yea, thou wouldst to shed o' the blood o' me and then hand unto the wraith o' me the blood blade to wipe.
> Prince: That's dodging!
> 'Patience': 'Tis a merry put thou settest o' a wraith at, sirrah, that she doth do duck o' thy throw.
> Prince: Oh, go away!

and so on. Eventually Prince, exasperated, declined to carry on unless Mrs Curran consented to be hypnotised. She refused – fearing it might lose 'Patience'; and the investigation ended.

James Hyslop offered a better prospect than Morton Prince, as not only had he collaborated with Walter Franklin Prince in the presentation of the Doris Fischer case, and consequently was knowledgeable about multiple personality; unlike Morton Prince he accepted clairvoyance, and had been convinced by the evidence for survival after bodily death. Unluckily, Hyslop allowed himself to be swayed by Morton Prince's verdict that there was 'nothing of scientific importance or interest in the case'; and when the Currans declined to come east again for another investigation, Hyslop felt his suspicions had been justified. When, in 1916, Casper Yost's *Patience Worth: a psychic mystery* was published, Hyslop took a hatchet to it in the ASPR *Journal*, conceding that it was readable, and that some of it might be genuine, but refusing to allow that it had any significance for psychical research.

'We are asked to swallow without hesitation the superficial statements and beliefs of a newspaper editor who boasts his ignorance of psychic research, and of a publisher who desires to sell his wares,' Hyslop complained. There was no evidence whatever 'that a scientific man would regard as conclusive, regarding the origin of the material'. From the point of view of a psychical researcher, this was not unreasonable; but Hyslop went on to cast doubt on the trustworthiness of the Currans, alleging that Curran had cast around to secure the endorsement of academic figures until 'some of them discovered that he was only seeking their interest and endorsement for the purpose of advertisement'; that Curran was familiar with the works of Chaucer, and had briefed his wife accordingly; that Mrs Curran knew the Ozark dialect, which would have helped her, as it contained archaic words; and that these damaging facts had been deliberately suppressed by Yost.

These accusations were vigorously rebutted by Yost, and others who had been convinced by 'Patience'; and in 1926 Walter Franklin Prince, re-examining the evidence, was compelled to admit that Hyslop had been grossly unfair. Curran had not been familiar with Chaucer – nor would it have affected the issue even if he had, as there was no resemblance between 'Patience's' writings and Chaucer's. Nor, for that matter, was there any resemblance between hers and the Ozark dialect. Far from seeking academic endorsement for the purpose of advertisement, the Currans had had to be persuaded to submit to investigation, and had regretted it. Contemptuous of any unscientific or evasive handling of psychical research, Prince explained, Hyslop sometimes 'gave utterance to expressions not so carefully verified as were his conclusions on the basis of experimentation'; and sometimes 'a little too readily listened to the unverified assertions of other inimical persons'. Hyslop, Prince nevertheless insisted, had maintained that he had never condemned the phenomena of 'Patience Worth', and 'never declared them spurious'.

If Hyslop had made such a claim, he was himself being evasive. In his review of Yost's book he had denounced the case as 'a fraud and delusion'; in a passing reference to it a year later he had remarked that it might have been useful, 'but deception of the public will make more money than the truth'; and in 1918 he had referred to 'Patience's' 'lying literary productions'. Hyslop could have argued that he had never denied the *existence* of 'Patience'; that he was simply criticising the way in which the Currans had exploited her. But the intemperate language which he used, and the readiness with which he accepted unsubstantiated gossip about the Currans, came oddly from a man professing to be concerned for the maintenance of strict scientific standards.

The outcome was that 'Patience' was not investigated by psychical researchers in the years when she had most to offer. Her second, and most successful, book – *The Sorry Tale*, woven around the story of Jesus – the *New York Times* reviewer thought, 'increased the marvel of the first' simply as a feat of literary composition: well over 300,000 words, and 'all spelled out through

The USA

the ouija board during part of the evenings of the last two years'. In general the reviews were favourable, the *New York Globe*'s making the point that the mysterious nature of the authorship was soon forgotten; 'there is nothing queer or spooky about the story itself', and its dramatic construction was 'excellent'. Less than a year later it was followed by *Hope Trueblood*, a 90,000-word story of life in England in Victorian times; 'a masterpiece', the *Los Angeles Times* reviewer thought. It was well received even in England; attention was not drawn to the ouija board's role in its conception, and it was treated by most reviewers as just another novel – 'of decided promise', the *Athenaeum*'s critic thought; 'definite and clear cut characterisation, good dialogue, quaint and arresting turns of expression, and deep but restrained feeling'. 'Patience' in other words, was capable of producing books which were marketable in their own right, and which were close enough in their evocation of the periods with which they dealt to qualify as historical novels, though Mrs Curran had no familiarity with the background.

'Patience' was still in action when Walter Prince wrote his book, though her output was no longer saleable; as if in embarrassment, the literary world which had praised her had been quick to forget her. Prince was left in no doubt, however, that she was genuine. And this has since left a puzzling problem – several, in fact. They have been sensibly discussed in Irving Litvag's *Singer in the Shadows*, published in 1972; chief among them, whether 'Patience' can be fitted into the psychological, secondary-personality category which the two Princes established. Walter Prince himself argued that she could not: 'I know of no proof that a secondary personality, subliminal or alternating, can show ability so tremendously in advance of the primary or normal consciousness.' And his conclusion was that 'either our concept of what we call the subconscious must be radically altered, so as to include potencies of which we hitherto have had no knowledge, or else some cause operating through, but not originating in, the subconsciousness of Mrs Curran must be acknowledged'.

On the other hand, the idea that 'Patience' was the returning spirit of a deceased girl of that name presented an even more formidable problem: how, in that case, could she have written so perceptively about life in the time of Jesus, let alone about life in Victorian times? Various explanations have been presented, from cryptmnesia to an ability to tune into the collective unconscious; but no agreement has been reached. After immersing himself in the case for two years, Litvag had to admit that if asked, who was Patience Worth? 'I readily confess: I do not have an answer'. But he points out that 'Patience' herself did not want the question to be answered; and he ended with one of her farewell poems explaining why. It includes the lines

> Farewell is a jest
> A wasted word.
> Yesterday is now,
> Today is now,
> And tomorrow too
> Is now

– a curious foretaste of what some physicists were just beginning to present as a tentative explanation of the mystery of Time.

The Sceptics

With the members of the ASPR doing their work for them, sceptics had little need to worry about 'Patience Worth'; and Coover, in this period, had been carrying on at Stanford with telepathy trials along similar lines to those he had conducted earlier. To his satisfaction, they were producing similarly negative results. He published his findings in *Experiments in Psychical Research* in 1917, with the clear aim of impressing his academic colleagues that psychologists need no longer be tarred with the psychic brush: reviewing it in the SPR's *Proceedings*, F. C. S. Schiller remarked that it weighed three pounds and was 'hardly meant to be read, at all events by the general public, to judge by the lengthiness and diffuseness of its style, and the academic jargon in which it is written'. Unluckily for Coover, however, his new account of how he had conducted the trials exposed a crucial flaw in the design. His method of testing had been to have 100 subjects trying to guess what card the agent was looking at; each subject did 100 trials, in half of which the agent had in fact looked at a card, but in the other, control, half he had not turned the card face upwards, so that he did not know what he was 'sending'. Some subjects had scored significantly better than would have been expected by chance when the sender could see the card; but as they also scored significantly better when what Coover assumed must be 'pure guesswork' was involved, because the sender had not seen the

The USA

card, he concluded that 'no trace of an objective thought-transference is found as a capacity enjoyed in perceptible measure by *any* of the individual normal reagents'.

Schiller, however, had earlier conducted some experiments with an automatist who, in a trance state, had been able to score significantly above chance on 'pure guesses'; picking up the right card by, presumably, clairvoyance. The results of Coover's method of controlling his trials, in other words, could be interpreted as showing the absence of telepathic communication between agents and subjects; but it could also be used as evidence for the reality of clairvoyance. By this time, however, the Stanford authorities had accepted Coover's demonstration as confirming that there was no further need to apply the legacy for the purposes which the testator had designated; it was henceforth used in other projects.

Harvard had also been the recipient of a legacy designed to promote psychical research, the Hodgson Memorial Fund; but no use had been made of the money – not surprisingly, with Muensterberg in the Chair of Psychology – until another benefactor offered a further sum, sufficient to lead to the appointment of Leonard Thompson Troland as an investigator. He introduced a few innovations in the course of trials conducted in 1916 and 1917: subjects had to guess which side of a box was illuminated by lights switched on in a randomised order; and the method by which the subject made his guesses, pressing a switch, enabled them to be automatically recorded for comparison with the automatically-recorded light sequence. But though this looked as if it were an impressive new way of testing for psychic powers, this was not Troland's real objective. He was a monist, who assumed that if there was a psychic faculty, it must also be physical, a form of energy transfer; and although he did not expect results, he had the consolation that if he did get them, he could then go on to show they were not psychic. Like Coover, he did not attempt to differentiate between individuals; and when, after only 600 trials, he found that the proportion of correct guesses was slightly below chance, he decided there was no further need to continue the experiment.

This came as no surprise to Hyslop; in his *Contact with the Other World*, published in 1919, he quoted a Harvard student who, asked if he would undertake psychical research, replied 'not on your life': it would ruin his academic prospects. The 'will to disbelieve' was quite as prevalent as the 'will to believe', Hyslop lamented, and 'no more creditable'. For scepticism based on intellectual obstinacy and pride, he felt, there could be no excuse.

A few months after the book's publication, Hyslop died. He had rescued the American SPR after Hodgson's death, and kept it alive for fifteen years largely single-handed; but in 1917 he had taken on the assistant who was now to succeed him: Walter Franklin Prince.

Walter Franklin Prince

Prince had been led into psychical research by a curious combination of interests and events. Born in 1863, he had graduated from Yale and had studied abnormal psychology; he had then decided to become an Episcopalian clergyman, and might have remained one but for two episodes, the first being a nightmare he had in 1902. In it, he was looking at a train, part of which was in a railway tunnel. 'Suddenly, to my horror, another train dashed into it. I saw cars crumple and pile up, and out of the mass of wreckage arose the cries, sharp and agonised, of the wounded persons.' Then, smoke or steam burst forth, followed by still more agonised cries. At this point his wife, disturbed by his distressed noises, woke him up; and he told her his dream.

That morning, shortly after his dream, the rear coaches of an express which was standing partly in the New York Park Avenue tunnel (about seventy-five miles away from where he was staying) were run into by a local train which crushed them, killing and injuring many people. And a newspaper account noted how, some time after the crash, 'to add to the horror of it all, the steam hissed out from the shattered engine upon the pinned-down unfortunates'.

The second episode was an encounter with 'Doris Fischer' a case of multiple personality. Walter Prince and his wife took 'Doris' into their home, eventually adopting her as their daughter and restoring her to health; in the process making a close study of the different personalities involved, and discovering, among other things, that one of them was telepathic. His account of the case, in which Hyslop collaborated, appeared during the war in the society's publications; and it was then that Hyslop had taken him on as assistant.

In 1917 Prince had another experience of the kind he had had fifteen years before, even more disturbing. On the night of 27–28

The USA

November he dreamt that a young woman had come to him with an order for her execution, telling him she was willing to die if he would only hold her hand.

> Then the light went out and it was dark. I could not tell how she was put to death, but soon I felt her hand grip mine (my *hand*), and knew that the deed was being done. Then I felt one *hand* (of mine) on the hair of the head, which was loose and severed from the body and felt the moisture of blood. Then the fingers of my other *hand* were caught in her teeth, and the mouth opened and shut several times as the teeth refastened on my *hand* and I was filled with the horror of the thought of a severed but living head. Here the dream faded out.

Prince recounted the dream to the Secretary of the society, Gertrude Tubby, the following morning, as well as to his wife. On 29 November the *Evening Telegraph* described how – twenty-four hours after his dream – a woman had placed her head in front of the wheels of a train near a Long Island station and had been decapitated. Her name accounted for Prince's use of the italics: she was Mrs Sarah A. Hand.

The story had even more curious twists than simply the coincidence of the name, and what happened. Mrs Hand, it turned out, had been for some time deranged; and a letter she had written, 'to whom it may concern', explained that she had a theory her head was alive, apart from her body, so she was going to cut it off to prove her case. In his dream, Prince had had a vague notion that the execution was connected with the French revolution; and Mrs Tubby confirmed in her corroborative statement, written the day after the crash, how in describing the dream he had recalled an execution 'where the eyes had opened and closed several times after the head was severed'.

When he later came to relate his dreams, Prince was to make the point that it was not just the way his dreams were so closely paralleled in reality that made an impression on him; they also had 'qualities of emotionality and vividness of imagery to a superlative degree'. And although the dream of the 'execution', he thought, might be accounted for by telepathy, as the woman who died had been worrying about her head's separate life from her body and had evidently been planning to behead herself to prove her point, it could hardly be supposed 'that the events of the railroad collision were consciously or latently in the mind of any living person, several hours before the occurrence'.

'Senora de Z'

Prince, then, had good reason to be anxious to take the earliest available opportunity to investigate clairvoyance, telepathy and precognition more systematically; and shortly after he took over from Hyslop one came his way, as if providentially, in the form of a report of an investigation of a medium in Mexico by Gustav Pagenstecher, a German physician who had settled in Mexico City. One of his patients was 'Senora de Z.' – Senora Maria Reyes de Zierold – who had come to him to be treated for insomnia; finding that drugs did her no good, Pagenstecher had tried hypnosis, and in the course of the treatment she began to tell him of things which she could not have known about through her ordinary senses. Previously sceptical about the 'higher phenomena', he decided to experiment to see whether she could produce them to order; and he found that she could. She could tell him what he was doing, out of her vision; what he was looking at; what he was tasting. As she put it, it seemed to her that while in a deep trance her own senses were not merely blocked, 'but transferred to the hypnotist, to such an extent that I feel the pricking of *his* ears, I taste the sugar or salt put on *his* tongue, and I hear the watch put in the vicinity of *his* ears; I also feel the burning sensation whenever a match is brought near to *his* fingers'.

Such 'exteriorization of sensibility', as it had been described, under hypnosis had been extensively demonstrated in Europe in trials before the First World War; but with orthodox psychologists taking the same course as Pierre Janet and Morton Prince, and having nothing to do with the 'higher phenomena', the study had been neglected. Pagenstecher, however, had determined to carry on his research by seeing what else 'Senora de Z.' could do; and he began trying her out with psychometry – giving her an object to hold, and noting her reactions.

Spiritualist mediums often asked for, say, a ring or a handkerchief belonging to the 'communicator' with whom contact was desired, as if they helped to tune in the 'control'. Senora de Z. was able to describe the process. In her trance, she explained, her senses would be taken over by the hypnotist,

> but as soon as the psychometric vision is completely 'focussed', i.e. when catalepsy is complete and the vision clear cut, then a most interesting phenomenon has always been observed: all my senses seem to be concentrated on the 'associated object' only. I feel the pricking of the object with a needle, as if my fingers were being

pricked. When the object is moistened with alcohol, I have the taste of alcohol in my mouth, and when a match is brought near the object, I feel my fingers burnt.

Sometimes her accounts of the 'associated object's' past history and ownership appeared to indicate straightforward clairvoyance, but sometimes they were mixed with telepathy. Thus Pagenstecher gave her a piece of paper on which there was a design for a medallion which he and his wife had planned to have made for a friend, until they found that the friend was not to be trusted. Senora de Z. accurately described the friend, and what she was doing at the time; but she then described the medallion that the friend was wearing, and the description was of the medallion that Pagenstecher had had designed, but which had not in fact been made.

To Prince's obvious relief, Pagenstecher impressed him on his arrival in Mexico as 'a man of sincerity, an able thinker and patient investigator of a strong scientific bent'; and Senora de Z. as a woman of good sense who took a matter-of-fact attitude to her psychometric powers. Soon, Prince felt compelled to accept that ordinary thought-transference between her and her investigators had to be ruled out. He could give her objects in sealed covers, shuffled so that he did not himself know which was which, and she could describe them; and on occasions when he did know, or thought he knew, about the object, he would invariably find if she disagreed with him that she was right. When he handed her what he took to be a 'sea-bean', a seaweed pod which he had picked up on a beach, and she described its source as 'tall tropical trees growing in a forest near some water', Prince said she had got it wrong; Pagenstecher replied that from past experience 'I bet on her horse, rather than yours'. Pagenstecher won his bet; a botanist informed them that the object was not, as Prince had assumed, a seaweed pod, but a nut from a tree of the species she had described – a nut, too, of a kind that often fell into a river to be washed down to the sea and eventually cast up on a beach.

Again and again, Senora de Z. was on target in her psychometry. On one occasion, given a carefully wrapped object, she said it was a farewell message from a man on a sinking ship to his wife and children, and gave a description of the man. The object was in fact a piece of paper with the message, which had been found in a bottle washed up in the Azores; and the widow, when contacted, confirmed that the description of her husband was accurate, in particular the fact he was badly scarred above his right eyebrow. Even if

Senora de Z. had been able to read the paper, it would have given her no clue to the man's appearance; yet she had got it right.

The same applied in one of Prince's tests, where he gave her a letter which she 'read' placed between her hands. He had taken it from an old file, knowing only that a clergyman had written it; she not merely read the letter, and described the clergyman, but also made a number of statements about him, his church, his travels, and so on, to which the letter gave no clue. Checking on the thirty-eight statements, Prince found that three of them could not be verified, but the rest were all literally correct. A mathematician, asked to work out the odds against her guessing them by chance, reckoned they were around 5,000,000,000,000,000 to one.

Prince would have been justified in claiming that Senora De Z. had provided the best and most consistent evidence for mental psychic phenomena that had been acquired since serious research into them had begun. Manifestly she could not have cheated; nor could she and Pagenstecher have been in collusion, as his own tests had independently confirmed Pagenstecher's findings. All that sceptics could have argued was that he too had been in collusion with Pagenstecher and Senora de Z.; as doubtless they would have done, if pressed. But what happened in Mexico did not need to be taken too seriously. Pagenstecher was not a well-known figure in the world of science; and Prince was only starting on his career in psychical research. It was easier simply to ignore the findings.

William McDougall

Psychical research in America now welcomed a recruit whom it would not be easy to ignore: William McDougall.

Like W. H. R. Rivers, with whom he had many affinities, McDougall had trained both as a doctor and as an anthropologist before taking up psychology and making it his career; and as early as 1907, reviewing Morton Prince's work on 'Sally Beauchamp' in the SPR *Proceedings*, he had drawn attention to what he regarded as a flaw in Prince's interpretation of the evidence: 'To assert, as Dr Prince does, that Sally is a split-off fragment of Miss B. is to maintain that the part may be greater than the whole.' Prince, he thought, appeared to have 'set out with the conviction that every case of multiple personality is to be regarded as resulting from dissociation of a normal personality, and to have allowed this prejudice to limit the range of his search for hypotheses'. This,

The USA

McDougall argued, was a mistake: 'If we are to discuss these strange cases with profit, we must give rein to speculation.' There were no established facts in this area: there might be many psychic entities within each organism, but 'it may be that, as Mr. H. G. Wells has suggested in one of his weird stories, disembodied souls are crowding thickly about us, each striving to occupy some nervous system and so become restored to a full life of sense and motion and human fellowship'.

In *Body and Mind*, published in 1911, McDougall had preached a return to Animism – the theory that, as he defined it, 'those manifestations of life and mind which distinguish the living man from the corpse and from inorganic bodies are due to the operation within him of something which is of a nature different from that of the body, an animating principle generally, but not necessarily or always, conceived as an immaterial and individual being or soul'. In other words he was in the Vitalist tradition, which during the past century had come to be rejected in favour of materialism, except by a few fellow Animists – chief among them William James and Bergson. And like them, he looked with favour on the evidence for telepathy as adding support to his Animist theory.

The penultimate chapter of *Body and Mind* had been devoted to 'the bearing of the results of "psychical research" on the psycho-physical problem'. Although a great deal of evidence had accumulated pointing to the survival of the human personality after the death of the body, McDougall felt that it was not yet strong enough to convince an open-minded doubter, and consequently did not qualify as a verification of Animism. Still, psychical research had, to his mind, furnished one very important positive result by establishing the occurrence of 'phenomena that are incompatible with the mechanist assumption'; such as telepathy. Although he could not present all the evidence for telepathy in his book, 'it must suffice to say that it is of such a nature as to compel the assent of any competent person who studies it impartially'.

In particular McDougall was impressed by the evidence provided in the cross-correspondences. It was possible to argue the case that the messages came not from the surviving personalities of the deceased, but through some immensely complex interaction between people thousands of miles apart; 'unless, though, we are prepared to adopt the supposition of a senseless and motiveless conspiracy of fraud among a number of persons who have shown themselves to be perfectly upright and earnest in every other relation [and his personal knowledge of some of them rendered the supposition ridiculous], we must recognise that we stand before the dilemma – survival, or telepathy of this far-reaching kind'; and either was 'fatal to the mechanistic scheme of things'.

During the war, McDougall had served in the Royal Army Medical Corps; and after his return to academic life he received an invitation to take up the Presidency of the SPR, left vacant by the death of Lord Rayleigh. In his Presidential Address, McDougall felt bound to defend his sceptical academic colleagues, insisting that one of the reasons why most of them held aloof from psychical research was 'by no means discreditable': they felt a sense of responsibility to the public.

> Men of science are afraid lest, if they give an inch in this matter, the public will take an ell and more. They are afraid that the least display of interest or acquiescence on their part may promote a great outburst of superstition on the part of the public, a relapse into belief in witchcraft, necromancy, and the black arts generally, with all the moral evils which must accompany the prevalence of such beliefs. For they know that it is only through the faithful work of the men of science during very recent centuries that these debasing beliefs have been in large measure banished from a small part of the world; they know that, throughout the rest of the world, these superstitions continue to flourish, ready at any moment to invade and overwhelm those small areas of enlightment.

McDougall nevertheless insisted that psychical research of the kind the society had been doing was necessary. It did not increase the risk of a relapse into superstition,

> rather it is our best defence against it. For Pandora's box has been opened, the lid has been slightly lifted, and we are bound to go on and to explore its remotest corner and cranny. It is not only or chiefly the work of this Society that has raised the lid a little and exposed us to this danger. The culture of Europe has for a brief period rested upon the twin supports of dogmatic affirmation and dogmatic denial, of orthodox religion and scientific materialism. But both of these supports are crumbling, both alike sapped by the tide of free enquiry. And it is the supreme need of our time that these two pillars of dogmatism shall be replaced by a single solid column of knowledge on which our culture may securely rest. It is the policy of sitting on the lid of the box that is risky; a danger and threat to our civilisation.

McDougall had not been President long before he received an invitation to take over the Chair of Philosophy at Harvard – ironically, from Muensterberg, who for two decades had been the chief scourge of the psychical researchers in America. Reviewing

The USA

Troland's poor use of the Hodgson Memorial Fund, Schiller expressed the hope that McDougall would see that it was put to some more effective purpose; and as soon as he arrived, McDougall linked up with Prince, taking over the Presidency of the American society but leaving Prince to run it and to edit the *Journal* and *Proceedings*. Immediately they set about shifting the emphasis away from the search for evidence for survival, which had been Hyslop's main concern, to more mundane issues. Accordingly Prince went to Europe to attend the first International Congress for Psychical Research at Copenhagen in 1921, there to see what could be done to improve international co-operation; and McDougall set up an Advisory Scientific Council in Boston with a solid academic composition.

Psychologists, McDougall had realised, felt their responsibility to the public even more acutely than other scientists. That was why so few of them had joined the SPR. They might be willing to work with the society's 'right wing' – by which he had in mind those psychologists who, like Janet, Morton Prince and Bramwell, might still be members, but who had in effect moved themselves out of psychical research when their own field of research came to be granted a measure of academic legitimacy; perhaps also the Cambridge nucleus, with whom McDougall was well acquainted, and who could be trusted not to cause embarrassment by allowing themselves to be deluded by dubious mediums, as the 'left wing' were prone to do. Significantly, in his chapter on psychical research in *Body and Mind* McDougall had not even mentioned telekinesis, let alone the physical phenomena of mediumship. What the left wing were doing might be necessary, he conceded; but it must not be allowed to frighten away academic psychologists.

In setting up the council McDougall clearly aimed to implement these views. It would bring sceptical psychologists together with the right wing of the American society, together with a few of the more reasonable members from the left, such as Dr Elwood Worcester, who was academically respectable but had spiritualist affinities. Doubtless McDougall hoped that the rest of the left would be gratified, and with luck overawed, by the council's composition. Far from it: senior members who had shared Hyslop's views (and since he had been the dominant force in the society for so many years, many of them did) were aghast when they saw the list of psychologists on McDougall's council: among them Coover of Stanford, Troland of Harvard and Jastrow of Wisconsin. Jastrow, in particular, had long made it clear that his interest in psychical research was purely destructive: he had described telepathy as 'a complex conglomerate, in which imperfectly recognised modes of sensation, hyperesthesia and hysteria, fraud, conscious and unconscious, chance, collusion, similarity of mental processes, an expectant interest in presentiments and a belief in their significance, nervousness and ill-health, illusions of memory, hallucinations, suggestion, contagion and other elements enter into the composition'.

If a Lutheran community had been told that Torquemada was to become one of their bishops, they could hardly have been more appalled than the society's trustees. The fact that its headquarters were in New York enabled them to get together in 1923 to elect a new President, the Rev. Frederick Edwards, without consulting McDougall, though he was himself a member of the board; and Edwards promptly ousted Walter Prince from the editorship of the society's publications, taking the opportunity to write in praise of Conan Doyle, then on a tour of the United States promoting spiritualism and the physical phenomena of mediumship. McDougall resigned from the board; effectively the Boston group of which he was the leader, and of which Prince was to become the most active member, split off from the main New-York-based section of the society, though the formal breach was delayed for a couple of years.

'Margery'

What McDougall most needed was a project which would provide him with the chance to convince the doubters – and perhaps even some of the sceptics – on the council that psychical research needed to be taken seriously. By one of those quirks of Fate with which the history of parapsychology has been littered, an opportunity straightway presented itself in Boston, but of precisely the kind which he least cared about: a medium – a medium, too, not on the model of Mrs Piper or Mrs Osborne Leonard, but an exuder of ectoplasm which was alleged to form itself, as Eusapia's had done, into 'pseudopods', capable of playing silly tricks. Perhaps worse still, from McDougall's viewpoint, was that the medium's control, unlike 'Phinuit' or 'Feda', not merely had a recognisable identity as the medium's deceased brother; his voice and manner proclaimed him to be, if not the original, an uncommonly exact copy. Nevertheless McDougall had little choice but to undertake the investigation because 'Margery' and her brother 'Walter' quickly became the talk of Boston.

'Margery' was the name by which Mina Crandon was to become known to the public in articles, before her identity was disclosed; and as it was to stick, for convenience it can be used to refer to her in her trance condition, during seances. Born in 1888, Mina had grown up in Canada, her closest family tie being with her elder brother Walter until, in 1911, he was killed in an accident. By that time she had moved to Boston, and married; and in 1918 she obtained a divorce to marry LeRoi Goddard Crandon, a surgeon with an academic post at Harvard and a lucrative Boston practice. Although intolerant of religions, Crandon was impressed by a talk he heard Oliver Lodge give on spiritualism, and read the books Lodge recommended to him; among them Crawford's. He also began to listen more sympathetically to the spiritualist case, put by his friend Dr Mark Richardson; and on 27 May 1923 he invited a small group of friends to his Boston home to try a little table-turning. So striking were the table's movements that one of the company, it was realised, must surely have psychic powers. By a process of elimination – the sitters leaving the room one by one – the psychic was found to be Mina.

Soon, she was producing some of the phenomena Crandon had read about in Crawford's descriptions of his work with the Goligher circle – along with some that were even more startling. On one occasion the seance-room table harassed a visiting doctor, actually pursuing him out into the corridor and through to a bedroom, where it pushed him on to the bed: 'then, on request for more, the table started downstairs after him, when we stopped it to save the wall plaster'. The phenomena appeared to follow the instructions of 'Margery's' 'controls', one of whom was soon to dominate the proceedings – her brother 'Walter'.

'Walter' was a character, in the spirit as in life: rumbustious, argumentative, even foul-mouthed. He instructed the sitters in what they must do and what they must not do; described what was going to happen next; and provided an acerbic running commentary on the proceedings. Initially they were informal, but gradually the procedure was tightened up, to satisfy sceptical acquaintances and investigators; and for a decade, 'Margery' became the central issue of psychical research in the United States.

The 'Margery' case could fill several volumes – and indeed has; but a biography written half a century later by Thomas R. Tietze provides a useful short introduction. Of the three possibilities –

that 'Margery' was entirely genuine, that she was entirely fraudulent; and that the genuine and the fraudulent were mixed – he rules out the first, leaving it up to the reader to decide between the other two. At first sight this is puzzling, as the tone of the book is sceptical. Yet it was a wise decision, because should the physical phenomena of mediumship ever be demonstrated in ways sufficient to secure their acceptance even as a possibility, the 'Margery' case will have to be reopened and reassessed.

The chief interest of the 'Margery' story lies less in what it has to tell us about the physical phenomena of mediumship, than in its demonstration of the inability of researchers to investigate them satisfactorily. Partly this was because of the elusive nature of the phenomena; partly because few of the researchers had any experience in this field (and fewer still took the trouble even to acquaint themselves with the work of, say, Richet, let alone of Crawford). Those who were experienced, too, tended to bring their preconceptions and prejudices along with them, which left them incapable of detachment. Rival factions consequently developed, leading to internecine feuds. To an outside observer, Stewart Griscom of the *Boston Herald* was to comment, the 'Margery' saga was 'profoundly and sardonically humorous, with almost a Molière touch. It has mystery, veiled motivations, true tragedy, howling farce, and a pervading aura straight from *Alice in Wonderland*. Almost everybody involved shoots off at tangents; respected clergymen and savants suddenly become voluble liars; there are meaningless statements apropos of nothing; logic and normality take extended holidays.' For those involved there were more saddening elements. In particular, the American Society for Psychical Research was split apart, a wound which was not to be healed until the Second World War.

On two issues there was no serious conflict of evidence. The phenomena were striking, even if unoriginal: raps from all parts of the seance rooms; 'Walter's' voice; levitations; movements of objects; 'pseudopods', which touched and nudged sitters with ghostly fingers; ectoplasm, which was periodically captured on film, when 'red light' was permitted. And the Crandons were not the kind of people whom it was easy to suspect of trickery. Sceptics and believers alike found Mina attractive and engaging, and her husband a rock of good sense. They allowed precautions to be taken: investigators were encouraged to search the rooms in which the seances took place. Mina also allowed herself to be searched, before she put on a kimono, silk stockings and slippers, and made her appearance. Her 'cabinet' was rather more like a cabinet than mediums usually settled for, as it looked like a squat sentry box; but as it was open at the front, and large enough for an investigator who wanted to check on her to sit beside her, it was not too daunting. And although the seances were normally held in darkness, apart from an occasional flash of 'red light', the outline of Mina's body was picked out by luminous pins stuck into her kimono, and luminous bands round her wrists and ankles. Or, sometimes, her wrists and ankles were attached to the cabinet with picture wire. Control – confusingly, the term continued in use to describe the precautions, as well as spirit guides – was also maintained by investigators holding her hands or feet. What they observed and reported during the seances was recorded by a note-taker, and on a dictaphone; and the transcript was signed by all present, though sitters could make individual additions or qualifications if they wished.

There were certain features of the sittings, however, which militated against belief even by sympathetic witnesses that they were genuinely productive of psychic phenomena. One was that Crandon was usually (though not invariably) in control of 'Margery's' right hand and foot. In view of Crawford's findings of the way that Kate Goligher appeared to gather strength from her family circle, this was not so suspicious as it seemed; and Crandon was himself controlled on his right side, so that at the worst, all he could do was to let go of 'Margery's' hand or foot – a move which ought to have been immediately visible to other members of the circle, so long as the luminous bands were secured round her wrists and ankles. In any case, the fact that Crandon was sitting beside her, and was himself controlled on the other side, meant that he could not be held responsible for the distant raps, the music, the luminosities and the movements and levitations of objects rendered visible with luminous paint, which continually featured – unless the Crandons were using some gadget such as a telescopic 'arm', with a 'hand' and 'fingers', and no such elaborate contraption was ever found.

A more serious disadvantage, from the point of view of the investigators, was the darkness. Members of the circle might be able to satisfy themselves, thanks to the luminous paint and the occasional flashes of 'red light', that the Crandons could not have moved from their seats; but only rarely was the light permitted good enough for witnesses to see clearly what was happening. It had been the suspicion aroused, often rightly, at dark seances which had prompted Home to express regret, after his retirement, about the occasions when he had given them. He knew that the psychic force seemed more powerful, the less the light; but the doubts raised in sitters' minds had meant that this was offset by a more than equivalent loss in credibility.

The most disturbing feature of 'Margery's' seances, however, was that part played in them by 'Walter'. It was he who dictated whether the 'red light' could flash, or whether one of the sitters would be permitted to feel the 'teleplasm' emanating from the medium to move the distant objects. Here, sceptics and spiritualists alike could feel justified in being suspicious: the spiritualists because 'Walter's' behaviour and language were embarrassingly unspiritual; the sceptics because, hard though it would have been for them to accept the reality of telekinetic forces, they found the notion that such forces could be exploited by any spirit, particularly so earthy a character, as grotesque. Home had been spared this objection, as his 'controls', if he had them, did not obtrude themselves; and although Eusapia had her 'John King' he kept for the most part in the background. But 'Walter' was autocratic, full of himself and his powers; and inevitably this nurtured suspicion that his instructions were a device which the Crandons could exploit whenever they needed to extricate themselves from difficulties.

The First Harvard Investigation

However obnoxious the physical phenomena of mediumship were to McDougall, 'Margery' offered him an unusually satisfactory opportunity to test them, in that LeRoi and Mina Crandon were agreeable and hospitable, and unlike most mediums lived in a good house in a good neighbourhood. He was assisted by two of his students, Harry Helson and Gardner Murphy. The Crandons were co-operative; but 'Walter', as if amused by McDougall's clear assumption that trickery must be involved, took a perverse pleasure in laying on not only the usual effects, but others of a kind which would demonstrate to him that cheating by the medium was out of the question. Thus when McDougall elected to sit in the cabinet with the entranced 'Margery', the better to watch her, the cabinet was quietly dismantled around them, the screws being removed and put in a heap outside the circle.

The autumn of 1923 went by without any indication of how the tricks were perpetrated, in spite of the increasing rigour of the precautions taken to ensure that neither 'Margery' nor the Crandons nor anybody else could be physically responsible for what was happening. But eventually, following a seance in which a piano stool 'danced' to music, moving several feet in the process, Helson found an eight-inch piece of string on the floor. McDougall summoned Mina to his office, and told her they had caught her out at last: the movement of objects in the seances, they now knew, had been contrived by attaching string to them, which an accomplice could tug at through the ventilator in the wall. By her own account Mina left him in a fit of the giggles. Even if so obvious a device had not been detected in careful searches which the investigators had invariably made of the room, she knew that the ventilator had been blocked up years before.

The *Scientific American* Investigation

That same day, the Crandons were visited by James Malcolm Bird, associate editor of the *Scientific American*. Bird had had a scientific training – he had in fact taught at Columbia University; and becoming interested in the problems posed by psychical research, he had persuaded his publisher, Orson Munn, to put up a substantial prize – $5000 – to go to anybody who could produce conclusive evidence of psychic phenomena: half for the first person who produced a psychic photograph under controlled conditions, half for the first who produced visible psychic manifestations (telepathy, clairvoyance and precognition did not qualify). A number of hopefuls presented themselves for testing, but though some phenomena were observed, none was considered satisfactory enough to merit granting the award. But among those who had suggested the names of possible psychics to Bird was Conan Doyle; and one of his suggestions had been Mina Crandon.

Like almost everybody who met her, Bird found her most attractive, intelligent and amusing. Still chortling over McDougall's allegation, she showed him the long-blocked-up ventilator and jestingly invented various other ludicrous devices by which she proposed to deceive him and the *Scientific American* investigating team. 'My dominant impression of her,' he wrote, 'was of mental alertness; and she has a sense of humor quite as wicked as my own.' To show that she bore McDougall no grudge, too, she raised no objection to his being one of the *Scientific American*'s team.

To outward appearances, the team was well balanced: McDougall; Hereward Carrington; Walter Prince; Dr Daniel Comstock, a physicist from the Massachusetts Institute of Technology; and Harry Houdini. Houdini's commitments prevented him from attending the early sittings; but in view of the scepticism of both McDougall and Prince, there was no risk that the committee would be easily swayed in the medium's favour.

The members of the committee, however, were unlikely to reach an agreed verdict. By this time it was widely assumed that if an investigator had accepted that a physical medium was genuine, as Carrington had with Eusapia, he ceased to be impartial: he became a 'believer'. Carrington, too, was looked down upon in academic circles; he had a degree, but it had been purchased, in his youth, from one of the many colleges which traded in this commodity. It made no difference that his knowledge of mediums' trickery was encylopedic; and the fact that he was a prolific writer of books on psychical research for the popular market was a further strike against him. His opinion would count for little, unless it was critical. McDougall and Prince, though both sincerely believed they brought open minds to the investigation, were both so deeply suspicious of physical mediums that they would not find it easy to judge what they witnessed dispassionately. Prince attended few sittings; in any case, he should not have accepted the role of referee because he was very deaf, and as the seances would be largely in darkness, he would be deprived of the use of two senses. As for Comstock, his role was chiefly to find whether there was a physical force – electro-magnetic, say – which could be detected. Unexpectedly, the decisive voice in the committee was Bird's. As he was present at almost all the sessions, whereas the others attended only sporadically, he soon became the most active participant.

The phenomena were even more abundant for this team than for its predecessor. The sitters witnessed phosphorescent lights and movements of objects at a distance from the medium, as well as feeling touches from invisible hands while both Crandon and 'Margery' were under their control. In addition, 'Walter' made good his boast that he could manipulate a pair of scales which Comstock had brought along as a contribution to the tests, in light just good enough to show that nobody was touching them. Scores of times, too, 'Walter' managed to ring an electric bell in a box designed by the investigators, so that it sounded only when a telegraph-type key was pressed down, the key being out of the Crandons' reach – sometimes when sitters were actually holding the box in their hands. And when Bird decided to satisfy himself that 'Margery' could not be responsible for the effects, by sitting in the 'cabinet' alongside her, 'Walter' laid on an impressive demonstration for his benefit by ripping off the whole wing of the cabinet on the side where Bird was sitting, and then dragging the remains around the room, carrying the two of them in it.

Eventually 'Margery' began producing a pseudopod which felt like an extended arm, with a hand and fingers capable of touching and gripping objects. Although it was allergic to light, which inevitably aroused suspicion, the investigators could feel it, and observe that it appeared solid when it passed between them and objects lit by luminous paint. And they could satisfy themselves that it was neither Mina's real arm nor a telescopic extension, as it emerged while her hands were controlled – and could be seen to be controlled, from the luminous bands round her wrists. Carrington expressed himself satisfied; and Bird was sufficiently impressed to write a favourable interim report in the *Scientific American*. The story was picked up in the newspapers, one of them claiming that even Houdini had been baffled. As he had not been able to attend, Houdini was understandably indignant; and he arrived in Boston to take charge of the proceedings.

At this point the investigation began to fall apart. From every point of view except one, Houdini was admirably suited to be one of the investigators. He knew all, or nearly all, the tricks of his trade; he had considerable experience of unmasking spurious mediums; and he had observed physical phenomena with 'Eva C.' But by 1924 he had ceased even to pretend to himself that he could conduct a dispassionate investigation. His sole interest was in the exposure of what he took to be a wicked conspiracy to defraud the bereaved.

Houdini

Houdini was fifty, at the height of his fame. His Hungarian parents, Samuel and Cecilia Weiss, had christened him Erich; but when, in his teens, he read the memoirs of the most celebrated conjuror of the previous era, Robert-Houdin, he took the name Houdini, and resolved to become even greater. He was subsequently to regret that he had unwittingly lowered himself in his own and others' estimation by identifying himself with Houdin, whom he disparaged – revealing in the process that he could be unscrupulous in twisting evidence, the better to distance himself from the man he had so greatly admired.

Professional magicians had waged war with spiritualist mediums for years; partly because psychic powers, if they could be exploited, would put the straight conjuror out of business; partly because duplicating the mental and physical phenomena of mediumship on stage was both easy and lucrative; partly because exposing mediums was a good way to attract publicity. Houdini's attitude, however, was rather more ambivalent than most. He wanted to be regarded as the greatest stage magician of all time, which entailed repudiating any form of psychic assistance. But he did not reject psychic forces out of hand.

One of his tricks, in fact, was based on his use of what at the time was regarded as an occult power. Indian yogis could train themselves to go into a state of what appeared to be suspended animation: Houdini, using breathing exercises, followed their example so that he could remain alive in a sealed casket, dunked in a river, for far longer than seemed humanly possible. He must have some concealed source of air, his fellow magicians insisted. He could not persuade them that what he was doing was not a conjuring trick – merely an exploitation of a technique which had been used in India for centuries.

A psychic asset, according to Doyle, which Houdini possessed and exploited, though he did not care to admit to it in public, was an 'inner voice' which told him what to do. Very possibly Houdini did not regard it as psychic, either; he may have assumed it was the equivalent of the voice of conscience. He could take the risks he did – risks which no other magician has cared to take – because he was confident that his voice would assure him of his safety, so long as he obeyed it. The tricks, in other words, were tricks; but without the 'guidance', he would not have dared to play them.

Houdini was also interested in spiritualism for a personal reason. 'If God in his infinite wisdom ever sent an angel upon earth in human form,' he wrote in the introduction to his *A Magician Among the Spirits*, 'it was my mother.' After she died in 1913, he longed to continue to communicate with her. But although periodically he was offered communications from her, including one through Lady Doyle, they never satisfied him; and the obvious spuriousness of some of the messages helped to turn him against spiritualism.

The USA

For a while Houdini's respect for Doyle made him investigate physical mediumship seriously – or so he claimed in his correspondence. His real attitude, though, was probably better revealed in an episode described by Milbourne Christopher in *Houdini: the Untold Story*. Visiting the grave of his old friend the magician Lafayette, who had been buried, along with a dog which Houdini had given him, in an Edinburgh cemetery, Houdini brought flowers in two pots, and said, 'Lafayette: give us a sign you are here'.

> Both pots overturned, as if a spirit hand had swept them to the ground; Houdini set them upright. Again they crashed to the ground. 'This time they fell with such force that the pots broke. A spiritualist would have concluded that the ghost of the great illusionist had made its presence known. Houdini had a more rational explanation. 'It was all very strange, yet I do not attribute what happened to anything other than the high wind which was blowing at the time.'

Houdini was never at a loss for a rationalist explanation of this kind; but at least in this period he had been prepared to accept that some of the phenomena he witnessed were inexplicable in ordinary conjuring terms. Feeble though the phenomena which 'Eva C.' had been able to produce in her London trials in 1920, Houdini had been impressed, as he showed in his correspondence not just with Doyle, but also with Crawford, whom he had hoped to visit in Belfast: 'It is certainly a wonderful affair, and there is no telling how far all this may lead.' Unluckily he did not witness a seance with the Golighers, contenting himself with asking Crawford for photographs, as he was going back to America. And following his return there, he was to become more aggressively sceptical as time passed, incorporating material into his stage acts to show how fraudulent mediums did their tricks.

Although Houdini still insisted that he was not attacking spiritualism as such, and that he still wanted to believe in it, his book, *A Magician among the Spirits*, published in 1924, dredged up every scrap of evidence he could find to show that mediums were 'human vultures'. Much of the evidence, however, was dubious, and some of it false. Even Walter Prince, greatly though he admired Houdini – 'I knew him well, and the world seemed poorer when his big heart and eager brain were stilled' – had to admit that the book was 'strewn with blunders', a string of which he listed in *The Enchanted Boundary*. There were others which

Prince did not list; and his excuse for Houdini – 'bias is less reprehensible in a book which professes from the beginning to the end to be an assault, than it would be in what professes to be a history' – itself effectively disposed of any claim the book had to be taken seriously.

Houdini was by this time incapable of separating fact from invention. When George Valiantine, one of the best known mediums in America, offered to demonstrate his powers to the *Scientific American* committee, and it was found that during the manifestations he was not in his chair, Houdini not merely released the story to the press, in spite of the agreement that all accounts of trials were to be published first in the *Scientific American*; he actually boasted that *he* had exposed Valiantine, though he had not been responsible for the device which revealed that Valiantine was not sitting where he was supposed to be.

By the time Houdini arrived to investigate 'Margery' he had by his own admission already compromised himself, as he had told the publisher of the *Scientific American*: 'I will forfeit a thousand dollars if I do not detect her if she resorts to trickery.' Theoretically this left it open to him to admit that she did *not* resort to trickery. But in practice he had burned his boats; he had been on a lecture tour of the United States as advance publicity for his book, and on it he had vehemently denounced spiritualism as the cause of distress, madness and suicide. He could not, at this stage, have backed down; a mutual friend in fact showed Doyle a letter in which Houdini made it clear that his simple intention was to expose the Crandons.

He did not find it easy. In the first two sessions, although Houdini claimed he had proved 'Margery' had rung the bell in the bell-box by using her foot and moved the table in front of her by getting her head underneath it, his argument took no account of the possibility that the motive force might be supplied by pseudopods. He wanted to boast of his exposure; but the other members of the committee, who were not convinced, reminded him of his duty to the *Scientific American*, and it was agreed to hold further trials a month later.

This time, Houdini determined to run things his way. Bird, he insisted, must be excluded, as he had already committed himself to the 'Margery' camp (as had Carrington, who felt there was no further need to attend). Crandon must not be allowed to control either of 'Margery's' hands; and 'Margery' must be encased in a cabinet which Houdini and his assistant, James Collins, had designed. It looked like an old-fashioned steam bath, with a hole for her neck and two for her arms.

The box had been constructed, Houdini explained, to make it impossible for 'Margery' to get out; and as Walter Prince would be holding one of her hands and Houdini himself the other, she would be powerless to play her usual tricks. Hardly had the seance begun, however, when the lid burst open; and Houdini's explanation, that 'Margery' must have used her shoulders to heave it up, invited the question how she could have used such force without Houdini and Prince noticing any change in the tension of her hands. Then, when the lid was closed again, 'Walter' came through and denounced Houdini in unprintable terms for interfering with the bell-box. Examining it, Comstock found that a small rubber eraser had been wedged into it to make it harder to ring. Houdini disclaimed responsibility; but as he had been responsible for checking it, 'Margery' had clearly won the first round.

For the second, Houdini and Collins reinforced the lid of the 'cabinet' and 'Margery' was locked in. Again. 'Walter' came

'Margery' in the Houdini cage.

Science and Parascience

through with a volley of oaths: 'Houdini, you . . . blackguard! You have put a rule in the cabinet. You . . . ! Remember, Houdini, you won't live for ever. Some day, you have got to die!' The cabinet was opened, and there was a rule which, if her hands had been released, 'Margery' might in theory have been able to convey to her mouth and use to ring the bell in the box, and perhaps play other tricks. Again, Houdini denied that either he or Collins was responsible; but as only they had had access to the cabinet, he was reduced to blaming the woman he had employed to search Mina before the seance.

According to one of Houdini's biographers, Lindsay Gresham, Collins was later to admit: 'I chucked it in the box myself. The boss told me to do it. 'E wanted to fix her good'; and when reminded that Houdini had given his 'sacred word of honour' that the first he knew of the rule in the box was when 'Walter' had informed him, Collins replied 'There's one thing you got to remember about Mister 'Oudini in his last years. For 'im the truth was bloody well what 'e wanted it to be.' Milbourne Christopher, himself a magician – and a sceptic – has since dismissed the story as 'sheer fiction' on the ground that it had been reported by somebody who felt he had been disparaged by Houdini. Yet Christopher himself has provided a hitherto unpublished story revealing Houdini's attitude, provided by his old friend Willard B. Greene. Houdini had given Greene a roll of film taken during one of the sessions at the Crandons', with the injunction not to let it out of his sight until it had been developed, and then to send it on by registered mail. Examining the prints when they were developed, Greene found they were uninteresting shots of the medium and her investigators, except for one, when there was a strange blur, 'almost a halo', above the medium's head. When Houdini's pamphlet claiming to have exposed 'Margery' appeared, it contained one of the photographs – but not the one with the halo. Believers might think it was ectoplasm, Houdini explained. 'You know as well as I do, Willard, that she is a fake. Why should I help build up her following?'

Nevertheless Houdini would have been rash to entrust the rule to his assistant. The more probable explanation of its appearance in the box was that he himself, certain that she was 'a fake' but impressed by her skill, had put the rule into the 'cabinet' as a form of insurance, so that even if she did succeed in impressing Prince and Comstock during the seance, he would have a let-out.

If, at this point, the Crandons had declined to continue with the tests, they would have had a good case. From the start they had expressed their reservations about 'Margery's' ability to produce effects when totally enclosed. The other investigators, too, were irritated with Houdini, whom they had hoped would settle the issue; instead, he had botched it. One further seance was held. It happened to be a blank – not an unusual occurrence with 'Margery', as with other mediums; but it provided the excuse to terminate the investigation for the time being. As things turned out, it was not to be resumed.

Dingwall's Investigation

While the *Scientific American* committee was in suspended animation, Dingwall arrived in Boston to investigate 'Margery' on behalf of the SPR. He had been present at a sitting in London, when the Crandons were on a visit the previous winter; and in good light he had witnessed a table levitation which, as he was to recall in his report of his Boston enquiry in the society's *Proceedings*, was an indication – assuming that it was supernormal – of 'remarkable incipient mediumship'. In Boston his objective was to conduct tests through which he could satisfy himself whether it was supernormal or not. For him the case was 'perhaps the most important of its kind hitherto presented for the consideration of psychical researchers'; if genuine it would, he thought, be '*the* most remarkable hitherto recorded'.

The Crandons impressed Dingwall. Mina was a 'highly intelligent and charming young woman, exceedingly good-natured and possessed of a fund of humour and courage which make her an ideal subject for investigation'; her husband 'a hard-working and skilful surgeon, of wide reading, and possessing extensive knowledge of many social questions and problems'. If the phenomena were fraudulent – and there was 'little, if any, direct evidence in support of such a supposition' – the two must, Dingwall felt, be in collusion, and the only reason he could think of for this was that a hoax designed to discredit spiritualism might appeal to Crandon's 'fervent rationalism'.

Dingwall conscientiously supervised the arrangements for the sittings. There were some problems: the fact that Crandon usually controlled his wife's right hand meant, in effect, that it could not be regarded as properly controlled. Yet initially this did not greatly worry Dingwall, as he hoped that the phenomena might prove to be of a kind which carry conviction whether or not her right hand was controlled. As he was to explain, having arrived with two possible hypotheses in mind – that the phenomena were genuine, or that they were spurious – his aim was to start his investigation on the assumption that the first hypothesis was correct, and to concentrate upon witnessing and cataloguing the phenomena.

They were abundant – 'raps' from various parts of the room, luminescences, scents, musical sounds as if instruments were playing, automatic writing, table levitations, movements of objects at a distance, and touches of sitters as if by a human hand or finger. 'Walter' came through continually, sometimes to discuss plans with Dingwall for improving the quality of the performance. The chief problem was the absence of good light, most of the time, as 'Walter' still found it inhibiting. Still, luminous paint was extensively used, so that it was possible for all the sitters to observe the movements of everybody in the circle, and to watch objects being displaced, as if by the ectoplasmic arm; and at one sitting on 5 January 1925, at which Crandon was not present, Dingwall, his fellow-investigators Dr Elwood Worcester (the respected founder of the Emmanuel movement, an attempt to counter the growing influence of Christian Science by reviving Jesus's healing ministry in Protestant churches) and McDougall were given an exhibition which, in view of Crandon's absence, was particularly impressive. Dingwall had brought a sheet of cardboard which he had treated with luminous paint. It was placed out of 'Margery's' reach; her hands and feet were controlled by Dr Worcester and himself; yet the cardboard sheet bent over towards Dingwall at intervals throughout the seance.

Eventually Dingwall secured 'Walter's' trust to the point where he and other sitters were allowed to feel the ectoplasmic materialisation issuing from 'Margery' and even, sporadically, to see it. On 19 January, when there were four cameras, one stereoscopic, in the seance room, transcript notes ran:

> Deep trance came on at once, and with fairly good rapidity, accompanied by comments and directions from Walter; we were shown the actual production of the teleplasm from the abdomen of the psychic. From time to time the red flash light was allowed. A mass formed on the abdomen, which shortly differentiated itself into a fairly well-formed hand, fingers downward, attached from the wrist to the umbilicus by a cord apparently ¾" in diameter, all white.
>
> Later, Mr Dingwall put out the palm of his hand. A mass was thrown on it, and although the mass apparently did not move, Mr Dingwall could feel apparently another hand above it moulding the

The USA

mass. And sure enough, the next red flash showed a fairly well-formed hand lying on top of Mr Dingwall's hand, while at previous sight only the unformed teleplasm was seen.

In the photographs the 'hand' was unimpressive, like a badly stuffed gardening glove; but on later occasions the substance, taking various shapes, came and went while 'Margery's' own hands were securely held, as Dingwall ascertained for himself. In none of the transcripts of the twenty-nine sittings which were held was there any suggestion that this or the other effects could have been obtained by conjuring tricks; and in February, when the series came to a close, Dingwall presented a copy of *Revelations of a Spirit Medium*, a work originally written in 1891 but reprinted thirty years later, edited by Dingwall and Harry Price. The inscription ran

> To 'Margery', whose undaunted courage
> and unfailing good humour are only
> two of the many features of her
> remarkable mediumship
> E. J. Dingwall
> Boston, Mass.
> Dec. 1924–Feb. 1925

Dingwall also wrote enthusiastically to Schrenck:

> It is the most beautiful case of teleplasmic telekinesis with which I am acquainted. We can freely touch the teleplasm. The materialised hands are joined by cords to the medium's body: they seize objects and move them. The teleplasmic masses are visible and tangible upon the table in excellent red light. I held the medium's hands: I saw figures and felt them in good light. The 'control' is irreproachable.

The Crandons had every reason to feel gratified, as well as satisfied. Dingwall's report would surely place 'Margery' on a par with Eusapia and 'Eva C.', and in one respect ahead of them, as although there had been suspicion, as yet no serious accusation of cheating had been made against her. The report, when it appeared, was a shock. Dingwall had back-tracked after his return to England.

He gave the transcripts of the sittings; and read in isolation, there was nothing in them to suggest that the phenomena were other than genuine. But Dingwall had attached his own retrospective commentaries; and according to them, he had changed his mind half way through the series. Although there was no hint of it in the transcripts, Dingwall now claimed – he was writing his report six months later – that in the course of the thirteenth session, on 19 January, (ironically, the very session at which he had been provided with what had seemed adequate visual and tactile evidence of 'Margery's' ectoplasm) he had been given reason to switch to the second working hypothesis: that 'Margery' cheated.

His doubts had surfaced at the sitting two days earlier, when to prepare for the forthcoming demonstration of the ectoplasmic process, 'Walter' had directed that a flat piece of wood should be placed projecting a foot out in front of the medium's chair in case the ectoplasmic substance, emerging like a baby, might fall to the floor, 'the cord be broken, and a catastrophe result'. This, in Dingwall's considered view, was in flat contradiction to past experience with teleplasm with 'Eva' and Kate Goligher: 'I need hardly remind those who read this paper (and presumably are acquainted with the literature) that there are many instances in which the substance has actually fallen to the ground without any such catastrophic results.' And although Dingwall still conceded that the session two days later had been 'very important', because of the unique opportunities it had provided for observation, he now considered it had suffered from a fatal flaw: the fact that it was 'Walter' who dictated when the 'red flash' came and went and, as a result, they had never seen the entire process: only stages in it.

> What was wanted was not the finished or partly finished product, but the making of the production itself. These 'hands' are supposed to grow, to expand, to approach perfection. But we want to *see* these steps in operation; to *see* the growth progressing; to *see* the actual extrusion and reabsorption.

So although the sitting had provided unique opportunities for observation, and might have provided indisputable proof both that the ectoplasm was real and that its extrusion and reabsorption could not have been engineered normally, 'it did none of these things. Although all that occurred *could* have been interpreted in two ways, yet I was forced to admit to myself that the evidence in favour of the second hypothesis was stronger than that for the first.'

The next session had clinched matters. By this time 'Walter' had become so confident that Crandon had relinquished control of 'Margery's' right hand to Dr Worcester. According to the transcript notes:

The USA

>Trance came on quietly in two or three minutes. Within ten minutes Mr Dingwall heard oozing sound near Psyche's lap and then movements of her legs. Mr Dingwall felt usual cold mass on left thigh small; then Walter said, 'Turn red light on two seconds', and we saw mass-like elongated tuberosities in Psyche's left groin. Then left leg went up on table, and then Psyche put her left hand down and threw mass on table.

The red flash had revealed, and the photographs had confirmed, that a 'heaped knobby mass' had been extruded, two to three inches wide, four to five inches long and three quarters of an inch thick. According to McDougall, it felt like 'a soft resilient mass, like a membrane filled with some semi-fluid substance'; and to Worcester, this was by far the most impressive contact with the substance that he had had. But Dingwall, though he had been controlling 'Psyche's' ('Margery's') hand, and had been left in no doubt of the reality both of the extrusion and the re-entry of the substance, had again – or so he claimed – been made suspicious by its behaviour; or, rather, lack of behaviour.

>Now, then was the opportunity for it to display its qualities of self-mobility and climb upon the table. But nothing of the sort occurred. *Psyche put her left hand down, with D's still controlling it, and* threw the mass upon the table. Is it not exactly what we should expect on the second hypothesis? The mass may have been concealed in the vagina and thence expelled; thus the only course open would have been for the medium to throw it upon the table and then devise means of manipulating it there without the use of the hands.

And in a footnote, Dingwall explained that he had shown photographs to an eminent gynaecologist who had agreed it would be possible to pack 'a considerable portion' of such a substance into the vagina from which it could then be expelled by muscular contraction.

In his summing up, Dingwall referred back to this sitting as crucial, because of the evidence it supplied of the lack of ectoplasmic self-mobility. The only fact which was clearly in favour of the first hypothesis was 'undoubtedly the personality and position of "Margery" and her husband, and the improbability of their engaging in persistent trickery'. Because of his respect for them, he could not commit himself to the second hypothesis. He eased himself out of his dilemma by reiterating that 'Margery's' mediumship remained 'one of the most remarkable in the history of psychical research', worthy to be ranked with those of Home and Palladino as showing 'the extreme difficulty of reaching finality of conclusions, notwithstanding the time and attention directed to the investigation of them'.

Had Dingwall written his commentary while the investigation was in progress, rather than six months later, it would carry more conviction; but as it stands, it is riddled with inconsistencies – in particular, the reason he gave for switching from 'Hypothesis One' to 'Hypothesis Two'. It was true that the ectoplasm which had poured out of Kate Goligher descended to the floor without catastrophic results; but it was not true that at this stage in its extrusion, ectoplasm necessarily showed 'self-mobility'. On the contrary, it was precisely because it *looked* like lifeless regurgitated matter that the photographs taken of it had commonly given more comfort to sceptics than to researchers – as had the apparent lack of vitality in some of the developed forms which 'Eva C.' had produced for Mme Bisson, Schrenck and Geley.

That 'Walter' controlled the 'red flashes' was indeed a serious defect in the procedure; but if it played so decisive a part in Dingwall's decision to reject Hypothesis One, he could presumably without giving offence have made this clear at the time. He claimed in his report that he persistently urged that 'everything depended upon the growth and reabsorption being *carried out in red light*', but this persistence does not feature in the transcripts. His attempt at an explanation of how 'Margery' might have cheated, too, was feeble, particularly considering that he had been controlling her at the time; for as the gynaecologist he consulted pointed out, if she had extruded some hidden rubbery substance of the type Worcester and McDougall described, the muscular contractions involved would have been expected to be obvious to the sitters (he might have added that the substance, whatever it had been, could *not* have been expected to be cold, as the sitters reported). As for the subsequent disappearance of the substance, all that Dingwall could surmise was that it must have been hidden and then carried away by 'Margery' or Crandon. As he was controlling her, this could hardly have been accomplished without either total incompetence on his part, or his collusion.

In any case, the exhibitions of ectoplasmic hands represented only one manifestation, and on the evidence of the photographs a poor one. Dingwall hardly attempted to explain how 'Margery' could have produced all the other effects, even with the assistance of her husband, unless they were taking crazy risks. The ectoplasmic arm and hand, for example, which nudged sitters and moved or levitated objects at a distance: if it were not a genuine pseudopod,

The USA

it would have had to be smuggled into the seances in spite of Dingwall's precautions. If his suspicions were aroused, all he would have needed to do was clutch it: and although 'Walter's' instructions were that it was only to be touched when he gave his permission the Crandons, if they were cheating, could not have been confident that those instructions would be obeyed.

What, then, made Dingwall turn to Hypothesis Two? In his commentary on the sitting of 17 January he admitted that up to that point his provisional impression had been that the mediumship was genuine, and he had partly given his opinion to that effect to his colleagues and others: 'I now (July 1925) no longer hold this view, and admit my change of mind' – though he would modify it if fresh facts required him to do so. But it seems likely that his change of mind, or the beginnings of it, took place four days later, when he received a letter from McDougall, warning him that he could not expect McDougall's backing if he came out with a favourable report on the investigation:

> My testimony to it would, I venture to think, carry considerable weight, even in the scientific world; whereas a favourable report by you, if not supported or confirmed by me, might fail to do so. It is highly probable, or even inevitable, that when you report the ectoplasmic phenomena to be genuine you will be accused by the scientists of being an accomplice, of being in collusion with 'Margery'. Your best defence against this would be my concordant testimony and support. Further, I shall, no doubt, be expected to render some report to the English SPR: and it will be very unsatisfactory from every point of view, if your report and mine on the same series of sittings are in serious disagreement.

That Dingwall should have expressed his satisfaction with the reality of the ectoplasm, McDougall concluded, was all right so far as it went, but he did not think it went very far; 'it seems to me, you are bound to carry me along with you'.

To have pronounced 'Margery's' phenomena genuine without McDougall's *imprimatur* would indeed have been unsatisfactory. By reason of his academic standing, McDougall was psychical research's White Hope in the English-speaking world. But in any case, Dingwall had good reason not to commit himself. Neither then nor later did he regard himself as a psychical researcher, so much as a devil's advocate for scepticism, employed to make sure that the research was 'clean', the procedures arranged so that there would be the minimum risk of fraud. He had realised that he would be acceptable in that role so long as he avoided endorsing the physical phenomena of mediumship without qualification. Always he must suggest some kind of 'natural' explanation of the way a medium *might* have been able to cheat.

An embarrassment remained for him; he had not been able to bring himself to tell the Crandons of his intentions until he sent them the proofs of his article for the SPR *Proceedings*, innocently remarking about them that the people who had read them 'have all come to different opinions as to the real views of the author'. Crandon administered a crushing rebuke. If the purpose of the SPR was to remain always straddling, 'in order always to be right', it had been fulfilled, he replied in a note to the society; but 'what an unworthy contrast do we here behold to the courage of Richet, Geley and Schrenck-Notzing!' Dingwall, Crandon felt, must have reasoned that if he pronounced the phenomena genuine, and they were later admitted by the scientific world to be genuine, then he would be in clover; but if he pronounced them genuine and they were found to have been produced naturally, he would be 'laughed out of the psychic arena as a credulous yokel'. Therefore he must poise himself between the two so that in whichever direction the psychic cat jumped, he would be there. Crandon went through the list of the phenomena Dingwall had observed and been unable to account for; having failed to realise, Crandon sarcastically suggested, that they could easily have been accounted for by 'an accomplice, small in stature, clothed and hooded all in black, with felt slippers on', wheeling in a tea-wagon with well-oiled rubber wheels carrying all the necessary apparatus and impedimenta. 'I am tempted,' Crandon concluded,

> using the words in a purely Pickwickian sense, to lay down two hypotheses to explain Mr Dingwall's treatment of the subject as far as hypothetical explanation goes.
> Hypothesis 1. The author is a nut.
> Hypothesis 2. The author is a nut.

The society printed the letter in its *Proceedings*, adding a footnote explaining, for the benefit of British readers, that 'nut' was 'an American word meaning an amiable individual whose ratiocination is erratic'.

The Second Harvard Investigation

By the time Dingwall had finished his series of trials, in February 1925, it had become clear that 'Margery' was not going to receive

The USA

the *Scientific American* award. Carrington and Bird accepted that 'Margery' had been shown to be a genuine physical medium; but Carrington's verdict carried little weight, and Bird was not a voting member of the committee. Houdini claimed that the phenomena were faked: in a pamphlet, he boasted that he had exposed 'Margery' – a verdict which his colleagues on the committee repudiated. In a letter to the *New York Times*, McDougall explained that he did not say that 'Margery' produced no supernormal phenomena, merely that what she had been able to do was insufficient to carry complete conviction. Prince took the same line. Comstock held to his view that although the phenomena were real enough, he could not accept them without a scientific explanation for them. 'The psychic award,' Munn decided, 'will not be granted to "Margery"' – courteously adding that from the start she had made it clear that she would not accept the money which the *Scientific American* had offered, even if she won.

At this point the Crandons made what was to turn out to be, for them, a disastrous decision. Among those who had attended some sittings were two Harvard graduates, Hudson Hoagland and S. Foster Damon; and when they proposed a second Harvard investigation, the Crandons agreed without bothering about the credentials of their team. They were in fact amateurs, with no previous experience of psychical research. Had they satisfied themselves that 'Margery's' powers were genuine, their report could have carried no weight. The best the Crandons could hope to do was to provide them with such impressive evidence that more eminent academics would be drawn in, out of curiosity; and for a while, this looked to be a possibility.

At the first sitting on 19 May 1925 – held, at the investigators' request, not at the Crandons' but in Emerson Hall in Harvard – the sitters felt touches; objects were moved at a distance by what was described, in the notes which were being taken, as a psychic hand; a luminous 'doughnut' – a paper cut-out, doughnut-shaped – moved around the table, and levitated first to two feet, then to three feet. 'Walter' was in his element, telling sitters where they would find the objects which had moved, whistling, joking (he pulled Hoagland's hair 'vigorously'). Throughout the performance, which lasted over an hour, the dictaphone registered confirmation from the sitters holding Crandon and 'Margery' that control was 'perfect'; yet periodically the bell in the box rang, even when pushed well out of the Crandons' reach. As the Crandons stripped to be searched before and after sittings, and as the sittings were not in their home, the investigating group was unable to fault them either then or in subsequent sittings; and at one of these on 3 June they were joined by a more senior academic figure, Dr Edwin G. Boring, Associate Professor of Psychology at Harvard.

Boring took charge of the proceedings, and compiled the report following the seance; adding a note of his own to the effect that although in a session with eight people, no single individual could vouch for everything that was reported, to the best of his knowledge and belief the record was correct. The effects, in his view, could all be put down to the operation of a 'teleplasmic arm', which 'seemed to cause all the other phenomena by the same natural means that any arm could cause them, unless it should be added that I had the impression that the "teleplasmic arm" occasionally found objects in the dark more readily than one would expect a human arm to do under normal conscious control'.

That there was an arm, Boring felt, there could be no reasonable doubt. It could be seen, when it came between the viewer and illuminated objects; and it looked solid, to him much like a human arm: 'In handling the bell-box and other objects on the table, and in manipulating and pulling my hair, I was convinced that the "hand" was actuated approximately as would a normal arm extended from the medium'. It could push, or grip and pull: the force with which Boring's hair was pulled was hard enough to be painful.

Boring's was the most forthright tribute that 'Margery' had yet received; but he was careful to leave an escape hatch. 'I have no beliefs at all,' he wrote, 'in respect of the manner in which this hand was produced or caused to move' – though he was sure that it emanated from the medium. Assuming his diagnosis was correct, it followed that all the group needed to ascertain was whether the arm was artificial; and in view of the problems confronting 'Margery' if she were smuggling in any kind of telescopic gadget, this ought not to have been difficult. Yet in the later sessions, although 'Walter' continued to tell the members of the circle in advance what he proposed to do, moving or levitating objects, or ringing the bell in the box, the sitters were still unable to detect any deception on the part of either of the Crandons. And when one of America's leading astronomers, Professor Shapley, attended a session, and felt his hair being pulled, he admitted he had been impressed 'by the distinctness of the phenomena' as well as by the Crandons' sincerity and frankness. 'No evidence of trickery of any kind was observed,' he concluded, 'and no suspicious actions on the part of any one in the circle.'

The USA

Only in the fifth sitting did the members of the group observe anything which aroused suspicion. The medium wore luminous ankle-bands, so that even if she did succeed in freeing one of her feet from control, any sitter who was watching could immediately have pointed it out; and during the sitting one of the bands fell off. Although Mina herself complained that it was loose before the sitting began, this gave one of the sitters, Grant H. Code, his opportunity.

Of all the group Code, who was older than the others, had entered into the closest relationship with Mina, to whom he had begun to confide his personal problems. But he was an amateur conjuror; and now he took Hoagland and another of the group along to show them that he could play the same tricks as 'Margery'. He managed to free a foot from their control, unobserved; rang the bell in the box; levitated an object; and imitated the touches and hair-pulling. Damon and Hoagland agreed that he had successfully produced many of 'Walter's' phenomena and by showing them how he had done it, he also showed how 'Walter' could be rendered helpless the next day. All that was needed was that Mina should be asked to wear bands of adhesive plaster instead of the old illuminated bands of elastic tape for the next evening's sitting.

As if to lend confirmation to Code's thesis, Hoagland's dog appeared the next morning with one of the slippers which Mina had worn at the seance the night before; and on it were traces of a kind which showed that her foot had been dabbling in the clay. Or so it seemed to the investigators. Had they read Crawford or Thomas Mann on the subject they would have realised that they must take into account the possibility of pseudopods, acting as an extension of human extremities; Kathleen Goligher's feet and Willy Schneider's fingers had shown similar traces after similar experiments, when physical contact was not possible. But the investigators had not studied the evidence from the other side of the Atlantic. They simply assumed that they now had 'Margery' safely in their net.

They were in for a rude surprise. When the sixth sitting began that evening, a confident 'Walter' intimated that he was aware of their plot; he even repeated some of what had been said. And in spite of the controls, the phenomena were more spectacular than ever. While the Crandons were visibly under control, the luminous tapes acquitting them of any guilt, the 'doughnut' danced, the bell rang in the box, and the sitters, including two senior academics, felt 'Walter' tweaking them. According to the transcript, signed by Code, Damon and Hoagland,

Science and Parascience

(At 10.16) At Walter's request Dr Shapley put doughnut on table. There is a silhouetting of the fingers all over the doughnut. At Walter's request, Dr Ousterhout leaned forward and took the doughnut in his hand. He felt the fingers holding the doughnut. Dr Ousterhout said it felt like a cold, slimy and rather clammy finger, which felt as though it had bones in it, but too flexible for an ordinary finger . . .

(At 10.25) There are now two hands on the table. One hand is well formed. The other is a long extension, shaped like a cat's tail. Hoagland feels both the psychic's feet in slippers. Code verifies this . . .

And so it went on. Code was now in a dilemma. He had shown what 'Margery' might do by conjuring, but he had also claimed to be able to set her a task she could not do; she had done it, and more. Worse: his plot had been unmasked. Either he would have to accept that the phenomena were genuine, or he would have to think up some story which would account for them, and also explain how 'Walter' had come to know about the plan.

Calling the investigators together, Code confessed that after he had demonstrated how he could play 'Walter's' tricks, he had gone to see Mina to warn her the committee now possessed clear evidence of 'Margery's' trickery. Knowing her as he now did, he was sure that she was not conscious of deception; that she was a victim of auto-hypnosis, induced initially through her husband's fascination with psychic matters. But he had felt it his duty to tell her that, at the seance that evening, 'Margery' would be exposed, and this would be disastrous not only for herself, but for her husband, who, of course, was also unaware of what was happening. 'All my observations of Dr Crandon had pointed to his belief in the phenomena,' Code told his colleagues. 'I therefore feared that a sudden exposure on the part of a group of observers in which he had placed so much trust would give him a shock that might be dangerous.'

Mina's reaction, Code went on, had naturally been to deny that she had ever 'done any of these things'. To convince her he had asked her to hold a private sitting with him, in which he discussed the position with 'Walter'; and 'Walter' had begged him to allow 'Margery' to cheat ('Dont fail me, Code. Dont fail me'), so that the innocent Crandons would not be publicly humiliated. Accordingly Code had neglected to control 'Margery', allowing her to produce the phenomena unhindered.

It is difficult to think of a more ludicrously implausible story; but

The USA

Hoagland and the rest of his committee needed some excuse, any excuse, to escape from what had become an acutely embarrassing predicament. They did not want to accuse the Crandons, whom they had come to like and trust, of fraud; yet neither could they accept that the phenomena were genuine, if Code were going to continue to insist that they were produced by trickery. It would have been unwise enough for a group of young graduates aspiring to further their careers to give a unanimous verdict in 'Margery's' favour; a split vote would have made them look ridiculous, the more so as Code was a conjuror, whose word would carry the most weight. Hoagland agreed to prepare a report along Code's suggested lines, damning 'Margery' but exonerating the Crandons. Before it was ready, however, on 23 October, the *New York Times* broke the story, giving it a slightly different slant, indicated in one of the headlines: 'Harvard scientists now say hypnosis theory was advanced to spare the Crandons'; and this gave Hoagland the excuse he needed to publish his report, which he did in *Atlantic Monthly* in November.

Implausible though Code's version had been, in print Hoagland's sounded even more preposterous. He was asking readers to accept that the phenomena which 'Margery' had been able to produce in seance after seance had all been accomplished by a woman who, in a self-induced trance, performed conjuring tricks so skilfully that even so experienced an investigator as Dingwall had been unable to catch her out during seances, and had been reduced to speculating retrospectively how she might have done them. Even more absurd, the interpretation required that Crandon, sitting beside her at most seances and holding her hand, should have remained wholly unaware of what she was doing.

Hoagland had a further problem, Code had duplicated some of the phenomena: but even by fudging the transcripts of the seances, there was no way of accounting for others, short of the existence of a conspiracy among the committee members themselves. How, for example, could 'Margery' have concealed the 'teleplasmic arm'? Hoagland's solution was to attribute phenomena for which 'Margery' could not herself have been responsible to the sitters' unconscious collaboration. It had been proved, he claimed, that a heavy table 'could be moved rapidly about a room by a group of people all sincerely believing that their fingers no more than rested on its surface, though by physical methods it can actually be demonstrated that they have exerted considerable force'.

He was basing his argument on Faraday's 'exposure' of table-turning; but Faraday had demonstrated only that a loose table *top* could be moved by fingertip pressure, without conscious design. Neither he nor anybody was ever shown that *tables* could be moved in the same way. It was, in fact, the realisation that tables and other objects moved in ways which unconscious fingertip pressure could not account for, which had impressed Wallace, Crookes and other early psychical researchers.

Margery Harvard Veritas

The Crandons' supporters rallied to them, their ranks now reinforced by Bird, who had left the *Scientific American* to take up the post of Research Officer in the ASPR. Prince resigned in consequence; Bird, he complained, was a master 'of the employment of language that squints'. Bird was a little more charitable about Prince, whom he described as 'one of those people in whom rugged intellectual honesty sticks out all over, like spines on a cactus', so wedded to strict scientific procedure 'that he ignores all observation and all results other than his own'.

In *Margery Harvard Veritas* Bird, Crandon and some friends took Hoagland's report to pieces. All they needed to do was to print the transcripts of the seances, with the descriptions which Hoagland, Code and the others had made during them, to show just how inadequate the sleight-of-foot explanation was. The writers of *Veritas* also could not resist poking fun at the earlier investigators: McDougall had wavered between admitting that 'Margery' had produced 'a very considerable quantity of evidence of supernormal phenomena', and saying that she had 'failed to convince us of the supernormal character of any of her phenomena'; and Prince was so deaf that he could not hear the bell in the box ringing even when it was ringing in his lap. But the chief venom was reserved for Code. Mina had insisted that his story of his chat with 'Walter', on which the Harvard committee's conclusions were largely based, was a fabrication. Code *had* come to see her, Mina explained; he had told her of the committee's view that while she and her husband were innocent, 'Margery' was cheating; and he had offered, in order to spare her blushes, to let go of her hand so that 'Margery' could continue to cheat. But she had angrily rejected his offer; there had been no visit to the seance room, and no private conversation between him and 'Walter'.

On this issue, it was Mina's word against Code's; but Bird had found fresh evidence to show that it had been Code who was lying. In an attempt to convince Bird of the truth of his version, Code had been unwise enough to try to repeat the demonstration he had given to the committee of the way 'Margery' played her tricks; and although conceding that Code played some of them skilfully, Bird found that he was unable to reproduce others – a failure 'made the worse by his complete lack of appreciation that he had fallen short'. Even more damning, Bird had discovered *how* Code had been able to reproduce one part of 'Margery's' repertoire: the ringing of the bell in the box. Code had abstracted a box used by the committee to test her, and had 'incorporated in it a trick wiring which enabled him to ring the bell by touching externally two particular screws which, in appearance, were merely part of the structure of the box'. Foolishly, Code had not troubled to dismantle the wiring later. In his absence, and unaware of the trick, Hoagland had sent the box, along with other bits of apparatus which had been used in the sittings, back to the Crandons. Taxed with the deception, Code could only lamely reply that he had meant to tell the Crandons what he had done, and had telephoned them; but they had been out when he rang.

Code, in other words, had confessed to cheating his colleagues. To show them how 'Margery' cheated, he had used a trick that she could not have used. And on the other point – Code's inability, as a conjuror, to reproduce the phenomena – Bird had support from an unexpected quarter: another *Atlantic* article, this one by Edwin Boring.

In 'The paradox of psychical research' Boring made an unusually detached contribution to the subject, emphasising the problems which psychical researchers faced; in particular their need to decide whether the phenomena were genuine or fraudulent, an issue which scientists were not ordinarily required to worry about. In the course of the article, however, Boring described how he had been detailed to control Code's left hand in the seance when he was showing how he could perform 'Margery's' tricks. Boring's instructions had been that if he realised how Code was getting his effects, he must say so at the time. He *had* realised; and in retrospect, he admitted he ought to have reported it, 'but it never occurred to me to do so. It was only after I had gone home and thought it over that I realised that the desire to have Code succeed had won out over the desire to control him rigidly.' The moral, Boring suggested, was that people 'who have the "will to believe" in the supernatural do not make good investigators of psychic phenomena'. It evidently had not occurred to him that people who had the will to disbelieve might make even worse investigators – as he himself had so effectively demonstrated.

Comparing Hoagland's report with *Margery Harvard Veritas*, Everard Feilding was shrewd enough to realise that the report, 'somewhat magniloquently described by the *Atlantic Monthly* as "the Climax to a Famous Investigation"', was 'not a climax at all'; and in the SPR *Proceedings* the following summer he argued that before the report's validity could be accepted, certain questions needed to be answered. Had Code told the truth? If so, Code's belief that Mrs Crandon could have been innocent of any deception in a case of this kind, where obviously 'long, elaborate and skilful preparation' was indispensable, struck Feilding as arguing 'an unsophistication of intellect, to put it mildly, which I can scarcely believe possible in a Harvard graduate'. Apart from this, Code's conduct struck him as 'little less than pathologically peculiar'. To save 'Margery' from an exposure 'he leads her – it must be assumed under a pledge of secrecy – into further fraud, and then immediately, that very night, splits on her. Further, by way of assisting his friends in their investigation, he stages an elaborate deceit in which he himself takes part, without a word of warning beforehand.'

In any case, Feilding noted, if Mrs Crandon was as alertly intelligent as had been generally remarked upon, that she should have walked into Code's trap was at least as unbelievable as Code's theory of her 'sweet natural guilelessness' if the phenomena were fraudulent. Besides, had Code really proved them to be fraudulent? According to Bird in *Margery Harvard Veritas*, Code had not been able to duplicate all of them satisfactorily. These were questions which, Feilding admitted, he himself was not in a position to answer; but he felt that they ought to be answered, if necessary by a fresh series of trials.

It was a typically shrewd assessment; and Feilding's standing was such that even on the other side of the Atlantic, the Harvard investigators realised they would have to reply. Hoagland and Code both sent in rebuttals: Hoagland's chiefly concerned with omissions and distortions in *Margery Harvard Veritas*; Code's with providing proof that his private conversation with 'Walter' really had taken place. That the compilers of *Veritas* had made it into a polemic was undeniable; not merely did this weaken their own case, it gave Hoagland the opportunity to shift the argument away from his team's incompetence in the investigation of 'Margery' to

The USA

justification for his criticism of *Veritas*. And this helped to distract attention from the fact that Hoagland no longer accepted the premise upon which he had originally based his report. His former eulogies of Crandon, and his acceptance in his *Atlantic* report of Code's proposition that Mina was unconscious of her trickery, were forgotten; he now described the Crandons as 'masters of the psychology of deception'.

In theory this ought to have irrevocably discredited Code, whose credibility should have been finally punctured if the Crandons were taken to be cheats. In Boston this mattered little, as the anti-Crandon element had never really bothered with the notion of unconscious cheating: the assumption had been that the Crandons must be frauds. But Feilding was a different proposition. He had clearly smelled a sewer rat. Code had to wriggle out of the charge that he had betrayed the Crandons by permitting the publication of the report; this was not his doing, he claimed, but Hoagland's, to whom he had protested. And to vindicate his side of the story, he produced the notes of the private seance with 'Walter'.

For once, Feilding allowed himself to be conned. In view of Code's explanation, he wrote in a letter published in the *Proceedings* the following January, though he questioned the wisdom of the course Code had pursued, 'I, personally, without expressing any view on the major issue of whether there are still grounds for a belief in the "Margery" mediumship, find it impossible any longer to doubt the good faith of Mr Code.'

Even if there had been no other reason to doubt Code's good faith, his 'notes' of the private seance ought to have confirmed Feilding in his suspicions. Code claimed he had written them down from memory within twenty-four hours; but he presented them as if they were a transcript taken from a dictaphone. They were far too detailed, and too pat, for comfort; with 'Walter' begging him to allow 'Margery' to cheat during the evening's seance:

>Walter – Don't let it be a blank, Code
>Code   – No, Walter
>Walter (Pause) – And let her hand move a little
>Code   – All right, Walter

and so on. In any case, Feilding apparently had not noticed Code's back-tracking, or had not appreciated its significance. Code now claimed he had never contended that the entire mediumship was to

Science and Parascience

be explained by innocent subconscious fraud: 'Dr Crandon has frequently stated in my presence that he considers it justifiable to help out when normal means fail.' If Crandon had in fact stated this, why had Code never mentioned it before? Yet, in his letter Code maintained his faith in the innocence – or as he more cautiously now described it, the 'disingenuousness' – of the Crandons. For Feilding's consumption, at least, Code had to distance himself from Hoagland. What Feilding did not know was that this, too, was simply a pretence. In the course of research into 'Margery' Tietze, years later, found letters Code had written to Walter Prince; and months before the letter to Feilding, Code had not merely made it clear that he took for granted that the Crandons had been in collusion; he had described to Prince the way in which they had been able to produce the materialisations which had so puzzled the investigators. Crandon, Code claimed, had made surgical alterations to his wife's 'most convenient storage warehouse', because 'a slight surgical enlargement of the mouth of the uterus would make it a more convenient receptacle'.

The only plausible verdict on the second Harvard investigation is

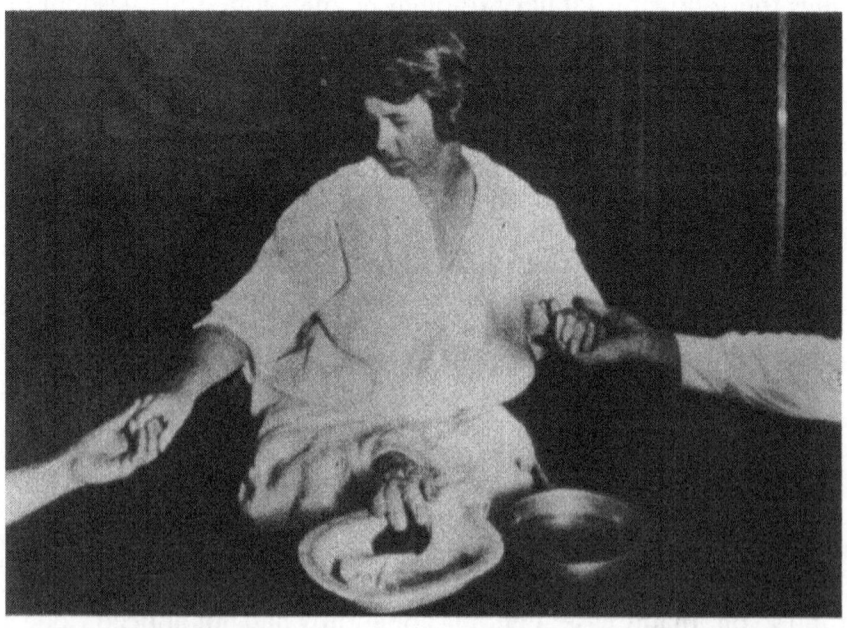

'Margery' extruding an ectoplasmic hand from what Code described as her 'most convenient storage warehouse'.

that it was a put-up job, stage-managed by Code, who successfully deceived both his colleagues and the Crandons. As a contribution to eliciting the truth about 'Margery', it was farcical. Yet it was decisive – more so than its predecessors. It marked the turning point in the 'Margery' case, Tietze has noted. The public was now 'confident that the Harvard report had put an end to this very disturbing question'; henceforward 'Margery' was to be of concern only to psychical researchers, 'playing their harmless game'.

The McComas Enquiry

They were to go on playing it for some years. Even before the final flurry of the correspondence with Feilding (as soon as he had backed down, the editor of the *Journal* thankfully closed the correspondence; it was reopened only briefly to publish Mina's statement on oath before a notary public that there had been no private seance with Code), Bird had suggested that Henry Clay McComas, a psychologist at Princeton, should join the American SPR's staff, and conduct tests; and in 1925 McComas set up a committee consisting of himself and two men from Johns Hopkins, Professor Knight Dunlap, a psychologist, and a physicist, Dr R. W. Wood.

As usual there was no lack of manifestations; but a crisis arose when Wood, feeling a 'teleplasmic rod', squeezed it – which according to Crandon, made 'Margery' ill for some days. The fact that Wood appeared drunk at some sittings gave Crandon the excuse to ban him; and Dunlap's fitness to serve on it was put in doubt when it was revealed that a few months before, he had stated his belief that the physical phenomena of mediumship could be accounted for only by fraud. The investigation was terminated, the committee eventually reporting that the 'Margery' mediumship, though 'a clever and entertaining performance', was unworthy of the society's serious consideration; Crandon's whole attitude to the committee and its enquiry being 'sufficient indication that no investigation by competent investigators employing the methods and checks required in all scientific research is likely to be permitted'.

It sounded damning; but McComas was prevaricating. He had been so baffled by some of the phenomena that he had felt compelled to try to enlist Houdini's assistance. Remarkably, considering that Houdini had been boasting all round the country that he had exposed 'Margery' (and had published a pamphlet to show how he had done it, in spite of his *Scientific American* committee colleagues' refusal to back him), the Crandons agreed. So did Houdini, presumably in the hope that this time, he really would catch them out as he was sure he could. But he had learned caution. If he could not catch them out during a seance, he told McComas, he would need to find a way to duplicate the tricks; so it would be as well to know in advance what particular tricks were being used, as 'the lady is subtle and changes her methods like any dexterous sleight of hand performer or any medium I have examined'. He must then, he insisted, have time to make the necessary arrangements.

When McComas came back the next day, to report to him what 'Margery' had done at the seance, Houdini was taken aback. She had been wired into a glass-sided 'cabinet' with only her hands outside; and they had also been wired, so that although they could be withdrawn into the 'cabinet', they could not be used to move objects at a distance from her. Yet objects *had* moved: the luminous paper 'doughnut' had levitated, as had a luminous basket, which had floated around the room.

According to Milbourne Christopher, Houdini realised that he was up against a new trick, and he would need new equipment to duplicate it. 'If someone had slipped a collapsible reaching rod into Margery's right hand, wired at the wrist though it was, she could have used it to lift the basket'; then, once the basket was in the air, it would slide down to her hand. But what about the lifting of the 'doughnut' and the basket, together? This might indicate the use of two rods; or could one, perhaps, be designed which would do the job? Anyway, preparing the gadgetry would take time – and, Houdini realised, he would need a confederate among the sitters: 'If Dr McComas's account were correct, certainly someone had secretly aided Margery – by giving a reaching device to her, then taking it away later.'

If McComas's account *were* correct, it represented a clear victory for 'Margery', as so many of her seances had been conducted in circumstances where she had no confederate – for, contrary to Houdini's assumption, these were not new tricks, nor had she changed her methods. The manifestations varied from seance to seance, and occasionally there were new ones; but the levitations had been familiar from early on in her career. But whether Houdini would have been able to duplicate them successfully with a confederate, if he had managed to bring one in, was not to be tested. Crandon sardonically agreed to Houdini's request for delay – 'the only value which could possibly be attached to your presence at Lime Street would be because it would afford amusement to watch your attempts to duplicate these phenomena' – but insisted that he must work in with McComas; and McComas, deciding that enough was enough, had decided to give up his ASPR post and return to academic life.

Less than a month later Houdini broke a bone in his ankle during a stage performance. Under the stress of having to continue to perform while in great pain, he allowed a student to strike him in the stomach – one of the acts he had developed to show his stomach-muscles' strength – before he had prepared himself for the blow; and his appendix ruptured. With characteristic determination he went on with his performances until it was too late; an operation removed the appendix, but by that time peritonitis had taken hold and on 31 October he died, at the age of fifty-two.

It had been singularly unfortunate that, at this crucial stage in psychical research in the United States, so justly famed a magician should have devoted his talents not to exploring, but simply to discrediting mediumship; worse, that he had become so paranoid on the issue that he felt no holds need be barred. He had even gone behind McDougall's back to President Lowell of Harvard, warning him that the reputation of the university would be jeopardised if any of its staff were connected with the 'Margery' investigation. 'I do not question the sincerity of his motives and intentions,' McDougall wrote of him; 'but it must be admitted that he has by his actions and utterances clearly shown his conviction that supernormal phenomena do not and cannot occur, and that the sole function of the psychic researchers is to discover the fraudulent means used to produce alleged psychical phenomena.'

Nevertheless the myth that Houdini exposed 'Margery' has lingered; and with it, a widespread impression that when a conjuror shows that he can duplicate seance-room phenomena with the help of tricks, the phenomena cannot be genuine. The absurdity of this assumption ought immediately to be apparent, for it carries the implication that mediums must be skilled conjurors – in 'Margery's' case, extremely skilled. How had she learned her craft, without ever giving away a hint of her ability to her friends?

Science and Parascience

The Clark University Symposium

Had he lived, Houdini was to have spoken at a conference in November at Clark University. The idea had been jokily mooted two years earlier at a lunch he had had with McDougall and Carl Murchison, Professor of Psychology at Clark, and doubtless would have come to nothing, had not Murchison known of a bequest which had been made to the university in 1908, for use in psychical research: the Smith-Battles Fund, which had not been used for psychical research, or indeed for anything else. It occurred to Murchison that if two or three thousand dollars were expended on a symposium, a book could be made out of the lectures which would bring in a considerable profit; and as he explained to the president of the university, the money could then be transferred from the Smith-Battles Fund 'where it is of little value' to other purposes, such as the Stanley Hall Fund – which would have been maliciously appropriate, as Hall had been a thoroughgoing sceptic.

Murchison, in short, was advocating the cynical policy adopted at Philadelphia and Stanford. But if the project were to raise money through the sale of the book, he needed big names from the psychical research field, believers as well as sceptics; and in this he succeeded. The team included Coover, Crandon, Doyle, Hans Driesch, Jastrow, Lodge, McDougall, Gardner Murphy, Walter Prince and Schiller. And the outcome was a book which gave, and still gives, a fascinating survey of the condition of psychical research at the time.

For once, the believers could not complain of bias against them. Murchison divided the speakers into four categories. Six were 'Convinced of the multiplicity of psychical phenomena' (they accepted most, though not necessarily all), including Lodge, Doyle and Crandon. Four were 'Convinced of the rarity of genuine psychical phenomena': McDougall, Driesch, Prince and Schiller. Two were 'Unconvinced as yet': Coover and Murphy. And two were 'Antagonistic to the claims that such phenomena occur': Jastrow and Houdini. Coover, admittedly, was stretching credibility when he claimed to be unconvinced 'as yet'; but so was Murphy, in the opposite direction, as he showed that he had in fact been convinced. Houdini's death meant that he had to be represented by extracts from *A Magician among the Spirits* – more of an embarrassment than a comfort to sceptics in academic surroundings; so scepticism was heavily out-gunned.

McDougall, too, as if anxious to compensate for his protracted

The USA

hedging about 'Margery', launched into a remarkable plea for the introduction of psychical research into the curriculum at university level. He praised Clark for being the first university ever to open its doors to the subject, an action for which it would certainly be severely criticised; in his view, psychical research would provide a far more valuable training than many established courses, because as an intellectual and moral discipline it ranked 'very high, perhaps the highest of all possible subjects of university study'. Among the intellectual disciplines it imposed was that of 'attacking problems patiently and resolutely, in spite of uncertainty that any solution may be attainable'; of 'observing exactly and recording faithfully phenomena presented to our senses' – a higher form of observation, he pointed out, than was required in chemical experiments; and of 'the reasoning processes by which conclusions were drawn from the phenomena observed' – which again imposed much more severe intellectual demands than the other sciences. And if 'by reason of the complexity and delicacy of its problems', McDougall went on,

> psychical research rivals all other branches of science, it far surpasses them all in respect of the character discipline which it affords. It requires a perfectly controlled temper, and a large and understanding tolerance of human weaknesses of every kind, intellectual and moral alike; and infinite patience in face of renewed disappointments; a moral courage which faces not merely the risk and even the probability of failure, but also the risk of loss of reputation for judgment, balance and sanity itself. And, the most insidious of all dangers, the danger of emotional bias in favour of one or other solution of the problem in hand, is apt to be infinitely greater for the psychical researcher than for the worker in any other field of science; for not only is he swayed by strong sentiments within his own breast, but he also knows that both the scientific world and the general public will react with strong emotional bias to any conclusion he may announce.

Conan Doyle was unable to attend, and sent only a short paper chiefly concerned to justify his belief in ectoplasm; and Lodge, though he attended, also spoke only briefly. But the quartet in the 'Convinced of the rarity' category all made worthwhile contributions.

Schiller, who was shortly to leave Oxford to become Professor of Philosophy in the University of California (Los Angeles), was chiefly concerned to show the fallacy in what was becoming the sceptics' stock defence of their position: that no matter how much evidence accumulated for, say, telepathy, they were not prepared to accept it. All they required, they claimed, was one single cast-iron case which would provide them with absolute proof.

This, Schiller pointed out, was not merely contrary to established scientific practice, which banked on cumulative evidence; it was also 'logical foolishness to expect it', because, as experience had already demonstrated, 'assumptions of incompetence or fraud can always cast a slur upon the most impressive evidence, and render it inconclusive'. Too many psychical researchers, too, had decided to reject cumulative evidence, Schiller had come to suspect, because it enabled them to discard whatever phenomena they did not *want* to accept.

Trained as a biologist, Hans Driesch had become convinced by his experiments that the mechanists were wrong, and that the Vitalists had been right. There were forces yet to be discovered; in particular 'a unifying non-material mind-like something' which provided 'an ordering principle' – a theme which Rupert Sheldrake was to take up and develop over half a century later into his theory of morphogenetic fields. Driesch's concept of entelechy, derived from Aristotle, won more respect than Vitalism ordinarily achieved among biologists; as the great historian of medicine Henry Sigerist pointed out, it had developed from laboratory observation, 'and is no more and no less speculative than the assumption that in far off times we may succeed in a bio-chemical explanation of life'. And it was particularly welcome to psychical researchers, because Driesch, like Bergson and McDougall, found room in his brand of Vitalism for paranormal phenomena.

Driesch had been appointed Professor of Philosophy at Cologne University in 1919 – specialism had not yet hardened sufficiently to preclude such a switch. He had joined the SPR earlier; in the 1920s he began to attend psychical research conferences, and to relate his theories to the phenomena; and in *The Crisis in Psychology* in 1925 he criticised people who had made up their minds that the phenomena 'never are and never will be', whom he likened to those 'who were with God when he created the world, and who know what he was able to do and what not', a species which 'never die out'.

Most textbooks or essays on psychology did not deal with parapsychology; 'nor, for that matter, even with "abnormal" normal psychology, such as hypnotism, if a paradoxical expression may be allowed'. But in every science, Driesch argued, 'the problematic side is more important for its advancement than the side which is well established', which was why he had thought it necessary to include psychical research. There were problems, he admitted; among them the foreseeing of the future, which for him was 'the greatest enigma of parapsychology'. He had long hesitated before accepting its reality but had become convinced partly by what he had read, partly by two extraordinary cases which 'careful and critical scientists' had related to him. He felt it was useless, though, to say anything more about a problem 'which we are sure we *cannot* understand in our present form of mentality'.

Grateful for the backing of so well-established and well-armed a campaigner, the SPR had made Driesch its President in 1926, and it was in this capacity that he was invited to contribute to the Clark symposium. Although he was not at his best in the English language, his paper was interesting in that it offered the germ of an explanation for materialised forms. One of the problems confronting any researcher who tried to persuade sceptics (or for that matter the general public) of materialisations was the common conviction that matter did not, in ordinary circumstances, materialise 'out of thin air'. But was this correct? Driesch cited Emile Coué, then at the height of his international reputation with his 'Every day, in every way, I get better and better' on hundreds of thousands of lips the world over. Coué's belief was that the imagination, if roused, could promote physiochemical changes (it was not until half a century later, with the discovery of the endorphins, that he was eventually proved right – they were the mechanism by which pain was relieved. But by then it had been forgotten that he was the prophet.) In the same way, Driesch suggested, there appeared to be 'mind-like agents' which could affect matter:

> They are not only able to affect physiological processes, to direct and regulate the genesis of the normal form, they may also provoke *abnormal structures* under the guidance of imagination. This is what may be called an *enlarged* Couéism.
>
> Let us keep well in mind that the action of what I have called *entelechy* in biology does not 'create' matter, but is only *ordering* pre-existing matter. And it is only this action of ordering, of directing, which we have to assume also in parapsychology, matter being everywhere. Mere assimilation, then, would be the most simple instance of a long series of events of which so-called materialisation would be the end.

Science and Parascience

Compared with these contributions, Coover's was shoddy: largely a rehash of Podmore, ignoring the strongest evidence for psychic phenomena, or traducing it with evasions and half-truths. Jastrow, however, was unusually thoughtful, arguing the case against psychic phenomena on metaphysical, or psychophysiological, grounds. Science, he claimed, had been progressing steadily from occultism 'to the discovery of material cause and effect in the naturalistic scheme as we moderns know it'. The story of the development of thought was 'the story of the long struggle and slow emergence of the single-threaded scientific view of things as they present themselves to an objective observation, detached from a personalised interpretation of the meaning of events and forces'. It sounded plausible; but the timing was unlucky. Only a few months later, Heisenberg was to state his principle of uncertainty, showing that 'objective observation, detached from a personalised interpretation', was impracticable at the sub-atomic level – and thereby subverting the 'single-threaded' view of things.

When Jastrow descended to details, too, he gave himself away. As one of the 'exposers' of Palladino, he felt secure in criticising Richet's acceptance of her in his *Thirty Years of Psychical Research*. 'Must one assume,' he asked, 'that Richet does not know that Palladino was repeatedly caught in the act of lifting the table telekinetically by the aid of her left leg and the broad flange of her flexible shoes?' Nobody knew better than Richet what Eusapia did when she was allowed to use her feet, as he had seen her do; nobody had attended more trials of her mediumship than he had; nobody had been harder to convince, until the series of tests he put her through in 1894 with Lodge, Myers and Ochorowicz in France had finally convinced him.

Where the sparks flew, in the book Murchison edited after the meeting, was not the result of sceptics and believers beating vainly on each other's armour, but in the resumed battle between Crandon and Walter Prince. In his contribution at the conference itself Prince had kept off the subject. Instead, he had made a spirited justification of his connection with psychical research. Because of his association with the ASPR, he was assumed to be a believer; but he begged the Clark audience not to accept so superficial a judgment; rather, to examine his attitude as they might examine a biological specimen.

> Put me under the microscope as the bug some people think I am. Reputed to be excessively cautious, and regarded by the Spiritualist

religious cult as a hard-hearted skeptic; formerly thoroughly skeptical all along this line; always occupied, during a curiously varied career, from the boyhood days when no mechanical or other puzzle was ever given up unsolved, in the analysis and resolution of one kind or another, in history, sociology, abnormal psychology etc., up to psychical research; one to whom accuracy is a religion, and minute analysis is an obsession, so that it is an agony to terminate the testing process and write a report; intolerably detailed in reporting and in presenting the subject in hand at every possible angle; alive by experience and study to the various pitfalls of illusion, delusion and deception – all this has made me a kind of scrutinising, analysing and rationalising monster, quite unpleasant to the tender-minded.

For years in this capacity, Prince pointed out, he had been asking people to examine his reports, to point out any precautions which he ought to have taken, any flaws in his methods, any weaknesses in his reasoning; yet few had accepted the challenge, and 'none has more than entered mere formal *a priori* objections, or uttered a few oracular and evasive generalities'.

The longest and most detailed contribution to the symposium came from Crandon. It was in no way an apologia; on the contrary, it exuded confidence that the mass of evidence which had been accumulated through the 'Margery' investigations, which he summarised, could withstand any attempt to explain it away. Henceforth it would be a question of exploring the phenomena scientifically. People might ask, for what purpose? Certainly not a religious purpose; psychic research, Crandon insisted, 'has about as much to do with religion as golf' – though it would affect some religious concepts and beliefs. The researchers were not propagandists for a 'new revelation', he insisted; all they wanted of scientists was 'a simple effort of good will – yes, let us say it, of honesty; for it is not honest to deny without trying to examine fairly'. The truly scientific mind, Claude Bernard had said, 'ought to make us moderate and tolerant'; but too often the critics had been 'the same old gang who tortured and burnt the free-thinker; they are the members of the Sanhedrin who cried, Crucify! Crucify! and they have carried it out, physically, if they could, but otherwise mentally, professionally and socially'.

It was not, however, the 'same old gang' whom Crandon was having to contend with at this time: it was Prince, who persuaded Murchison to include in the book, published under the title *The Case for and against Psychical Belief*, the scathing review Prince had written for the *American Journal of Psychology* of *Margery*

Harvard Veritas, and Bird's *Margery the Medium*. It was unashamedly a counter-polemic, designed to destroy the good reputation of the Crandons. Yet the review exposed Prince's own limitations. Unable to explain how the phenomena at the second Harvard investigation seances could be accounted for, he was reduced to generalisations – 'darkness may be required by a "psychic law", but it is also convenient' – and objections to 'Walter's' autocratic ways.

6   The SPR in Decline

'Feda'

The reluctance of the Cambridge nucleus to become involved in the investigation of physical mediums, and the negative nature of the report on 'Eva's' London series, again took the SPR out of the mainstream of psychical research in the 1920s. Significantly, the two contributions made by members at the 1923 Copenhagen international conference both dealt with the mental mediumship of Mrs Osborne Leonard. Work with her was continuing to produce positive results – about the only success which the society could claim.

Mrs Leonard's reputation had remained unblemished, and 'Feda's' ability to provide 'communicators' undiminished. She even won over Robert Blatchford, editor of the *Clarion*, long a leading campaigner for Socialism. 'Throughout my thinking life I have been a convinced materialist; even a militant materialist,' he wrote in his *More Things in Heaven and Earth*. 'I believed that the personality was bound up in the structure of the brain. As I have expressed it more than once, "the brain is the man".' As a letter he had written shortly before he went to Mrs Leonard showed, he went sceptically. What he heard converted him: his dead wife came through, and spoke to him as she had when she was living.

Blatchford also noted what other sitters had sometimes remarked upon: 'some curious acoustic facts', as he described them. 'Feda's' voice did not reach him as if Mrs Leonard was her mouthpiece. It sounded initially as if 'Feda' was speaking from above and behind Mrs Leonard. Later, it was as if she had moved in front, slightly to Mrs Leonard's left; so that when he was speaking to 'Feda', he was turning away from Mrs Leonard: 'When my wife spoke to me with the direct voice, she seemed to speak from a point between the medium and the control.'

Although 'Feda' expressed a preference for getting to know sitters, claiming that this helped her to obtain better results, from the society's point of view her most impressive feats were with first-time sitters whom she could not know about in advance; as in a case history provided by Mrs Dawson-Smith, the mother of a young officer, Lieutenant Frank Dawson-Smith, who had survived the war, including Passchendaele, only to be murdered in Somalia in 1920 by supporters of the 'Mad Mullah'. That autumn his mother went anonymously for a sitting, taking notes of what 'Feda' relayed from the 'communicator' – 'Frank'. Mrs Dawson-Smith passed the notes on to lodge, and Mrs Salter later published extracts from them in the SPR *Proceedings*. At the first of Mrs Dawson-Smith's sittings, her notes ran:

FEDA: The communicator says: 'Have you got the snapshots?'
Mrs D-S: I have those you sent me before you passed over.
FEDA: He says: 'Ah, but there are more to come. Will you remember what I say? You will laugh over it and I want you to laugh. Don't forget it. I feel strongly you will get it and you will see what I mean. I am taken in such a funny position . . .'

He calls you by such a funny name (more whispering, 'No, no, not that'). He must mean Mum. Not – well, but the other is nothing. (Pause). He says he calls you MOTH – that spells 'moth' (pronouncing as written), but he says 'No, no, ask her, she knows, don't you, Moth?'

Mrs D-S: It is short for mother.
FEDA: Just a piece of a word. He says, 'Yes, just a piece of mother', and he laughs . . .

He keeps calling 'Eric, Geoff!' (Feda shouted the two names) and 'Eric!' He says, 'All right, put that down and I'll explain afterward' . . .

He says you have some books of his with funny language. He was studying them. He says 'I started to learn the two languages. I have dabbled with many, but these two were different. I could speak one fairly well – but I know little or nothing of the other' . . .

He is pleased about the memorial. You know what he means? His name and a date – and he likes what you have put on it. He says, 'Something else is being done which you will know soon, not a private one but a public one.'

Two months after this sitting, a brother officer brought two packages to Mrs Dawson-Smith, in one of which were some prints. 'I laughed when I saw the one he evidently meant me to notice,' she commented in her letter to Lodge; it had turned out to be a picture taken of him surf-bathing, at an awkward moment. Frank had always called her 'Moth', pronouncing it as in 'mother'. Eric and

The SPR in Decline

Geoff were close friends, both of whom had been killed in the war. Frank had been learning Swahili, before leaving for Africa, with the help of a dictionary; and he had started to learn Somali just before he was killed. A white marble tablet was erected in his memory in his home church, and although at the time of the sitting she did not know it, a memorial tablet was also to be put up in a church in Nairobi.

There were to be further sittings in 1921, and the 'preview' element became even more marked. On 10 January 'Frank' said there was another snapshot of him: 'He is trying his best to get it to you,' 'Feda' told Mrs Dawson-Smith. 'He is going to try and impress the person who has it to send it to you. It may take some time.' The snapshot, the last to be taken of him, had been picked up by a brother officer, who had written to a man in Ireland to tell him about it; the man in Ireland told Mrs Dawson-Smith; and in July, when the brother officer returned to England, he met her to hand it over.

Another communication in that January sitting, was even more remarkable. According to 'Feda', 'Frank' wanted his mother to look for 'an old purse with a receipt in it, a tiny paper'. He described it as a counterfoil: 'Try and unearth it.' He knew his mother still had it, he told 'Feda'. Close to it was a long narrow strap, which he had noticed 'accidentally'; and he reiterated that it was important for her to find it.

In her box-room, Mrs Dawson-Smith found a trunk over which a long strap was hanging. It contained, among other things, an old leather purse, 'and in it a worn old counterfoil of a money order', which she took out and put in her desk, 'thinking the importance might be found later'. It was – but not until nearly four years later. On 23 November 1924 she wrote to tell Lodge what had happened:

> I had a letter from the 'Enemy Debt Clearing Office' demanding a sum of money said to be owing to a Hamburg firm, which was incurred in July 1914 – before the war. I *knew* my boy had paid it, as I remembered how anxious he was to send the money before war was declared, as he owed it and wanted to pay as a debt of honour. So I wrote to the Controller and explained that the account had been paid ten years ago. Then the Hamburg people said they had not received it, and if I had no proof other than my memory, it would be pressed (the claim). *Then* I remembered my boy's message at Mrs Leonard's and I hastened to look at the counterfoil and found it, the identical paper needed to prove the account had been paid. Needless to say I sent a complete account of the transaction to the Controller, and he

of course verified it in every particular, and wrote to apologise for having caused me so much worry and trouble, and to say no further action would be taken in the matter.

With the meticulousness which had become second nature to her, Mrs Sidgwick asked for the evidence to be sent; and after inspecting the counterfoil and the correspondence, she formally confirmed that they bore out Mrs Dawson-Smith's account.

This evidence 'certainly suggests that the communicator's memory was the source of the knowledge shown', Mrs Salter commented. But could it be classified as *fore*knowledge? The caution psychical researchers had learned to display showed itself in her appraisal. 'The emphasis laid upon the importance of the counterfoil, though interesting in view of the sequel, does not seem to imply any more exact knowledge of the future than would be within the scope of any person who had the circumstances of the case clearly in his mind,' she remarked. 'Obviously it *might* be of importance to be able to prove payment of such a debt, and documentary proof was therefore worth preserving.' To such an extent had the Cambridge clan been conditioned to look gift horses in the mouth.

The Death of Barrett

There were few gift horses around, however; largely for a reason which Barrett's death, in the summer of 1925, underlined. The last survivor of the founders of the society, he had been the most open-minded, striving to broaden the base of its research.

Barrett had been the first to confront the British Association in the paper which he read at its 1876 meeting. In a paper 'Reminiscences of fifty years' in 1924 he recalled with some pride that among the few scientists who had supported him in the subsequent furore, four – Crookes, Rayleigh, Wallace and William Huggins – were to receive the Order of Merit. It was Barrett who, six years later, had brought together the men who were to found the SPR; and two years after that had performed the same service in Boston, setting up the American society. 'One of the first of those distinguished physicists who have contributed so much down the years to its work and to its intellectual standing,' Renée Haynes has said of him in her history of the society. 'He combined great vitality with great intellectual gifts, and an insatiable – and wide-ranging – scientific curiosity with stubborn perseverance.'

The SPR in Decline

It must have irked Mrs Sidgwick that she could not keep Barrett's reports out of the society's publications, as she would often have preferred. Dowsing, for example, was regarded with disfavour by those members who were determined at all costs to preserve the society's image as a strictly scientific organisation. To them, the mind's-eye picture of a country bumpkin walking over fields holding a forked hazel twig savoured of superstition. Barrett had carried out careful, thorough research, the results of which had been published in the *Proceedings* in two long articles; they represented the first serious attempt to investigate the subject from a scientific standpoint, but they brought him no credit in the nucleus.

His report on a poltergeist haunting at Derrygonyelly, though eminently sensible, was also unwelcome; the Sidgwicks shared Podmore's view that poltergeists could and should be explained away in terms of some member of the family making mischief. For Barrett even to have investigated Crawford, let alone to have insisted that the Goligher circle were not fakers, was calculated to irritate Mrs Sidgwick still further. And even worse must have been his claim, in his swan song, to have had 'indubitable' evidence that psychic photographs could be genuine.

Although Barrett was a simple-minded man, in many respects a journeyman physicist rather than an academic, he was much shrewder in his speculations about the phenomena he was researching into than the nucleus gave him credit for. Even before the society had been founded, in his early exploration of the 'higher phenomena' of mesmerism, he had realised that straight 'thought transference' was a misleading concept, because it seemed to suggest 'a transmission of ideas between two persons across material space', whereas 'space', he thought, 'does not seem to enter into the question at all'. He had suggested 'transfusion of thought', which comes closer to current opinion.

One last service which Barrett rendered to psychical research has only recently been recognised as anything but a geriatric aberration. In his uncompleted *Death-bed Visions*, published posthumously, he provided a collection of cases of people who shortly before death had appeared to meet old friends and relatives coming, as it were, to help them across to the spirit world. Even Richet pronounced his evidence 'disturbing' – disturbing, that is, to anybody who shared Richet's materialism. Interest in this phenomenon has revived following the publication of Raymond Moody's *Life after Life*; and its implications have since been examined by several writers – among them Robert Kastenbaum, who in his survey of the evidence for and against survival has commented that 'more than half-a-century later, Barrett's little book remains a classic for its demonstration of astute scientific reasoning applied to a phenomena that some would regard as beyond empirical investigation'.

Gilbert Murray

Although the SPR's record of investigations in the mid 1920s was poor, apart from Dingwall's efforts and the continuing work with Mrs Leonard, there were two unusual investigations in which the society was involved at second hand, both of which produced interesting results. The first was a report by Mrs Sidgwick in 1924 on the 'guessing game' which had been played over the years by Gilbert Murray, Regius Professor of Greek at Oxford, in his family circle.

Towards the end of the nineteenth century a party pastime had become popular which involved sending a subject out of the drawing room; selecting an object in the room; bringing the subject back and inviting him, or her, to guess what or where the object was. There were many variations: sometimes those playing the game silently 'willed' the subject to find the object; sometimes the subject was blindfolded and led around the room by a 'guide'. Groups playing the 'willing game' were often astonished at the speed with which subjects found the object – as, indeed, were the subjects themselves; and arguments would arise over whether telepathy was responsible, or Cumberlandism – named after the explanation provided by Stuart Cumberland for his own success at the game, which he exploited professionally: he claimed the ability to pick up tiny clues by observation, or by his 'feel' of the muscular reactions of the 'guide'.

Murray had often played the game with his family and friends; but theirs was the sophisticated version he had described in his Presidential Address to the SPR in 1915:

> I go out of the room, and of course out of earshot. Someone in the room, generally my eldest daughter, thinks of a scene or an incident or anything she likes, and says it aloud. It is written down and I am called. I come in, usually take my daughter's hand, and then, if I have luck, describe in detail what she thought of.

The kind of scenes or incidents which his daughter or other 'agents' thought up for Murray to guess virtually ruled out Cumberlandism as an explanation. After a time the family had begun to record them, and Murray's guesses: and at the first session for which the record had been preserved, held on 17 April 1910, his daughter (Rosalind, later to be Mrs Arnold Toynbee), who was acting as 'agent', had suggested:

> Dad's little German hairdresser cutting Dennis's hair.
> *Murray*: A funny little man walking down a street knocking on doors – he looks foreign – he's just like my little German hairdresser.

Following Murray's Presidential Address the records, which had been kept since 1910, were examined by Mrs Verrall. Out of five hundred guesses, broken down into three categories, 33 per cent had been 'hits', 28 per cent 'near-misses', and 39 per cent 'misses'. In one respect this underestimated Murray's achievement: some of the near-misses were very close to being hits.

> *Agent*: Alister and Malcolm MacDonald running along the platform at Liverpool Street, and trying to catch the train just going out.
> *Murray*: Something to do with a railway station. I should say it was rather a crowd at a big railway station, and two little boys running along in the crowd. I should guess Basil.

How did Murray 'guess'? How did the information come into his mind? He did his best to explain: it came 'not through any particular sense, but through what I may call a sort of indeterminate sense of quality, or atmosphere. For instance I almost always, if I am going right, get first a feeling of the country in which the scene or incident is set. I say, "This is Russian," "This is Italian," "This seems tropical" or the like.' Murray could also usually sense whether the subject came from life, or from a book – the 'taste' from a book being particularly strong, so much so that he might pick it up even when he had not read the book. Sometimes there would be mind's-eye pictures, or mind's-ear sounds, or even mind's-nose smells: when the subject had been Savonarola's Florence, with the people burning their possessions, he had at first felt 'This is Italy', then 'Not modern', and then he had smelt burning oil or paint 'and so got the whole scene'.

A possible explanation, Murray thought, was 'hyperesthesia'; hyperacuity of the senses – of hearing, in his case, as when in a crowd of people, 'if your name is mentioned in another part of the room, you do not consciously hear the name but you turn and give attention'. Mrs Verrall found some examples in the transcripts which lent support to this idea. Once, when the subject which his daughter had chosen was 'a walk round by Mansfield', he had received 'a faint impression of Masefield'. Significantly, too, on occasions when the subject had been written down, but left unspoken, Murray had been unable to guess it. Nevertheless the hyperacuity of hearing notion did not fit all the evidence. Sometimes Murray picked up what was in the agent's mind even when it had been left unspoken.

> *Agent.* Dr M. in a white coat in his X-ray room examining a Russian with a red beard.
> *Murray.* I wonder if this is right. I get a picture of someone with a cough being examined by a doctor – I think your doctor in Geneva or somewhere, in a white coat, and the patient who is consulting him is rather like Tolstoy, but isn't. Ought I to know the person?

Tolstoy had not been mentioned; but it was Tolstoy whom Rosalind had had in mind. Whatever the explanation, Murray observed, he was sure that what he was picking up was not information, but rather a feeling, which then unleashed the information. It was noteworthy, he thought, that he had no success with, say, playing cards, or with any subject that 'was not in some way interesting or amusing'.

Eleanor Sidgwick's 1924 paper reported the results of further experiments. The outcome of her analysis was strikingly similar to Mrs Verrall's; Murray had registered a slightly higher proportion of hits and of misses, and a slightly lower proportion of partial successes. The 'feelings' were still reaching his consciousness in various ways: 'smell' had guided him on two occasions. When the subject was a lion trying to grab a piece of meat outside its cage, he got 'a sort of smell of wild animals – carnivorous animals'; and a fantasy offered by his daughter about an opium den off Piccadilly Circus Underground, with red sofas, dancing and a man in a skull cap had prompted him on his return to the drawing room to say it was odd, but he had picked up the smell of 'some incensy stuff – I should think it was opium, or hashish'. The subject was 'like a sort of opium den' with red settees; it was in London; and people were going 'down into it'.

Again, there were occasions when it was as if Murray had heard the subject: for 'Sir Francis Drake drinking the health of Doughty before he was led out to be hanged', Murray got 'a faint feeling of

The SPR in Decline

Arabia, or desert', for which the most likely explanation was that he had heard 'Doughty' but that it had brought the author of *Travels in Arabia* into his mind. Again, however, there were occasions when he appeared to have picked up the agent's thoughts even when the agent had left them unspoken.

Murray's description of the game in his Presidential Address, and Mrs Verrall's study of the records, had been published in wartime, and only for members of the SPR; they had attracted little attention. In 1924, however, the fact that the Earl of Balfour was in the audience when Mrs Sidgwick read her paper, and expressed the view that it effectively disposed of the hyperesthesia theory, led to its being reported in *The Times*; most of the account, under the headline 'Lord Balfour on Telepathy', was devoted to his contribution. And three days later the physiologist J. S. Haldane weighed in with a letter to the editor of *The Times* presenting his explanation. Murray was picking up ordinary sound waves; hyperesthesia was indicated, partly by his inability to guess what the subject was unless it was spoken; partly by the fact that the mistakes 'are very evidently such as arise from imperfect hearing'. He even claimed that this was Murray's own view.

Had Haldane attended the meeting and heard Mrs Sidgwick's paper, Lodge mildly protested, he would have realised that hyperesthesia did *not* fit the facts; and a controversy started up in *The Times* correspondence columns, Barrett and Donkin again entering the lists, as they had done half a century before following Barrett's paper to the British Association. But in *Psyche*, a journal devoted to the propagation of Behaviourist ideas, 'A.M.' – Adelyne More – gave the dispute a new twist by rejecting both telepathy and hyperesthesia.

As originally presented in the 1840s, the hyperacuity of the senses theory had been an attempt to account for the way in which certain individuals, when hypnotised, would react to signals made behind their backs. They must be feeling the tiny currents of air made by a beckoning or pointing finger, James Braid had argued, and moving in response to it. The advantage of the theory was that it required no additional sensory channel; all of us, the assumption had been, are capable of sensing such minute currents, but we are not ordinarily aware of them, any more than we are aware of our clothes touching our bodies. Hypnosis, Braid believed, enabled subjects to register sensory information which was available but not as a rule noticed. W. B. Carpenter had appropriated Braid's idea and fashioned it into a general theory of hyperesthesia; and

Science and Parascience

Faraday had gratefully adopted and adapted it to account for table-turning, by suggesting that it accounted for the way in which people were causing the tables to move without being aware that they were exercising muscular force.

As Lord Rayleigh was to point out in 1942, no scientific evidence had ever been offered for hyperesthesia. Undoubtedly some people had particularly acute hearing; but as nobody had ever demonstrated the existence of the kind of hyperacuity which Murray would have required for success in his game, Rayleigh dismissed the idea as a myth; it was simply a convenience for those who, like Haldane, wanted to dispose of telepathy, but found it hard to dismiss the evidence for Murray's faculty out of hand – understandably, as Murray by 1924 was a respected figure, and not just in academic circles; he was President of the League of Nations Union (a post carrying considerably more prestige than its equivalent, which he was also to hold in the United Nations Organisation, when it was set up after World War Two).

Adelyne More, however, a disciple of the behaviourist J. B. Watson, was not prepared to accept the existence of any process whereby information could be filtered through the unconscious into awareness. The results Murray obtained, she felt, could be accounted for by 'the hypothesis of conscious hearing plus successful guessing plus similar associations in the minds of the medium and his family'. 'The medium' could only be intended as an insult, as mediumship to a behaviourist was necessarily spurious. Murray, she was alleging, was using his ears in the normal way, when he could, and eking out what he heard with the help of a kind of Cumberlandism. And although she did not accuse Murray outright of deliberately deceiving his family and friends, and later the SPR, by pretending that he was picking up a 'feeling', whether by telepathy or hyperesthesia, when in fact he was consciously hearing what was said in the drawing room, she obviously knew that this would be inferred, as she went on to echo a point which Donkin had made in his controversy with the founders of the SPR: that in all scientific enquiries, the good faith of those concerned 'should form no part of the data on which the conclusion is to rest'. The evidence in cases of this kind should not be allowed to rest upon social or personal distinction, she argued. 'Rather, it must rest upon the solid foundation of controlled and rigid conditions under which the experiments are conducted.'

This attitude, logical enough in those branches of scientific research where all the subjective elements could be eliminated,

The SPR in Decline

could hardly apply in Murray's case. He had admitted in his Presidential Address to the SPR that 'the least disturbance of ordinary method, change of time or place, presence of strangers, controversy and especially noise, is apt to make things go wrong'. It would therefore have been legitimate for sceptics to make the point that Murray's faculty, whatever it might be, could not be scientifically tested, for much the same reason as the condition of being in love could not be scientifically tested. But as telepathy was a threat, they preferred to continue to insist that it would only be accepted if it could be demonstrated by some method acceptable to scientists. And in the meantime, they could have it either way: hyperesthesia, or cheating.

Murray's own belief was that his faculty was telepathic. There were so many occasions when he picked up what was in the agents' minds, rather than what they actually said, that he had been compelled to reject the hyperacuity hypothesis. But for some reason, he did not express this point of view at the time, keeping it to himself until his Presidential Address during his second term of office in 1953. As a result, hyperesthesia continued to be advanced as the explanation.

Adelyne More's viewpoint also attracted some support. By the mid 1920s Houdini was devoting much of his time and effort to proving that mediumship, in all its guises, was faked; and Murray's performances goaded him into demonstrating how the trick was done, in a performance specially laid on in his New York home for Ralph Pulitzer, Bernard Baruch, Walter Lippman and others. While the subjects he was to guess were being decided, one of the guests escorted Houdini to a room two floors above, and stood guard over the door. Houdini failed with the first subject, but when Baruch suggested 'Don't give up the ship', Houdini got 'water and shipwrecks'; and when the subject was 'the statue of Buffalo Bill in Wyoming', Houdini got 'oxen stampeding', and then switched to 'buffaloes' – much as Murray used to do.

Conan Doyle was to use this tale as one of his illustrations of Houdini's psychic powers, so sure was he that Houdini was only pretending that he had accomplished it by 'scientific trickery', as he claimed to do. But the more common interpretation was that Houdini had found how Murray did the trick; and this might still be the accepted view had not the secret been given away, years later, by Houdini's brother, who had been with the guests downstairs. When a subject was chosen, he had repeated it out loud, as if to help them to concentrate on it. Unknown to the others, the room was 'bugged' so that Houdini could listen in. 'Bugging' was then in its infancy; nobody would have suspected that there could be a concealed microphone.

The Black Box

Convincing through Murray's evidence was for anybody who accepted the possibility of telepathic communication, a family game hardly helped the SPR to advance its claim to be recognised as a body engaged in serious scientific investigations. The trials of a diagnostic gadget undertaken in 1924 were a different matter: they were as scientific as, at that time, their investigators could make them.

The leaders of the medical profession were still smarting from a calculated snub which it had received two years earlier, when the celebrated bonesetter, Herbert Barker, had received a knighthood. Because he practised without medical qualifications, he had been subjected for years to sour attacks in the medical journals, and harassment in the courts; and the General Medical Council had struck a doctor, Frederick Axham, off the Medical Register for assisting him by giving anaesthetics to his patients. Following Barker's knighthood the GMC had incurred further odium by refusing to reinstate Axham; and the profession's monopolistic powers had come under attack in the press. If the profession were to hold its privileged position, some of its members felt, the public needed reminding that the GMC's powers were for the good of the community, as a protection against quackery; and the arrival in Britain of the diagnostic instrument invented by an American, Albert Abrams, appeared to offer an ideal opportunity.

Practising in California, Abrams had established his reputation as a physician and neurologist, and in the course of his practice he made what struck him as an intriguing discovery: that when he used percussion, tapping a patient's body with a delicate hammer, the sound varied according to the direction in which patients were facing, and the disorders from which they were suffering. A possible explanation, he realised, was that in some unexplained way, the body reacted to the earth's magnetic field. Experimenting further, Abrams made the curious finding that if a healthy person held a piece of diseased tissue, it was possible to detect its presence by using percussion. From this he moved on to experiment by setting up a circuit, of the kind that would ordinarily be used for electrical experiments, to see whether the – presumed – electromagnetic component could be exploited to provide an objective diagnosis of disease in the absence of the patient, simply by including a piece of the patient's tissue, or a drop of the patient's blood, in the circuit; and when Abrams found the method worked, he began to manufacture and market his invention in the form of the gadget which came to be known as the 'Black Box'.

If the 'box' had actually incorporated and used an electric current, it might have been taken more seriously; but the fact that the 'current' which it measured by means of resistances was biological – on the analogy of animal magnetism, rather than of straight magnetism – led to its being damned by the medical profession in the United States. The profession in Britain would ordinarily have ignored its introduction; but this chance to expose quackery was too good to miss. Not merely did the 'box' look spurious, because it appeared to be an electrical device, yet did not use electricity; better still, there would be no need to test it on patients (which would have contravened the GMC's regulations), because Abrams had claimed that *any* biological or chemical substance could be diagnosed with its assistance.

In 1924 a committee was formed under Sir Thomas Horder – later, as Lord Horder, physician to King George V – to carry out tests of the 'Box'. It was a fairly high-powered group, though Whately Smith, by this time working at the Air Ministry, was the only member who had had any experience of investigating unexplained phenomena; there was his colleague, Major H. Lefroy, head of wireless research at the Air Ministry; Dr C. B. Heald, medical adviser to the Director of Civil Aviation; and M. D. Hart from the War Office. Together they prepared a simple but carefully thought-out test procedure requiring that the operator of the 'Box' should identify the contents of packages containing a variety of substances. They would be passed to him immediately before he was asked to make his diagnosis, so that he would have no opportunity to play any tricks, such as substituting his own.

The tests were carried out not on an Abrams' 'Box', but on a variant working on the same principle, which was being used by a homeopathic physician practising in Glasgow – W. E. Boyd. Relating what had happened to an audience at the Royal Society of Medicine on 16 January 1925, Horder described Boyd's technique. It involved 'a human subject standing at right angles to the horizontal component of the local magnetic field'. A receiving plate was connected to the subject through 'a variable condenser in series' by an electrode strapped to his forehead; the specimen to be diagnosed was handed in through the hatch on a holder, of which one side was earthed, and put on the receiving plate. Boyd then percussed the subject, making his diagnosis with the help of tuning 'by varying the value of the inductance'.

Repellent though quackery of any kind was to orthodox doctors, quackery masquerading as science was particularly resented; and as Horder's audience must have been largely composed of men 'in whose nostrils', as he put it, 'the subject has an odour which is quite unsavoury', they presumably had settled down to enjoy themselves at Boyd's expense – especially as they heard that when Boyd had come to London to give a demonstration, it had been a failure. Boyd's excuse had been that the London laboratory had not been screened to exclude extraneous magnetic impulses; so it had been agreed that Whately Smith should go to Glasgow, to conduct tests in a screened lab there.

The condition in which the tests were held, Whately Smith had found, were satisfactory. In the first test, Boyd and his emanometer were required to distinguish between two substances placed in their packets on the plate. In a run of twenty-five trials, the results were 100 per cent correct: the odds against this happening by chance, Horder noting, being 33,554,432 to one. In other tests, Boyd had to identify which specific substance, among a number, was on the plate. Again, he was right every time. Only in one of five tests did he slip up, being wrong in two out of twenty trials; but in these, Whately Smith had to admit, there was a possibility that the mistake might have been his, rather than Boyd's.

Either Boyd's technique worked, and worked spectacularly well, or he must have found some way of duping Whately Smith; that he should have secured Whately Smith's collusion in trickery, Horder hastened to say, was unthinkable. It might be unthinkable to Horder and those who knew Whately Smith, but as those who did not know him would inevitably suspect that he must be either dupe or rogue, Horder and Heald themselves went to Edinburgh, to repeat the tests, this time bringing with them Dingwall – already the acknowledged expert in planning fraud-repellent investigations – so that he could recommend any additional precautions he might think necessary. Dingwall was broadly satisfied with the earlier arrangements; he suggested a few minor modifications, and the tests began again. Horder did not go into detail about them in his report to the audience at the Royal Society of Medicine; he

The SPR in Decline

contented himself with saying that the same level of success had been maintained.

The effect on the audience can be imagined. After Horder sat down, the chairman asked whether it was the audience's wish to discuss the report there and then, or whether it would prefer to leave discussion until a later date. The meeting, as the *Lancet* succinctly reported, 'decided against each alternative'.

What, then, was the explanation? Boyd himself soon found that the emanometer did not provide consistently accurate diagnostic information; and although mistakes could be attributed to a failure of screening, this was of little benefit because, as he found, there was no way to make his screening system reliable. Yet chance could surely be ruled out; as could fraud, given the precautions. Interestingly, too, both Horder and Heald had been able to hear the changes in the percussion 'note', whenever a different substance was passed through the hatch. More than that: when they took the place of Boyd's assistant, and were themselves percussed, they could 'definitely feel an alteration in the abdominal muscles', even when a specimen was being withdrawn, and another one put through the hatch, without their knowledge. If Boyd had somehow managed to substitute his own specimens for those which the investigators had brought with them, in other words, this could not have accounted for the way in which their stomachs reacted differently to the different specimens, providing a different 'note' when percussed. It was this, in fact, which had been chiefly responsible for their verdict that 'no more convincing exposition of the reality of the phenomena could reasonably be desired'.

The other possibility was that Boyd was picking up the information psychically. Ever since, variants on the original 'Black Box' have been used, often for a time with such striking success that the practitioners of Radionics, as it has come to be called, have been led to think that they have found a way to get objective diagnostic information consistently. Always, however, these hopes have been dashed; it is as if the 'Box' requires a psychic link to work satisfactorily.

Radionics was not a field of research in which Horder would have cared to involve himself. He had a let-out; it would be unsafe to use the gadget, he argued, until it was known how it worked. Years later, Beverley Nichols, encountering Horder – by this time a peer – at a dinner, asked him why the 1924 investigation had never been followed up. 'I have rather a guilty conscience about it,' Horder replied. He must have known that for him or any other ambitious young member of the medical profession to have accepted even the possibility of a psychic component in diagnosis, let alone argue that it should be investigated, would have put a blight on a promising career.

The Chaffin Will

The SPR continued to perform one useful function: its *Journal* and *Proceedings* included a flow of case histories of telepathic or other experiences. By this time the accumulation of such anecdotal material had reached the stage where, from the point of view of converting sceptics, it was a waste of time to add any more; a few, however, were of unusual interest, such as the Chaffin Will case, the details of which, though it was American in origin, appeared in the *Proceedings*.

The story, as unfolded in documents sent by a North Carolina lawyer, J. M. Johnson, to the SPR, concerned a will made by a farmer in that state, James L. Chaffin. Chaffin had four sons; and for some reason which the documents did not go into, in a will he made and had attested by two witnesses in 1905, he left the farm to his third son, Marshall, whom he also made sole executor, leaving out the rest of the family, including his wife.

When James died in 1921, Marshall duly came into the inheritance. Four years later, however, the second of the four brothers, James Chaffin Jr, began to have vivid dreams about his father; culminating in one where his father, wearing a black overcoat, told him he would find his will in the overcoat pocket. The overcoat was in the possession of the eldest brother; examining it, James found that the lining of the inside pocket had been 'sewd together'. Cutting the stitches, he found – not the will, but a message in his father's writing on a roll of paper tied with a string: 'Read the 27th chapter of Genesis in my daddy's old bible.'

At this point James was sufficiently impressed, or shaken, by the corroboration of his dream to take the precaution of getting a neighbour to come with him to his mother's house. There (he wrote in his formal statement),

> we had a considerable search before we found the old Bible. At last we did find it in the top bureau drawer in an upstairs room. The book was so dilapidated that when we took it out it fell into three pieces. Mr Blackwelder picked up the portion containing the Book of Genesis, and there we found two leaves folded together; the left-

The SPR in Decline

hand page folded to the right and the right-hand page folded to the left forming a pocket, and in this pocket Mr Blackwelder found the will.

– a version which Blackwelder corroborated. The newly-found will read:

> After reading the 27th chapter of Genesis, I, James L. Chaffin, do make my last will and testament, and here it is. I want, after giving my body a decent burial, my little property to be equally divided between my four children, if they are living at my death, both personal and real estate, divided equal; if not living, give share to their children. And if she is living you all must take care of your mammy. Now this is my last will and testament. Witness my hand and seal.
>
> <div style="text-align:right">James L. Chaffin
This <i>January</i> 16, 1919</div>

The second will, in other words, had been written fourteen years after the first, and two years before his death; and Genesis 27 gave a clue to the reason for the change of mind, as it deals with Jacob's filching of his brother Esau's birthright. Why the testator had not told his family was not clear; but the fact that he died suddenly as the result of an accident suggested the possibility that he had preferred not to disclose his intentions until on his deathbed.

The beneficiary of the first will, Marshall, was no longer alive; but on the new will being tendered for probate, his widow prepared to contest it on behalf of her son, a minor. On being shown the will, however, and in the knowledge that a number of witnesses were prepared to testify that it was in James L. Chaffin's handwriting, she withdrew her opposition – the fact of its being in the testator's writing, even if not attested, making it valid under the state's laws.

The lawyer, Johnson, who sent the documents to the SPR, explained that he had tried to find out whether the discovery of the will could be accounted for by, say, some subconscious knowledge of its existence; but the members of the family were unanimous that it had never been mentioned in the testator's lifetime. The writer of the unsigned commentary in the *Proceedings* of the SPR drew attention to the fact that it was not the actual will which was in the overcoat pocket, as the second son had been told in his dream; but this could hardly be held to cast doubt on the son's veracity. And as Johnson emphasised, he himself had no suspicions; he had been 'much impressed with the evident sincerity of these people, who had the appearance of honest, honourable country people, in well-to-do circumstances'.

The case aroused interest not simply because of the satisfactory outcome – dreams from which financial benefit accrued to the rightful owner, though rare, had been reported before – but for the scope it gave for controversy over whether it could best be accounted for by the return of the father's spirit, penetrating his son's mind in dreams; or by delayed telepathy; or by cryptomnesia – the son's memory of something his father had said or done being jogged in his dreams. The commentary in the *Proceedings* recalled an episode from Myers' *Human Personality* in which a woman, coming out of a swoon after hearing of the death of her father, said that he had appeared to her while she was in it, and told her that there was some money sewn inside the shirt he was wearing at the time, which turned out to be correct; but this could be attributed to a telepathic impression conveyed to her before his death. 'In the present case, nearly four years intervened between the death and the apparition, so that the hypothesis of delayed telepathy is hardly applicable.'

The Easing-out of Dingwall

By the mid 1920s, though its journal continued to provide records of such cases, the Society for Psychical Research was providing very little evidence of activity on the part of its members – apart from reports of the continuing ability of 'Feda' to impress investigators: among them the Rev. W. S. Irving, 'a model sitter' – in the view of the exacting Mrs Salter, who had charge of the *Journal*, in her introduction to his account of a series of trials with Mrs Leonard in 1925 – 'in respect of the trouble he takes to verify and check every statement made, so far as he possibly can'.

'Feda' was still concerned to show that she was not reading her sitters' minds. Much of the information which, she claimed, was coming from Irving's wife, who had died in 1918, continued to be trivial; but it was often of a kind likely to impress him that it really was his deceased wife who was communicating. And frequently there could be no question of 'Feda' mind-reading; not, at least, reading *his* mind. From time to time her 'communicators' would describe what was happening at the SPR – as well they might, in view of the society's interest in her. On 29 January 1924 she told Irving that his 'wife', who had 'visited' the SPR, had reported among other things that somebody in the society's offices had unexpectedly received some red flowers. Asked whether this was correct, the SPR's secretary replied that on the day of the sitting, 'Mr Dingwall brought me a plant of red azaleas in full bloom. The gift was entirely unexpected. Mr Dingwall has never given me a plant before.' What Dingwall thought of this unexpected exposure of him in the role of a gallant is not recorded.

The evidence which Mrs Leonard was continuing to provide, however valuable it was for those who were interested in debating the issue whether telepathy or survival after death could be held responsible for 'Feda's' capabilities, was hardly enough to justify the SPR's existence as a research organisation; and this was beginning to foment discontent, as J. G. Piddington – a longstanding member of the Cambridge nucleus, a close associate of Mrs Sidgwick's, and the society's Treasurer – realised. In his Presidential Address in 1924 he remarked on the existence within the society of two schools of thought: the 'High-and-Dry', who wanted to maintain the most rigorous of scientific standards, and the 'Not High-and-Dry', who took the line that 'so much has been established beyond cavil that we can now safely relax to some extent the stringent precautions' and 'generally adopt a less suspicious and more genial attitude to mediums, automatists, dreamers of dreams, seers of apparitions, corroborating witnesses and so forth'.

The issue was not in fact so simple. The chief threat to the survival of the SPR was that the Cambridge nucleus's determination, which Piddington whole-heartedly shared, to keep it High-and-Dry, had left it bankrupt of new ideas for research, and increasingly uneasy about involving itself in what had become the major preoccupation of researchers on the Continent, physical mediumship; and here, chance came to the nucleus's aid with the death of Geley and the decline in the powers of the best known mediums, first 'Eva' and then Willy Schneider.

In the winter of 1924 Dingwall had held another series of seances with Willy Schneider, in London; and they had been disappointing. 'It can hardly be denied that the phenomena occurring in the presence of Mr Schneider have been diminishing, both in quantity and quality, in recent years,' he reported. 'There is nothing like the range and power which were noticeable in 1922 and even later. The phenomena are weaker and negative sittings more common.' Even so, had Willy been a new and untried medium his performances would have been considered quite striking.

Science and Parascience

As before, Willy had two controllers, one on either side; ordinarily there were four or five witnesses, and a note-taker to record their comments. Except in the occasional blank sitting, the familiar manifestations were repeated: cool breezes wafted past; the table moved about; sitters felt themselves being touched. Sometimes the cardboard strips reared up on end; a handkerchief, placed on the table, took on different shapes; the tambourine trembled so that the attached cymbals tinkled. At one sitting the tambourine rose up, and then fell. Later, a cardboard strip 'rose completely from the table several inches and oscillated up and down in the air several times, while remaining horizontal'. And following another session, a well-known magician, Douglas Dexter, who had been asked to represent the Occult Committee of the Magic Circle, had to admit he could think of no way by which either the medium or any of the sitters could have used physical force to achieve the results without instant detection.

As usual, Dingwall conceived it to be his duty to advance some hypothesis which might conceivably account for the phenomena, even if his fellow-conjuror admitted himself baffled. In the case of Willy, however, Dingwall's surmise was so preposterous that he can only have presented it as a matter of form; almost as a tease. 'The movements of the table,' he suggested, '*may* conceivably have been effected by the medium's head.' The medium's head, in his trances, was usually flopped on the hands of the controllers who were holding his hands: how he could have used it to move the table without their noticing was not explained. 'No doubt it is possible,' Dingwall went on, 'that skilfully directed air currents, after the manner of the production of smoke rings, or even actual blowing, may have caused the tinkling of the cymbals on the tambourine.' Willy, in other words, would have had to lift his head, turn it at right angles, and blow sufficiently hard through the gauze not just to make the cymbals sound, but sometimes actually to move the tambourine; all this without anybody noticing. In any case, the levitations of the luminous rings and strips could not be so easily accounted for, as Dingwall admitted:

> In order to raise an object two to three feet distant from him, the medium must have had concealed in his mouth an extensible apparatus workable by the mouth alone and by this means have supported a flat object lying on the table and raised it into the air from below. This feat must have been accomplished without any obvious interference, with his breathing or speech; and when completed, the rod must have been in some inexplicable manner with-

drawn and again concealed in the mouth. We frankly do not believe such a device exists, and therefore are driven to the conclusion that the only reasonable hypothesis which covers the facts is that some supernormal agency produced the results.

Even so, caution prevailed: 'We are fully prepared to abandon this hypothesis,' Dingwall concluded, 'if contrary evidence is offered.'

Dingwall was manifestly a High-and-Dry: considerably higher and drier than some members of the Cambridge nucleus. For all his experience with mediums whom he had accepted as genuine, such as Ossowiecki, his cast of mind was becoming increasingly sceptical, as his reviews in the society's publications in this period revealed. He dismissed *The Facts of Psychic Science*, by Campbell Holms, as unworthy of serious attention, on the ground that the author did not adopt a sufficiently rigorous attitude to the source material; though what was interesting about the book was precisely the fact that the author, a Not-High-and-Dry, was less concerned with whether the phenomena he surveyed had, or had not, been genuine, than with showing just how wide a range they covered – and, by implication, how narrow the SPR's concept of the range of 'respectable' research had become. Yet Dingwall could take seriously writers such as von Gulat-Wellenburg, still the leading sceptic on the Continent, in spite of the fact that – as Dingwall himself showed – their prejudices were leading them to gross distortions and falsifications. After pointing out just how feeble Gulat-Wellenburg's efforts to discredit certain mediums were, Dingwall could still recommend his book as 'one of the most important critical surveys of physical mediumship which has hitherto appeared' – the most important 'since that made by Mr Podmore'.

When Schrenck, Oesterreich and Tischner published their reply to the sceptics, too, Dingwall's reception of their case, in spite of the fact that he had to endorse some of it, was unsympathetic. The value of their book, he concluded, was that it had revealed the 'unanswerable character' of one of the main contentions of the sceptics, which had been that up to that time, 'no adequate evidence had been adduced which would lead a critical mind to accept the existence of physical phenomena from a mere acquaintance with the literature alone'.

This was tantamount to conceding victory to the sceptics, as 'the literature' presumably included Dingwall's own reports. He was in effect granting the demand which sceptics so often made, that they would accept the phenomena only if they could see them; if this were accepted, it would be pointless to continue to test mediums in the way that Richet, Schrenck, Geley and Dingwall himself had tested them. And in fact it was at this time that Dingwall's continental excursions on the society's behalf came to an end.

Harry Price had bounced in to try to fill the vacuum the Cambridge nucleus had created. He had not succeeded in his aim of making himself a force within the SPR; and in 1925 he set up the National Laboratory for Psychical Research, the better to pursue investigations on his own account. Dingwall would have been a natural ally; but though Dingwall admired Price's energy, and recognised that he had an 'exceptionally keen and ingenious mind', his acquaintanceship with Price had shown him that Price was a Not-High-and-Dry, who would find it easier to work with the College of Psychic Science, where Conan Doyle and others had found the atmosphere less repressive than the SPR.

For a while, however, Price appeared to be conducting research with an energy and an ability that promised to make his National Laboratory the leading psychical research organisation in Britain. In particular, he had discovered a physical medium, Stella Cranshaw, who could produce phenomena reasonably consistently, even in the presence of sceptical witnesses; some of them striking, such as a fall in temperature in the seance room of over 20°F – significant not only because although 'cold breezes' had been the commonplace of seance rooms, they had not as a rule registered on thermometers, but also because, as Lodge observed, 'it is easy for hocus-pocus to send a thermometer up; but it is by no means easy to send it down'.

'Stella C.', as she was described in reports, could move objects at a distance from her, and sometimes break them into pieces; and her mediumship so impressed Dr E. J. Tillyard, the Australian entomologist, that in 1926 he dealt with it in *Nature* in a review of Conan Doyle's *History of Spiritualism*. Critical though Tillyard was of the book, he urged that the case for psychical phenomena was strong enough to merit more investigation: a courageous attitude, in view of the predictably hostile response from Sir Horatio Donkin and other sceptics in *Nature*'s correspondence columns.

Tillyard was also a witness of Price's investigation of another medium, the Roumanian Eleanore Zugun. 'Stella C.' reported that objects near her sometimes moved, as if of their own accord; Eleanore Zugun was actually plagued by such movements, as if she

The SPR in Decline

were the storm-centre of a poltergeist outbreak, and the investigators were able to observe 'apports' materialising (one materialised in Tillyard's pocket, on his way home after a seance). That Tillyard, a scientist of sufficient eminence for the editor of *Nature* to solicit his contributions, should be devoting time to work with the National Laboratory, rather than with the SPR, was the measure of Harry Price's achievement in this period.

By contrast the SPR had embarked on only one fresh initiative, and that arose from an idea which had been proposed earlier by Harry Price and by Dingwall, following a radio experiment in Chicago. In 1927, the British Broadcasting Corporation allowed itself to be persuaded to help the SPR with an experiment to find out if listeners, or some of them, had telepathic abilities; Lodge was to be in charge.

The aim of the programme was 'to discover whether any evidence could be obtained of the telepathic transmission of ideas' to people who would know nothing more than that a small group of 'agents' would be seeking to transmit information at stated times. Five objects – a playing card, a Japanese print, a bunch of lilacs, another playing card, and a picture of a man wearing a mask – were exhibited to the 'agents' at the society's premises, at five-minute intervals between 11 p.m. and midnight; while Lodge, at the BBC's Savoy Hill headquarters, told listeners to record their impressions, have them witnessed where possible, and post them to the society – the 'agents' being kept in the society's premises all night and until after the first postal collection in the morning.

Nearly twenty-five thousand replies were received; but the only clear outcome of the test was the realisation that such experiments needed more careful thought if they were to provide reliable evidence for, or indeed against, telepathy. The guesses showed a strong tendency among listeners to choose an ace, for example, particularly the ace of spades; and to prefer odd-numbered to even-numbered cards. The chances of a correct guess in any such trial, in other words, would vary according to what card was chosen, or turned up when the pack was cut. It was also impossible to decide, in the case of a picture, what should count as a 'hit'. Should 'flowers' serve, in the case of the bunch of lilac? Or 'feeling of amusement', which no fewer than 499 viewers had in connection with the jokey picture? Dr V. J. Woolley's cautious conclusion in his report to the society was that the records showed 'the great difficulty of reaching any definite statistical result in tests of this kind'.

Science and Parascience

A positive result would have given a considerable fillip to the SPR; the lack of it left the society where it was before, living on its past. Soon there were signs of dissatisfaction, and not just among the Not-High-and-Dry school. The appointment of Woolley to be Honorary Research Officer (Dingwall had been paid a salary) had itself shown which way the tide was flowing; Woolley hardly bothered to conceal his impatience with physical mediumship. However High-and-Dry Dingwall might be, his past preoccupation with physical mediums rendered him suspect with the Cambridge nucleus; and in 1927, he was informed that the SPR council had decided to dispense with his services.

The council also decided to return Harry Price's library of books on magic, left to the SPR on permanent loan, giving as its reason shortage of space; the more likely reason was the growing mistrust of Price, coupled with the fact that a new librarian had been appointed, who had decided upon a complete reorganisation of the society's own collection. Theodore Besterman was something of a prodigy. In 1924, at the age of twenty, he had brought out a bibliography of the works of Annie Besant – he was later to make an international reputation as a bibliographer – and a history of crystal-gazing which, though dry in its presentation, showed an enviable knowledge of the sources. He had then collaborated with Barrett in *The Divining Rod*, a survey of the evidence for dowsing.

Besterman identified himself with the High-and-Dry element in the society, and he made no attempt to conceal his impatience with those who did not share his views. With his appointment in 1929 to succeed Helen Salter as editor of the society's publications, he had the chance to air them without restraint – so long as they would be shared by the Cambridge nucleus. And in a review of Gwendolyn Hack's *Modern Psychic Mysteries*, dealing with the work of, among others, the leading Italian psychical researcher, Ernesto Bozzano, Besterman claimed that to take it seriously would be 'to bring our subject into contempt and disrepute'.

Conan Doyle

In a letter, a copy of which he sent to every member of the society, Conan Doyle complained that the review was full of misrepresentations and innuendos: 'My only resource is, after thirty-six years of patience, to resign my own membership, and to make some sort of public protest against the essentially unscientific and biased work of a society which has for a whole generation produced no constructive work of any kind, but has confined its energies to the misrepresentation and hindrance of those who have really worked at the most important problems ever presented to mankind.'

A few months later, Doyle died. 'A simple-hearted bluff man,' Lodge was to describe him, 'who having begun by a training in medicine and as an agnostic, ultimately became an almost undiscriminating enthusiast for what he believed to be spiritual truth.' Yet Doyle could display a robust common sense which members of the society too often lacked. The fact that 'Eva C.'s' materialisations looked so spurious, he pointed out, far from being an indication that she or anybody else had smuggled them in, was a strong argument in favour of their being genuine; for nobody who was going to cheat would choose to cheat in the very way that would make her *appear* to be cheating.

Carlos Mirabelli

It was arguable, as the Cambridge nucleus believed, that the credulous Conan Doyle had been a liability to psychical research. It would have been difficult for them, however, to rebut his criticism of the SPR for its failure to undertake 'constructive work' and its 'misrepresentation and hindrance' of some of those who *were* doing constructive work, through the investigation of physical mediums. And the unwillingness to accept physical mediumship was now to have a particularly unfortunate consequence. A remarkable medium had emerged in Brazil; but there was no enthusiasm for any project to investigate him.

Carlos Mirabelli had been born in Brazil in 1889, of Italian parents (his father, curiously, was an Italian Lutheran clergyman). Undistinguished at school, Carlos had become an assistant in a shoe shop; and in this capacity, he began to be the centre of poltergeist-type disturbances. The shoe boxes took to leaving their shelves and flying around the shop, sometimes even accompanying him out into the street. Before long, he was locked up in the local lunatic asylum.

The psychiatrists in charge appear to have been unusually broad-minded. Instead of putting him into a strait-jacket, they gave him tests, which showed that he could move objects at a distance. He was not normal, one of them reported; but neither was he crazy. What happened in his vicinity appeared to be 'the result of the radiation of nervous forces that we all have, but that Mr Mirabelli has in extraordinary excess'. After a few days, he was discharged.

The discovery that he could himself control the psychic forces made all the difference to Mirabelli. Although he was not averse to accepting money for demonstrations of his powers, he preferred to earn his living in property-dealing, for which he showed considerable talent; but he enjoyed his fame as a physical medium, which soon spread, the more so in that he could put his telekinetic powers to entertaining use. At a banquet he was attending he enlivened the proceedings by causing an invisible hand to play a military march on a row of bottles and glasses; and when he played billiards, he did not need actually to make contact with his cue to send the billiard balls scuttering round the table.

During the 1920s a succession of reports of his phenomena were published in Brazil; Helen Salter predictably characterised them as 'preposterous' in the SPR *Journal*, of which she was still editor in 1927. In the following issue, however, Count Perovsky felt compelled to modify his, by this time, profound scepticism, after reading a report on Mirabelli which had appeared in Schrenck's *Zeitschrift*. Startling though the phenomena recorded might be, Perovsky noted, they were attested by 300 observers – politicians, professors, doctors, and business men. Fearing the possibility that the report was a hoax, Schrenck had taken the precaution of showing the list to the Brazilian consul in Munich: seventeen of the signatories, the consul had said, were personally known to him, including a former President of the Republic, a Secretary of State, and a Professor at the university of São Paulo. 'Such evidence as this cannot be ignored,' Perovsky felt. 'This amazing personality ought to be tested on European soil.'

Unluckily the European soil at the time was not receptive. The psychical research societies lacked the funds for costly enterprises. Schrenck was fully occupied with his own work; Osty, at the Institut Métapsychique, was wary; and the Cambridge nucleus were unlikely to take up Perovsky's idea with any enthusiasm. The obvious step would ordinarily have been for American psychical researchers to undertake an investigation; but they were split by the 'Margery' affair, and had no funds for such an enterprise. Nothing was done.

What psychical researchers missed, by their inability to conduct research into Mirabelli's mediumship, was revealed in 1930 in two

The SPR in Decline

articles by Dingwall in the *Journal* of the American SPR under the heading 'An Amazing Case' – a case 'in which the most extraordinary occurrences are recorded', Dingwall observed; 'so extraordinary indeed that there is nothing like them in the whole range of psychical literature'. His information was taken from the original documents in Portuguese, in which the occurrences were described in considerable detail, and vouched for by numerous witnesses of good standing.

Naturally sceptics had poured ridicule on the stories which had spread about Mirabelli, particularly when it was claimed that on one occasion, while waiting at a railway station, he had suddenly vanished, to reappear almost instantaneously ninety kilometres away. But so striking had the stories been, vouched for by so many citizens in good standing, that eventually a committee of twenty had been set up, consisting of men in established positions in the community, to decide what, if anything, should be done about Mirabelli. Having heard the witnesses, they had accepted the evidence as genuine, on the ground that it was vouched for by so many people whose word could not easily be doubted, and because what was described could not be accounted for by any form of trickery, as it took place often in the open air, in public places, and usually in broad daylight. The committee recommended that Mirabelli should be more fully investigated, by people better qualified to find out more about the phenomena.

The investigation was carried out in Santos by the newly founded Academia de Estudos Psychicos. Mirabelli was subjected to controls of the kind to which mediums in Europe had become accustomed. The investigators divided themselves up into three groups: one dealing with spoken mediumship, which had 189 positive sittings; one with automatic writing, which had 85 positive and 8 negative sittings; and one with physical phenomena, which had 63 positive and 47 negative sittings. The reports on the spoken and written evidence showed that 'the medium spoke 26 languages, including 7 dialects; and wrote in 28 languages, among them 3 dead languages, namely Latin, Chaldaic and Hieroglyphic'. This was remarkable enough, as Mirabelli had had so little formal education; but the physical manifestations surpassed any that had ever been reported, anywhere.

Of the sixty-three positive sittings, forty were held in daylight and twenty-three in bright artificial light, with the medium clearly visible to all witnesses, sitting tied up in his chair in rooms which were searched before and after. Yet in these conditions, a variety

Science and Parascience

Mirabelli used to levitate, and remain floating for minutes at a time, in the presence of witnesses.

of staggering phenomena were observed and recorded. The report cited six examples. In the first, a chair with Mirabelli in it rose into the air until it was two metres above the floor, where it remained for two minutes. In the second, in a room of about a thousand square metres with stone walls and locked doors, three knocks came from a table and a childish voice cried 'Papa'. It was recognised by one of the investigators as that of his daughter, who had just died; and gradually her form materialised, in the dress she had been buried in, to be embraced by her weeping father. Apart from looking deathly pale, she seemed to be just as she had been when alive; a doctor who was present felt her pulse, and she answered his questions tonelessly but sensibly. She was photo-

The SPR in Decline

The look of alarm on the part of Dr Carlos de Castro (right) is accounted for by the fact that a deceased poet (centre) has just materialised between him and the entranced Mirabelli, in the course of a test seance at the Cesare Lombroso Academy of Psychic Studies.

graphed (her picture appeared in the commission's report) before floating into the air, and after more than half an hour, dematerialising. The investigators – ten of them – all testified to what had happened.

The third and fourth examples had happened immediately afterwards. A noise came from a closet, as of something beating against the doors; they opened and a skull emerged, floating and gradually accumulating bones until it became a complete skeleton, when it began to stumble round the room. The bones were hard and damp to the touch, and it stank like a corpse. After twenty minutes the skeleton gradually disappeared, leaving the skull to descend on a table.

Then, a sweet smell as of roses preceded the formation of a glowing mist in the room, which suddenly dissipated to reveal a materialised bishop who had been drowned not long before in a shipwreck. He, too, responded to medical examination as if he were living, before he slowly dematerialised. Only then did Mirabelli – all this time visible, and tied up – come out of his trance.

Science and Parascience

For the fifth example, there were no less than sixty witnesses. It consisted of a number of materialisations, one of a man well known in the community; he spoke as if alive and, according to the doctor present, he responded to tests as if alive. One doctor, who grasped at the materialisation when it began to float into the air, fainted and awoke to find himself in a different room. And the sixth example was from a seance at which Mirabelli himself dematerialised, to be found later in another room, though the seals put on his bonds were intact, as were the seals on all the doors and windows of the seance room.

'What,' Dingwall asked rhetorically, 'are we to make of these amazing reports?' They were attested by over five hundred people, of whom about a hundred were foreigners; and their statements were supported by numerous photographs. Dingwall had to confess himself at a loss. 'It would be easy to condemn the man as a monstrous fraud and the sitters as equally monstrous fools,' he admitted. 'But I do not think that such a supposition will help even him who makes it.' The fraud hypothesis might be advanced if the seances had been held in darkness or even semi-darkness, but not in light. Mass hallucination? What then, of the photographs? Collusion? It would be easy to assert that the 'materialisations' were really the medium's confederates, 'but confederates are human beings, and human beings do not usually rise into the air, dissolve into pieces and float about in clouds of vapour'. No: certain events had clearly happened, and had been described by witnesses. 'That the whole case is of enormous importance cannot be denied by anyone who is at all acquainted with the history of alleged supernormal phenomena.' The full story, he felt, would be of surpassing interest.

Dingwall realised, however, that the full story was not going to be told. 'The chaos in which psychical research finds itself at present prevents any really valuable systematic work being done,' he lamented. 'Jealousy, spite, self-advertisement, incompetence and even downright lying are now so common that research is relegated to a back place.' The fact that his articles appeared in the *Journal* of the American Association, and not of the SPR, lent mute testimony to the state of affairs in London: and perhaps also in America; Walter Prince would have been even less likely to accept it for his Boston journal.

How, then, could Mirabelli be investigated? Orthodox science was not going to help; the SPR, Dingwall sourly commented, 'torn almost in two by internal dissensions, is not likely to add anything of permanent value unless drastic changes are made in the administration'; and the American societies lacked both the means and the staff. The Santos report would 'go down to history merely as a curious specimen of psychical literature', unless its findings were confirmed by an independent and competent commission; but no commission could be formed. 'Such is the state of psychical research in the year of Grace, 1930.'

Cassandra could not have foretold the future with greater accuracy. As it was known that Hans Driesch had visited Mirabelli while in Brazil in 1928, he was asked for his recollections; but though he had observed what appeared to be some telekinetic effects and some apports, he did not feel justified in claiming that they were psychic, and he contented himself with adding his voice to Dingwall's, urging full-scale investigation. But no investigator was sent to Brazil; and it proved impossible to raise the money that would have been required to attract Mirabelli to Europe.

An Experiment with Time

The only work to appear in Britain in this period which was destined to make a lasting impression as a contribution to the evidence for psychical phenomena was J. W. Dunne's *An Experiment with Time*, published in 1927; yet ironically, Dunne went out of his way to try to dissociate himself from psychical researchers, insisting in his opening words 'this is not a book about occultism'. In his lifetime Dunne had had a number of dreams which had foreshadowed future events of a kind he could not have foreseen. He wanted to show that this was natural; it could be explained by his theories about the workings of time.

Cases of prevision – or precognition, as it was coming to be described – had been endlessly reported throughout recorded history, and scores of accounts had already accumulated in the files of psychical research societies. Many of them were in dreams, which had impressed even Podmore: 'It is precisely amongst the dreams that the clearest and best-attested cases are to be found.' He was careful to add that there was a problem in dealing with such cases: 'We have little security that the "misses" have been recorded as well as the "hits".' Billions of dreams are dreamed every night: might it not only be the ones which happen to be coincident with future events that are remembered and recorded?

Other attempts had been made to account for precognition, with the help of variations on the theme of Laplace: 'If there was an intelligence which, at a given instant, knew all the forces of nature, and could analyse the data,' he had suggested, 'nothing would be uncertain to it and the future as well as the past would be present to its vision.' Early in the 1900s Gabriel Tarde had gone even further along this road, arguing that the future could actually influence the present, on the analogy of gravity: plants, and animals, might be learning to adapt to the 'pull' of the moon, say, in advance. But always present was the complication which Maeterlinck had commented upon, in connection with the dire predictions which traditionally had come from the spirits through mediums, seers and sybils: 'Either these beings predict to us a misfortune that their predictions cannot avert, and in that case what is the use of predicting it; or, if they announce it to give us the means to prevent it, they do not really see the future and they predict nothing, since the misfortune may not take place; so that in either case their action seems absurd.'

Such speculations, however, made less impression on the public than a rooted uneasiness about anything which savoured of predestination – and consequently an erosion of free will; coupled with a feeling that to know about the future was an affront to common sense. 'To make contact with that which does not yet exist,' as Gardner Murphy put it, 'is, for many, a contradiction in terms, a philosophical paradox, an outrage; or even may be held to come under the category of an "impossibility".'

There was no reason to expect that Dunne's book would shake this conviction. Although he had been a talented aeronautical engineer – the designer, in fact, of the first British military aircraft to fly before the war – his name was not known to the reading public: his only previously published work had been on fly-fishing. *An Experiment with Time*, too, was unpretentious, with its string of dreams, most of them unexciting, and an abstruse theory to account for them. And although it received generally favourable reviews – H. G. Wells thought it 'fantastically interesting'; even *Nature* described Dunne as 'a careful, sane experimenter' – and sold well enough to go into a second edition two years later, it might then have been forgotten had not Richard de la Mare of Faber & Faber persuaded his firm to take it over and publish a new, expanded edition. This time it took off, and apart from a brief spell in the 1970s it has been in print ever since.

If anybody could tell what qualities a book requires to succeed in this way, he would be a millionaire; it is only possible to speculate. With hindsight, however, it is possible to single out three advantages which *An Experiment with Time* had over the countless books on psychic, occult and esoteric phenomena which were published between the wars; one of them being that Dunne took care in his introduction to insist that it was *not* in any of those categories (he added that it was not about psychoanalysis, either; a reminder that Freud was then widely regarded as a cross between Cagliostro and Svengali). Readers who would not have gone beyond the first page if they thought they were being lured up any psychic path were consequently reassured.

The book's second merit was that Dunne clearly was not sensationalising his material: very much the reverse. He related some sensational dreams; but he was careful to treat them coolly. One concerned a nightmare he had had in a remote army camp in South Africa:

> I seemed to be standing on high ground – the upper slopes of some spur of a hill or mountain. The ground was of a curious white formation. Here and there in this there were little fissures, and from these, jets of vapour were spouting upwards. In my dream I recognised the place as an island of which I had dreamed before – an island which was in imminent peril from a volcano. And when I saw the vapour spouting from the ground, I gasped: 'It's the island! Good Lord, the whole thing is going to *blow up*!' For I had memories of reading about Krakatoa, where the sea, making its way into the heart of a volcano through a submarine crevice, flushed into steam, and blew the whole mountain to pieces. Forthwith I was seized with a frantic desire to save the four thousand (I knew the number) unsuspecting inhabitants.

And the nightmare had become worse as he found that the authorities – they were French – would not listen to his plea to evacuate the inhabitants.

A few days later, a batch of papers arrived at the camp; and in one of them, the *Daily Telegraph*, the centre spread caught his eye.

VOLCANO DISASTER IN MARTINIQUE
TOWN SWEPT AWAY
AN AVALANCHE OF FLAME
PROBABLE LOSS OF OVER 40,000 LIVES

> One of the most terrible disasters in the annals of the world has befallen the once prosperous town of St Pierre, the commercial capital of the French island of Martinique in the West Indies. At eight o'clock on Thursday morning the volcano Mont Pelée, which had been quiescent for a century . . .

and in another column there was a headline

A MOUNTAIN EXPLODES

– the eye-witness describing how Mont Pelée appeared to split open all down the side.

Dunne was careful to make the point that his dream had not been entirely accurate. The newspaper headline had estimated 40,000 deaths.

> I was out by a nought. But, when I read the paper, I read, in my haste, that number as 4000; and in telling the story subsequently, I always spoke of the printed figure as having been 4000; and I did not know it was really 40,000 until I copied out the paragraph fifteen years later.

The actual mortality figures in fact bore no resemblance either to his figure or to the newspaper's, which led him to wonder whether he might not have been a victim of what had been called 'identifying paramnesia', one of the hypotheses psychologists had presented to explain *déjà vu*, 'I have been here before', experiences; the idea being that reading the newspaper report had put a false idea that he had had the dream into his mind. But soon, he found that identifying paramnesia simply could not account for his glimpses of the future, because he became careful to recall his dreams on waking. And probably it was a piece of advice which he gave readers which was to be the third reason for the book's influence, and its subsequent staying power. Most people, Dunne knew, forget their dreams within seconds of waking. Even when dreams are remembered, it is usually only specific episodes which can be recalled; and the glimpses of the future might be among the forgotten trivia. The only way to ensure that they were not missed was to keep a pad and a pencil handy: 'Immediately on waking, before you even open your eyes, you set yourself to remember the rapidly vanishing dream.'

That many of his readers did, and that some of them were successful, was to be discovered years later by J. B. Priestley, who had been greatly influenced by the book. On a TV programme, he asked viewers to send in examples of any experiences they might have had which would challenge the conventional view of Time. Replies poured in, and they revealed how many people had followed Dunne's advice. If they had not done so, Priestley estimated, 'a third of the best precognitive dreams I have been sent would never have come my way'.

The SPR in Decline

Dunne's glimpses of the future in his dreams, sometimes dramatic, often trivial, prompted him to ask himself a question. Were they, as they had been regarded, abnormal – psychic? Might it not be 'that dreams – dreams in general, all dreams, everybody's dreams – were composed of *images of past experience and images of future experience, blended together in approximately equal proportions?*' And if so, might not the standard notion of the future as inaccessible be 'due to a purely mentally-imposed barrier which existed only when we were awake?' There must, Dunne decided, be a second self. We do not, after all, merely observe what is happening around us; we observe that we observe what is happening. From this he constructed a theory which enabled him to present the second self, the observer in the background, as being capable of moving forward as well as backward in Time, but only able to get the information across to us, scrappily, in dreams and visions, when the mentally-imposed barrier is lifted.

Dunne's 'serialism' sounded impressive, backed as it was with mathematical formulae; but to the great majority of his readers it was incomprehensible, and the tiny minority who claimed to understand it rejected it. The dreams themselves, however, could be held to constitute evidence for psychic precognition, regardless of Dunne's disapproval; as they were by Dame Edith Lyttelton.

Dame Edith Lyttelton

Edith Lyttelton was yet another member of the Balfour family, though a different branch from Eleanor Sidgwick's. The widow of a former Colonial Secretary, she had made a career for herself in various social activities; as a tireless worker on behalf of refugees, as one of the promoters of the English-Speaking Union, and as a British delegate to the League of Nations. She had been a member of the SPR for many years – as 'Mrs King' had been one of its contributing automatists (it was she who, before the war broke out, had written 'Lusitania' adding 'Foam and fire'); and she had joined the SPR Council in 1928. Although on the Cambridge side of the, by this time, barbed-wire fence between the High-and-Dry and the rest, her book *Our Superconscious Mind*, published in 1931, showed her to have a breadth of vision which could help to resolve some of the conflicts which were racking the society.

Our Superconscious Mind could have been read as a tactful reminder to members of the SPR that their proper function was not, as too many of them seemed to assume, to test mediums to destruction and then delight in their exposure, but instead to follow Myers's course, and begin to prospect for gold ore among the dross of the subliminal mind. 'Superconscious' was a term she had thought up for the ore-bearing seam herself; but after she had finished the first draft, she found that it had in fact been used earlier by one of 'Feda's' 'communicators', Drayton Thomas's father:

> All your mind is not in or acting upon your brain at once. You have your conscious and subconscious mind . . . I think that a better term for subconscious would be superconscious, for 'sub' suggests that which is under, a subservient mind, which it is not. It is the more powerful of the two. I would rather speak of it as the *over*-mind and not the under-mind.

Edith Lyttelton's thesis, briefly stated, was that 'the unconscious mind has a wider range of knowledge than the conscious mind' and that certain manifestations seemed to her 'to reveal the existence of a superconsciousness as well as a subconsciousness' (such divisions, she agreed, might be arbitrary, but they were convenient). Clairvoyant or precognitive dreams, hallucinations of sight or hearing, automatic writing and mediumship might sometimes be evidence of forgotten memory – cryptomnesia; but they could also be the mechanism 'by which the message or the knowledge of the superconscious mind is conveyed to the conscious mind'; and her book was designed primarily to give examples of the superconscious at work, providing information – usually trivial, but sometimes valuable – of a kind which could not have been obtained through the normal senses, 'such as knowledge of what is passing, or has passed, at a distance in time or space; what is about to happen; and the kind of vision which is either called prophecy or inspiration'.

She had herself been given an example, she recalled, by Mrs Rogers – formerly Mrs Curran, whose automatism was still relaying the utterances of 'Patience Worth'. A few hours after arriving in St Louis, Edith Lyttelton had been confronted with 'a remarkable instance of superconscious knowledge, expressed without hesitation in verse – knowledge relating to myself which could not possibly have been in Mrs Rogers's normal consciousness'. It was of too intimate a nature to repeat; Edith Lyttelton felt, in fact, that 'Patience Worth' – or Mrs Rogers's superconscious – knew too much about her for comfort. Still, she could testify that the material was of a high literary quality. 'Judged by any standard,' she claimed, there was 'a singular beauty and originality in many of her sayings and some of her poetry; and in all her work, diffuse and obscure as much of it is, occur flashes of insight and passages of beauty, making her a good example of a medium who, had she possessed a better-organised normal brain, would have been acclaimed as a genius.'

Edith Lyttelton gave other examples of trance poetry, including one by a writer who was not a professional medium, but who occasionally went into 'a sort of dreamlike state', in which he spoke, and composed prose and verse, while hardly remembering afterwards what he had said or written. His belief was that a discarnate personality was responsible, trying to explain why communication from the other side was so difficult:

> To all who wait, blindfolded by the flesh
> Upon the stammered promise that we give
> Tangling ourselves in the material mesh
> A moment while we tell you that we live,
> Greeting and reassurance; never doubt
> That the slow tidings of our joyful state,
> So hardly given, so haltingly made out,
> Are but the creaking hinges of the gate . . .
> Beyond, the garden lies; and as we turn
> Wond'ring how much you hear, how much you guess
> Once more the roses of glad service burn
> With hues of loving thought and thankfulness;
>
> Once more we move among them, strong and free,
> Marvelling yet in our felicity

The value of the superconscious mind was not limited to its artistic productions, Edith Lyttelton insisted. It could act as a protector – much as Socrates' daimon, or the guardian angels of the Christian tradition, had been reputed to do. Twenty years before a friend of hers, a countess, had suddenly had an overwhelming feeling that she must stop a man she knew from going on a projected sea trip. Pushing the idea aside, she had gone for a walk from her London hotel; and 'almost without being aware of what she was doing, she found herself in a post office, and this time she yielded to her impulse and telegraphed her friend. The ship he would have been on sank, with only one survivor.'

Edith Lyttelton knew enough about the SPR to realise that a tale of that kind would be dismissed with a shrug unless backed by attestations; and she had asked the countess whether it would be

Science and Parascience

possible to obtain confirmation from the friend whose life had in all probability been saved. It was: he replied to her letter recalling how he had actually paid for his ticket, and was about to join the ship when he received her telegram. Although he could not remember what she had said, it had persuaded him to give up the idea; 'You may imagine what I felt when I read in the papers that the ship had been lost, only one man saved.' From the company's records, Edith Lyttelton confirmed that the story of the wreck was accurate.

Whence came this superconscious information, these superconscious abilities? From the spirit world? Or from some source within us? Edith Lyttelton preferred the inner source hypothesis. 'Once the idea is firmly grasped that part of our being is in possession of knowledge of which another part is not conscious,' she argued, 'and that occasionally fragments of that knowledge reach our consciousness in various and undependable ways, much of the confusion and some of the contradictory results of psychical happenings are accounted for.' Among them, she suggested, was 'dramatisation' by a secondary personality, such as 'Feda'. The mixture of truth and fiction that such personalities purveyed had commonly been attributed in the past to the struggle between good and evil spirits, or to delusion, or to the fact that the communicating spirit's message was garbled in transit. If she had to make a choice, she would prefer the last interpretation; 'but if we concentrate on the idea that a part of our own mind is the transmitter, and for some reason cannot be understood by the conscious mind in a normal way, but has to resort to all sorts of devices, some clumsy, some obscure, some clear enough, like dramatisation, but all essentially unreliable, we begin to have an idea of the complexity of the process'. She was not, she insisted, rejecting the possibility that disembodied intelligences might also be at work; the superconscious portion of the mind might be in touch with them, and transmit their communications. But the trivial nature of so many of the communications pointed 'not to messages from the discarnate, but to communications from a part of our own mind'.

To Edith Lyttelton, precognition was just another demonstration of the psychic power of the superconscious mind; and in her book, she reported the case of a man she knew who had eight precognitive dreams 'of little individual value, but when taken together confirmed the evidence collected by Mr Dunne'. The best had been a dream of being alone in the middle of an empty street when a car suddenly swept by, just missing him. A month later, finding himself alone in the middle of the crossing of Cannon Street and Queen Victoria Street, he noticed that they were empty of traffic and pedestrians, and recalled his dream. 'Suddenly a car rushed in on my left, and turned towards me, and it was almost upon me before I realised I must get out of its way.' It was not the fact he was nearly run over that impressed the narrator – that might easily happen to anybody walking in the city: it was that 'such an isolation in the middle of a busy thoroughfare is very rare'.

In *L'Avenir et la Prémonition*, also published in 1931, Richet took a similar line, providing about one hundred and fifty case histories of precognition, which he defined as 'knowledge of the future by means other than the ordinary sensory channels'. Lodge, in his Presidential Address the following year, sought to redress the balance in favour of spirit communication of the future, by citing an experience of his own when a medium had given him an uncannily accurate picture of what the future held for him:

> A church door and some other details were mentioned as belonging to a house in which it was said I was going to live, and in which I am now living. The prediction was made at a time when I knew nothing of the existence of the house and when, as afterwards transpired, no door was there. A church door was independently, and so to speak accidentally, added by the landlord, who was not the landlord at the time of the prediction, and who knew nothing about it. Nor did I know anything about the house or enter into its occupancy until a period of some seven years had elapsed.

Such incidents, he remarked, could hardly be explained as prediction based on inference; 'They may possibly be contemplated in terms of planning, but it would need to be a supernormal planning on the part of intelligences in a spiritual world.'

For the High-and-Dry element in the SPR, however, dreams of the kind Dunne described were not evidence of a kind which they cared to accept. Doubtless, too they were irritated that in his introduction he should have been dismissive of psychical research. S. G. Soal gave *An Experiment with Time* a sniffy review, lamenting that the author had failed to take the elementary (by SPR standards) precaution of getting his written accounts of his dreams attested before the events which they foreshadowed had come to pass. All that Soal would concede was that the method Dunne advocated for dream recall could be useful if proper attention was paid to corroboration and evaluation; and Besterman set up a trial, in which SPR members were invited to emulate Dunne, using the proper precautions. Out of forty-five possibles sent in, Besterman reported, eighteen dreams might be held to provide some prima facie evidence for precognition; but of these only two provided good evidence, and his personal opinion was that the results were inconclusive. Dunne, perhaps relieved that the SPR was not going to muscle in on his territory, contented himself with complaining that Besterman had not given members the correct instructions.

Neither the critical attitude of the SPR nor Dunne's determination to keep precognitive dreams out of the psychic category made any difference to the public's reaction. Precognition continued to be regarded as psychic; Dunne's account of his dreams continued to carry conviction, in spite of his failure to have them attested. Perhaps even more influential than *An Experiment with Time* itself were the plays which Priestley wrote around the Time theme in the 1930s: *Dangerous Corner*, *I Have Been Here Before*, and in particular *Time and the Conways*, a West End hit in 1937.

Having lunch with his sister and discussing old friends – Priestley was to recall in *Rain upon Godshill* – 'suddenly I saw that there was a play in the relation between a fairly typical middle-class family and the theory of Time, the theory chiefly associated with J. W. Dunne, over which I had been brooding for the past two years'. The play almost wrote itself; 'it seemed to cost me no more thought and trouble than if I were dashing off a letter to an old friend', and the complex second act, in particular, written in a couple of days, was to be produced as he had written it with scarcely a correction. In that act the action moved forward to 1937; the Time warp was that in the third act, it moved back to the year where the play had started in the first, in 1919. Although Priestley did not try to explain Dunne's serialism through his characters, the basic notion was put across, and very effectively; *Time and the Conways* has remained a repertory standby ever since, as well as enjoying a West End revival and a TV showing, thrusting precognition into the minds of great numbers of people who would never have read Dunne's book.

7 Mind over matter

Aware that the SPR was in difficulties, Harry Price thought to take advantage of the situation by offering to merge his National Laboratory with the society. When the offer was rejected by the SPR Council, he moved over to the attack, seeking to have its ruling overturned at its next meeting. And although this move also failed he had had a stroke of luck, which he was now able to exploit. 'Stella C.', who had been his most successful subject, had married and ceased to give seances; he badly needed a replacement. In 1929, Schrenck died; and Price seized the opportunity to take on his star subject, Willy Schneider's brother Rudi.

This was made easier by the fact that Schrenck's method had been virtually to adopt the brothers. He had dominated psychical research in Germany for many years, thanks largely to the wealth which marriage had brought him; he had subsidised and edited the *Zeitschrift*; and although there were able young researchers, notably Tischner and Oesterreich, in Germany, he had continued to conduct his own research in his own way, concentrating on testing individual mediums.

The waning of Willy's powers had caused Schrenck and his associates little concern, because Rudi had shown similar psychic capabilities, and was as willing as his brother had been to have them tested. The phenomena were much the same: movements of objects at a distance; draughts of cold air; the touching or nudging of sitters. In addition, in the early stages of his career Rudi almost invariably levitated; and his phenomena in general were even more striking than Willy's. 'Bells and a cardboard figure named "August" would sail through the air,' the original records of the seances, later transcribed by Anita Gregory, showed. 'A broken-down musical box would play, a typewriter would type by itself, invisible hands would trim a bonnet, a boot would be torn off a foot with some violence, windows would be shattered, and a "hand", visible or otherwise, might be described as playing tug-of-war with an object such as a wastepaper basket, or a handkerchief, which might be torn in half by the struggle.' Rudi had been tested by

Science and Parascience

Schrenck and a number of other investigators, most of whom found no reason to suspect that he might be using sleight of hand; and examining the allegations which a few witnesses made, Mrs Gregory found that none of them could be taken seriously.

The one which had attracted most attention was a claim by two professors at the University of Vienna that they had 'exposed' Rudi. All they had in fact done was provide a simulation of the phenomena; and they had been able to provide it only by dispensing with the controls that were always employed by Schrenck. Taxed with this deception, they had to admit it. More damaging, at first sight, was that Walter Prince, on a visit to Europe, came to the conclusion after attending tests that sleight of hand was being employed. But he did not actually detect Rudi in any trickery; and in view of his long-standing prejudice against physical mediumship it seems reasonable to suppose that his mind was still closed. To have accepted that Rudi was genuine simply because he could think of no way in which the medium could be cheating, after all, could have been interpreted as an admission that he might have been wrong about 'Margery'; he had never been able to catch her out, either. And although it was surprising that Malcolm Bird, too, should have been sceptical about Rudi, Bird attended only one sitting, and his explanation of the way in which he thought the manifestations might have been faked – that a confederate had been admitted in the seance room – merely indicated incompetence on his part, as he was supposed to have made sure that the door was locked and sealed.

For years, Rudi had continued to produce physical phenomena at seances; but in Britain, thanks largely to the Cambridge nucleus's hostility, his reputation was little known. Price, however, had attended seances with him, and had been impressed; and hearing of Schrenck's death he went immediately to Germany to offer to take Schrenck's place – even, up to a point, to take on his guardianship: Rudi was to call him 'Onkel'.

No medium had ever had the publicity which Rudi, thanks to Price's contacts with the press, enjoyed on his first visit to Britain in the spring of 1929, when he gave six seances. The reports in popular newspapers, usually so ready to find an excuse to jeer at (or denounce) mediums, were friendly; and Price was adept at finding ways to obtain additional publicity, such as issuing a £1000 challenge to conjurors to perform the same feats, under the same controlled conditions. There were no takers; but when the second series was held later in the year Will Goldston, President of the

Magicians' Club, publicly admitted his conviction that 'no group of my fellow magicians could have produced those effects under those conditions'. Over a hundred people in all, including some well-known scientists, attended the two series, and although Rudi's effects were not so striking as they had been five years earlier, the movements of objects at a distance were well defined, and none of the sitters publicly expressed any doubts. 'If Rudi were "exposed" a hundred times in the future,' Price felt able to claim, 'it would not invalidate or affect to the slightest degree our considered judgment that the boy has produced genuine abnormal phenomena.'

The press publicity, and Price's biography *Rudi Schneider*, gave Price a lead over the SPR in the public estimation. 'There is not a man, woman or child in Great Britain,' he boasted, 'who has not read about Rudi, his phenomena, and the conditions controlling the experiments.' At the same time, he was able to deliver a back-hander to the SPR – 'the British public has learnt more about scientific psychical research in the last few months than it did in the previous fifty years' – while distancing himself from 'the mire of charlatanry'; the public was at last beginning 'to realise the difference between modern organised scientific psychical research and "spiritualism"'.

The Besterman Rumpus

At this point, the new year of 1930, Price had good reason to hope that what was emerging as his main ambition – to set up a psychical research organisation in which all others would merge – might be fulfilled, as the SPR appeared to be falling apart. At the Annual General Meeting on 26 February, with Lodge in the Chair, Dingwall moved a resolution 'that this meeting views with grave concern the decline in the prestige of the Society both at home and abroad, and is of the opinion that a change in the administration is desirable'; and although the proposal was rejected on a show of hands 'by an overwhelming majority', it was becoming increasingly unlikely that the society could survive under its established leadership. And at this critical stage, 'that young swine Besterman', as Price described him, provoked another crisis by rushing into print with *Some Modern Mediums*, a brash and superficial survey of physical mediumship based on a short tour of the Continent he had made the year before, which also disparaged the research which Richet, Schrenck, Geley and others had carried on earlier.

Science and Parascience

Besterman's treatment of 'Eva C.' was typical. He had simply dredged up the allegations which had been made against her by Gulat-Wellenburg and others, ignoring the rebuttals. 'I do not say that "Eva C." did the things I have suggested she may have done,' he oleaginously claimed. 'All I maintain is that the things I have described *could* easily have been done.' Her mediumship, he concluded, 'if not conceived in deliberate fraud, was certainly continued in fraud, lived its life in fraud, and ended in fraud'.

Besterman provided no evidence to sustain this very damaging allegation – the reasons he made it did not become known for many years; but the full story, when it eventually emerged, provided a telling illustration of the self-destructive tendency which the Podmore attitude engendered among psychical researchers, leading to a willingness to believe, and almost to expect, the worst of other psychical researchers, however distinguished, on flimsy grounds. In this case, suspicion had been aroused retrospectively about 'Eva C.' when Osty, who had not been involved in testing her, took over the Institut Métapsychique after Geley's death and found some photographs which appeared to show that some of the materialisations had been faked – attached to her by threads, or wires. He showed them to some psychical researchers, but did not publish them; on the advice, he claimed, of Schrenck and Richet. Thirty years later Rudolf Lambert, a German who had been a psychical researcher in the 1920s, explained what had happened in a letter to the society. According to Lambert, Osty had shown him the photographs but pledged him to secrecy about them on the ground that it would be disastrous if the story reached the ears of the 'dangerous negativist', Count Perovsky, whose prejudice against physical phenomena was notorious. 'Eva C.' by this time had left mediumship, to marry; but so certain was Osty that Mme Bisson had been involved with her in fraud that he had excluded her from the third international conference, held in Paris in 1927. Inevitably the rumour had spread that she and 'Eva C.' had been exposed, leading Perovsky to demand unsuccessfully to be told what was going on. Perovsky's death in 1954, Lambert claimed, released him from his pledge.

Lambert's letter appeared to settle the issue. The photographs Osty had found must surely have shown that the phenomena had been faked. All the research carried out with Marthe Béraud in her role as 'Eva C.', it was assumed, must be set aside as discredited. Yet as Lambert himself unwittingly disclosed, the assumption that Geley had suppressed the photographs because they showed that

'Eva C.' cheated was unjustified. Many of the photographs which Mme Bisson and Schrenck had used in their books, after all, had given the strong impression of faking; Schrenck himself had noted and commented upon that fact – with, as Lambert admitted, 'surprising frankness'. And judging by the photographs Osty had shown him, Lambert had to concede that in the main, 'no stronger suspicions attached to Mme Bisson after Osty's discovery than at the time of Schrenck's publications'. In other words, though this had clearly not occurred to Lambert, no more suspicion should have attached itself to Madame Bisson and 'Eva C.' after Osty's discovery of the photographs than it had before.

Osty's mistake, assuming Lambert's recollection was reliable, had been to consider the photographs without reference to any accompanying text. This was all the more unwise in that Richet had specifically warned against it, from his own long experience. Photographs could provide useful testimony, he had observed; but those taken of psychic phenomena often looked spurious, and in any case they could be 'so skilfully counterfeited that I should make no conclusions at all on any such shown to me, unless the circumstances under which they were produced were given with such precise detail as to make all trickery impossible'.

Lambert, too, was being misleading when he claimed to have kept quiet about the photographs: it was he who had told Besterman about them, giving Besterman the excuse to denounce 'Eva C.' and by implication denigrate those who had investigated her; and as R. H. Thouless pointed out when Lambert's account appeared in the SPR *Journal*, he had waited until all those who could have challenged his version were dead. But even if that version were substantially correct, there were other possible explanations for Geley's decision not to publish the photographs; the most plausible being simply that Geley had already filled his books with such pictures, some of them just as suspicious-looking.

The outcome, however, was that 'Eva C.' was effectively discredited in psychical research circles, along with her investigators. Yet again, as with 'Margery' and others: if 'Eva C.' were so supremely skilful a conjuror, able to deceive scores of investigators week after week for twenty years without ever being detected in trickery, why did she put up with all the humiliations imposed upon her in the form of controls, for no financial benefit except the bed and board provided by Mme Bisson, unless she hoped to establish the genuineness of the phenomena?

In a letter to Schrenck, written in the course of the London series, she told him that she had grown weary of the investigations. As three out of the first five seances had produced some positive results, she was still hopeful; but her chief hope was that this series would finally settle the issue. She had done her best, she felt, for science: there was nothing more she could humanly do. It had often required courage, because her investigators were not always considerate and the controls imposed on her were painful, 'for I am really a bit of a savage, and all these exhibitions of my person are really hateful'. She had accepted all the conditions, as she realised they were necessary; but 'after this, I believe I shall have done my duty'. She had, indeed. All her investigators, even the contemptuous Sorbonne group, had paid tribute to her co-operativeness. But now, her labours had brought psychical research no advantage. On the contrary, she appeared to have added yet another black mark against it.

Osty at least realised that 'Eva C.' could not have produced her phenomena unaided; but all that this meant was that Mme Bisson's years of research were taken to testify only to their collusion in fraud. Again: to what purpose? Mme Bisson had obtained even less credit than 'Eva C.', and an equal share of suspicion and derision. The most plausible explanation why she persevered after 1914 is that, with 'Eva C.', she felt that she must demonstrate that the phenomena were genuine. If they were not, the two of them could have made a fortune, and been far more widely acclaimed, as magicians.

In any case, what Osty had not realised – he had not himself been involved in the trials – was that the phenomena had been witnessed and photographed at times when Mme Bisson, there to hypnotise Marthe, had not been present at the seances. Or perhaps Osty did realise this, but also realised that to admit it would be tantamount to admitting that Geley, too, must have been involved, along with Richet, Schrenck and others, which he could not accept. Yet ironically, he did just as much damage by fostering suspicions of 'Eva C.' and Mme Bisson. Geley could henceforth be condemned both as a dupe, for allowing them to fool him for so long, and as a rogue, for suppressing the photographic evidence of their dishonesty.

The SPR Indicted

Besterman's contemptuous dismissal of the researches of Richet, Schrenck and Geley would ordinarily have been regarded as his own business: the SPR did not hold corporate opinions, and its members were free to express their own views on such matters. But as he was in charge of the society's publications, Besterman was in an invidious position. 'The utterances of the editor of the SPR,' Stanley de Brath observed, 'inevitably react on the Society which has appointed him, and whose matured opinion he is naturally held to represent.'

Besterman's work was far from mature; his essays, de Brath complained in a letter to H. Dennis Bradley, were the 'hasty impressions of a young man who presents his suspicions as universal fact'. Bradley himself had good reason to be indignant. Something of a loner, he had put in a great deal of work over the previous decade investigating mediums, and had little positive to show for it. Now, here was this whippersnapper presenting himself as an expert after spending a mere four months investigating them.

In a broadside, *An indictment of the present administration of the Society for Psychical Research*, Bradley had no difficulty in showing that the book was a travesty. Besterman dealt at length only with five mediums, and of these he had himself actually investigated only two. His account not merely revealed his inexperience, but showed he had been 'utterly incompetent', his approach being that of a representative of an amateur detective agency 'obviously predisposed to regard all forms of phenomena as doubtful or fraudulent'. The book, however, was for Bradley chiefly an excuse to enable him to belabour the society – one of the obstacles, he complained, in the way of scientific research.

> It possesses a seance room which is never used. Never does it hold sittings; never does it conduct investigations. All published accounts of phenomena it treats with contempt, and never does it attempt analysis or constructive criticism. In its bovine incredulity this pseudo-scientific Society appears to me to be equally as stupid as are the great bulk of spiritualists in their credulity.

Here, then, was Price's opportunity. Although the council of the SPR had denied that Doyle's defection had led to any serious falling-away of support, membership was declining: in 1930 it had little more than half its 1920 total, and this latest row might drive more members over to the National Laboratory. Yet it was at this critical stage that Price began to lose the initiative he had won. Rudi Schneider had been invited by Osty for trials at the Institut Métapsychique; and he was succeeding under conditions more calculated to impress scientists than those under which Price had tested him. Doubtful as Osty had been about physical mediumship, he had perfected a gadget which, he had decided, could settle the issue one way or the other; and so far as he was concerned, it had.

In his Frederic Myers Lecture to the SPR in 1933, Osty was to describe how with the help of his son, Marcel, a physicist and technician, he had been able to install apparatus 'capable of registering photographically, automatically and at great speed', any telekinetic phenomena produced by mediums in total darkness. Two types of rays were employed: infra-red, 'to guard the object it was hoped to have displaced'; and ultra-violet for the photography. An infra-red projector directed an invisible beam, reflected by mirrors placed in different positions, at a photoelectric cell; the cell controlled the opening of a shutter to flood the laboratory with ultra-violet for a tenth of a second, simultaneously causing a photograph to be taken. The photographs would give away a medium (or any sitter) who used physical force; and if objects were moved at a distance, the infra-red apparatus might give some clue to the identity of the force which was moving them.

The 1931 trials with Rudi pointed to the existence of a telekinetic force emanating from him. He 'exteriorises, in the direction of the object to be displaced, an energy which is not photographable by white light and which is not visible', Osty explained; but it 'behaved like an invisible substance which arrests a varying proportion of certain infra-red radiations'. It had been 'very moving', during the early sittings, when an electric bell inserted into the relay circuit gave warning that the invisible telekinetic substance was entering into the infra-red, while at the same time the medium could be heard describing what he was doing and feeling; and to check afterwards from the photographs that he was in his place, and that there was no visible source of interference with the infra-red rays. There was no way by which the medium could have cheated, even if he had known the disposition and direction of the rays, which were varied for each session; the camera would have betrayed him. In any case the telekinetic interruption of the infra-red took a different form from physical interruptions. The only persons who could be suspected of fraud, Osty had been able confidently to claim, were the investigators themselves – 'that is, my son and I'.

On past experience, they would certainly be suspected; but the combination of photography and infra-red would at least make it virtually impossible for anybody with sufficient knowledge of the apparatus involved who attended a seance to doubt the validity of the phenomena, if they occurred. And paradoxically, the man to whom this discovery was least welcome was not a sceptic, but Harry Price, who felt that his earlier work with Rudi was correspondingly devalued.

In furtherance of his design to have a monolithic psychical research organisation, Price in 1929 had offered to merge his National Laboratory with the Institut Métapsychique, an offering which Osty had politely turned down; and their relations, previously cordial, had soured. It did not improve matters when Osty ignored Price's signals, in his letters, intimating his wish to be present at the seances with Rudi. And what made things worse was that Besterman, who had been critical of Price's trials with Rudi, had finally been won over by Osty's. 'Although as you know I have not hesitated to express myself in very critical terms of paraphysical phenomena as such, I must acknowledge myself convinced,' he wrote to tell Osty. 'On the basis of your report I am fully persuaded of the genuineness of the phenomena.'

The 1932 Trials

Price had been upstaged, and he did not like it. Nor did he care for Rudi's growing independence. Rudi had acquired a fiancée, Fräulein Mitzi Mängl; and when Price proposed a third series of trials in London, Rudi refused to come unless she came too. Price jibbed, on the ground of expense; but he must subsequently have reflected that this would be handing Rudi over to Osty, and perhaps also to the SPR. Early in 1932 he gave way, and Rudi and Mitzi arrived again in London.

For this third series Price had installed an automatic camera, designed to take pictures whenever objects moved; and on 22 March, Dr C. C. L. Gregory, Head of the Department of Astronomy at London University, and a research student, C. V. C. Herbert – later Earl of Powis – brought along an infra-red installation, to see whether Rudi could repeat his Paris success. He did. Blank sessions were becoming increasingly frequent, but occasionally Rudi succeeded in moving objects at a distance, tying a handkerchief in a knot, and producing faint materialisations, while photographs revealed him slumped in a trance in his chair; and a telekinetic force was registered on the apparatus.

In the course of the series, however, a row broke out in Price's organisation which was to wreck his prospects for restoring his reputation as Rudi's impresario. It arose out of Price's growing hunger to have his name and his work constantly in the public eye, which had led him to embark on two projects that were to bring him more publicity even than he had obtained over Rudi: the investigation of the haunted Borley rectory; and an ascent of the Brocken mountain, to test an old Walpurgisnacht legend attached to it. And for the Borley research, he had brought along Lord Charles Hope.

Hope had been content to stay in the background; the full extent of his involvement in psychical research was not made apparent, in fact, until Anita Gregory's 'Anatomy of a Fraud' was published in *Annals of Science* nearly half a century later. 'Few people,' she wrote, 'were, or are, aware of the years of effort and patience, and of the large sums of money, that he devoted to psychical research'; his correspondence in this period 'bears eloquent testimony to his industry, his accuracy, his tact, his caution and his scrupulous fairness'. He was initially drawn to Price because Price was at least active, while the SPR appeared moribund. But on his first visit to Borley with Price, something aroused his suspicion that Price was not above assisting the production of psychic phenomena with the help of physical force.

How far psychical researchers had already come to realise that Price was not to be trusted as an investigator is hard to judge, as suspicions could not be published, and might be unwise to express even in correspondence. Conan Doyle had smelled him out, Gagool-fashion, two years before, telling Osty about a seance during which he had decided that Price must have been cheating; and in a letter to W. H. Salter following the publication of Price's *Rudi Schneider* in 1930 Mrs Sidgwick, too, surmised that Price might have had a confederate to help fake the manifestations at the London sessions – though in view of her attitude to physical mediums, she might have made the same charge against anybody who had presented the same evidence as Price did.

Fearing that further trials with Price might compromise both Rudi and himself, Hope decided that to be on the safe side he would set up a series with Rudi independently. Taking advantage of Rudi's presence in London, he arranged to hold it with Lord Rayleigh – the physicist, who was following with such distinction in his father's footsteps – that autumn. Hearing about the arrangement, Price denounced Hope for conspiring against him; 'it is like the host at a dinner party having his throat cut by his guests'; and at an angry meeting of the Council of Price's National Laboratory, Hope resigned.

The loss of Hope's support, however, was quickly counterbalanced by the gain of an important new recruit: Dr William Brown, Wilde Reader in Mental Philosophy at Oxford, a consultant of the Bethlem Royal Hospital, and the author of a number of works on psychology and psychotherapy. Brown was in the Vitalist tradition of Myers and McCullough; in 1927, when he was President of the Psychology section of the British Association, he had not hesitated to discuss psychic phenomena in his paper at that year's meeting on 'mental unity and mental dissociation'.

The following year he had returned to the subject in lectures given at Yale, later published as *Science and Personality*; it had two chapters on 'Personality and Psychical Research' in which Brown described some of his own experiences, notably some sittings with Mrs Leonard which had greatly impressed him. Although he was sure she could not have known who he was, 'Feda' clearly did, as the four 'communicators' she produced were 'just the four people I would be interested in hearing from. There are very few people on the other side that would interest me, but these four certainly would.' As usual, there was some material that was wrong, and some that could not be checked, but a sizeable proportion was so convincing that Brown had been compelled to rate it 'far beyond the possibility of chance'. On whether the communication was telepathic, or spiritist, or a mixture of both, he was not prepared to be dogmatic. Still,

> as regards the telepathy part of it, what one feels is that there is so much that might be expected to come through telepathy – emotional experiences that you are only too anxious to hear of again, just the sort of things that would move you most – and these are just the things that you do not get. All through, you have the feeling that the person on the other side is trying to find something that isn't obvious to your own mind.

Brown's book had struck Lodge as 'extraordinarily well-informed'; seldom, he had noted, 'do we find a writer apparently almost equally at home in psychology, mathematical physics and psychical research'. For Price to have persuaded Brown to come to a session with Rudi was itself encouraging, as psychologists who would risk identifying themselves with far-out psychical research were rare. But he came, and was so greatly impressed that Price managed to persuade him to write to *The Times*, describing what he had witnessed: curtains billowing about, a cold breeze, and 'a loud bang from a far corner of the room' – when the lights were turned up, they found that the detachable top of a table there 'had been hurled over our heads'. Brown had found no evidence of trickery, but rather a strong sensation of 'a power for which I could imagine no mechanical or pneumatic contrivance was a cause'; undoubtedly the phenomena were 'worthy of the closest scientific investigation'.

To Price's huge delight, not merely did Brown's letter appear in *The Times* on 7 May, it was followed up by another from a witness who had also attended seances; Dr D. Fraser-Harris, a former Professor of Physiology and a well-known authority on the working of the body's senses. Fraser-Harris described how what might have been invisible hands had tugged a basket out of his grasp, and placed a cigarette in his fingers. He wanted to make it clear that he was 'not a "Spiritualist"', but he had seen enough to convince him that there was a need for more research; not the least convincing part, to him, being that two out of every three seances in the series had been blank, 'not at all what one would expect from a fraudulent person'.

Price had never before seen his work featuring in so prestigious a medium. It constituted, he boasted, 'the commencement of a new epoch in psychical research'. His delight was to be short-lived. The time had come for the most spectacular of his publicity stunts to take place, based on the legend that if a goat and a virgin were brought together on the Brocken at midnight, with the appropriate mumbo-jumbo, the goat would change into a handsome young man. That Price was claiming that he wanted to prove the legend to be a superstition can have fooled nobody, but the venture was ridiculous enough to attract coverage in the popular press, thereby wrecking Price's chances of establishing his National Laboratory as a scientific institution, and leaving the scientists who had been working with him in the lurch.

'Dr Brown has since been having rather a time of it at Oxford,' Hope wrote to tell Gregory on 13 May, 'being laughed at by Lindemann and even Einstein, among others. Of course they will not ever hear of such phenomena being genuine.' Brown, abashed, wrote a further letter to *The Times* in which although he reiterated his point about Rudi's manifestations being worthy of the closest scientific study, he added the qualification 'whether genuine or spurious'; urged the necessity for 'much more stringent scientific investigation'; and suggested it might be carried out at the SPR –

all of which was calculated to enrage Price, who wrote him a furious letter.

Price, however, could not now avoid his Walpurgisnacht. Accompanied by C. E. M. Joad – head of the Department of Philosophy at Birkbeck College, and later to be one of the pundits of the BBC's 'Brains Trust' – along with over a hundred assorted reporters, feature writers and photographers, the virgin, and the goat, the farcical Brocken ceremony went off, to the accompaniment of a fanfare of internationally hilarious publicity. Nothing happened.

The Hope/Rayleigh Series

Had Price not succumbed to the heady attraction of being constantly in the news, his National Laboratory would by this time have been well placed to win over many SPR dissidents. But he now had to make the decision whether to play along with Osty in Paris, and Hope and Rayleigh in London, with the aim of restoring their confidence, or to fight them; and he chose to fight. He began to put it about that the results Osty had obtained with Rudi could not be relied upon, because he had allowed Rudi to bring his fiancée, Mitzi, with him to seances. This was correct; but as Osty pointed out, she had attended only a few, and 'before, during and after the brief interlude of his fiancée, Rudi produced identical phenomena' – whereas in London Price himself had 'let her assist at every seance'.

Price could do nothing to prevent the SPR from capturing Rudi, that autumn; Hope and Rayleigh held their series under its auspices. And although 'on the whole, the phenomena noted were weaker and less frequent than those reported as having taken place with the same medium elsewhere', Hope claimed 'the results obtained go far to support the claims put forward by Dr Osty'. As an additional precaution, Rudi had been enclosed in a specially constructed cage of wood and muslin, so that he was isolated both from the sitters – except for his controllers – and from the infra-red ray apparatus and the galvanometer. And Gregory and Fraser-Harris expressed themselves well satisfied with the new precautionary measures.

There were a few striking manifestations. While Rudi was being controlled by Fraser-Harris, Gregory heard a loud bump, and immediately the room was illuminated by the lamp which was the source of the infra-red beam. What had happened, it was then ascertained, was that the table which stood in front of the 'cabinet' had been turned upside down; this had caused the filter attachment to fall off. The outcome interested Hope, because with Rudi, as with other mediums, the 'control' – in this case 'Olga' – had warned against lights being put on as dangerous to the medium; and when the light came on, Rudi slumped to the floor. But when he recovered he did not know what had happened, and felt no ill-effects. 'Olga-Rudi', Hope thought, seemed disposed 'to blame "herself" more than us for the accident'.

For the most part, however, Fraser-Harris had the impression that his fellow-investigators were little concerned 'with spectacular experiences'. Their primary interest was in the effects registered on the instruments in use. The physicist Professor A. F. C. Pollard, who attended eight of the twenty-seven sittings, reported that on nearly every occasion there were movements of a galvanometer which, confirming as they did Osty's discovery, were 'very remarkable, and of greater scientific value than the telekinetic phenomena'. In addition 'the bell in series with a selenium cell rang on two or three occasions, indicating an absorption of at least 50 per cent of the infra-red radiation'. There could be no question of room tremors being responsible, 'since the tracings caused by interference due to the medium are *unilateral*, and can be picked out from such tremors or irregularities imposed on the zero line of the records by fluctuations of the voltage on the mains'. Similarly the variations of the current in the galvanometer circuit could not be due to any disturbance other than the absorption of the infrared radiation; 'in view of the distance of the medium from the apparatus and the fact that he was always under vigilant control [Pollard had himself acted a number of times as the controller] it would appear that this absorption is due to some agency, at present unknown, emanating from Rudi himself'.

Hope was preparing the records and commentaries for publication in the SPR's *Proceedings* when, on 5 March 1933, the *Sunday Dispatch* published an article by Harry Price, denouncing Rudi as a cheat. It was clearly designed to publicise the issue of the *Bulletin* of his National Laboratory, which came out the next day. Giving records of the seances of a year before, along with photographs, Price claimed that two of them, taken immediately before the seance, showed that Rudi had managed to free one of his arms from control, at the same time as the handkerchief which he was trying to move telekinetically was displaced.

Mind over Matter

It was not, as 'exposures' of mediums go, particularly damning. 'Supposing that at that particular seance Rudi pushed the handkerchief off the table by very normal means, either deliberately, since his powers were undoubtedly waning, or possibly because his secondary personality induced him to do it,' Anita Gregory has commented, 'this still left a large number of occasions to be explained when he did not free an arm, and phenomena were recorded.' Scores of the phenomena recorded in the long series of trials, in fact, could not have been accomplished even if he had been able to free an arm at will. But this was only the beginning of the mystery. The man who was supposed to be controlling Rudi's arm was – Price. Why, unless he were a confederate, had he not reported the loss of control? Still more mysterious: if he had immediately, as he claimed, realised that the photographs proved Rudi to have cheated, why had he waited almost a year before the exposure?

During that time he had given no hint that anything was amiss. He had even sought financial support for a fresh series of sittings with Rudi, and he had failed to tell even the members of his own council. 'Not that Mr Price was silent,' Hope sarcastically complained,

> as to the results of these sittings. In several newspaper articles written by him between the close of these sittings and the publication of his report he wrote in eulogistic terms of Rudi and his phenomena. In the *Empire News* for 8th May 1932 he says 'For three years he has been under laboratory tests in England and France and has emerged unscathed from his very strenuous ordeals'; and again in *Light* of 20 May 1932 he writes 'This is the third time he (Rudi) has been in England, and on each occasion he has added to his laurels. For three years Rudi has been subject to the most stringent laboratory tests in England and France and has passed every one with flying colours.'

Other similar statements by Price, Hope claimed in his report of his own series with Rayleigh, could be quoted, some of them even more recent; and he went on to make a point about the timing of the 'exposure'. Not only was the Hope/Rayleigh report about to appear; Rudi was again in Paris for a joint investigation by the Institut Métapsychique and the SPR, to which Price had not been invited. 'Mr Price cannot complain,' Hope remarked, 'if in the circumstances stated above this belated "exposure" is received with reserve.'

What, then, was Price's motive? In 'Anatomy of a Fraud' Anita Gregory – she became the wife of C. C. L. Gregory – has provided a detailed reconstruction of the episode which leaves no doubt at all that Price delayed publication of the photographs the better to be avenged on Hope and Osty. He had told his secretary, Ethel Beenham, and Mrs K. M. Goldney, joint Hon. Treasurer of the National Laboratory, about the photographs, pledging them to secrecy. Mrs Goldney was subsequently to explain that she was shocked, but felt she could not break her promise to keep it quiet – though she later regretted that decision: she resigned, along with Fraser Harris and other members of Price's National Laboratory Council, following the *Sunday Dispatch* 'exposure'. Miss Beenham, who had also been worried, was in no doubt about Price's motive: 'He was terribly spiteful against Lord Charles,' she told Mrs Goldney after Price's death. 'He was waiting for a chance to hit back at him, and used this report for that purpose.'

From Price's correspondence, Mrs Gregory was easily able to show how in trying to justify his decision, he merely enmeshed himself in a web of lies. So much so, in fact, that it aroused her suspicions about the photographs themselves. Fraser-Harris had pointed out at the time that it might have been the flash of light for the photograph that had caused Rudi to jerk his arm back; and in 1967 C. V. C. Herbert – by this time the Earl of Powis – recalled that a photographic expert had told him that the photograph of Rudi with his hand free from control was probably the second of the two – not, as Price had claimed, the first. Price, in other words, might simply have taken advantage of the opportunity to transpose the pictures.

But there was a further possibility, which Osty, understandably angry with Price, hinted at: that Price had actually faked the photographs. And examining the negatives in detail, Mrs Gregory realised there were good grounds for this suspicion. They were to be confirmed by Colin Brookes-Smith, a photographic expert, whose opinion was that in the photograph which Price used to damn Rudi, Price had superimposed the extended arm with the help of a double exposure. This interpretation was to be challenged in the correspondence in the SPR *Journal* following the publication of 'Anatomy of a Fraud', and the issue may never be finally settled; but nobody, reading the evidence, could now doubt that Price used the photographs to mislead the public into believing that Rudi had cheated.

It cannot have been Price's intention utterly to destroy Rudi's credibility. To have done so would have been to destroy his own. 'Price never had any intention of dismissing all Rudi's phenomena,' Mrs Gregory argues. 'His case, stated baldly, now was that Rudi's powers had since 1929 waned to such an extent that he had ever since resorted to fraud, and that consequently the Osty and the Hope-Rayleigh investigations, both of which claimed positive results, were worthless.' But Price, master though he was of press relations, had failed to realise that the press and the reading public would take very much the same line as Sidgwick had imposed on the SPR: 'Once a cheat, always a cheat.' 'It may well be the case,' Mrs Gregory considers, 'that psychical research has never had a more serious set-back than the Price-Schneider scandal.' Rudi could stage no come-back; his powers were almost gone. Effectively the 'exposure' killed off serious research into physical mediumship for over forty years.

On the evidence, however, of the Osty and the Hope/Rayleigh trials, it is hard to see how anybody who is prepared to accept at least the possibility of telekinesis can doubt that Rudi displayed it. And Osty, who had himself been so dismissive of the physical phenomena, now felt compelled to answer those who, while accepting that Rudi could influence infra-red rays, felt that this was unimportant compared to what had been learned from telepathy and precognition. Rudi, 'a motor mechanic by trade and of little education, incapable of understanding any problem of physics, or chemistry or biology', would certainly not be able to understand what was being said by any group of scientists. Yet when asked to move an object at a distance, without contact:

> It is enough for him momentarily to suspend his conscious activity to put himself into a special physiological state, called a trance, which endows him with exceptional powers over matter. Then this ignorant being behaves as if he knew the intimate and primordial resources of life and processes of creation . . . like the paranormal knowledge of reality in time and in space, the paranormal knowledge of the organising process of life reveals that behind the uses of the mind in feeling, in thinking and in acting on matter there is another intelligent plane of being, usually not manifest, which very probably represents the fundamental reality of ourselves, and forms part of a plane of life quite different from that in which we exercise our ordinary intelligence.

In that case, it also became more difficult to dismiss the other phenomena which continued occasionally to erupt, even in the closing stages of Rudi's career. In a paper William Brown read to the SPR, he described how, among the blank sittings, there had been one occasion when he had not merely seen the top of a small table move, on the other side of the room from the medium, but had seen an apport: flowers had appeared, and then disappeared. His account of his experience, he admitted, could not be expected to carry conviction; 'All one can say is that the phenomena occurred, and one is boggled.'

Even if a number of scientists of established reputation were to test a physical medium, and obtain results, 'they alone would believe such results', Brown feared; 'other scientists would refuse to believe them'. Lodge, who was in the Chair, agreed; the other scientists would remain convinced that physical action at a distance was impossible. 'So am I,' Lodge remarked:

> But I do not regard telekinesis as physical action at a distance. If a thing moves, it is always because something is in contact with it and making it move. The point is to ascertain what that something is. It may be an ectoplasmic emanation from the medium, or from the sitter; but the effect is not going to be contrary to the laws of physics. The laws of physics are all right. It is the laws of physiology that want explaining. We do not know everything that an organism can do, we have got to find out, and it is no use shutting our minds to experiments which show that an organism can do this sort of thing, by saying that it is physically impossible.

In his paper, Brown also drew attention to an aspect of Rudi's mediumship which had not had much attention: the fact that his breathing was at a rate ten times or more faster than the normal, yet he could keep it up for a couple of hours at a time. This would ordinarily be regarded as impossible: it presented a physiological problem which, Brown argued, 'needs and will repay investigation', not just on that account, but because the rapid breathing was actually related to the interruptions to the infra-red rays. And this was a point which Rayleigh was to draw attention to in his Presidential Address to the SPR in 1937. The graph on the photographic recording drum, he recalled, had revealed a link with the medium's breathing which made it clear that interceptions of the beam, though the photographic evidence showed there was nothing material in its path, was linked with Rudi's muscular movements. Those graphs, Rayleigh thought, were 'one of the most valuable contributions ever made to our subject'. Yet scientists had ignored them.

Whether it would have made any difference had Price not published his 'exposure' is impossible to tell; the likelihood is that it would not, in view of Rudi's waning powers, and the absence of any other medium capable of producing physical phenomena. The determination of scientists to disbelieve had been strengthened by the Walpurgisnacht affair; and although for the public in general, Price remained their mind's-eye picture of the dedicated psychical researcher, he had destroyed his chance of achieving his life's ambition.

The SPR's Jubilee

Whatever prospect Price might have had of absorbing the SPR had also vanished. 1932 was its jubilee year, which restored some of its self-esteem. Lodge was elected President for the year, with Eleanor Sidgwick, now in her eighties, as 'President of Honour'; and an address she wrote in that capacity was read for her by Lord Balfour – Gerald, who had succeeded to the title on his brother's death two years before.

It made depressing hearing, as Balfour had to admit: 'Some of you may have felt,' he remarked, 'that the note of caution and reserve had been over-emphasised.' This was putting it politely. Mrs Sidgwick laid weight upon the society's negative achievements, such as its members' determination to expose fraudulence; in particular, she was unable to resist disparaging physical mediumship. The society's investigators, she claimed, had not encountered much trickery except among physical mediums, 'among whom it is unfortunately common'. Listing them, she cited Eusapia, making no reference to the point so often argued by Lodge and others that what Eusapia did in her trances, if she was allowed to, should not be regarded as cheating. The final sittings at Naples, Mrs Sidgwick claimed, were 'apparently pure trickery' – which even the sceptical Count Perovsky, who had attended them, had not claimed.

Lodge had, in a sense, already made his contribution to the jubilee in the form of his autobiography, published in 1931. It was conventional, a little old-fashioned, but it brought out clearly his tolerance and good sense, and showed how convinced he still was that psychical phenomena represented an integral part of physics, as his colleagues must surely come to accept. 'Whatever the hostility now,' he asserted,

> I feel convinced that, in due time, science will take them under its wing, will recognise their truth, and will bring them into more serious consideration. So will it ultimately find that these facts contain the

germ of a vast development; they open a new department, a new province, of knowledge; one that will immensely enlarge our scope, and give us a clearer apprehension of the majesty of a universe of which as yet we know so little. Whatever the outcome, the study must surely prove of the utmost significance to the hopes and destiny of man.

In the jubilee year Lodge's old friend and fellow-worker, J. Arthur Hill, brought out a volume of his letters. 'He has been a hard and unselfish worker,' Hill observed, "and thinking of the whole of his activities I should be tempted to use the word "saintly", if it did not savour of smugness.' It was the quality of reverence in Lodge which had brought that term to Hill's mind, but even that was not entirely suitable: 'Sir Oliver is rather too human for it.' He had been a true prophet and revealer; 'future generations will probably realise this even more vividly than we do'.

Looking back, it is clear that Lodge held the SPR together in that critical period, binding up the festering wounds following the faction fights. It had been typical of him that when Doyle died in 1930, he took the opportunity in his obituary to emphasise the need for members of the SPR to co-operate with such men, who must have sacrificed something to enter upon so unpopular a line of enquiry. 'He was doing his best according to his lights, and though he may seem to us deficient in judgment, he was abounding in energy, and put some of us to shame. We need not accept the results of such men or believe their doctrines. But I think we should be careful not to alienate them, and turn them from criticising friends into implacable enemies.'

Thoughtography

Lodge may have had in mind another example of negativism which surfaced in the society's jubilee year. In 1930 a book had appeared presenting the most convincing evidence which had yet been provided for the ability of mediums to sensitise photographic plates: T. Fukurai's *Clairvoyance and Thoughtography*. Twenty years before, Fukurai, a Professor of Psychology at the Tokyo Imperial University, had tested a clairvoyant, coming to the conclusion that her powers were genuine. His curiosity aroused, he began testing another medium, and in the course of trials discovered that not merely could she guess what was on undeveloped film: in her effort to do so, she appeared to be affecting the film.

Mind over Matter

She was even able to imprint thought-forms on photographic plates, which did not need to be in a camera; they could be presented to her wrapped in opaque paper. But in the course of the trials the medium died; and when reports began to circulate about what he had been doing, Fukurai was denounced in the press and forced to resign from his university chair. Undeterred, he had continued to experiment; in 1928 he had come to England to conduct tests with William Hope; and he set out the evidence he had accumulated in his book.

In the universe, Fukurai argued, there must exist some psychic power, of which ordinary physical forces are only one part. Some mediums had the ability to tap the power and, among other things, impose their thoughts on photographic negatives. He had found that it was possible for a medium to put a thought-form on one out of six plates, leaving the rest unaffected; or to put thought forms on two plates, so that they meshed like pieces of a jigsaw; or to put a thought-form on one particular section of one of the rolls of film which had come in to common use in box cameras in the 1920s, without disturbing the rest of the roll.

That 'thoughtographs' could be imposed on a negative without the use of a camera was not a new idea. In *Photographing the Invisible* James Coates had described them, distinguishing between them and spirit photographs, and claiming that they could be 'obtained independently of the lens and of the camera'; he could not explain how, but he surmised that it must be through some process like crystal-gazing. Later, Stanley de Brath had conducted some experiments in which photographs were obtained when the medium had no access to the plates, and had come to the conclusion that they were not obtained by any process analogous to normal photography: 'There is ample proof that the lens plays no part in the production of the image.' De Brath, however, still favoured the spiritualist explanation. Either the image was ideoplastic – a thought-form projected by the medium, or the sitter or both; or it must be the work of a discarnate entity. He preferred the discarnate entity hypothesis, on the ground that as, in some cases, the image on the plate corresponded to nothing that the medium or the sitters were thinking about, 'only very complicated hypotheses of thought-transference can be offered a solution'. The notion that a discarnate agency might be 'acting on some specially ideoplastic kind of ectoplasm' seemed to him more plausible.

The common assumption had been that if apparently psychic matter appeared on film, either spirits must be responsible, or they were faked. Fukurai's was the first work to appear dealing primarily in thoughtography. So far as sceptics were concerned, however, the notion that not merely could the camera lie, but that film could lie at the behest of somebody's thoughts, without even being inside a camera, could only be a joke. Psychical researchers for the most part shared their scepticism, but were less amused. It was difficult to dismiss Fukurai as a charlatan: he had, after all, given up his career rather than renounce his opinions; and he had made no attempt to cash in on his discoveries – the book was presented as a serious contribution to psychical research. But the common impression was that Hope was a rogue, and consequently that Fukurai must either have been deceived by him, or in collusion with him.

Yet Hope had passed a number of tests made by investigators who knew their business, such as Carrington. The fact that he had been 'exposed' by Harry Price could hardly now, in the eyes of some members of the SPR, be regarded as decisive; in any case Price's view, if it were worth anything, had been that Hope had genuine psychic powers, but cheated occasionally in order to supplement them. Fukurai was out of reach, but Hope could be exposed again; and in 1932 he was denounced by Fred Barlow, who earlier had been one of his chief supporters, and Major W. Rampling-Rose, who described himself as 'a sort of detective', employed in the photographic industry, though normally his job was to track down defects, rather than fraud. Between them, they provided evidence in the SPR *Journal* which appeared to confirm that Hope had been cheating, and showed how he could have been doing it. As Barlow put it, he was not arguing that no medium had ever produced a genuine 'extra'; but to carry conviction, the evidence would have to be much more definite than any which he had been able to obtain.

Again, however, concrete evidence that Hope had cheated was missing; and some of their arguments indicated that they had not appreciated the possibility of a thoughtographic component. Barlow had been a believer because he had assumed that the 'extras', the spirit forms which appeared, really *were* spirits; what had disillusioned him had been the discovery that the 'extra' had sometimes been 'an exact copy of some existing photograph or painting'. But ten years earlier Coates, believing as he did that 'all these extraordinary super-mundane appearances of the living and the dead have been observed only through the sudden functioning of the psychic faculty' had urged that there was nothing surprising about the way in which the 'spirits' had so often resembled the deceased persons, not as they might have been expected to look – that is, how they had looked around the time of their deaths – but often as they had looked when they were much younger, or in portraits. All that this demonstrated, Coates argued, was that the 'spirits' were simply thought-forms, which could be expected to be based on actual recollections of the person or the portrait. To regard them as spirits, he asserted, was 'as absurd as the vacuous conclusion that they are fraudulently produced'.

This second Hope 'exposure' was the kind of thing that Lodge was worried about. Though he himself had for a long time regarded Hope with suspicion, he had gradually become disposed to accept that he was genuine; not from personal experience, but from the common-sense viewpoint that Hope could not, or would not, have gone on and on producing bogus spirit photographs, commonly without seeking remuneration, year after year. In a letter to J. Arthur Hill in 1929 he remarked that to his mind, 'the probability is strongly in favour of simplicity and honesty now that he has been going on for so long.' Surely, Lodge argued, the appeal of fraud as a motive would long since have evaporated? But 'The atmosphere of suspicion naturally attaching to all physical demonstrations,' he feared, 'greatly hampers their rational investigation.'

8 Extra-Sensory Perception

In 1934 a book was published which was to revolutionise both psychical research and public attitudes to psychic phenomena: Joseph Banks Rhine's *Extra-Sensory Perception*. 'It has become our contention,' Seymour H. Mauskopf and Michael R. McVaugh have remarked in the introduction to *The Elusive Science* – in which they unravel the tangled history of the events leading up to the book's publication (and the sometimes even more confusing repercussions which followed) with exemplary detachment – 'that during the quarter-century after 1915 psychical research was transformed from what had been a rather disorganised amateur activity, mixing spiritualism with attempts at experimentation, into a more coherently structured professional and research enterprise and began to gain, not general acceptance, but a degree of toleration from psychologists and other scientists.' And although some of the research which helped to bring about this transformation was conducted by others, they feel that 'the activity of J. B. Rhine at Duke was critical in bringing about this transformation'; a verdict with which it would be hard to disagree.

Rhine himself was always careful to acknowledge the work of his predecessors in the field of laboratory-type exploration; even Coover's initial research at Stanford, though Coover had failed to realise the significance of the contribution he had made to the subject. It had been Coover's critics who had observed that of the twelve highest scorers in his telepathy section and the ten highest scorers among his controls, five were the same, which had given the vital clue that this might indicate either that while acting as controls, they were guessing correctly through clairvoyance, or that while obtaining what could be interpreted as telepathic 'hits', clairvoyance was in fact responsible. 'While, then, Prof. Coover did not prove anything at all,' Rhine commented, 'he unwittingly opened up some very interesting suggestions.'

Extra-sensory Perception

The Experimenters: Warcollier and Gardner Murphy

A variety of experiments had been made after the war, using different techniques, such as the trials Brugman had reported at the first international conference and the experiments of René Warcollier. Before the war, Warcollier had become fascinated by certain unsolved problems of animal life, such as mimicry – from twig insects to the changing colours of the chameleon – and the ability of certain species to reconstitute portions of their anatomy, as lizards grow new tails; and some of the evidence for psychic phenomena had suggested to him that the forces involved might be related. He had therefore embarked on a series of experiments with telepathy, designed not to demonstrate its existence but to try to discover its mechanics – he was an engineer by training – in the hope of finding ways to facilitate transmission and reception; and his *La Télépathie: Recherches Expérimentales*, published in 1921, gave details of his findings and their implications.

Telepathy, Warcollier claimed, represented transference of subconscious thought and feeling. Conscious thought only got in the way – which was why, in his view, the Coover tests had produced such largely negative results; the subjects had not been in suitably relaxed states of mind. Some degree of rapport between transmitter and receiver, Warcollier believed, was also desirable, though not essential; and boredom should be avoided.

In 1920 Warcollier had organised small groups to test his theories. At set times one group would seek to transmit a word, or a drawing, while the others would see if they could pick up the 'transmission'. In this way he was able to test whether groups were more likely to be successful than individuals, and also whether distance made any difference to the results. Groups did work slightly better; and disconcertingly – in view of the determination of orthodox scientists to sustain the inverse square law – distance seemed rather to improve the results.

At the international conference in Warsaw in 1923 Warcollier met Gardner Murphy, who was later to be, with Rhine, the dominant influence in psychical research in the United States. Murphy had grown up in a part of Boston where, as he was to recall in an autobiographical sketch, 'individualistic and heterodox opinions were encouraged'. His grandfather had for a time been Mrs Piper's attorney, and it was in his grandfather's library that, at the age of sixteen, he read Barrett's *Psychical Research*; 'From that moment the quickened flame never abated.' It happened that in Murphy's first graduate year at Harvard, Troland was the beneficiary of the Richard Hodgson Fund, and asked him to help, which prompted Murphy to do some extensive reading of reports of earlier work on telepathy. He joined McDougall in the abortive first Harvard investigation of 'Margery'; and, thanks to McDougall, he himself had the support of the Hodgson fund from 1922 to 1925 to do experiments in telepathy, including the first trial using the new medium, radio. On 2 March 1924 a test broadcast from a Chicago station attracted 2500 guesses from listeners: of these, however, only two were strikingly accurate, and the general level was slightly below chance.

Measured quantitatively, the trans-Atlantic trials with Warcollier were also unimpressive; but there were intriguing demonstrations of the importance of the point which Warcollier had been emphasising: the need to regard telepathy as communicating not what the transmitting agents wanted to communicate, or thought they were communicating, but some component, of which they might not be aware. Thus one of the 'senders', who was herself one of the more successful 'receivers' whom Warcollier had discovered, was handed an object in darkness, and asked to say what it was. She thought it was 'the horns of a little deer, or rather of a roe', eventually deciding it was a stag's horn. In another room, one of the recipients drew three sketches, all on the same theme: a pitchfork's prongs, a claw, and antlers. The actual object was the lower jawbone of a woman. The same evening – 14 March 1925 – Warcollier himself was to try to send a message from France to an American group sitting in New York; and as he wanted to banish

The compote glass with 'stag's horns'.

the memory of the earlier experiment, he tried to visualise a glass funnel which he had seen that morning. 'At the same hour a percipient in New York drew a sort of funnel with handles, which he called "a Visigoth helmet, upside down"; and another of the New York percipients drew a large compote glass with handles, remaking that it was "like the horns of a stag".'

These findings did not attract much attention at the time; understandably, in view of the emphasis on the physical phenomena of mediumship in the Geley-dominated era. But they were to be valuable to Murphy, intimating as they did that if the reality of telepathy was ever to be demonstrated quantitatively, to try to meet the specifications laid down by orthodox science, the subjective element must be taken into account. Experiments might work if senders and receivers were in rapport which would not work if they were unknown to one another. It might be necessary for both to be in a certain frame of mind, if communication was to be established. And the decision whether a result was a 'hit' or a 'miss' would have to be put on a rather different basis from that of the shooting range. Not merely might a receiver describe, or draw, an object which was not the same as the one the sender was holding, but was the same general size, shape and colour: there could also be displacements. In one experiment, in which a sender had knelt in an armchair and joined his hands to see whether the receiver would pick up 'prayer', the subject reported 'a curtain of heavy material and dark colour, right along the wall, not drawn, but held back by a curtain-band'. This was, in fact, an exact description of the background to the room in which the agent was sitting.

In 1925 Murphy caught influenza and, as so often in that era, its after-effects were both disturbing and lingering; for a time he even went blind. He already had a part-time teaching post at Columbia University; and he decided that in view of his poor health he had better accept Columbia's offer to make it full-time, even though this meant giving up the Hodgson Fellowship. 'In no way did I slacken interest,' he insisted, 'but life forced on me temporarily an orthodox path.' There was, however, to be one divergence from that path: his contribution to the Clark University symposium, important both because he was the only representative of the younger academic generation – he was thirty-two – and for its content.

In 'Telepathy as an experimental problem' he surveyed past work and indicated, with remarkable prescience, the difficulties which were likely to be encountered in the future, illustrating them from his own work, and Warcollier's, with some striking examples. On one occasion a man who was acting as a sender in a long-distance trial had been sitting in a restaurant with green hangings where three men at the next table were talking loudly, eating roast capon with bread sauce, while a pianist strummed away in the background. Suddenly waking up to the fact it was time to 'transmit' a diagram, he left the restaurant and, five minutes later, performed his task. The receiver, hundreds of miles away, recorded at that time in automatic writing 'Roast capon, bread sauce, three men, much talk, green hangings, somebody strumming'.

Among the trials to which Murphy referred in his paper were those which had been conducted by his successor as beneficiary of the Hodgson Fund at Harvard, George Estabrooks. Estabrooks had reverted to Coover's card-guessing system, separating the senders from the receivers by a partition, the receivers being notified when to guess by a clockwork device; and their scores in the first of the series were spectacular. Out of 1660 guesses, the odds against chance being responsible for the number of correct guesses of the card's *suit* were 900 to one; of the card's *colour*, no less than 8,000,000 to one. The next in the series, however, produced much less impressive scoring, and in the third, where senders and receivers were in two rooms at a distance from each other, the subjects scored below chance.

Estabrooks had been more sympathetic to psychical research than Coover, and more perceptive. 'In the laboratory,' he had noted 'we cannot get the intense emotional state which seems so necessary for a really conclusive demonstration.' Consequently the need was to search for a technique which would 'take that very weak tendency and magnify it until we can claim proof'. Trials of the kind he had conducted, he realised, created their own problems in that the atmosphere might not be conducive, and boredom or fatigue appeared to weaken that very weak tendency still further. But this laboratory demonstration of the way in which initially good scoring fell to chance, or even below, was important, Murphy pointed out, because it was so 'extraordinarily consistent': the best results had been obtained in the first five experiments, the next best in the next five, and around the fifteenth, 'the results drop to what we should expect from chance'.

Eleanor Sidgwick also realised the significance of these findings, suggesting as they did 'that some capacity was at work which rapidly deteriorated with use'. They were more suggestive than that. The way in which psychic powers or faculties declined both in trials and, in the case of mediums, with advancing years, was already well established; but the natural tendency of sceptics had been to claim it provided additional evidence for the spuriousness of psychic phenomena. Estabrooks's results confirmed that this line of reasoning was untenable. The fact that the success rate was higher when senders and receivers were separated only by a partition might have been attributed to the fact that the subjects had somehow overheard what the cards were, either directly or through hyperesthesia; but this could not account for the way the success rate had fallen in the initial trials, while they were in the partitioned room. Had any of the receivers found a way to cheat, too, their scores would have been more likely to improve, rather than fall off. And if Estabrooks himself had wanted to cheat either for or against telepathy, he would hardly have cheated in such a way as to produce the results which appeared in his report. Henceforth the decline effect ceased to disturb psychical researchers – though it continued to sadden them, because it meant that so many of the most promising receivers lost their receptivity. It also remained an irritant, in that the more ignorant critics continued to try to use it as it were as an argument in their favour.

The Jephson Trials

Decline effect was to be a feature of the next reported series of card-guessing trials, conducted by Ina Jephson in Britain. She dispensed with agents, allowing individuals to monitor their own clairvoyance by the simple method of shuffling a pack, drawing a card from it, guessing what the card was, writing the guess down on a score sheet and then writing down beside it what the card had actually turned out to be. The advantage was that anybody could volunteer and conduct the experiment in his or her own time; the obvious disadvantage, that any of the subjects, – about three hundred volunteered to participate – could easily cheat. But what was impressive about the results was that not merely were there no indications of cheating, such as suspiciously high scores: the marked tendency was for subjects to score well at the start of their 'runs', but for their guesses then to sink to chance level, and below. Fatigue? Boredom? Some other cause? Ina Jephson did not know. But at least cheating, easy though it would have been, could be ruled out. Her subjects would hardly have consistently rigged their own guesses in such a way as to show a gradual decline; the decline effect's consistency could consequently be regarded as unconventional but interesting evidence for the existence of ESP, in the absence of any obvious alternative way of accounting for it.

Was there any point in experiments of this kind, in view of their revelation that what Estabrooks had described as the 'very weak tendency' to guess correctly by psychic means became relentlessly weaker as trials progressed? In the *Journal* of the American society, René Sudre argued that there was not, claiming that the performances of individuals with striking powers were more likely to carry conviction. Ina Jephson's reply was that what scientists were demanding was replicability, and this might be achieved in the mass in a way that it could not be, or at least had not been, with individuals. Rhine was to settle for the statistical approach. It did not, after all, preclude research with gifted individuals; it could identify them.

J. B. Rhine

Joseph Banks Rhine had grown up in a remote mountain region of Pennsylvania where, according to his wife, he acquired and never lost 'the marked and definite independence of mind, a freedom from, and even an unawareness of, social pressures, especially in regard to the opinions of others'. His cast of mind was sceptical; in college, and later while serving with the Marine Corps, he acquired the mechanist outlook which he was never entirely to shed; and having graduated in botany, and married another botany student, Louisa Weckesser, he could easily have settled down to an academic career. Reading Bergson's *Creative Evolution*, however, convinced them both that what science needed was extension beyond its – by this time – rigid materialist boundaries. They decided to do research 'on the rim of the great problem of the nature of life'; and Myers's *Human Personality* pointed them towards psychical research.

Their initial idea was to investigate mediums; and in the summer of 1926 they went to a seance with 'Margery'. They were ready to give her the benefit of the doubt, Rhine insisted; but 'when I found this poor bunch of tricks at the back of all these investigations and publications, it was a tremendous jolt', he complained in a letter to the ASPR; 'I am disgusted, not only with the case but with the attitude our journal has taken on it, sponsoring it before the scientific world.'

Extra-sensory Perception

The report of the seance which the Rhines attended appeared in Morton Prince's *Journal of Abnormal Psychology*, and it shows how Rhine's disgust had got the better of his judgment. Many of the familiar phenomena occurred, and the Rhines had to admit they were impressive; but certain observations 'led us to discover that the whole game was a base and brazen trickery'. The Rhines could not explain, however, how the trickery was carried out. They could only speculate; and their speculation showed that they were unfamiliar with the reports of some earlier investigators – for example, in relation to pseudopod manifestations; and they were unwise enough to cite Code's findings in support of their argument.

The Rhines' verdict might be unfair, but it was decisive in terms of their future, partly by encouraging them to concentrate upon research into the mental, rather than the physical phenomena: partly by leading them into the Prince/McDougall camp. It happened that the President of Duke University, William Preston Few, who was looking out for a psychologist, had asked McDougall for his ideas; and McDougall, who had never really settled down at Harvard, offered himself. He made the move in 1927; and that autumn the Rhines joined him at Duke, to assist him in his courses, and to pursue psychical research.

It was some time, however, before Rhine settled down to the laboratory-type research with which he later came to be identified. In the winter of 1927–8 he and Louisa investigated a 'mind-reading horse', Lady, who answered questions her owner put to her by pointing to letters or numbers with her nose; and the fact that she sometimes correctly answered questions to which her owner did not know the answer suggested that there must be more to it than unconscious sensory signals, of the kind which had been held to account for the success of an earlier horse and owner combination. A year later, when the Rhines returned for a further investigation, Lady only responded to signals – theirs, or the owner's; so the enquiry had to be abandoned. In this period, however, the Rhines read the available literature of psychical research intensively and extensively, and began to work out projects and procedures; and in 1930 he began a series of experiments with students to test them for telepathic perception.

Rhine's reading initially pointed him in the direction Richet had taken, to experiments in which suggestion under hypnosis was used to try to put the students in a suitable frame of mind; in *New Frontiers of the Mind* he was to recall that though the project which he and his colleague, Professor Helge Lundholm, tried out was relatively short lived, it was 'extremely important in that it was the foundation for later, more successful work'. And at this point, a book appeared which gave him and McDougall much-needed encouragement, because it helped to counteract the prevailing impression that psychical research in the United States had been dealt a mortal blow by the exposures – as they were taken to be – of 'Margery': a remarkable and surprising study of some experiments in telepathic communication.

Mental Radio

The surprise lay in the authorship: it was the work of Upton Sinclair, who had made his name before the war with his novel *The Jungle*, exposing the horrors of working for the Chicago meat-packers, and whose later books had firmly established him as the most articulate of American Socialists. Socialists were generally regarded (and generally regarded themselves) as dedicated materialists, hostile to occultist notions of any kind. *Mental Radio*, however, turned out to be a plea for the recognition of telepathy (Sinclair remained doubtful about clairvoyance) on the strength of a series of trials he and others had carried out with his wife.

Mary Craig Sinclair, Sinclair explained, had been a sensitive even as a child, in that when her mother told a servant to go and find her, 'the child would know her mother wanted her, and would be on the way'; and sometimes she had shared dreams with her mother. The faculty had continued: Sinclair recalled an occasion when she had become very worried about Jack London, saying she felt he was in great mental distress; they learned a couple of days afterwards that he had committed suicide. Later, Sinclair and his wife had experimented with 'hand healing'; he could 'take on' her headaches, he found, and she 'take on' his indigestion. But as he was 'busy trying to reform America', and she had 'the most intensely materialistic convictions', it was only gradually that her psychic faculty was uncovered and developed.

Sinclair was under no illusions that his account of that faculty, and the experiments with which they had tested it, would be easily swallowed. His followers would be a little shocked: 'You have come, after thirty years, to the position where you accept me as one kind of "crank", but you won't stand for two kinds.' Yet there was nothing for it, he had decided, but to come straight to the point, and describe the experiments.

Extra-sensory Perception

In their everyday trials Sinclair would take an object, or make a drawing of anything which came into his head; Mrs Sinclair would be called in and lie down; the object, or the drawing, wrapped up, would be placed on her solar plexus; and she would try to empty her mind of thoughts, to allow a picture of the target to come in. Frequently she got the answer exactly correct: but some of her guesses were striking even when they were not quite correct. For example, when he drew a running fox, she drew two crossed guns and a hunting horn.

There were also occasional displacements. Unbeknown to the Sinclairs, a visitor to his office who had heard about the tests decided to 'give her some that will stump her', and drew two pictures. They were slipped into a series she was working on: and when she picked up the first of them, she wrote:

> Some sort of a grinning monster – see only the face and a vague idea of deformed neck and shoulders. It is a man, but it looks like a cat's face, cat eyes and whiskers. Don't know just how I know it is a man – it is a deformity. Not a cat. See colour of skin, which is deep, flat pink, as of a coloured picture. The face of the creature is broad and weird. The flesh of neck or somewhere gives effect of rolls or creases.

Opening the envelope, she found it was a drawing of a leg and foot on a roller skate, which was marked as a 'miss'. But later in the series she was guessing, 'some sort of a grinning monster' did indeed appear. Not merely was her earlier guess a startlingly

'Some sort of grinning monster.'

accurate description of the drawing; it turned out that the drawing was one of the two which had been done by the visitor in Sinclair's office. In other words, she had got the 'Happy Hooligan' (the drawing was of a cartoon character of the period in a comic supplement; when Sinclair looked it up, he found that the face was indeed pink), but in the wrong envelope. She had accurately picked up what had been drawn, but not where it had been put.

In a series of 290 drawings, her 'hits' numbered 65 – nearly a quarter, almost the same proportion as her total misses. Coincidence? There was no way of estimating the precise odds against so many 'hits' occurring by chance, but to Sinclair, 'a million years would not be enough for such a set'. Understandably, Sinclair thought these results worth publishing; but as his wife was reluctant to face the publicity, and feared it would damage his reputation, he agreed to circulate his account of the trials to friends, before committing himself. Some of them begged him not to publish; one of them unkindly anticipated publication in a syndicated article under the title 'Sinclair Goes Spooky'. But McDougall's comments, which were to appear as a preface to the American edition, were encouraging; and Sinclair went ahead.

Mrs Sinclair's account of her condition while guessing struck McDougall as particularly interesting, falling in line as it did with what so many other sensitives had described. It was a state, she explained, of 'simultaneous concentration and relaxation' – though that might appear to be a contradiction: 'Perhaps we each have several mental entities, or minds, and one of these can sleep (be blankly unconscious) while another supervises the situation, maintaining the first one's state of unconsciousness for a desired period, and then presenting to it some thought or picture agreed on in advance, thus restoring it to consciousness.' Whatever the explanation, 'When I practise this art which I have learned, with my mind concentrated on one simple thing, it is a relaxation as restful, as seemingly "complete", as when I am in that state called normal sleep.'

Knowing how sceptics, inside as well as outside the societies for psychical research, were likely to react, McDougall recommended that Mrs Sinclair should undertake some more formal trials by scientists. Sinclair was aware that, as he put it 'much of the evidence which I am using rests upon the good faith of Mary Craig Sinclair'; and as a sceptic might well have added that much of it also rested on *his* good faith, too, they were anxious to co-operate. But the problem arose that had blocked formal trials with Gilbert

Murray. Her state of 'simultaneous concentration and relaxation', she found, could easily be disrupted by things which ordinarily did not bother her at all, light and noise; and she was uneasy in case the presence of strangers, 'sceptical or possibly hostile', might also make a difference. The trials were not held.

Nevertheless the results the Sinclairs had achieved, McDougall felt, were 'so remarkably successful as to rank among the very best hitherto reported'. They could be rejected as conclusive evidence of 'some mode of communication, not at present explicable in accepted scientific terms', only by assuming 'that Mr and Mrs Sinclair either are grossly stupid, incompetent and careless persons, or have deliberately entered upon a conspiracy to deceive the public in a most heartless and reprehensible fashion'. He was not, he admitted, intimately acquainted with them personally; but a knowledge of Sinclair's writings 'suffices to convince me, as it should convince any impartial reader, that he is an able and sincere man, with a strong sense of right and wrong, and of individual responsibility', which should ensure that his book received a respectful hearing.

The Zener Cards

In 1930, Rhine began to experiment with card-guessing, helped by his colleague, Dr K. F. Zener. For a while the results were obstinately negative, until Rhine, doubtless mindful of the possibility that something more stimulating might be desirable as target material, asked Zener to design special cards for the tests; and he came up with five: a plus (or cross), a circle, a rectangle, a star, and three wavy lines. Later the designs were to be slightly modified, and the term 'ESP cards' was introduced; but the term 'Zener cards' caught on. They were the same size and shape as ordinary playing cards, with plain backs, and they were produced in packs of twenty-five. The packs would be shuffled, and Rhine or one of his assistants, acting as agents, would work down through them, while the receivers, or subjects, tried to guess what each one was, the agent noting down the guesses. At the end of the run, the guesses would be compared with the cards.

'This simple, monotonous procedure Rhine was to recall, seemed 'an almost childish way to investigate the possibility of the human mind's possessing powers not recognised by scientists or the majority of laymen'. It lacked drama, and needed to be endlessly repeated, day in, day out, over years. But it had the great advan-

Science and Parascience

The 'Zener Cards'.

tage that it *was* simple. Chance expectation would be five 'hits' in each run; and though there might be considerable variations on individual runs, they would be expected to even out over, say, a hundred runs, whereas anybody who had clairvoyant powers could be expected to show up by scoring frequently or consistently above chance. And this was what happened. In the spring of 1931 one of the students, A. J. Linzmayer – 'our first really striking subject', as Rhine gratefully described him – got nine straight 'hits', not once but three times. He scored equally well when tested for 'pure' clairvoyance – that is, when the agent did not know what the card was – as he did when tested for 'undifferentiated extra-sensory perception' – the term Rhine adopted, from Tischner, for perception which might be attributed either to telepathy or to clairvoyance. On his last day at Duke, before he left for his summer vacation, Linzmayer agreed to set aside the whole of the day for tests; and in one of them he ran up a score of fifteen consecutive 'hits', and a total of twenty-one 'hits' out of the twenty-five-card run.

Gratifying though this performance was, it was unlikely to make

Extra-sensory Perception

any impression on sceptics, as the tests had not been carried out with sufficiently rigorous precautions to rule out cheating. That Linzmayer had not been cheating was, in fact, soon indicated by the setting in of decline effect; when he returned later to Duke for further trials, his results were far less spectacular. Nevertheless he continued to score regularly at slightly above chance level, guessing six or seven cards right, on average; and this in itself was encouraging, because his consistency over so many trials – around three thousand in all – was in a sense a more impressive demonstration that some factor other than chance must be involved than the occasional high score. And in 1932 another subject turned up at Duke who was able consistently to produce even higher scores: a divinity student, Hubert Pearce.

Tested by Gaither Pratt, who had become one of Rhine's assistants, Pearce in his first 5000 trials averaged the astonishing number of ten 'hits', twice as many as chance expectation. Once he even 'shot a possible', guessing all twenty-five cards in a run correctly. But this was exceptional: his chief value, Rhine realised, lay in his consistency. Pearce, too, was able to score *below* chance when asked to do so, for purposes of demonstration. He would get only one out of the twenty-five right, or none at all. And his scoring was unaffected by precautionary checks. The then celebrated magician Wallace Lee, invited to be an observer, conceded that there was no way in which Pearce could have been picking up sensory clues, whether consciously or unconsciously.

Pearce's consistency made it possible to conduct a wide range of experiments; for example, to find whether distance made any difference. In one trial in 1933 Pratt in one building on the campus picked up cards from a shuffled pack, without looking at them, at intervals of a minute; while Pearce, in another building a hundred yards away, made his guesses. Over 300 runs, Pearce averaged just under ten 'hits' in each. When the distance was extended to 250 yards, his scoring remained high. Tests with different subjects at even greater distances confirmed that scoring could be high even with 250 miles between agent and subject.

The Monograph

In the autumn of 1933 Rhine put together a monograph providing a general historical introduction to the subject, giving the results of the experiments with Linzmayer, Pearce and others, and discussing their significance. He sent it to Walter Prince, who published it in the spring of 1934, with an introduction by himself and a foreword from McDougall, on behalf of the Boston Society for Psychic Research. Only 900 copies of *Extra-Sensory Perception* were printed; but, as Mauskopf and McVaugh have commented, the contents were to revolutionise psychical research and to make its title 'literally a household phrase'.

The term 'extra-sensory perception' – or, more commonly, simply 'ESP' – was quick to catch on. Rhine felt the need to justify his decision to adopt it as preferable to 'supernormal perception', to Richet's 'cryptesthesia', or to 'metagnomy', which Osty and Sudre were seeking to popularise. It had gradually become clear, Rhine argued, that telepathy and clairvoyance did not constitute a hitherto unrecognised sensory process; his interpretation was that ESP was 'perception in a mode that is just *not* sensory' – rather than not recognised. Sudre was to fight a rearguard action against it: 'perception', he argued, was misleading, because 'the telepathic image does not have the characteristics of a perception: it emerges like a memory from the subconscious mind', and because it ignored the transmission element. Rosalind Heywood later added that 'perception' might be a misnomer, 'since the response to such communication does not always appear to be a conscious one' (as on the occasions when people have reported that they have been 'taken over' – stopped, say, as if by an invisible hand from exposing themselves to what turned out to be some hidden danger, without their comprehending why). But as so often has happened in the creation of the terminology of psychical research, the term which caught on was not the one which purists would have preferred. 'ESP' has stayed the course.

The monograph, too, had an immediate impact, not just for the evidence it provided for ESP, but because Rhine had been careful to reply to some of the more obvious lines of criticism in advance, in a chapter of 'Elimination of negative hypotheses'. The most obvious was that 'we would be as likely to go below chance average, if we ran 90,000 more trials, as we would be to go above'. Rhine had no difficulty in showing that even in that unlikely event, the results already obtained would be enough to satisfy any statistician that chance could not account for them.

Fraud, then? Incompetence? Unconscious sensory perception? Rational inference? The diverse circumstances under which the trials had been conducted made each and all of these implausible, Rhine argued. For example, there might be a number of ways in

Extra-sensory Perception

which by looking at the backs of the cards it could be possible in time to get to know what was on the front of them; but some subjects preferred to keep their minds and their eyes elsewhere: Pearce, for one, rarely looked at the cards while guessing, and in some trials neither the cards nor the agent were in view. Fraud? Was it really likely that the people involved, as agents or subjects or observers, were all in a conspiracy to produce the results? If anybody had been cheating, the results would presumably have been better in *un*witnessed tests; but 'those subjects who have not been wholly witnessed throughout have in many cases shown better results when witnessed than when unwitnessed'. Incompetence? If there had been poor observation or evaluation, the results would have been best when they had begun the trials, and were inexperienced; the reverse was the case, as the results with some subjects had improved at the same time as they were finding ways to tighten up their investigative procedures, at least until decline effect set in.

Repercussions

Not the least remarkable outcome of the publication of *Extra-Sensory Perception* was its reception in the American press. As psychical research had long been of interest to the editors of newspapers and magazines, it was not surprising that the work at Duke should have attracted their attention; but in addition, the *Scientific American* had not been frightened off by the 'Margery' experience, and in fact in 1933 had initiated a series of trials for telepathy, with its readers' help, under Walter Prince's supervision. The initial findings, he reported, were encouraging; and although the eventual outcome was disappointing, the editor suggested that this pointed to the need for trials 'conducted under controlled laboratory conditions'. As this appeal was in the January 1934 issue it seems highly probable that he knew, from Prince, that such trials had been conducted at Duke, and had been strikingly successful. Rhine could be sure of an ally, there.

Less predictably, the *New York Times* 'science correspondent, Waldemar Kaempffert, described the Duke research at length, and respectfully, in his column 'The Week in Science', treating it as he would have treated similar research in physics or chemistry. In the *New York Herald Tribune*, too, E. E. Free suggested that just as Faraday's discoveries were remembered, a century later, as the outstanding achievement of his time, so in 2034 Rhine's might well be singled out for the accolade. Writers in other newspapers and magazines followed their example: and for the first time psychical researchers were widely treated as contributors to scientific knowledge rather than dabblers in the occult.

The publicity which Rhine's research obtained in the press gave him another boost, though a disconcerting one: a tidal wave of correspondence, 'much of it helpful', as he acknowledged in his *New Frontiers of the Mind*, 'and some of it extraordinarily so'. Through it, a network of co-workers could be established throughout the country, in which experiments along the same lines, or variations on them, could be undertaken. Some of them were conducted by men such as Dr C. R. Carpenter of Bard College who admitted that his hope was that he would find flaws in the procedure, if the tests were put on a regular, objective basis, without fussing over the subjective needs of the subjects. But one of them survived the ordeal, for a while scoring almost as well, and as consistently, as Pearce, until his investigator was forced to admit that he could find no explanation except ESP.

Other trials were conducted by men and women who were already interested in the subject, but who were triggered into activity by hearing or reading about the work at Duke. As Mauskopf and McVaugh found, examining the correspondence, what was most noteworthy about them was their heterogeneity. They included engineers, schoolteachers, a manufacturer, a psychiatrist, a pediatrician and a professor of philosophy; and their letters revealed that some of them were 'uncommonly perceptive and purposeful' – they were far from being the kind of mystics and cranks whom the critics of psychical research claimed were its chief adherents.

Rhine's most pressing need was more funds; and here, too, fortune favoured him. In 1934 a young Irish medium, Eileen Garrett, came to Duke to be tested, sponsored by a rich Cleveland woman, Mrs Frances Bolton. Mrs Garrett had been building up a reputation in Britain, where researchers had found her 'surprisingly different in appearance and manner from any other medium', as one investigator, E. Clephan Palmer, noted in 1927; 'very modern, Eton-cropped and humorous'. She had a 'control', the oriental-sounding 'Uvani', who spoke through her – but she had decided that 'Uvani' was a phenomenon to be investigated, with a view to understanding it, rather than accept that his was a voice from the spirit world. To this end she put her mediumship at the disposal of serious researchers, gaining their trust and admiration.

Following the disappearance of Captain Walter Hinchliffe on his attempted east-west Atlantic flight in 1928, 'Uvani' had given a detailed account of the way he had crashed; and although there was no way in which it could be confirmed, some of the incidental details given were impressive in their accuracy. Even more impressive were the details 'Uvani' gave two years later at a seance where the intention had been to obtain a communication from Conan Doyle, who had just died, but where the 'communicator' introduced himself as Flight Lieutenant H. Carmichael Irwin, captain of the airship R 101, which had crashed in France two days before.

'Irwin' presented a string of reasons why the airship had foundered, many of them highly technical. The transcript revealed that it would have been difficult for Eileen Garrett to have collected the information even if she had been intimately involved in the project – the construction of the R 101, the disputes, the difficulties – from the start; and although not all the information was accurate, as John G. Fuller has shown in his reconstruction of the case, it was strikingly close to the truth.

In her trials at Duke, Eileen Garrett revealed that she could score extremely well in tests both for clairvoyance and for telepathy, the telepathy results being the better of the two: in 625 trials she guessed 336 cards correctly, an average of over 13.4 out of each run of 25 Zener cards (tested in her trance state, when 'Uvani' did the guessing, the score was lower, but still well above the chance level of 5 out of the 25). By this time, however, the arrival of yet another good scorer was of less importance to Rhine than the contact with Mrs Bolton. Mrs Bolton's interest was primarily in securing evidence for survival after death; and Mrs Garrett, combining as she did the ability to make contact with 'communicators' and to do well in straight test conditions, was the ideal go-between. Research of the kind being undertaken at Duke, Rhine suggested to Mrs Bolton, was necessary to provide the groundwork for research into survival; and it could be much more effectively conducted if it had more adequate funding. McDougall's support helped to persuade Mrs Bolton to promise a $10,000-a-year grant, for a probationary period of three to five years, a sum which was to enable Rhine to attain an almost independent status within Duke, and to found the *Journal of Parapsychology*.

For a time, the main criticism of Rhine's work came from other psychical researchers. So far as the American SPR was concerned he was a heretic. As he was out of the society's reach, he could not be excommunicated, but he could be ignored; *Extra-Sensory Perception* was not accorded a review in the *Journal*, and two years passed before its pages contained any reference to the research at Duke. And in Britain the book's reception was guarded. The SPR gave the book to R. H. Thouless, Lecturer in Psychology at the University of Glasgow, to review, presumably because he was a High-and-Dry. He had not even fully committed himself to acceptance of supernormal phenomena – an asset, from the High-and-Dry point of view, as his views would carry more weight in academic circles, in which he had a growing reputation: he was to be President of the British Association's Psychology Section in 1937. Thouless welcomed Rhine's innovations, such as the Zener cards and the tests designed to try to distinguish telepathy from clairvoyance. But he complained that it was 'generally quite impossible to discover in any particular experiment what the experimental conditions were'; and where it *was* possible, the experiments were not free from objections. The best that could be said for them was that they were simple, so that 'those who are not convinced may try the matter out for themselves'.

That Thouless was unaware of the importance of *Extra-Sensory Perception* was also clear from the fact that the major part of his review was devoted not to Rhine's experiments, but to Coover's. This was because the work of R. A. Fisher, the leading statistician of the era, had begun to assume great importance in High-and-Dry circles, as he had been willing to co-operate in analysing the results of tests, and could be trusted, when sceptics claimed that the researchers' statistics were unreliable, to give an impartial verdict. It was largely thanks to Fisher that members of the society were becoming proficient in this subject; and some of them, going over the Coover ground as an exercise, were discovering that Coover's research, far from casting doubt on the reality of extra-sensory perception, had produced even stronger evidence for it than Schiller had realised at the time. If some of the participants in Coover's tests had continued to score at the same rate as they had been scoring – in other words, provided decline effect had not set in – the 50,000-to-one odds would very soon have been reached, Thouless was able to show, and surpassed. Gratifying though this information was to Rhine, because it showed that his own results need not be attributed simply to his unguarded enthusiasm, in the letter he wrote to the SPR he was understandably a little miffed at his book's cool reception; but he contented himself with correcting Thouless on a point of detail.

S. G. Soal

Thouless was not the only member of the SPR to treat Rhine's work with a measure of suspicion. S. G. Soal, Senior Lecturer in Mathematics at Queen Mary College, London University, was more outspokenly critical, writing to Prince to express his doubts, and preparing to undertake research in Britain which would demonstrate that the experiments at Duke had been slipshod, and the results untrustworthy.

Soal was a prickly academic, with a relish for demolishing the work of others; and over the previous fifteen years he had emerged as one of the highest and driest of the society's active members. Yet he was regarded as a man of refreshing intellectual integrity, largely because of his role in one of the strangest cases reported in the society's publications: the 'Gordon Davis' affair.

In the early 1920s, soon after he had joined the SPR, Soal had investigated a clairaudient, Mrs Blanche Cooper, who practised at the College of Psychic Science. One of the 'communicators' was Soal's deceased brother, Frank; at the start of one seance, Soal was told that 'Frank' had brought along somebody who knew him; and 'a voice well articulated and extraordinarily clear and strong began to speak'. Soal had heard a number of different voices emanating through the medium, but in none of them, not even that of 'Frank', had he recognised any of them as the voice of somebody he had known. This one was different: he knew it was familiar, though he could not immediately place it. Eventually 'Gordon Davis' identified himself, and Soal realised he was hearing the voice of an old schoolfellow. 'Can you really be Gordon Davis?' he asked. 'I had heard you were killed.' 'The same – what's left of me,' 'Gordon Davis' replied, and he went on to remind Soal of the old School, and of the last conversation they had had together.

Soal had not known Davis well at school, and could not recollect having spoken to him in the fifteen years after he had left it until they had met by chance in 1916, waiting on a station platform for a London train, in which they had had the conversation which 'Gordon Davis' had recalled. Afterwards he had heard Davis had been killed in the war. Curious, he asked Mrs Cooper's 'control', 'Nada', at the next sitting if she could get in touch with 'Davis' again, and he was rewarded by information about his 'house' and its contents – what it looked like from the outside, the pictures in the living room, and downstairs, 'two funny brass candlesticks' and 'a black dickie-bird on the piano'.

At the time, Soal claimed, he dismissed the description of the house as 'the purest fiction'. Four years later, however, he heard by chance that Davis was still alive, and working as an estate agent in Southend. Intrigued, Soal visited him there – and found himself going into the very house which 'Nada' had described, even the pictures on the walls; and the brass candlesticks downstairs. And what was still more startling, at the time of the seance Davis had not been living in the house. He had not even been inside it, though the possibility that he might buy it could have been in his mind.

The curious combination of a misplaced 'spirit' – a living man coming through as a 'communicator' – an unprecedented type of precognition, naturally attracted interest, the more so because Soal, though himself an automatist, was so rigorous in his evaluation of mediums. Had Conan Doyle, say, told the 'Gordon Davis' story, it would have been unhesitatingly dismissed. As it was, doubts were cast upon it at the time by H. Dennis Bradley, who thought Soal's evidence flimsy. Soal also got his dates muddled up (another brother signed a statement that he had read the 'communications' at Christmas time in 1921, though the seance was held later); and Alan Gauld has since uncovered further grounds for suspicion. Soal's reputation in any case lies in ruins following the recent discovery that he fiddled the results of a card-guessing series in the 1940s. But at the time, the general good impression was confirmed by his later reports, which were in the High-and-Dry tradition.

Not merely was Soal critical of investigators whose work did not come up to the most exacting standards; he had no hesitation in casting aspersions on them as dupes, or even as rogues. Underlying all Crawford's work with the Golighers, he claimed in a letter to the *Journal* in 1931, was a fundamental assumption which Crawford had never adequately verified 'and which grew more and more tacit as time went on'. The tacit assumption, of course, was that the levitating agency was a supernormal force 'and not a human leg' – a statement which could only be read as implying that Crawford, if he were not in collusion with the Golighers, had deliberately ignored the possibility of fraud on their part.

Soal had also been contemptuous of what he regarded as Warcollier's casual research methods, and the difficulty of making a firm assessment of their results if experimenters were allowed to claim partial success when there was some associative connection between the percipient's guess and the object to be guessed. 'If, as M. Warcollier seems to believe, telepathy often works by very obscure associations apparent only to the percipient himself,' Soal complained, 'then it is difficult to see how science is going to deal with it objectively at all.' The words 'apparent only to the percipient himself' were a subtle distortion of Warcollier's argument: there might indeed be occasions when only the percipient could point to an association – for example, if he had guessed an object which for some subjective reason was intimately linked with the object which was being 'sent'; but Warcollier had been chiefly concerned to emphasise the possibility that a percipient might pick up a mind's-eye picture of an object which had a clear *objective* resemblance – say, in its shape.

Inevitably, Soal had been critical of Ina Jephson's experiment, the more so as his own trials to find potential telepathic subjects had been unproductive. With Besterman, he ran a second trial along similar lines, but with the precaution that the cards were sent to the volunteer percipients enclosed in opaque envelopes; and this time there were no positive scores and no decline effect. Soal's conclusions, which he stated with ill-concealed relish, were that people with telepathic faculty were extremely rare, and that evidence to the contrary was chiefly based on the experimenters' wishful thinking.

Rhine's results consequently came as an irritating surprise. In his letter to Prince on the subject Soal was sourly critical of the work at Duke because of the failure, as he thought it, to take adequate precautions. He enclosed a list of specific criticisms, to be sent on anonymously to Duke; but by the time the letter reached the Boston society, Prince had died, and both the letter and the enclosure were forwarded to Rhine. It was the measure of Rhine's self-confidence, by this time, that he contented himself with a cool reply, forcing Soal to excuse himself by claiming that unlike Dingwall, who had reached a condition of not wishing to get any positive evidence for psychical phenomena, he at least kept an open mind. So he did; but he would not have been sorry to demonstrate that Rhine's results were unreliable, and he set up trials which, if they continued to produce the negative results he had been obtaining under properly controlled conditions, would suffice to render Rhine's suspect.

In the summer of 1934, Soal circularised the people who had

already taken part in some of his experiments, some because they had had psychic experiences. Twenty-three of them took part in experiments on the Rhine model. The results were negative. The following year a further appeal for volunteers, reinforced by the promise of money prizes, failed to lure anybody capable of scoring significantly above chance. In 1936, spiritualist mediums who had been invited to show their capabilities fared no better. Finally he tested Mrs Garrett. Although before the results were made known she expressed her satisfaction with the test conditions, in over 12,000 guesses she 'did not show a glimmer of any paranormal faculty', whether Soal or anybody else was in charge.

G. N. M. Tyrrell

By 1937, however, Soal's negative results were of relatively little concern to Rhine; he had so much else going for him. In his *New Frontiers of the Mind* he had no difficulty in disposing of his English critics: including one who had claimed that he could accept the evidence for telepathy but, as he could not accept clairvoyance, felt bound to dismiss the evidence for it as fallacious; and another who believed that the explanation for the good results at Duke was that his assistants, subjects and colleagues had all been engaged in pulling his leg. In any case, only the High-and-Dry element had been hostile; some psychical researchers had been profoundly impressed, and were seeking to follow Rhine's example.

One successful series of trials with card-guessing had already been reported in England by C. W. Olliver, who described them in *The Extension of Consciousness: an introduction to the study of metapsychology*, published in 1932; but his work was disregarded by the SPR, not even obtaining a review in the *Journal*. The most interesting of the trials on the SPR's behalf, from the point of view of finding new ways to test and monitor ESP, was being undertaken by G. M. N. Tyrrell, formerly a radio engineer with the Marconi company, who had retired early in order that he might concentrate on psychical research. He was one of the mellowing influences within psychical research because, as Rosalind Heywood was to recall in *The Sixth Sense*, he had a rare combination of qualities: 'scientific training, the power to generalise from a number of apparently unrelated particulars, and an encouraging personality which never inhibited a timid percipient'. He was also an agreeably lucid writer, as he was to show in *Science and*

Extra-sensory Perception

Psychical Phenomena, published in 1938, in which he described his research.

In the early 1920s Tyrrell had found that his adopted daughter, Gertrude Johnson, 'possessed the extra-sensory faculty in a marked degree', as it constantly showed up in her everyday life; and he began to test her with playing cards, which she was able to guess successfully. Rhine's work prompted him to try something different, in 1934, based on the knack she showed of finding lost objects. He set up a row of five small boxes, open on his side: choosing a box at random, he would insert a pointer, saying 'IN' and Gertrude, on the other side of a screen, had to guess in which box it was. In 30,000 trials Gertrude had over 9000 hits, as against chance expectation of 6000 – odds of 'billions to one' against chance. And in trials with six other 'senders' her results, though less spectacular, were also 'billions to one' greater than chance.

Heartened by these results, Tyrrell had begun to cast around for ways in which to remove all possibility that sensory cues could influence the results. The randomisation could be made mechanical; the operator could be kept in ignorance of which box was being indicated (which would also mean that telepathy between operator and subject could be ruled out; if the findings were positive, it would be through clairvoyance on the subject's part); the guesses and 'hits' could be recorded automatically, to eliminate the possibility of human error; and 'the whole operation should be proof against possible fraud or misuse'.

In each of the five boxes, Tyrrell installed a small electric light bulb, wired up so that any one of them could be lit by a gadget which switched them on in a mechanically randomised sequence; when the operator pressed the key, he would not know which box would be lit. The results were automatically recorded on a strip of paper, moved by clockwork every time a box was selected by the percipient; a single mark was registered on the paper if the guess were wrong, a double mark if it were right.

By throwing a switch, too, Tyrrell could arrange that the light would not be turned on until the percipient actually opened the lid, ensuring that the percipient could not be helped by any leakage of light or heat from the box. With these refinements installed, Tyrrell tested Gertrude again. In 1700 trials, the odds against her obtaining her successes by chance was a thousand million to one when the light was already lit at the time she guessed, and a million to one when it was lit by delayed action.

Gertrude's ability to score above chance, in other words, was not affected by the fact that Tyrrell did not know which box was selected. She must be using clairvoyance. And this could not be by 'seeing' the light go on in the box, because she was still scoring far above chance when the light did not go on, because of the delayed-action switch. Could the explanation be that precognition, rather than clairvoyance, was responsible? This was easy to check: all that Tyrrell had to do was get Gertrude to select and open the box *before* he pressed the key which would select the (randomised) number and light up the bulb. In 2255 trials Gertrude had 539 hits as against a chance expectation of 451: the odds against this being obtained by chance again being many millions to one.

Summing up the results of his experiments, Tyrrell took the opportunity to rebut the contention of a 'a certain class of critic' who wanted consistent 100 per cent successful results if they were to accept that a medium was exercising extra-sensory powers. If the faculty existed, the critic would ask, why could it not be used at will?

> The answer has, I think, been sufficiently indicated. It is because normal perception tends to oust the supernormal and keep the field to itself. In order that the deep mental stratum which has the supernormal knowledge may use the normal motor mechanism to get this knowledge externalised, there must be some very delicate liaison work between the two types of consciousness involved, which is hard to establish and easy to derange.

On similar grounds, it was absurd to expect that positive results could be repeated at will.

> Try the same experiment with a humorist, that the above type of critic wishes to try with the sensitive. Say to him: You said some very witty things at dinner last night. Tonight I have got some people coming to hear you make some more jokes and take them down! Note the result. The very fact that an experiment is being tried tends to inhibit a faculty which depends on spontaneity. Because the subject-matter of physics is dependable and certain, this type of critic insists that psychological phenomena *ought* to be the same. There is no reason for this, except a mental inertia, which refuses to change its habits of thought; but the attitude is extremely common.

As Gertrude showed signs of nervous strain when guessing, Tyrrell surmised that her faculty ran in uneasy double harness with her normal faculties – 'the tendency is for the two to alternate rather than co-exist' – and there was always a difficulty in externalising the extra-sensory aspect, 'which lies in some department of the mind, on the fringe of normal consciousness'. But she showed no sign of instability, he insisted. Her integrity was 'quite unquestionable, and her attitude towards psychical phenomena in general one of robust commonsense tinged with healthy scepticism' – a testimony that was to be echoed by Rosalind Heywood, herself a shrewd judge of character. After their house was bombed in the blitz, the Tyrrells and Gertrude were to spend three years with the Heywoods; the family atmosphere had 'extraordinary serenity', Rosalind Heywood found, and Gertrude was 'no temperamental "psychic", but a sensible, practical and equable woman'.

Research on the Continent

Tyrrell's reports of his work left Rhine 'reasonably confident' that it had 'a sound basis and a brilliant future'. He was also delighted with the research of Hans Bender, a young psychologist working at the University of Bonn: 'Although this work was done independently of the experiments at Duke, and followed a quite different method, its confirmation of the American findings is clear at many points in Bender's report.'

Bender used twenty-seven cards, on which were the letters of the alphabet, and a full stop. The cards were put in opaque envelopes, and hidden from the percipient 'Fräulein D.' in, say, a box or pinned behind a curtain; and she would guess them in much the same way as Ossowiecki, sometimes hesitantly drawing the letter, in a manner which suggested she was groping towards it. The results were best – again like Ossowiecki's in Poland ten years earlier – when she was allowed to handle the envelopes; and here, Bender used an additional check: he put the card in cellophane, and allowed her to handle it under a cloth. In these trials 'Fräulein D.' got 37 correct out of 134: chance expectation was five.

Ossowiecki was himself maintaining his record, unblemished. The SPR's *Proceedings* in 1933 contained an account of an experiment along the same lines as the one which Dingwall had conducted ten years before, though this time Besterman was in charge, and as Dingwall was out of favour, no mention was made of his results.

Besterman had been introduced to Ossowiecki while on a visit to Warsaw in the spring, and Ossowiecki had agreed to 'read' the contents of a sealed envelope which would be sent to him from England. The first attempt failed because the Polish censors, their suspicions aroused, opened the envelope. A second envelope reached its destination; and as Lord Charles Hope was going to Warsaw in the autumn, it was agreed that he should monitor the proceedings.

The envelope contained a light-tight reddish-orange envelope in a light-tight black envelope, enclosed in a manila envelope doubled in two and sealed with surgical tape; each of the envelopes was sealed with private and invisible marks which would make it impossible for anybody to open them and then seal them up again undetected. This package, enclosed in yet another envelope, had been handed to Ossowiecki by the President of the Polish psychical research society, who had two sessions with him in August. In the first of them, Ossowiecki said that there were four envelopes; and in the second that the enclosure was not, as he had thought at first, an illustration cut from a paper.

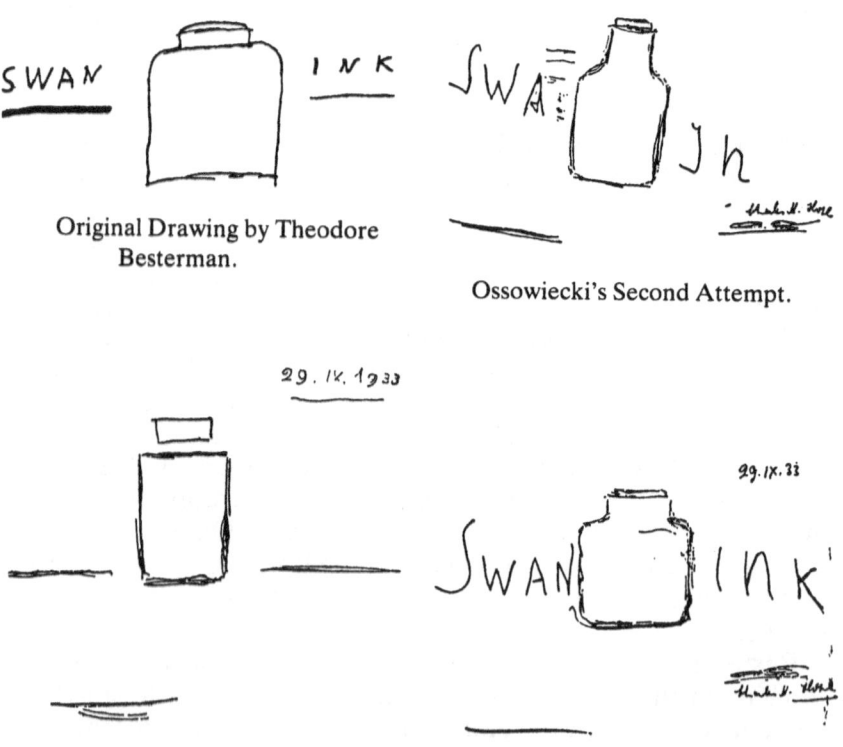

Extra-sensory Perception

It is a drawing made on a big piece of paper, this drawing is 5 × 6 cm.

There are three envelopes – one exterior, the next black, the third coloured – as it is neither yellow, nor blue, nor red, I think that it is rose, but I do not see very well.

Beside the drawing there is something written.

It represents something like a goblet, closed with a cork, and there is something written, not only the goblet, but around it – I see a W – I see a capital I – I also see an S and something red and something blue. That makes me confuse it with the letters.

It had been agreed that the envelope would be opened in the presence of both Besterman and Ossowiecki: this being impracticable, the decision was taken to open it on 29 September, with Hope standing in for Besterman. Another 'reading' was held, the envelope remaining in Hope's pocket while Ossowiecki described the circumstances in which Besterman had made the drawing and prepared the package. It was a mixture, Besterman subsequently explained, of accuracies and inaccuracies; but Ossowiecki then did three drawings, each one coming closer to the original. Hope then opened the envelopes, taking care not to destroy the sealing, and displayed the original.

Like Dingwall before him, Besterman could detect no flaw in his precautions. Inspection of the seals and the private marks convinced him that the envelopes could not have been tampered with, and they would have resisted any known form of penetration, such as X-rays. A point to be noticed, he added in his report, was that the paper had been folded in such a way as to destroy the form of the bottle, and the word 'SWAN'; yet this had not affected the reading, which was 'almost an enlarged facsimile'. The experiment, Besterman had to admit, had been 'almost completely successful'.

The record of Pascal Forthuny – Georges Cochet, well-known in France as novelist and critic – was hardly less impressive than Ossowiecki's. 'A cultured writer and accomplished artist', as his friend Sudre described him, his psychic abilities had been described in a book by Osty in 1926, and he had continued to give private sittings, or to demonstrate at the Institut Métapsychique. Like Ossowiecki, he made no attempt to profit from his faculty.

He had realised its existence while he was writing; his hand began to doodle on its own, at first making random strokes, and then producing words and sentences, indicating the influence of a 'communicator' who turned out to be his son, who had been killed in an air crash. For a while the information Pascal Forthuny received was commonly inaccurate, but when he found that he could pick up information better through psychometry, he submitted to experiments at the institute, with impressive results: Osty, who ran them, calculated that a third of his guesses were correct and a third in part correct. This was much the same proportion as Murray achieved; and it was obtained, according to Forthuny, in much the same way as Murray's, through the senses – sometimes the mind's eye, sometimes the mind's ear. The visual images were not defined enough to qualify as hallucinations, but the auditory sounds were: he could hear them clearly.

In his demonstrations at the institute Forthuny's method was simple and effective, even if not calculated to impress a High-and-Dry, let alone a sceptic. He walked among the audience, stopping when an idea struck him to say whatever came into his head to the person sitting in front of him: the facts, revealed in fragments, were sometimes indiscreet, but he was always careful to present them allusively, so that the individual alone would recognise them; and Forthuny would know when to stop. He did not pretend to be able to perform in this way with anybody, and he knew that he was sometimes led off along false trails; but his ability to provide a mass of information to, and about, complete strangers was unquestioned.

Forthuny's demonstrations were of interest to Sudre for another reason: they illustrated certain problems in connection with proving the reality of extra-sensory communication. Sometimes he would feel drawn to a person, and begin to give him names and details which would turn out to be applicable not to him, but to the man sitting next to him. Or the names would turn out to be puns: one young man who was told he was a 'cardinal of the Curia' turned out to be an assistant of Mme Curie's. In any controlled trial these would have gone down as errors or coincidences; but they happened so often that displacement seemed a more likely explanation for many of them.

There were also a few indications that some of the more open-minded scientists were ready to make public their acceptance of ESP. In Germany Hans Berger, the discoverer of 'brain waves', which he recorded on an electro-encephalograph, announced that he accepted telepathy; partly because of a personal experience. As a young man, after he had fallen into the path of a mounted battery and narrowly escaped being crushed to death, a telegram arrived from his father – the first, and only, telegram Berger ever received from him – asking if he was all right, as his sister had a strong feeling that he had been involved in an accident. Later, experiments with students convinced him that 'the parapsychological phenomenon of *'Gedankenübertragung'* between one brain and another must be recognised as fact; as he suggested that the electrical manifestations related to perception represented the conversion of electrical into psychic energy, which could be transmitted through space, and act upon the recipient telekinetically.

This was courageous of Berger, as his work on 'brain waves' had yet to win orthodoxy's respect. It was a little easier for Alexis Carrel, as he had won a Nobel Prize in physiology in 1912 – the year before Richet's. Carrel's *Man the Unknown*, published in 1935, was an international best seller; and in it he disclosed that as a medical student in the 1890s he had conducted his own psychical research, and made his own deduction from it. Clairvoyance and telepathy, he had decided, 'are a primary datum of scientific observations'. As a faculty they developed only in a few people; but they were widespread in a rudimentary state, demonstrating that 'knowledge of the external world may come to man through other channels than his sense organs', and that thoughts could be transmitted:

> These facts, which belong to the new science of metapsychics, must be accepted just as they are. They constitute a part of the reality. They express a rare and almost unknown aspect of ourselves. They are possibly responsible for the uncanny mental acuteness observed in certain individuals. What extraordinary penetration would result from the union of disciplined intelligence and of telepathic aptitude!

We know only one of the aspects of intelligence, Carrel concluded, which is 'but a small part of a marvellous activity consisting of reason, judgment, voluntary attention, intuition, and perhaps clairvoyance'.

9 Backlash

The publication of Rhine's *New Frontiers of the Mind* in the autumn of 1937 marked parapsychology's highest point. In it, Rhine was able to deal effectively with his critics by elaborating on the precautions which had been taken at Duke to prevent error or fraud, and by showing that his results had been repeated in other trials, elsewhere. The *Journal of Parapsychology*, too, launched earlier in the year, showed that new percipients were being found; including the most successful of them all, in this period, a young woman music teacher who was tested by Bernard Riess, a psychologist at Hunter College, New York. Riess, sceptical of Rhine's claims, made sure that she did not see the cards or pick up any sensory clues by having her conduct the trials in a house a quarter of a mile away; but in a series of runs of the Zener cards, conducted weekly over a period of months, she amassed the staggering total of almost 1350 'hits' out of the 1850 guesses: 18 correct, on average, in each run, against the chance expectation of 5.

As *New Frontiers* was heavily promoted not only as the choice of the Book-of-the-Month Club, but on Zenith Radio, which ran a series of programmes on ESP, along with tests, at a peak listening hour, Rhine became a household name. At the same time, however, his research and his reputation became a threat to those academic psychologists who had brushed aside or ignored ESP; and he now began to feel the backlash.

Predictably, Jastrow had been hostile. His complaint about *Extra-Sensory Perception* had been that Rhine did not always specify the precise procedure adopted in trials; and other sceptics had joined in, picking on different aspects of the research. Chester E. Kellogg, a psychologist at McGill University, chose to denounce Rhine's statistical apparatus: as a result of it, he feared, 'the public is being misled, the energies of young men and women in their most vital years of professional training are being diverted into a side-issue, and funds expended that might instead support research into problems of real importance for human welfare'. Unluckily for Kellogg, all he succeeded in doing was irritating the

Backlash

statisticians, a new academic breed who resented being taught their business by outsiders. 'Dr Rhine's investigations have two aspects, experimental and statistical,' the President of the Institute of Mathematical Statistics explained in a formal press release. About the experiments he had nothing to say; 'On the statistical side, however, recent mathematical work has established the fact that, assuming that the experiments have been properly performed, the statistical analysis is essentially valid. If the Rhine investigation is to be fairly attacked, it must be on other than mathematical grounds.'

The publicity in connection with the controversy over his work had earlier been conducted chiefly within the academic fold. Once it had spread outside it, his critics could feel justified in denouncing, and even smearing, him and his colleagues; and Rhine-baiting was to become a minor industry.

A foretaste of what was to become common was provided in Science Service, an agency which had been set up with the aim of keeping the public informed about scientific developments with the help of its bulletin, *Science News Letter*, which was circulated to libraries, schools and private subscribers. Ordinarily it concentrated on providing information, eschewing controversy; but its editor and its psychology editor, Marjorie van de Water, came to hear about a discovery made by the rising young behaviourist, B. F. Skinner, that some packs of Zener cards had been so imperfectly made that it was possible, in certain lights, to detect the pattern on the front through the back. Skinner had written to Rhine to tell him; although he had not published the information he had not kept it to himself, and it had found its way to Marjorie van de Water, who published photographs of the cards with an article which, to the casual reader, carried the implication that here was the explanation of the Duke results.

Rhine had, as it happened, been well aware of the danger of subjects learning to detect the symbols on cards by examining their backs, though for a different reason. Half a century before, sceptics had accounted for success in card-guessing by claiming that the percipients were learning to identify cards from their backs by memorising, perhaps unconsciously, tiny indications *on* their backs. So quite apart from the fact that not all Zener cards were faulty, and that few of the tests with those which were faulty would have been carried out in light sufficient for the patterns to have been detected through the backs, precautions had in fact been taken in formal trials to ensure that percipients could not see the backs. In any case, in many trials percipients were asked to guess down through an undisturbed pack. Yet the fact that the defect in the cards had not been noticed could be made to sound damning; and although the editor of *Science News Letter* was reprimanded by Science Service's trustees for so blatant a departure from objectivity, the damage had been done. The discovery of the faulty cards was seized upon with relish by those psychical researchers who for one reason or another were unimpressed by Rhine's reports. 'It is, I think, to be desired that our colleagues in America should try to pay a little less attention to the statistical analysis of their results,' Dingwall wrote sarcastically in the SPR *Journal*, which he could still use as a medium for correspondence in spite of his estrangement from the SPR Council, 'and should try to take the trouble, however arduous it may be, to train themselves properly to conduct and report the experiments on which they base analyses.'

The Fatal Thumbprint

By this time the High-and-Dry element in psychical research had become so corroded by scepticism that it was often more sour even than outside critics, such as Jastrow; in America and in Britain, the SPRs were tearing themselves apart. The year which launched ESP, 1934, also saw what turned into the death throes of research into physical mediumship, because of what appeared to be damning reports from investigators.

In Boston, 'Margery' had continued to give seances, and the American SPR had continued to report them. This alliance had survived even the defection of Bird, who for some reason which was never satisfactorily explained decided in 1930 to level an accusation against Mina not for what she was doing at the time, but for something which he claimed she had tried to do at the time of the Houdini investigation.

Mina, Bird claimed, had asked him to collaborate in a trick designed to baffle Houdini. 'She sought a private interview with me and tried to get me to agree, in the event that phenomena did not occur, that I would ring the bell-box myself, or produce something else that might pass as activity by "Walter".' At another seance in 1924, he claimed he had seen displacements of the table 'produced by the normal use of the psychic's feet'. Bird was not suggesting that all the phenomena were faked: half of them, he thought, had been genuine. 'If he admits half a ghost,' 'Walter' commented, when told, 'that's as good as a whole ghost!' But the damage was done – not so much to 'Margery', as to Bird. If he had noticed cheating, why had he not said so at the time? For propagating this heresy, Bird was sacked from his job as the ASPR's research officer; and when he approached the Boston society in the hope of having his paper published, Walter Prince would have none of it. Bird faded from the scene (Tietze, who tried to find out what had happened to him subsequently, drew a blank).

Two years later, however, another member of the ASPR produced information which discredited the Crandons more effectively than any of their previous investigators had been able to do. One of 'Walter's' accomplishments was his ability at seances to put his thumbprint on wax in a bowl placed out of 'Margery's' reach. It was assumed to be 'Walter's', because a man who claimed to be a fingerprint expert had compared it with a print found on an old razor belonging to Walter in his lifetime; and nobody had thought to double-check until E. E. Dudley, aggrieved by the appointment over his head as 'research consultant' of a man who had been his assistant at the ASPR, decided to compare 'Walter's' prints with those of people who had attended seances from the start – 1923. Among them was the dentist who had shown how 'Walter' might make his prints on wax; and Dudley found that the prints which had been attributed to Walter were, in fact, those of the dentist.

Dudley was careful to state, in his report to the ASPR, that this was not in itself proof that the prints had been faked. 'From a strictly scientific standpoint, identification has very little bearing on the question of supernormal versus normal origin,' he wrote: 'Walter', perhaps, might be able to explain why they were not his own? But when his article was turned down for the ASPR *Journal*, he passed it to the Boston society. Prince had mistrusted Bird, but he had nothing against Dudley, and the article appeared in the Boston society's *Bulletin* in the autumn of 1932. It looked damning; and the immediate reaction of the President of the American SPR only made matters worse. He accused *Dudley* of substituting the dentist's prints for Walter's. Unluckily for this line of defence, the thumbprint feat had been performed while the Crandons were on a visit to London. In 1934, investigation of the London prints showed that Dudley's accusation had been well-founded; they were the dentist's.

This discovery brought 'Margery's' career to an end, for investigative purposes. Yet as some High-and-Dry members of the SPR noted, with characteristic perversity, it did not in itself discredit her mediumship. Even Mrs Sidgwick, commenting on Dudley's charges, had been careful to point out that discoveries about the identity of the thumbprint did nothing to explain how they had been imprinted on the wax at a time when 'Margery' was supposed to be firmly controlled. What still needed to be explained was why the supposedly strict controls had not worked. Besterman agreed; whoever's the thumbprints might be, 'the phenomenon would be of extraordinary importance if it were really supernormally produced'. It was not easy to see how 'Margery' could have escaped from control time after time to produce them – including at the strict London seances – without ever being detected.

Nevertheless the discovery effectively ruled out any prospect the Crandons might have had of restoring their credibility among psychical researchers. This was unlucky, as 'Walter' had just found a new way of baffling his critics at seances by interlocking two separate rings made of wood, leading the ASPR *Journal* to claim that the passage of matter through matter had at last been experimentally confirmed. It had been described by the German physicist, Johann Zöllner, in the 1870s, following demonstrations by the medium, Henry Slade, that he could 'ring' a table leg in such a way that the ring could not slide on and off; but when, following the Seybert report, it had been wrongly assumed that Slade had been exposed, Zöllner's high reputation as a physicist had been gravely damaged. Now, 'Walter' was able to produce several interlocked wooden rings.

A carpenter, it was pointed out, could fashion interlocked rings from a single piece of wood. Lodge, asked for his opinion, suggested that the matter could be settled by seeing whether 'Walter' could interlock two rings made of different kinds of wood; and he had two made, one from pine and the other from teak, for the test. 'Walter' triumphed: but when the rings were sent back to Lodge to receive his benediction, by the time they arrived they were useless as evidence, as one had broken.

This was not uncommon. Many witnesses – W. B. Yeats among them – saw the interlocked rings, and they were photographed; but then, they would disintegrate, or disappear, or crack apart. In 1934 Hannen Swaffer – one of Fleet Street's leading columnists, in spite of his evangelical Spiritualism – was shown the last surviving ring in Boston, sealed in a glass case. When he returned two years later, and the case was taken out again for inspection, 'the law of frustration' had been at work; one of the rings had fractured.

Rhine's *Extra-Sensory Perception* appeared just in time to distract attention from the Crandons' final humiliation; and understandably, psychical researchers have tended to regard the 'Margery' affair as an embarrassing interlude, best forgotten. There have been few takers for the point of view presented at the time by Gwendolyn Hack; that they should be numbered among psychical research's long line of martyrs. 'One occasionally finds persons so imbued with the spirit of sacrifice in the cause of science that they will undergo any kind of humiliation inflicted on them,' she observed in *Modern Psychic Mysteries*; and she praised the Crandons for having 'submitted to all kinds of tests, and endured untold indignity in order to convince the men of science'.

There is one other possibility. Tietze, summing up, rejected the Hack view, but did not rule out the 'straddling the fence' proposition; conceivably, the mediumship was sometimes genuine. He left it to his readers to decide. That Tietze, for whom Walter Prince 'was (if anyone in this incredible affair was) the hero of the Margery case', should have been left with any doubts at all might seem surprising. But anybody who reads the evidence without a preconceived determination to find the Crandons guilty will find such uncertainty understandable.

What has tended to be forgotten is that during ten years of seances, night after night, week after week, the Crandons were never actually detected in fraud. On the few occasions when individuals claimed to have seen how the tricks were done, as Houdini and Rhine did, they claimed only to have seen her foot do what other investigators, just as sceptical – Boring, for one – also saw, but realised might be done by a pseudopod, if such psychic limbs existed. In any case, the kind of trickery which Houdini and Rhine claimed they had witnessed could not begin to account for the staggering range of phenomena which 'Margery' (or 'Walter') produced; a range which can only be appreciated by a study of the transcripts, each of them signed by the sitters present, showing that even those who could not bring themselves to accept the paranormal component, such as McDougall, did not dispute that objects moved at a distance, tables turned somersaults, apports came and went, and 'Walter's' voice boomed out from different directions – even when, as Comstock testified, he had his hands over the mouths of both Crandons.

If there were fraud, it would be hard to disagree with Prince's verdict, which he gave shortly before his death, that the 'Margery' case must be regarded as 'the most ingenious, persistent and fantastic complex of fraud in the history of psychic research'. But this presents another problem. Nobody now, reading the transcripts, could take the Code/Hoagland hypothesis of *un*conscious cheating seriously. Both Crandons must have been deeply involved – and without assistants, as often they had only investigators to contend with. But reading the accounts of the early stages of Mina's mediumship makes it very difficult to accept the idea that the two of them had secretly perfected their conjuring act in advance, before trying it out on their unsuspecting friends. And if they *were* prestidigitators, cunning enough to have won Houdini's admiration, why should they have gone on giving private seances, as they were to do even after they had ceased to be involved in investigations? There was no money in them; and if fame was what they were after, they could have had it far more easily, and with no back-biting, from conjurors, by performing *as* conjurors. That they should have continued for so long to give seances for psychical researchers, simply to gull them, would be hard enough to account for; what is surely inconceivable is that they should have continued week after week, year after year, to give seances for their own circle of friends. What would have been the point? For Mina, in particular, the seances frequently involved discomfort. Why persevere, unless they hoped eventually to prove that the phenomena were genuine?

With hindsight, it is easy to see that because the seances were conducted in near darkness, there was never any real prospect of their providing conclusive evidence for the phenomena, in the absence of gadgetry which would have satisfied investigators that the Crandons were physically incapable of playing tricks. But here, the responsibility for their failure must rest chiefly with the investigators themselves; Prince in particular. Far from being the hero of the case, he should never, in view of his deafness and his incurable antipathy to the physical phenomena, have allowed himself to become involved in the actual investigations.

Prince lived just long enough to witness the downfall of the Crandons, following the news from London that the thumbprints were not Walter's; and also to have the satisfaction of launching Rhine's monograph, and savouring its welcome in the press. In a biographical note in 1976 Tietze was to describe him as 'a great man, perhaps the greatest man American psychical research has ever had on its side'. Greater than Rhine? In his handling of the evidence for the mental phenomena he was certainly outstanding; and *The Enchanted Boundary* remains the most effective demolition of scepticism of the era. But unluckily the physical phenomena were his blind spot – as they were McDougall's – at the very time when unprejudiced investigation was needed.

Mirabelli revisited

In the winter of 1933 a member of the American society, on a visit to Brazil, was able to make contact with Mirabelli, who by this time was in Rio. Mary S. Walker attended three seances with him; and she was impressed by the fact that he was still submitting to tests by scientists – and by the fact that the scientists were themselves impressed.

By this time, the phenomena were no longer so spectacular as they had been in the 1920s; but they were better calculated to convince doubters. They consisted mainly of the movement of objects at a distance from both Mirabelli and his investigators, including objects which she knew could not have been planted, as they belonged to her: her camera, and her hat. A fan, placed on her palm, 'began to wriggle about as if alive, before falling off'; and bottles of water on a table began to shake, until one of them fell. There were also a number of apports, both inside and outside the house; and she watched while flowers in a window box were uprooted as if by an invisible hand. 'Watched' was the operative term; Mirabelli's telekinetic powers still worked in light.

Mary Walker could not stay long enough to test Mirabelli more systematically; nor, in view of the collapse of confidence in the American society, could her report in its *Journal* be expected to carry much weight. By 1934, however, the British SPR had managed to make sufficient funds available to despatch Besterman on a trans-Atlantic tour designed to take in Mirabelli, the Rhines and other researchers; and Besterman's High-and-Dry reputation would make it more difficult to reject favourable verdicts, should he give them.

He did not give them. His assumption that the phenomena must be fraudulent, he told a meeting of the society after his return, had been confirmed in the few seances he had attended. Yet he could not account for some of the telekinetic phenomena he had seen; and in his anxiety to account for others he was compelled to out-Dingwall Dingwall in his devil's advocate role. When bottles on a table began shaking and clinking together, with Mirabelli some yards distant, Besterman had to admit he could not say definitely how the trick was done 'but I strongly suspect a black thread'. Could a black thread have escaped the vigilance of the investigators, examining the bottles before and after? Mirabelli, Besterman surmised, must have been able to throw the thread in such a way that it looped around a bottle: 'If this is done, it is only necessary to let go one end of the thread, which can then be recovered and secreted.' How this feat could have been achieved with thread so thin as to be invisible to witnesses, Besterman did not attempt to explain.

He also had to admit that he had not bothered to contact Mirabelli's earlier investigators, his excuse being that their testimony would have been of relatively little value because 'these gentlemen have in most cases had no experience with mediums other than Mirabelli, and they have no notion of the conditions under which psychical research should be conducted'. Ordinarily the council of the society, as then constituted, would have been expected to greet this verdict with relief. But Besterman, pleading ill-health, had cut short his stay in the Americas, failing to carry out his promised visit to Duke and to other centres on his planned itinerary. Feeling that he had let the society down, the council requested his resignation as Research Officer, and he had to comply.

That no serious investigation of Mirabelli was undertaken by researchers with experience of the continental mediums was indeed a blow; and although Besterman's successor, C.V.C. Herbert, reported some positive findings he had obtained in the course of a tour of them in the autumn of 1935, including some with Rudi Schneider, physical mediumship was by this time under a cloud. 'Straight' telekinesis – or as Rhine and his followers began to call it, psychokinesis, or 'PK' – shared its obloquy. Rhine began to investigate it in 1934, following a visit from a young gambler who claimed to be able to influence the fall of the dice, and soon obtained positive results; but it was some years before he cared to publish them because, according to Louisa Rhine in her *Mind over Matter*, the first priority was to win acceptance for ESP, and 'if now another revolutionary concept like PK were to be announced, coming as it would from the same laboratory, it might even tend to slow up whatever measure of recognition of ESP might be coming with the passing of time, and the accumulating of more experimental data'.

Backlash
The Demise of Physical Mediumship

Once only was the evidence for physical mediumship presented by a scientist whose views it was not easy to deride, as he had gone some way towards achieving the high reputation of his father in orthodox circles. When Lord Rayleigh, the fourth baron in the line, became President of the SPR in 1937, he chose as the subject of his Presidential Address 'The problem of physical phenomena in connection with psychical research', and although he was careful to say that he felt the society's turning away from them to concentrate upon the mental phenomena was justified – 'if I occupy your attention with a somewhat unfashionable topic, it is only because I happen to be less ignorant about the other and more fruitful branches of the Society's work' – he insisted that

> there seems to be an appreciable residue which has not been successfully dissolved by the acid of destructive criticism which has been poured over it. The evidence seems to stand, and if we dogmatically reject it we shall be open to the reproach of laying down what ought to be the order of nature, instead of observing what is . . . If it is difficult to reconcile with our other notions, that may only be because these require to be revised or extended. Physical science has had to make adjustments of that kind often enough in the last few decades, and it would be rash to conclude that we have reached finality.

Critically but sympathetically, Rayleigh used Crawford's research with the Goligher circle to illustrate his thesis. He had been sufficiently impressed by Crawford's accounts of his experiments to pursue enquiries about him, finding that he had also favourably impressed scientists who had known him. As Eleanor Sidgwick was no longer alive, Rayleigh could bluntly reject her speculation, echoed by Fournier and Soal, that the 'cantilever' which had levitated the table was not a pseudopod, but Kathleen Goligher's foot. Crawford's account showed that he had been careful to exclude that possibility, and he could see no reason for doubting Crawford's accuracy and candour – even Fournier, after all, had not impugned them.

To Rayleigh, Fournier's explanation – that Crawford had relaxed his vigilance prematurely – simply did not fit the facts. Crawford's accounts showed that he had continued to take all the precautions which Fournier had accused him of omitting to take. If Fournier had meant what he said when he wrote that he had 'no reason to doubt the conscientious and accurate character of Dr

Crawford's observations and records', why, then, had he accused Crawford of failing to take the very precautions which Crawford's records revealed that he *had* been taking? Crawford's books provided a complete answer to Fournier's general criticism, Rayleigh argued; and he was 'unfavourably impressed by Fournier's failure to notice this'.

Rayleigh, however, could not accept some of the evidence from some other researchers who had tested physical mediums. He assumed that full-form materialisations must have been fraudulent, 'deliberately produced by impudent impostors'; he was disturbed by Fournier's photographs 'showing the woven texture of what purports to be a psychic structure', and he could not accept Crawford's hypothesis about ectoplasm's ability to be either fluid or – in its cantilever role – stiff. Still, at least Crawford had boldly faced these problems. 'The candid way in which specific questions are faced produces a favourable impression, compared with the mysticism of so many writers on these subjects,' Rayleigh concluded. 'Dr Crawford's theory perhaps raises more difficulties than it answers; nevertheless, if work of this kind is ever satisfactorily built into the scientific edifice I do not doubt that he will rank as a pioneer.'

Rayleigh's Presidential Address turned out to be a graveside oration for physical mediumship. His predecessor in office had been Charlie Dunbar Broad, yet another Trinity man, who had been appointed Knightsbridge Professor of Moral Philosophy at Cambridge; and in a paper to the Aristotelian Society in 1937, in which he put forward a plea for precognition to be taken seriously, he dismissed the physical phenomena as unworthy of philosophers' serious attention: 'I do not doubt that at least 99 per cent of them never happened as reported, or are capable of a normal explanation which, in a great many cases, is simply that of deliberate fraud.' Even Tyrrell, whose *Science and Psychical Phenomena* was published the following year, devoted only one brief chapter to the physical phenomena. He had to concede that the results obtained by Osty and his infra-red apparatus suggested there must be 'some emanation of a quasi-physical kind, which issues from the organisms of the mediums when in a trance, obeys their volition and absorbs certain kinds of radiation'; and it was also perhaps unlikely 'that identically the same kind of phenomena should have been repeated over and over again in many different countries, unless there had been a nucleus of supernormal fact for the accretion of fraud to grow upon'; but he excused himself for not having gone

Backlash

into more detail on the ground that although they possessed an undoubted interest, 'the evidence is conflicting and the honesty of most of the mediums so far tested is at least doubtful'.

Soon, it was to be almost as if parapsychologists were treating the researchers into physical mediumship much as Stalinist historians treated those Bolsheviks who had been liquidated in the purges, expunging them from the record – at least in connection with their work in this area: Crookes, as a renowned physicist, and Richet, as a Nobel man, could not be omitted from lists of those scientists who had accepted physical phenomena. In *The Sixth Sense* – an important book, coming out as it did in 1959, when parapsychology was at its nadir in Britain – Rosalind Heywood managed to avoid the embarrassing subject. Two years later Gardner Murphy, in his *Challenge of Psychical Research* – also influential, as he had established himself as one of America's foremost psychologists – dismissed it in a sentence: 'Investigations of "physical mediums" from the 1870s to the 1930s were in general rather discouraging', before going on to deal with Rhine's research with dice. In her *Mind over Matter* in 1970 Louisa Rhine gave some space to Fukurai and thoughtography, none to the physical mediums. It was not until the advent of Uri Geller, and the renewed interest in the subject by physicists, that the taboo was to be gradually, and reluctantly, lifted.

10   Balance Sheet

As if in response to the wind of change, sweeping away the old-style psychical research to make way for new-style parascience, the last years before the outbreak of the Second World War saw the disappearance from the scene of the old guard.

Charles Richet died in 1935, at the age of eighty-five. He had been active as an investigator of mediums, and as a collector of case histories, for over half a century; the range of his interests had been even wider than Barrett's and his formidable reputation in orthodox scientific circles, and his Nobel Prize, had made him the chief spokesman for psychical research on the Continent. From the High-and-Dry SPR point of view he was a little slapdash in his writing. Eleanor Sidgwick feared he was careless over particulars, as indeed he could be; he declined to allow any weight to the ouija board communication from 'Hugh Lane' at the time of the sinking of the *Lusitania*, for example, on the ground that the sitters had known Lane was on board, whereas the incident's significance lay in the fact they had *not* known. He had not been 'trained up to SPR standards', in this respect, Lodge noted, a little patronisingly.

Nevertheless Lodge greatly admired Richet as 'an especially accomplished man of science, and an orator whom it was a privilege to hear; he was a brilliant conversationalist as well as a renowned physiologist and one who did not scruple to pursue truth into regions which his colleagues, and indeed he himself, regarded as unpopular and absurd'.

Immediately following Lodge's obituary of Richet in the society's *Proceedings* was 'In memory of Everard Feilding' by an old friend, E. N. Bennett. Feilding, too, had been involved in research into mediums for nearly half a century. His cast of mind was sceptical, but he was prepared to accept good evidence when he encountered it – and also to shrug his shoulders in wry amusement when he did not. 'He was always ready,' Bennett recalled 'to disregard the waste of time and money, to laugh at the exposure of trickery, and to suggest by way of consolation that after all we had gained some further knowledge of mediumistic psychology.' Years

Balance Sheet

Eleanor Sidgwick

Gladys Osborne Leonard

Sir Oliver Lodge

Sir William Barrett

Camille Flammarion

Dr W. J. Crawford

later, Dingwall was to add his tribute to 'the most acute and well-balanced investigator I ever encountered, and in addition one of the noblest characters I ever met'. But Feilding was one of a vanishing species, the gentleman of leisure with an income sufficient to enable him to pursue mediums and apparitions as part hobby, part life-interest, and the social connections to provide introductions, where they were needed. Henceforth few men could follow his example, except after retirement.

Feilding died on 8 February 1936: two days later, Eleanor Sidgwick followed at the age of ninety-one. 'An admirable administrator,' Renée Haynes has described her, 'she also contributed many reports to the Society, reports which exemplified her clarity of thought, her energy and her enormous industry.' In connection with subjects about which she had an open mind, her ability to set out the evidence lucidly and fairly was unequalled; 'I never knew anyone,' Mrs Salter said of her, 'less liable either to accept or reject evidence from any emotional bias.' But this only applied to evidence for phenomena which she *could* accept; and the narrowness of her range of acceptance had played a large part in promoting the SPR's decline.

McDougall died two years later. As an investigator of 'Margery' he had revealed his chief limitation, an inability to recognise and accept the physical phenomena of mediumship. In 1926 he even admitted that he simply had not been able to believe that 'ec', as he distastefully called ectoplasm, could both move objects at a distance, *and* appear like a crude human hand: hardly a sensible attitude in view of the considerable quantity of evidence that ectoplasm could do just that. Yet his role in establishing parapsychology in the United States, in spite of the 'Margery' fiasco, was all-important: his use of the Hodgson Fund to finance psychical research at Harvard, and then his work at Duke.

In Europe Osty's death, also in 1938, removed the chief prop of the Paris Institut Métapsychique which he had run virtually single-handed (and, in Sudre's view, high-handedly). It did not recover, closing down for the duration of the war in 1940. Psychical research on the Continent had in any case gone into a decline. The international gatherings at Athens in 1930, and in Oslo in 1935, were far less productive of interesting papers than their predecessors. In Germany, Tischner and Oesterreich had hoped to found a properly constituted research society after Schrenck's death, but lacked the funds to set it up; and the advent of Hitler proved destructive, as the Nazis' fascination with the occult did not extend to support

Balance Sheet

for research into ESP and telekinesis – Oesterreich lost his Professorial Chair at Tübingen for refusing to divorce his Jewish wife. He was to survive the war and to be restored to it; but in Poland, Ossowiecki was less fortunate. According to Sheila Ostrander and Lynn Schroeder in their *Psi: Psychic Discoveries behind the Iron Curtain* he turned down the chance to leave Poland when the Germans invaded, and spent the war using his psychic gift to help the resistance. 'On the day of the Warsaw uprising, he remarked "I see that I shall die a terrible death. But I have had a wonderful life!" Shortly, the Nazis machine-gunned Stefan Ossowiecki to death.'

In Britain there were valuable replacements for the old guard, as the succession of new presidents in the late 1930s showed: Charlie (as he still styled himself) Broad, Knightsbridge Professor of Moral Philosophy at Cambridge, Lord Rayleigh and Henry Habberley Price, Wykeham Professor of Logic at Oxford, were men of unquestioned academic distinction. But their interest was primarily in the theoretical aspects of psychical research; they were little concerned with investigation of the phenomena. And those members of the society who were concerned, with a few exceptions – Tyrrell and Whately Carington (he had changed his name from Whately Smith) chief among them – tended to be imbued with negativism.

Lodge, who had done so much to hold the society together, died in 1940. 'Where success can be measured,' his biographer W. P. Jolly has written,

> he was successful. In science his ideas are incorporated in millions of pieces of equipment working all over the world and beyond it in space. His university flourished. His books were read by millions and his lectures attended by hundreds of thousands. Some things which were 'imponderables' when he first studied them are now, like wireless waves, commonplace . . . he hoped that spiritual imponderables would too be shown to have an understandable reality. He died contented, and confident that this was so.

What gave Lodge his confident serenity is not easy, in retrospect, to understand, all the indications being that the latest developments in psychical research at Duke and elsewhere, promising though the results had been, were going to suffer the same fate as the careful research he had undertaken with Eusapia and with Mrs Leonard: outright rejection by the academic world. It would easily have been possible, in fact, at the time of the outbreak of the Second World War, for a sceptic to argue that in his lifetime, psychical research had accomplished nothing.

This would not, however, have been correct. One of the disadvantages under which psychical researchers laboured was that when they were successful – when some phenomenon which had been in the supernatural or paranormal category was naturalised – they were not given the credit. Yet they could reasonably have claimed the credit in connection with hypnosis, and with multiple personality.

Hypnosis and Multiple Personality

It had taken a little over a century for the mesmeric trance state, or in James Braid's purged form, 'hypnosis', to obtain recognition; and as it happened, this was conceded just at the time when psychical research was being put on an organised basis. Nevertheless its reclassification as fact, rather than occult fiction, was largely the work of psychical researchers, even if they had not begun to take that name until the 1860s. And their role in establishing dual or multiple personality is documented in the pages of the *Proceedings* of the psychical research societies, where the reports which eventually led to its acceptance were originally published – notably Morton Prince's work with 'Sally Beauchamp', which has retained its hold on the public imagination ever since (a new edition of his *The Dissociation of a Personality*, first published in 1905, has appeared recently), and Walter Franklin Prince's study of 'Doris'.

Neither of these developments, however, redounded to the credit of psychical research. In both cases, acceptance of the reality of the phenomena was contingent upon their being presented as forms of mental disorder. Hypnosis was 'induced hystero-epilepsy' – Charcot's way of persuading the French Academy of Medicine to recognise it; and although it acquired recognition, in the process it forfeited status – what self-respecting doctor would want to induce hystero-epilepsy in his patients? – reverting in practice to much the same standing as it had held before recognition, being practised mainly by travelling showmen and backstreet hypnotherapists.

Morton Prince's work with 'Sally' had a more immediate outcome: it helped to establish the notion that certain individuals, in certain circumstances, can take on different personalities. Because

Balance Sheet

of its historical association with diabolic possession, the possibility had been rejected (as the hypnotic trance had been) as 'put on'. That anybody might, without being aware of it, turn into a different person, had been dismissed as a superstition. Prince's work, however, coupled with that of Freud and Flournoy in Europe, had an important consequence during the First World War. From time to time soldiers who had been in the trenches would be found wandering behind the lines, suffering from loss of memory; but as in other respects they appeared to be in full possession of their faculties, they risked being shot as deserters, as some were. Thanks, however, to a few courageous psychiatrists – W. H. R. Rivers, in particular – who had come to accept that such men were suffering from a personality dissociation, 'hysterical fugue' – which sometimes meant acquiring a new personality – the authorities were persuaded to accept that this could be a consequence of honourable men pushing themselves too far (it tended to be the keen, dedicated soldiers, not the shirkers, who were affected).

As 'hysteria' and 'multiple personality' were still not considered a respectable enough diagnostic label, the disorder had to be described as 'shell-shock', and classified as neurological rather than psychiatric; but with the return of peace it became possible for the medical profession to grant the syndrome recognition in its own right. Before the war, Henry Habberley Price observed in his Presidential Address to the SPR in 1938, the idea that anybody could be two different people would have been dismissed as nonsense: 'Yet nobody (with the exception of a few old-fashioned philosophers) would now object to the concept of Dual or Alternating Personality, or deny that they have thrown great light on some of the most obscure phenomena of the human mind.'

Psychical research, however, won no kudos from the acceptance of either hypnosis or multiple personality. Instead, there was a repetition of what had happened when meteorites were transferred from the supernatural to the natural category: the process which Herbert Mayo, Professor of Physiology at Kings College, London, had caustically described in 1851. Any new truth had to face three stages of opposition, he warned in his *Letters on the Truths Contained in the Popular Superstitions*: 'In the first, it is denounced as imposture; in the second – that is, when it is beginning to force itself into notice – it is cursorily examined, and plausibly explained away; in the third, or *cui bono* stage, it is decried as useless, and hostile to religion.' Yet having gained admission, the new truth 'passes only under a protest that it has been perfectly known for ages'.

The particular truth which Mayo was seeking to establish was the dowsing faculty. It would not be the dowsers, he knew, who would receive the credit if and when their faculty were accorded recognition; it would be hailed as a triumph for orthodox science, performing a rescue act by snatching dowsing from its obscurantist occultist jailers. This was precisely what was to happen with hypnosis and with multiple personality. In both cases the process was assisted by researchers who had been initially on the occultist side of the barrier reef, but who realised that they might retain the credit only by steering them through to orthodoxy's shelter.

When psychology was establishing itself in the 1880s as an academic discipline independent of philosophy, hypnosis and other aspects of psychical research featured prominently on conference agendas. By the turn of the century hypnosis featured rarely, psychical research not at all; and the few orthodox psychologists who continued to work with hypnosis were taking care to distance themselves from the psychical researchers with whom they had so recently been closely identified, and with whom they had had to suffer from orthodoxy's derision. The first standard English textbook on hypnosis – published in 1903 and still being reprinted over half a century later – was written by a member of the SPR, J. Milne Bramwell; but he insisted that in all his years of research into hypnotism he had 'seen nothing, absolutely nothing, which might be fairly considered as affording even the slightest evidence for the existence of telepathy, or any of the so-called "occult" phenomena'; and although he claimed that he retained an open mind on the issue, in an appendix he took the line that spiritualist seances were a danger to health, and claimed that believers in clairvoyance could be divided into two categories: the deceivers and the self-deceived.

Hypnotism had for so long been identified with the 'higher phenomena', however, that the efforts of those who, like Bramwell in Britain and Pierre Janet in France, hoped to purge it of such associations, met with failure. Psychologists who hoped to advance their academic prospects realised they would be well advised to avoid any connection with it: still more, with its 'higher phenomena' aspect. Periodically orthodox scientists gave them reminders of the wisdom of this course. When the programme was being prepared for the 1914 meeting of the British Association for the Advancement of Science, Vernon Harcourt, a professor of chemistry, actually opposed the idea of admitting psychology as one of the topics, because if psychology was allowed in it would be impossible to keep 'psychics' out.

As a result, hypnotism all but reverted in academic circles to its former occult status. An academic who continued to investigate it was likely to find that his results would only be published, if at all, in the psychical research journals. A few individuals courageously refused to be daunted, notably Sydney Alrutz, Professor of Psychology at the University of Uppsala, whose careful and well-documented investigations produced fresh evidence before and after the war for clairvoyance under hypnosis; but in the 1920s the High-and-Dry influence in the SPR, increasingly absorbed with the need not to offend orthodox susceptibilities, was turning against evidence obtained in this way. When Eric Cuddon's *Hypnosis* was published in 1938, as part of a series put out with the society's backing, it was clearly an attempt to divorce hypnosis from its unwelcome mesmeric association by playing down the 'higher phenomena'.

The same uneasiness characterised research into multiple personality. As suitable subjects such as Morton Prince's 'Sally Beauchamp' were rare, investigators might have been expected to use mediums, who could induce the symptoms. But to consort with mediums, even with impeccable scientific intent, would have courted misconstruction: Prince, who had used the societies' publications to put his case, backed away from identification with psychical research as soon as the case had been made. He investigated Mrs Curran, but with ill-concealed distaste; and as editor of the *Journal of Abnormal and Social Psychology* he was well placed to insist that multiple personality and dissociation must be regarded as mental disorders, with no psychic content.

There had been one other possibility: that the mysteries of multiple personality might be explored by anthropologists. The tribal shaman, witch doctor or medicine man was ordinarily chosen for his ability to dissociate: to enter a trance in which he would either be possessed by a spirit (so it was assumed) or could communicate with the spirits, to obtain information not available through the senses – often of a kind which struck Western observers as clairvoyant. 'We must not mind taking hints from quarters which are accounted scientifically disreputable,' H. H. Price urged in his 1939 Presidential Address to the SPR; and he cited the phenomena associated with Eastern mysticism (the yogi's abilities, from surviving for hours in airtight boxes to levitating, were still derided as a myth). 'I even think that the humble savage may have something to teach us,' Price went on. 'The most cursory reading of anthropological literature is sufficient to show that anthropologists have collected a whole mass of material which falls within our province, though their scientific orthodoxy has usually led them to assume it must somehow be explained away as fraud and delusion.'

Half a century before, Andrew Lang had urged the need for such research; but like the psychologists, anthropologists had shied away from it. In France César de Vesme collected what evidence he could find in his *Primitive Man*; but it was scanty, largely because of the influence of Sir James Frazer, and the theories he had propounded in *The Golden Bough*, which in spite of Lang's efforts had not yet been, as they were later to be, exploded. As Frazer had dismissed the psychic faculties of shamans as spurious, to have taken them sufficiently seriously to set up tests, with a view to discovering whether clairvoyance was involved, could effectively have destroyed any chance a young anthropologist might have had of academic advancement.

Parapsychology

Far from advancing the cause of psychical research, then, its two major achievements had set it back. The hypnotic trance state and multiple personality could now be presented as cleaned-up versions of mesmerism and possession. Extra-sensory perception, however, remained a worry to orthodox psychologists. The growing quantity of evidence for its reality made it hard to ignore; and the public interest which had been aroused was not going to be satisfied by the old argument that it was contrary to the laws of nature. If a radio transmission from Sydney could be heard almost simultaneously in Stoke-on-Trent and Seattle, why should minds not be able to tune into each other in the same way? The analogy might be fallacious, but it was attractive; and this posed the threat of a revival of interest in the anti-materialist ideas of Myers and William James.

'It will be a great day,' Flournoy had written in his *Spiritism and Psychology*, 'when the subliminal psychology of Myers and his followers and the abnormal psychology of Freud and his school succeed in meeting, and will supplement and complement each other. That will be a great forward step in science and in the understanding of our nature.' And the two schools were gradually to come together; but with little appreciable effect on the development of parapsychology in the years between the wars, in spite of the fact that Freud and Jung were both corresponding members of the SPR, and both deeply interested in the subject.

Freud was warned off publicly expressing his interest in telepathy by his disciple and biographer, Ernest Jones, a deep-dyed sceptic, with the result that the paper he wrote on 'Psychoanalysis and Telepathy' in 1921 was not published until after his death. Invited by Hereward Carrington in 1921 to act as co-editor of a periodical devoted to psychic matters, Freud refused, but added 'if I had my life to live over again I should devote myself to psychical research rather than psychoanalysis'; but as Jones was able to show in his chapter on occultism, Freud was ambivalent on the subject, wavering between interest and doubt, and the extent of his interest was not appreciated until the biography appeared in 1957.

Jung's fascination with the subject began when he was a student in the 1890s and in his *Memories, Dreams, Reflections* he was to provide a vivid account of his experiences then and later; some of them of the poltergeist type, as when, hearing a 'deafening report', he went to investigate and found that a breadknife had unaccountably snapped into several pieces. And a similar bang accompanies the best-known of his psychic experiences, on the occasion in 1909 when Freud, still in his materialist phase, was pouring scorn on them.

> While Freud was going on in this way I had a curious sensation. It was as if my diaphragm were made of iron, and were becoming red-hot – a glowing vault. And at that moment there was such a loud report in the bookcase, which stood right next to us, that we both started up in alarm, fearing the thing was going to topple over on us. I said to Freud: 'There, that is an example of a so-called catalytic exteriorisation phenomenon.'
> 'Oh, come!', he exclaimed, 'that is sheer bosh.'
> 'It is not,' I replied. 'You are mistaken, Herr Professor. And to prove my point I now predict that there will be another loud report!' Sure enough no sooner had I said the words than the same detonation went off in the bookcase.'

Freud, not surprisingly, looked 'aghast', and the subject was not referred to again. But though Jung made no secret of his interest in the subject – a paper of his on the psychological background to belief in spirits was read at an SPR meeting in 1919 – his ideas had no appreciable influence until much later, and his experiences remained unknown, except to intimates, until the 1960s.

Science and Parascience

In any case, neither Freud nor Jung had much influence on academic psychology, as distinct from psychiatry, in the inter-war years. The majority of psychologists holding university posts were in the mechanist, materialist tradition, uncomfortable about psychic phenomena partly because of the link with spirits, demonology and superstition in general; partly because of the widespread assumption that the laws of nature had been discovered, and did not allow for ESP, let alone for telekinesis; partly because psychology had only with difficulty moved across the great divide between the Arts, where it had been philosophy's ward, and the Sciences. The move, in fact, was not yet complete; many scientists were (as many still are) unimpressed by psychology's claims for recognition. 'It is in loyalty to the spirit of science that I must deplore the animus of psychical research,' as Jastrow explained. 'The trial is on. It is either psychology alive and metaphysics dead, or vice-versa.'

Lodge had realised what the orthodox reaction to fresh evidence was going to be. If psychical researchers hoped that positive results obtained in laboratory trials would convert sceptics, he warned in *My Philosophy* in 1933, they were in for a disappointment. So long as the prevailing view remained entrenched, that psychic phenomena did not exist, and that reports of them consequently could not be genuine, experience had shown that positive findings pointing to their existence would inevitably be rejected, regardless of whether they were reported by a single investigator, or by several. However strict the precautions taken to eliminate error and fraud, Lodge feared, they would make no impression. In the case of Crookes's experiments with mediums such as D. D. Home, for example, nothing that he could have done would have made any difference: the phenomena he reported would not have stood a chance of being accepted even if 'every member of the company had been searched and handcuffed and chained up or controlled mechanically in any desired manner, with all their utterances recorded on a gramophone and all their movements on revolving drums'.

Far from impressing critics, Lodge went on, more elaborate precautions would simply provide them with a different excuse for rejecting the reported results. Any practised conjuror in such circumstances would take care to see that an investigator was kept preoccupied with apparatus, for then it would be unnecessary 'to take trouble to distract his attention'.

From the point of view of the medium, too, Lodge felt, the concentration on controls was unwise, and partly because 'a

Balance Sheet

genuinely sensitive physical medium, induced to sit among these strange surroundings, could hardly help being affected by them'. Controls of the kind which critics insisted upon could not provide for all contingencies; precautions taken in a telekinesis experiment could not rule out the possibility of an apport. With psychic phenomena, a critic reading the record would always 'assume that some precaution was after all neglected, and that if he had been there, things would have been different'.

It did not prove necessary, however, for academic psychologists to line up behind Jastrow to do battle with parapsychology. A simpler solution was to ignore the evidence. When Troland published *The Mystery of Mind* in 1926, he had shown the way. He felt compelled to admit that 'the psychologist and the physicist may conceivably be forced by facts to alter their views in future', but he proposed to leave the subject out of consideration, excusing himself a little lamely by saying that it was still not clear if the phenomena were mental; that there were doubts over their authenticity; and that he was going to deal with a different aspect of mind.

Boring, in McDougall's old Chair at Harvard, took a similar course. Initially impressed by Rhine's results in 1936 he put the Hodgson Fund to use, again, to stage a colloquium where Rhine could put his case, which he did successfully, answering all the criticisms which were advanced. Yet Boring continued to put up objections. The work at Duke had been shown to be statistically sound; but did statistically significant results in themselves prove the existence of ESP? And when Rhine enquired about the prospects of reviving psychical research at Harvard along the Duke lines, Boring, though he admitted that using the Hodgson Fund for this purpose would be 'just what the donors intended', confessed that he had not the energy to make the move 'if the Department is not back of it', a clear intimation that the department, although Rhine might temporarily have silenced it, had not been convinced.

Boring also advanced two more excuses, as if uneasily aware that he was being unreasonable: they were very short of space in the department, and 'I have lots of other things that I am much more interested in'. Like so many of the new breed of academic psychologist, Boring did not want to know about ESP. Unlike most of his contemporaries and successors, he had seen and heard enough of the evidence not to reject it out of hand; but there were plenty of rationalisations to help him ease his conscience. His contemporaries and successors in academic psychology had no need to worry.

Science and Parascience

It was extremely unlikely that pressure would be put on them to introduce parapsychology into the curriculum, or to conduct research into ESP; they could either ignore the subject or, like Jastrow and Skinner, examine it with the intention of finding flaws.

A problem arose only when, as at Harvard, a fund existed which the donor had presented specifically for psychical research; and then only if there was somebody in a position of sufficient influence to make trouble if it were not used for that purpose. William James's son, Henry, had helped draft the deed of gift in 1912; a quarter of a century later he was one of the Fellows of the Harvard Corporation, and influential enough to push Boring into action. The action, however, consisted of the setting up of a committee consisting of sceptics; a let-out was found, the Fund being devoted to research into the homing of a species of seabird, Leach's petrel, by K. S. Lashley – a disciple of J. B. Watson – and his graduate student, Donald Griffin. After all, as Lashley put it, the homing was almost extra-sensory, as nobody had been able to discover what sensory clues were used. But neither of them took the ESP possibility seriously.

At Stanford, Coover was on the point of retirement in 1937, when the pressure came on to investigate ESP; but he, too, was able to ensure that his replacement as Fellow in Psychical Research would concentrate on finding chinks in Rhine's armour. And in other universities in the United States there was no need for psychologists to concern themselves with ESP, unless they wanted to. It was not as if pressure would be put on them, by their colleagues in other disciplines. 'Even if telepathy were proved to be true,' an eminent biologist had told William James, 'savants ought to band together to suppress and conceal it,' because it would upset the uniformity 'without which scientists cannot carry on their pursuits'; and perhaps it was this feeling – that the existence of ESP, if admitted, would threaten all the new academic disciplines, as well as some of the old ones, which was decisive in ensuring that there would be no campaign to procure its recognition.

This applied even more forcefully in countries where the universities were in the hands of self-perpetuating and largely self-governing oligarchies, as at Oxford and Cambridge, and their power tended to extend to the scientific journals. *Nature*, establishing itself as a high priest in the temple of science, rarely permitted itself even to consider psychical research.

One of its few attempts at a dispassionate look at what the SPR was trying to do, in 1926, had been calculated only to irritate psychical researchers with its claim that the distinction between what they were doing and spiritualism was 'a somewhat artificial one', and it was characteristic that a letter from Harry Price defending the work with Rudi Schneider in 1932 was refused publication, whereas the letter he wrote following his 'exposure' of Rudi the following year was printed. Ironically, as Anita Gregory was to show, the text of the first letter, had the editor of *Nature* remembered it, would have revealed that Price was lying in the second, as in it he made 'a completely conflicting set of assertions about the same set of events'.

As a result scientists, who were becoming more and more specialised in their own fields of research, rarely heard about the results of psychical research except in journals where they were presented for popular consumption. In their own journals they could expect to read about it, if at all, only when evidence in favour of ESP was challenged. The need, therefore, as Whately Carington had been quick to realise, was for fraud-proof trials. He had immediately appreciated the significance of Rhine's work, on reading *Extra-Sensory Perception*: 'an extraordinarily important book,' he had described it to Walter Prince, 'quite the most important that has ever been done in this field'. But he had also written to Rhine to tell him, 'speaking frankly and brutally' that his critics would not be silenced 'until and unless you have systematically closed and rivetted and clinched the door of leakage until not the minutest crack remains'. And gradually, it was to become apparent that there were no watertight doors in parapsychological research.

Experience was to show that there were no watertight doors in research in psychology, either: that there were a host of variables and unquantifiables which could never be safely tied down, or excluded from the reckoning. In any case, parapsychologists were to find – as Sidgwick had warned – that even if it had been possible to lay on the perfect foolproof, fraud-proof test, its results would still be suspect, as there would remain the charge that all concerned, investigators and witnesses as well as subjects, were in collusion.

Paraphysics

Parapsychology represented only one of the routes which the psychical researchers could have taken in their quest for recognition. An obvious alternative was paraphysics, a term Hans Driesch used in his paper to the Clark symposium. Much of the effort in the first half century of psychical research had, after all, been expended upon physical phenomena; might it not have been better to concentrate upon breaking down the physicists' resistance – the more so as their defences were collapsing?

In the nineteenth century it had been physicists – Faraday, Tyndall, Lord Kelvin – who had been in the van of the opposition to psychical research. They regarded it as an absurdity, in view of what they took to be the immutable laws of nature; and, in Tyndall's case, of his faith in matter as the only reality. But apart from those physicists who accepted psychic phenomena because they had witnessed them, there were also some who regarded 'matter' as an abstraction. According to Flammarion, Henri Poincaré had often assured him in their conversations that 'as he doubted even the reality of the external world, he believed only in spirit'; and with Einstein's discoveries, followed by those of the quantum physicists, it became possible to see what Poincaré had been getting at. In his Gifford Lectures in 1927 Arthur Eddington, Professor of Astronomy at Cambridge, made his celebrated claim that, putting it crudely, 'the stuff of the world is mind-stuff'; and the following year Alfred North Whitehead could claim, without the risk of being derided as a crackpot, that the materialist foundations of physics were crumbling. 'Time, space, matter, material ether, electricity, mechanism, organism configuration structure, pattern, function, all require re-interpretation,' he wrote in *Science and the Modern World*. 'What is the use of talking about a mechanical explanation when you do not know what you mean by mechanics?'

Lodge was the first to grasp the implications of the new physics for psychical research. 'I and many others of the older generation are now being left far behind,' he admitted in a letter to J. Arthur Hill in 1928; but unlike some of his generation, he had nothing but admiration for the work of Heisenberg, Bohr and the other 'leaders of the revolutionary school' – not surprisingly, as they made nonsense of the arguments that Tyndall had used to defend his materialist faith. They also offered a way back to respectability for the spiritistic hypothesis, which 'in its simplest and crudest form', as Lodge put it to the SPR the following year, 'is that we are spirits here and now, operating in material bodies, being, so to speak, incarnate in matter for a time; but that our real existence does not depend on association with matter, although the index and demonstration of our activity does'. And when in 1931 Sir James Jeans claimed in *The Mysterious Universe* that there was a wide measure of agreement, 'which on the physical side of science approaches almost to unanimity, that the stream of knowledge is heading towards a non-mechanical reality: the universe begins to look more like a great thought than a great machine', it looked as if materialist science was dead.

More than that: Jeans gave heart to psychical researchers by citing 'action-at-a-distance': it was as if 'every bit of the universe knew what other distant bits were doing, and acted accordingly'. If so, how could the old *a priori* objection to telepathy or telekinesis be sustained? William Brown, too, had drawn attention to the significance of Bohr's discovery that electrons could move from one orbit to another without, apparently, traversing the intermediate space. This was just what apports, so familiar in seances, appeared to do. Even Heisenberg's indeterminacy principle, Besterman pointed out, was significant – 'of paramount importance', in fact, because 'if paraphysical phenomena exist, nothing seems more certain than their failure to appear when subjected to stringent tests'. Besterman, needless to say, was not using this to excuse the failure of mediums under strict test conditions; he was arguing that it was futile to expect proof of telekinesis from trials when conducted with sophisticated equipment.

The hopes of the psychical researchers were quickly dashed – as were Whitehead's. In *Nature and Life* in 1934 he complained that although every single feature of what had been regarded as the common-sense notion of physics, derived from materialism, had been dethroned, the common-sense notion 'still reigns supreme in the workaday life of mankind. It dominates the market place, the playgrounds, the law courts, and in fact the whole sociological intercourse of mankind.' The result was 'a complete muddle of scientific thought', even among scientists; their attitude was 'a touching example of baseless faith'.

Certainly the leading physicists showed no disposition to permit their theories to be pressed into parapsychology's services. 'I am at one with the materialist,' Eddington insisted, 'in feeling a repugnance towards any form of pseudo-science.' Einstein felt the same way. He agreed to write a preface to the German edition of Upton Sinclair's book, because he thought it was 'out of the question in the case of so conscientious an observer and writer as Upton Sinclair that he is carrying on a conscious deception of the reading world; his good faith and dependability are not to be questioned';

but he was later to claim in a letter to Jan Ehrenwald that he had written it in such a way that his lack of conviction was not indicated, 'without having to sacrifice honesty'. Einstein's scepticism, however, was fuelled by his hostility to the quantum physicist's action-at-a-distance' theory, because he thought it would entail either acceptance of telepathy or a denial of independent action. He would have had to think again had he lived to hear that action-at-a-distance had been confirmed by further research.

Of the leading physicists only Wolfgang Pauli, who worked with Jung on synchronicity, was prepared to venture into psychical research in this period; and if the physicists held aloof, it was not surprising that scientists in other disciplines continued to feel they need not bother to study the evidence. The belief, amounting to a faith, that science was still proceeding in an orderly fashion towards the goal of a materialist explanation for everything remained widespread. And this, as Jules Romains, poet, novelist and playwright realised, posed a dilemma. He put his thoughts into an article, 'The answer to the greatest question of all', in *La Nouvelle Revue Française* in 1939.

Fifteen years earlier he had written *Eyeless Sight*, a study of the evidence for the ability to 'see' without the need for eyes. 'Are we sure of having eliminated, once and for all, the hypothesis formerly held that one and the same nervous organ could, if need be, assume more than one function?' he had asked, and had gone on to cite tests which had seemed to demonstrate extra-retinal vision, and to make the point that sleepwalkers have often been observed to guide themselves 'with a remarkable ease, with their eyes closed'. The book had attracted little attention, and in his article he showed he had realised why: the human mind finds it hard to work on two levels of reality, as it was required to do when materialist assumptions were faced with psychic phenomena. He did not think that conventional science should feel threatened,

> yet it may one day be confronted with results by methods vaguely termed 'psychic' that are so coherent and conclusive that they cannot possibly be dismissed as null and void. When this happens, many people think there will be nothing to prevent so-called 'positive' science from continuing peacefully as before, while tolerating the development outside its own frontiers of an entirely different kind of knowledge which at present it either dismisses as pure superstition, or relegates to the realm of the 'unknowable', or of what it contemptuously describes as metaphysics. But it will not be as easy as all that. Some of the most important results obtained through psychic experi-

ments, as soon as they are confirmed (if they have to be) and officially recognised as 'true' will be a threat to positive science *within its own frontiers*; and the human mind which up to now, shrinking from its responsibilities, has pretended to ignore the conflict will then be obliged to arbitrate. This will create a serious crisis – no less serious than that provoked by the application to industrial techniques of discoveries made in the realm of physics. It may even change the whole of human life. I believe this crisis is not only possible but probable, and may even be with us very soon.

Romains's diagnosis was accurate; but not his prognosis. He had underestimated the power of 'positive' science to continue peacefully as before, containing quantum physics in spite of the fact that it made nonsense of so much of conventional teaching.

The Demolition Squad

Difficult though the task of psychical researchers was in the 1930s, as the academic world resisted acceptance of the results, it was made far harder by the presence within the SPR of members who devoted much of their time to the demolition of any positive results obtained; in particular Rhine's, but also those of British investigators. Soal was carrying out his series of experiments whose negative results inevitably suggested either that Britain lacked any subjects with ESP abilities, at a time when the United States seemed plentifully endowed with them – an improbable hypothesis – or that the Duke results were untrustworthy; and a new gadfly recruit, G. W. Fisk, managed to find a weakness in the tests which Tyrrell had been doing with Gertrude Johnson.

Unwelcome though his discovery was at the time, it was valuable in that it revealed just how careful researchers would have to be to provide foolproof and fraud-proof techniques. While Fisk was being tested to find whether he too could guess more often than by chance which box had a light on inside it, he found that if he went on choosing the same box, opening it until he guessed correctly, and then switched to another box and went through the same procedure, he could score consistently higher than chance. Evidently Tyrrell's attempt to ensure that he was choosing the boxes at random was not proof against a system – much as in roulette, a gambler might realise that there is some fault in the wheel which makes it likely that certain numbers will come up more often than others.

Science and Parascience

'No better example could be staged of the kind of thing which it is the paramount duty of the experimenter to guard against,' Tyrrell commented. He added 'or of anything more likely to create a subconscious resistance against the experiments as a whole'; because although it was clear that Gertrude had not been using the Fisk method – it could not work in trials when the targets were mechanically randomised, or when the subject did not know whether or not the guesses were right, in both of which she had also been successful – the shock of finding that she could have cheated in some tests, and the knowledge that this might be held against her by sceptics, not only made her ill, but also sent her scoring down to chance level.

This in itself had important implications for psychical research, Tyrrell realised. Following the publication of *Extra-Sensory Perception*, the immediate reaction of doubters in the SPR was that judgment should be suspended on the Duke results until they were confirmed in similar trials elsewhere; a point which Thouless made in his review. Thouless might think this an easy matter, Tyrrell observed; 'but what I wish to stress is that anyone who "repeats" them without reproducing the psychological atmosphere has not really repeated them at all'. The psychological atmosphere 'is elusive, but it is clearly of the greatest importance; and if the investigator disregards it, nature will not'.

If Tyrrell were right, this would be of no help to the cause of psychical research, as Dingwall almost gleefully pointed out in a reply. The same argument, he recalled, 'has been used to defend every clumsy experiment or blatant imposture'. Tyrrell claimed that Gertrude Johnson's scoring went down after an unpleasant experience; but how did he know that was the reason? 'How does he know that it was not because Miss Johnson's tea was not the right temperature, or because his bacon was not of the right brand, or because the moon was not in the right quarter?' The situation, Dingwall complained, was becoming farcical.

With critics in the SPR ready to pounce upon and maul any positive result, it was not surprising that the only work done by members which could be held to offer positive evidence for psychical phenomena was by Edith Lyttleton and H. F. Saltmarsh, collecting and, as far as possible, checking accounts of precognition. Within the society, however, these aroused little interest, as by this time there was a surfeit of such anecdotal case histories. Some way was needed to produce precognition in formal trials; but at a time when the British experiments with ESP following the

Balance Sheet

Duke guidelines were producing negative results, it hardly seemed worth while to pursue precognition in the laboratory.

This was, however, what Rhine himself was doing. He had noted the high proportion of cases of precognition, notably in dreams, which had reached him in correspondence (his wife Louisa was to take on this side of the proceedings, and later to present some valuable analyses of the evidence they provided). He had also been impressed by Dunne's account of his dreams, and still more by Saltmarsh's collection; and he had begun trials to see whether he could demonstrate precognition by using the same card-guessing methods as he had used for clairvoyance. When setting them up, however, he had been compelled to recognise that, confusingly, what at Duke they thought they had safely classified as clairvoyance might be attributable to precognition: to the percipient guessing the cards in advance. This had given him pause; and he had decided, as with psychokinesis, to delay publication until he had sorted out the problem. Still, the question whether the mind was able to 'overcome the barriers of time, as it has those of space' was important, he observed in *New Frontiers of the Mind*. It was not too much to say that it might prove to be 'the greatest question science has ever investigated'; but at Duke, they were beginning to think that 'it might also prove the hardest to solve'.

The University Council

With the SPR apparently unable to settle down to effective research, there seemed just a chance that Price might be able to redeem himself. His 'exposure' of Rudi Schneider might damn him in the eyes of other psychical researchers, but it redounded to his credit among academics who did not know the background facts; and he was now pursuing a course of action which, he hoped, would restore his ascendancy. In 1933 he had conceived the idea of offering his library and equipment to the University of London, along with an annual grant, provided that the university would recognise psychical research as a legitimate object of academic study; and this had been accepted. No college could be induced to provide suitable premises; but a quasi-formal University Council for Psychical Investigation had been formed, with Joad and Soal among its members, and this represented the first toehold Price had been able to secure in the academic world.

Price was by this time too dedicated to keeping himself in the public eye for the enterprise to have much chance of success; some of his gambits, such as a test of fire-walking, were too obviously publicity stunts rather than serious investigations. But the chief wrecker, on this occasion, was Soal. Dingwall at least made no secret of his growing hostility to psychical researchers (back firmly in his devil's advocate role, he did not consider himself one of them); but Soal was devious, as well as sour. At a meeting of the 'Ghost Club', which Price had revived in 1938, he launched an intemperate attack on the research at Duke, implying that it was useless because of the Rhines' failure to take even elementary precautions; yet in a review for the SPR a few weeks later of Kellogg's denunciation of Rhine, Soal contrived to give the impression that Kellogg's criticisms were unjust.

Soal was also playing a double game by passing on information about the SPR – which he was able to do, as he had retained his membership of their council – to Price. When Fisk suggested a further SPR test with the BBC, Soal warned Price; as a result Price's University Council got in its application first (in the SPR Council, Soal had to lie his way out, pretending that Price had thought of it first). Soal's diatribes against the SPR shocked his colleagues on Price's council – even Joad, who had been alarmed to find that Soal was accusing Gilbert Murray of cheating in playing his family telepathy game.

In 1938 Joad himself was made a laughing stock by an article he wrote for *Harper's* in which he described what had happened to him following a seance with the 'poltergeist' girl, Eleanore Zugun. On the train home he had taken up a new book, to find that some of the pages had been left uncut.

> I felt in my pocket for my penknife; the feel of it was certainly unusual and, pulling it out, I found that a crescent-shaped piece of metal – in point of fact the metal letter 'C' – encircled the knife in such a way that so long as the letter was there it could not be opened.

Reviewing Joad's article for the SPR, W. H. Salter recalled that in the *Proceedings* of Harry Price's National Laboratory eleven years earlier, Professor E. J. Tillyard had described how following a sitting with Eleanore Zugun, he had taken up a new book on the train home, to find that some of the pages were uncut,

> so I opened my greatcoat, put my hand down into the left pocket of my coat, and felt for my knife to cut the pages with. Then a curious feeling came over me. The knife did not feel like my knife at all. I drew it out and found, firmly attached to the metal half-ring of the

leather case enclosing it, a white metallic C which effectively closed the case. I realised at once that it was the C which had been lost ten days before from the notice-board of the ground floor of 16 Queensberry Place, the loss of which had been generally attributed to 'Dracu' (a 'control' of Eleanore Zugun).

It was certainly strange, Salter observed, 'that Dr Joad and Professor Tillyard should both have experiences so strikingly similar on the same occasion'; and he suggested that Joad, in view of his academic standing, should clear up the matter. Joad, for once, decided that silence was golden.

The resignation of some members of the university council had in any case by this time made it obvious to Price that his aim, to win academic recognition, was not going to be achieved; and he had decided to wind it up. He did, however, leave his library to the university, expressing the hope that when the 'stately pile' then being erected in Bloomsbury was complete, space would be found for it there; as it was.

The library remains his only enduring monument. 'Through his immense energy, enthusiasm and ability,' Dingwall has recalled, 'he outstripped all other investigators in the variety and sensational quality of his work.' He had used his opportunities, however, not for the advancement of psychical research, 'but in order to forward the personal interests and ambition that dominated his life'. Dingwall's assessment appears in Trevor Hall's biography of Price, which did much to explain his erratic courses. Price, according to Hall, was a life-long fantasist: what he said and wrote about his family, childhood and much else was sheer invention. When fantasy and reality fused, he could do very valuable work: unfortunately it is no longer possible to be certain which of his reports can be relied upon, and which should be discarded.

Much the same applies, though not for the same reason, to the work of Hewat McKenzie's British College of Psychic Science. The college was much more active than the SPR in promoting mediumship; the college's function, McKenzie believed, was to discover and train mediums, and try to ensure that they continued to give satisfaction to their clients. But although he was aware that there were fake mediums, and some who occasionally cheated – from time to time he exposed them – he was not interested in subjecting them to controlled trials: 'he had not the slightest idea of the real meaning of scientific work,' Dingwall complained, 'and possessed little appreciation of what constituted good evidence.'

Although his direct influence on the course of psychical research was consequently small, indirectly it was considerable. Through the college, John F. Thomas undertook a trans-Atlantic protracted series of proxy sittings, with his deceased wife as 'communicator', in the 1920s; and it was Thomas's sincerity and conviction which so impressed Rhine that he changed his plans, deciding to go to Duke to work with him, under McDougall's supervision. Thomas eventually became the first-ever graduate to obtain a Ph.D. for his work in psychical research, described in his *Beyond Normal Cognition*, published in Boston in 1937.

It was Hewat McKenzie, too, who launched Eileen Garrett on her long career. 'Whatever integrity and seriousness I have been able to achieve in my attitude towards using my supernormal sensitivities,' she wrote after his death, 'I feel that I owe to the untiring patience and faith of this unflinching and courageous man.'

Spontaneous Phenomena

Perhaps the most serious of the adverse effects which the craving for scientific respectability had on the course of psychical research was that it distracted attention from the investigation of spontaneous phenomena. The trend predated the publication of Rhine's *Extra-Sensory Perception*; realising what was happening, Lodge emphasised in *My Philosophy* in 1933 that to carry conviction, evidence about psychic happenings must continue to be accumulated, of all kinds, at all levels.

> I take it that the real strength of our position lies in the phenomena themselves, namely that they can be experienced by a number of people, and by one person after another, as time goes on, until the cumulative evidence becomes overpowering. Moreover I hold that what are called 'uncontrolled' experiments are not to be despised. For sometimes, under what may be called, and are really, less than strict conditions, phenomena occur of such vigour, and of so simple and striking a character, that they overcome suspicion and constitute their own demonstration.

Lodge's advice went unheeded, as F. C. S. Schiller lamented three years later in what were to be the last communications from his pen to appear in the *Journal*; he died a few weeks later. Cases of spontaneous phenomena, he observed, were now rarely looked into and reported: 'I venture to think that this scarcity may be largely due to the treatment which the bearers of tales about the supernatural too often receive from the officials of the Society' – in marked contrast to the treatment which they had received from Myers and Gurney, half a century before.

The mistake which was being made, Schiller argued, was a mistake about the nature of scientific method. The belief had arisen that what was needed were single cases, each providing clear-cut proof; but 'proof', he insisted, 'is always *cumulative*, and only yields growing *probabilities*'. Hence the need was to continue to collect cases which, though individually inconclusive, would add to the stockpile – and at the same time to the popularity, numbers and resources of the society.

Schiller's claim that it would improve the society's prospects if it took more interest in matters which the public was interested in was also clearly well-founded. Harry Price was busy exploiting the keen appetite for tales of haunted houses, with his accounts of his work at Borley Rectory; and on another level Lord Halifax, who had been Viceroy of India and was about to become Neville Chamberlain's Foreign Secretary, provided an introduction in 1936 to a new edition of his father's *Ghost Book*, which proved so popular that he followed it up with a second collection. Yet in this period the society veered away from active research into apparitions. Reports about them were still coming in: what was missing was any sense of urgency in investigating them. As a result information about cases which could have been of considerable interest often did not reach the society until it was too late to investigate them.

One such case was the haunting of a house in Ramsbury, Wiltshire. Samuel Bull, a chimney sweep, had died of cancer in 1931; and that winter his apparition was seen many times by his widow, daughter, son-in-law and grandchildren, as well as friends. They all recognised him, and he looked and dressed as he had done in his lifetime; his widow actually felt him, as he had put his cold, but firm, hand upon her. 'Grandpa Bull', as the children called him, could be heard at any time of the day or night, but he was seen only at night, when sometimes he would be around for hours.

The family informed the vicar. The vicar informed Lord Selborne. Selborne eventually informed Gerald Balfour. Balfour sent a questionnaire, which found its way back to the vicar. Providing the answers, the vicar warned that the family were soon to move into a council house, 'so that if the SPR propose to make any investigation there is no time to be lost'. Five days later, Balfour and Piddington arrived in Ramsbury, only to find the family in the process of moving house; and when the move had been made, Grandpa Bull appeared no more.

All concerned, including the vicar, were convinced that the family had been telling the truth. Sometimes there had been as many as nine witnesses to testify to the reality of Grandpa Bull; and as he lingered around, unlike most apparitions, his would have been an unusually easy case to investigate, and might have provided evidence 'of quite exceptional value', as Sir Ernest Bennett observed in his *Apparitions and Haunted Houses*, published in 1939. But the chance was missed because of 'the *vis inertiae* of those who had knowledge of the facts over so long a period and failed to report or examine them, and those too who, at the most critical period in the history of the case, delayed their visit for a whole week until any practical research was almost useless'; a verdict echoed recently by Andrew Mackenzie in his *Hauntings and Apparitions*.

It was not only the investigation of spontaneous phenomena which suffered from the concentration of effort upon laboratory type research. Work with mediums, even with those whose reputations, like Mrs Leonard's, appeared to be firmly established, came to be regarded with uneasiness by some of the High-and-Dry element, and its results derided by Soal and those who shared his views. Research with mediums who were not established was left to outsiders, with the result that so far as the SPR was concerned, the feats of remarkable individuals such as Arthur Spray, about whose psychic faculties a book, *The Mysterious Cobbler*, appeared in 1935, were ignored. And it was the same in the United States: Edgar Cayce's powers as a clairvoyant and a healer were impressively documented in his lifetime – but not on the ASPR's behalf. The investigation of mediums, in fact, was beginning to be regarded by parapsychologists as slumming.

Dowsing, too, was neglected. Barrett had done his best to interest the SPR in the subject; and in France shortly before the First World War the biologist Armand Viré, President of the French Archaeological Society, had set up some trials in the expectation, as he was later to admit, that they would demolish the pretensions of the six dowsers tested, but in which they obtained positive results. Subsequently the craft had been developed in France for use in clinical diagnosis, with conspicuous – and for the doctors who participated in tests, embarrassing – success, by the Abbé A. Mermet and others; in *The Modern Dowser*, published in 1930, the Vicomte Henri de France, praising the 'modest country priests' who had kept dowsing alive during the period when orthodox scientists continued to look the other way, showed that it could be used for a range of other purposes, such as finding seams of mineral ore, and assisting on archaeological digs. 'One can foretell without any clairvoyance,' he wrote, 'that before many years the use of the dowser will have become a current practice.' Dowsing was in fact a common practice all over the world, and it would have been easy to investigate; but as the prevailing High-and-Dry view appeared to be that it would not be seemly to be found investigating the antics of forked hazel twigs held by yokels, the vicomte's plea was ignored.

The same fate befell advice given six years later, which ought to have made more impression upon psychical researchers, as it came from Sir Joseph Thomson. By this time Thomson's reputation as one of the founding fathers of nuclear physics was secure, with an Order of Merit to cap it; and although he had not taken an active part in psychical research since the day when he attended a sitting with Eusapia, he had remained a Vice-President of the SPR and kept an enquiring mind on the subject. 'The divining rod is perhaps of all phenomena which may be thought to be psychical, the one most favourable for experiment,' he wrote in his memoirs. 'The motion of the rod is a mechanical effect and gives an indication of the magnitude of the phenomena.' As the conditions under which the effect appeared could be controlled, and there was 'no lack of trustworthy people who possess the dowsing power', he regarded such experiments as 'well worth making'. But the only serious trials which were carried out in Britain in this period were by Harry Price; and although the results were impressive, by his account, they lacked independent confirmation.

Mediumship

Although psychical researchers could not claim to have made substantial progress towards fulfilling the objectives set by the founders of the SPR, by the time the Wehrmacht drove into Poland, there was one aspect of their work which sceptics, inside or outside the society, have been unable seriously to undermine: the evidence for psychic communications obtained through mediums such as Gladys Osborne Leonard, and through some automatists. The results were important on two levels: for the evidence they provided of the ability of a practised and manifestly trustworthy medium to provide information to sitters of a kind which she could not conceivably have picked up by ordinary sensory channels; and for the light they throw on the vexed issue which mediumship has always thrust upon sitters: whence comes such information? From the spirits of the deceased, surviving in another world? Or from what has since come to be called 'super-ESP'?

From the start, there had been leading psychical researchers who rejected the spiritualist interpretation of the evidence: Schrenck and Richet chief among them. In *Thirty Years of Psychical Research* Richet reiterated his materialist case for the phenomena; Lodge, in his review, did battle with him on the issue. But as Lodge noted in his obituary, Richet had confessed to him in private that 'he was sometimes nearly bowled over by the evidence'; and according to Ernesto Bozzano, the last letter he had received from Richet indicated that he had at long last been convinced by it.

From the 1880s up to the First World War, eminent Italian scientists had been active in psychical research, in particular Cesare Lombroso and Enrico Morselli; but after the death of Eusapia, and with the onset of fascism, the impetus had been lost and Bozzano had had to work almost single-handed. A spiritualist, he nevertheless based his argument not so much on the evidence from mediumship as on the evidence from evolution. The common explanation for the development of psychic powers was that the 'sixth sense' had in fact been the *first* sense, predating the others: it had been lost, Bergson had surmised, simply because the development of the others, and of sight in particular, had rendered psychic communication not only less necessary, but also a nuisance. But this, Bozzano argued, was improbable. Any species which had enjoyed the benefit of such faculties, he pointed out, would surely have made good use of them, and survived.

To Bozzano, the faculties were not earthbound. On the contrary, their possession was irreconcilable with human nature, and 'civil, social and moral institutions, far from deriving benefit from them, would be shaken to their foundations'. The faculties pointed to the existence of spiritual senses, he believed, existing latent in the human mind, but 'waiting to emerge and function in a spiritual environment after the crisis of death', or perhaps on earth, but only in the distant future. He illustrated his theme with a wealth of evidence from curious sources, such as cases of zenoglossy – the term Richet had coined for the way mediums sometimes spoke in languages which they did not know in their waking lives. And

Balance Sheet

although his theory was too far removed from the preconceptions of most psychical researchers to carry conviction generally, it had impressed Richet: 'What neither Myers nor Hodgson nor Hyslop nor Sir Oliver Lodge were able to do, you have accomplished.'

What was needed, clearly, was some way to probe the source of the messages which purported to come from the spirits; and Carington made a bold attempt to discover whether the 'controls' could be traced to mediums' secondary personalities by giving mediums and 'controls' word-association tests, and comparing the results. His initial statistical method, however, was torn apart by Thouless; and though the outcome pointed to there being no identifiable spirits – in the sense of 'Feda', say, using the same terminology while communicating through different mediums – they were not conclusive.

That there must be some source other than the medium's subconscious mind, however, was hard to dispute, owing to the build-up of evidence from the 'cross-correspondences', presenting as they did a startling demonstration of the existence of communication through a number of automatists who were not in communication with each other. They continued into the 1930s: the most striking of them being the 'Palm Sunday' case, in which mediums began to produce a string of references to Mary Lyttelton, a girl with whom Arthur Balfour had been in love, who had died of typhoid in 1875. Balfour, who never married, kept the anniversary of her death each year on Palm Sunday, almost as a religious rite; and the automatists kept providing information related to, and apparently coming from, Mary; to his love for her; and to keepsakes he cherished – a lock of her hair in a silver box, and so on – information of a kind which the automatists could hardly have picked up in their daily lives. Much of the material which they sent in, and which the analysts related to the 'Palm Maiden', was trite. 'The impatient reader,' Renée Haynes has observed, 'sometimes gets a feeling that people are searching for the beads of a broken necklace in a dustbin full of Christmas tinsel and cracker mottoes'; but 'the cumulative effect was impressive'.

The cumulative effect of the cross-correspondences as a whole, for anybody who could summon up the stamina to wade through them, was indeed impressive, as Gardner Murphy testified. As a young man he had assumed there could be no personality without a body in which to house it, and had despised 'the bio-cultural absurdities of heavens and hells, and the stupidity of the tradition in which the belief in individual survival, indeed immortality, had grown up'. But, likening it to an irresistible force striking an immovable object, he had recognised the evidence for 'a genuine continuity and a genuine purpose in the *pressure of the surviving individual to make real his presence to the living*', in certain cases of apparitions 'and in the intricate and never-to-be-evaded playfulness of some of the most exquisite of the cross-correspondences'.

As Rosalind Heywood remarked, surveying the available evidence in *The Sixth Sense*, it is hard for any dispassionate critic 'to avoid the conclusion that for thirty years in dozens of cases something was causing a number of automatists, not only to refer to the same topic – one often abstruse – but to make their references complementary'. But were the references complementary because 'Myers' and the other 'communicators' were feeding the information to the automatists? Or was there – as Alice Johnson put it (though she found it hard to credit) 'a sort of telepathic committee meeting of the subliminal selves of the automatists, at which they scheme together and settle on their different parts?'

At least with the cross-correspondences there could be no question of the knowledge being picked up, consciously or unconsciously, by the medium through the normal sensory channels; and the idea of a string of simple chance coincidences became too far-fetched to be taken seriously. In sessions with individual mediums, however, these possibilities were less easy to rule out; as was the charge, often levelled against mediums, that they owed their popularity to the fact that their 'hits' were remembered and their 'misses' forgotten. This notion, however, had received a blow when H. J. Saltmarsh, a member of the society who was to do much useful investigative service on its behalf, hit upon a method of testing it. He sent a transcript of some sittings which had been held with Mrs Warren Elliott to six people, who had not been to her, but who had had a similar experience to the sitter: each had been affected by the death of a young flying officer in the war. Marks were given on the basis of the accuracy of the medium's pronouncements. Two sets of sittings were marked:

	TOTAL POSSIBLE	ACTUAL MARKS	CONTROLS' MARKS
1.	5642	4107 (72.8%)	452 (8%)
2.	5554	3226 (58.1%)	487 (8.75%)

The marking, Saltmarsh admitted, had to be subjective, up to a point. There were complications when, say, a fact was wrong but was presented in a way highly characteristic of the deceased officer. Nevertheless the level of scoring was so much higher in the connection with the actual sittings than with the controls (R. A. Fisher, consulted, replied that the odds against the medium obtaining her totals by chance were in the region of 1,000,000,000 to one) that in this trial, at least, chance could be ruled out.

Another accusation commonly levelled at mediums was that they used 'fishing' to pick up their information as they went along. But this, too, became hard to sustain in view of the number of reports of cases of proxy sittings where the proxy did not know, and in many cases could not have known, the information which the mediums provided. In individual cases it was possible for doubters within the society to argue that the proxies might have known, or guessed, more about the subject than they claimed; but this line of criticism, too, broke down in connection with Mrs Leonard's career – recorded in hundreds of transcripts, each annotated by the sitter – revealing her astonishing consistency, and the way in which on occasions 'Feda' could produce information unknown both to the proxy and to the sitter, which the sitter was subsequently able to verify. And although Mrs Leonard eventually had to reduce the number of sittings she gave, the information from them showed no appreciable 'decline effect'.

Nor was there ever any ground for regarding Mrs Leonard as other than reliable. In 1964 her biographer, Susy Smith, found her in her eighties 'still a vital and interesting person, poised, wise and serene'. Never in her career was there any question even of her exploiting conscious knowledge: when through chance, or through putting two and two together, she guessed the identity of sitters, she would immediately inform them. Not merely did her friendly co-operation enable SPR members to study mediumship for over forty years, Rosalind Heywood commented; she also 'demonstrated that a medium can remain both honest and a person of normal common sense in daily life'.

Survival?

But did she – or the 'communicators' whom 'Feda' paraded for sitters – also demonstrate the reality of a world in which the deceased lived on in the spirit, renewing old friendships and family ties, and capable of watching over, and occasionally helping their friends and relations on earth?

For some researchers, such as the Rev. Drayton Thomas, the primary objective of psychical investigation was to settle this issue.

Others feared that too much concentration on Survival would distract attention from the more immediate purpose of establishing the reality of telepathy or telekinesis, and would also jeopardise the chances of convincing scientists of the legitimacy of psychical research. Some of those who might be induced to accept a 'super-ESP' explanation, with mediums and sensitives intercommunicating on some psychic wavelength, might well jib at spirit communicators.

One scientist who was prepared to accept the possibility was Sir J. J. Thomson. In his *Recollections and Reflections*, he described the issue of Survival and communication 'of transcendental importance'; and he expressed his agreement with Lord Rayleigh's view that telepathy with the dead 'would present comparatively little difficulty, when it is admitted as regards the living. If the apparatus of the senses is not used in one case, why should it be needed in another?' Such an attitude, though, was unusual among scientists and among academics in general; and spiritualism also raised hackles in other circles, particularly in the established Church. Combing through current Anglican writings, L. P. Jacks – a former editor of the *Hibbert Journal* and a past President of the SPR – found in the late 1930s that speculation about the nature of the life hereafter had all but ceased. Hymns and harps in heaven had ceased to attract; and it had become embarrassing that there was no promising alternative to spiritualism.

One attempt had been made to clarify, if not to settle, the issue. In 1934 Eric Dodds, shortly to succeed Gilbert Murray as Regius Professor of Greek at Oxford, threw down the gauntlet with a paper 'Why I do not believe in Survival' at a meeting of the society; and subsequently he agreed to take part in a trial. Drayton Thomas, it was decided, would act as a proxy for a friend of Dodds, Mrs Wilfred Lewis, whom Thomas did not know, at sittings with Mrs Leonard.

The transcript of the sittings left no doubt that 'Feda' had been able to supply a mass of accurate information about Mrs Lewis's father, F. W. Macaulay, his work, his character and his relations with his children; and some of it was of a kind which even if Thomas or Mrs Leonard had discovered who the sitter was, they could not have obtained. A typical 'hit' was 'Feda's' claim that there was somebody called 'Race . . . Rice . . . Riss . . . it might be Reece but it sounds like Riss', who had been linked up with the family in happy times in the past. Mrs Lewis recalled that while at school, her elder brother had hero-worshipped an older boy whose name was Rees, and she and her sister used to tease him about his insistence that this was how the name was spelt by singing 'Not Reece, but Riss', until her father had stopped them, 'explaining how sensitive a matter a young boy's hero-worship was'. The 'communicator' also gave 'Feda' a name 'like Puggy or Peggy'; her father had in fact sometimes called her 'pug-nose' or 'Puggy'. Out of ninety-four items, by Mrs Lewis's reckoning, seventy were correct.

Commenting on these and other proxy sittings, Dodds agreed that 'the hypotheses of fraud, rational inference from disclosed facts, telepathy from the actual sitter, and coincidence, cannot either singly or in combination account for the results obtained'. The medium had produced a substantial amount of accurate material at the first sitting, before she could have had any opportunity to make enquiries; in any case, he could not imagine how she could have found out about 'Riss' or 'Puggy', and the notion that such items were lucky shots was equally incredible. Mrs Leonard must have had supernormal access, Dodds decided, '*either* (a) to some of the thoughts of a living person or persons who had never held any communication with her *or with the sitter*; or *else* (b) to some of the thoughts of a mind or minds other than that of a living person'. He could see no way of escape

> from this staggering dilemma. Nor do I see any valid ground for embracing one horn of it and spurning the other, as Mr Thomas does. In the present state of our knowledge – or, rather, ignorance – about the mechanism of telepathy it seems to me impossible to specify the limits of its operation, though no doubt such limits exist and will one day be determined.

Even more striking evidence came from another case in the 1930s which provided a change from the usual seance-room diet in that the 'communicators' had something useful to transmit, and went on transmitting information over a period of years until the issue was finally and happily resolved. It was described by Baron Erik Palmstierna, the Swedish Minister in London, in his *Horizons of Immortality*. The main receivers of the information were the celebrated violinist Jelly d'Aranyi and her sister, using a ouija board and an upturned glass; the letters which it indicated, darting to and fro over the board, being taken down at the time.

Most of the material was couched in the high-flown language this method sometimes produced: when asked what the source was, the

Science and Parascience

reply was 'We are speaking from His light up here, to His light in every soul on earth'; but occasionally the source came up with useful information, the most striking example being from a 'communicator' who claimed to have been a composer in his lifetime enquiring about a posthumous work of his which had been lost. Asked who he was, the glass spelled out 'Robert Schumann'.

D'Aranyi had never heard of the missing work, and did not know how to proceed until a fortnight later 'Schumann' came through again with a reminder, adding 'Tell Tovey'. D'Aranyi wrote to Sir Donald Tovey, who replied that he had heard of a concerto which had not been played in Schumann's lifetime, but he had no idea where it was; and the 'communicators', when questioned, did not know, either. That August, however, a further instruction was passed: 'Remember to write to Palmstierna to go and look up in Berlin the work of Schumann'; and although the instruction was ignored, Palmstierna, who was in Sweden at the time, decided on his own account to return to England via Berlin, and while there, thought he might as well enquire about the concerto. He found it at the Prussian State Library, where it had been deposited by Schumann's daughter, who had forbidden its publication.

From this time on, the message transmitted through the ouija board concentrated on persuading d'Aranyi and the others to try to obtain permission first to copy the concerto, and then to give it a performance. The authorities, however, put difficulties in the way, insisting that the ban on publication must stand until the centenary of Schumann's death in 1956; and interest was sagging when in November 1936 a reminder, 'Remember Schumann', stirred the group into action again. They found on enquiry that a new librarian had been appointed; he agreed to release the concerto for publication and performance; and the following year, Jelly d'Aranyi was the soloist when it was performed at a BBC concert.

In sequence, the messages read as if composed by impatient instructors who are none the less uneasily aware that their range of information is limited. It is as if they, too, were groping towards the discovery of the whereabouts of the concerto on Schumann's behalf; and later, to try to find how to break the ban on publication. At each stage they were able to present some information which helped to take the procedure one step further. For example, they not merely contradicted a mistaken impression that the concerto was unfinished, but also explained how the mistake might have been made: 'It is possible that the library has not got the right copy.' So it proved: Schumann's own completed manuscript was found later.

In a letter to the editor of the SPR *Journal* following the publication of *Horizons of Immortality* Palmstierna emphasised that there was no way in which the information which the messages passed could have been in the conscious or subconscious mind of Jelly d'Aranyi or her sister: 'One is tempted to challenge those who insist on the presence of a subconscious mind in the particular case to define unambiguously what they really mean by that agency.' For once, the society's sceptics could find no adequate reply.

There was one other problem, which Tyrrell felt compelled to face. Difficult though it was both for spiritualists and supporters of the 'super-ESP' hypothesis to account for the nature of the 'controls', such as 'John King', it was even more difficult to account for the evidence, by this time attested, that mediums could appear to take on the personality of a deceased person about whom they knew nothing, talking like him, and even beginning to act and look like him.

To Tyrrell, this was the most baffling problem that mediumship presented.

> An actor plays a memorised part; the hypnotic subject does what he is told to do by the operator; but the trance-personality, if it is subconsciously acting, *extemporises* a part without a model. How does it do it? It gets its cue telepathically from the minds of living persons who did know the original, we might suppose. But 'telepathic leakage' could not do that. We should have to suppose that the subconscious mind of the person who had known the communicator in life was sending out to the medium a stream of stage directions. Or, if we think it more plausible, that the medium was subconsciously reaching out with some telesthetic faculty and observing a mental model of the communicator in the mind of the other, and basing its excellent characterisation on that. In either case we are postulating extra-sensory faculties of extraordinary range and power, and have moved a very long way from the idea of telepathy as 'thought-transference'

— so far away, indeed, that the telepathic theory, if thought through to its logical conclusion, 'turns out to be, not, after all, an alternative to the theory of Survival, so much as another and very odd version of that theory, namely the version that a deceased person can survive in the form of a psychic parasite on a medium'.

The most plausible solution, Tyrrell thought, lay in the existence of much more comprehensive mental and extra-sensory powers than had been recognised, deep in the subliminal self. The concept of 'I' would have to be greatly extended to accommodate them. Most of the anti-Survival arguments, he pointed out, arose from the incongruity of the familiar 'I' entering into such totally different surroundings. But this was to assume that this 'I' represented the full personality. Not so:

> When we look deeply into the nature of human personality we find that vistas of the self are hidden behind the scenes, possessing powers and qualities which science is unable to define or bring into line with other knowledge by its superficial methods. That, indeed, is why the deeper research called 'psychical' is so unpopular. It overturns the complacency of successful science, which has been dealing with the surface-appearance of things based on the finds of the sense. The principle of selfhood and the criterion of 'I' are far too subtle to be captured by a net of reason such as ours; they refuse to be held by our categories of thought; they transcend and elude every effort we make to grasp them. So do the faculties of extra-sensory cognition.

On this hypothesis, Tyrrell was able to present a possible explanation of mediumship. The lower type, he thought, consisted of little more than some extra-sensory faculty; but in higher types, the medium would be used by 'an entity animated by the still-existing self-principle of a deceased person'. At best, 'the inscrutable "I-principle" which animated the living person also animates the new person', but in the process of getting across to the living it might hark back 'to something more or less resembling its former terrestrial self, and while doing so, may even forget about its other-worldly state of existence'. Tyrrell, in short, accepted Survival – but not in the sense of assuming that the human personality simply moves unchanged into an after-life.

Summing up after his examination of the evidence in *Mediumship and Survival* Alan Gauld concedes its strength: 'I cannot dismiss this evidence *en bloc* as bad evidence, as entirely the product of fraud, misrecording, malobservation, wishful-thinking or plain coincidence. I can find no other decisive reason for rejecting it' and also the weakness of the alternative, because the evidence points not just to surviving memories of a kind which automatists might pick up by 'super-ESP' but to surviving personality characteristics, 'distinctive purposes, skills, capacities, habits, turns of phrase, struggles to communicate, wishes, points of view'. Nevertheless in this area 'what we know stands in proportion to what we do not know as a bucketful does to the ocean. Certainty is not to be had, nor even a strong conviction that the area of one's uncertainty has been narrowed to a manageable compass.'

Prince Bernhard's Crash

In the run-up to the Second World War there was no strikingly prophetic dream to compare with Mgr de Lanyi's about Sarajevo – or if there was, it did not reach the psychical research journals. But a dream which was described in the journal of the Dutch society, and in 1939 in the SPR *Journal*, came very close to the event it foreshadowed; and it was unusual in that it was described in a letter which reached the recipient – W. H. C. Tenhaeff, the first man ever to hold an academic appointment in parapsychology, at the University of Utrecht – *before* the event.

In her dream, 'Mrs O.' wrote, she had seen a level-crossing, a long road and a meadow, with a lorry behind a gate. 'A car came very quickly in a hurry to cross, but in the middle a tyre burst and the car drove full speed into the gate, and into the lorry.' Someone was killed: 'I saw him lying there, and it was Prince Bernhard.'

The letter reached Tenhaeff on a Saturday evening. Listening to the radio the following Monday morning he heard that Prince Bernhard had just been involved in an accident, which turned out to have been on a long road beside a railway, with meadows and a gate. Lorries were loading sand; and Prince Bernhard's car, travelling fast, had struck one of them. The Prince, taken from the car, had been laid on a blanket by the road.

The dream differed from the reality in that there was no level-crossing, and no burst tyre; the lorry had come out into the road, and Prince Bernhard survived. Nevertheless the similarity to a 'Dunne dream', with its attendant inaccuracies, was obvious; and the detail sufficiently close to make precognition (to anybody who accepted it) a more plausible explanation than chance coincidence.

Postscript

To return to my starting point . . .

I have tried to present the evidence about, rather than for, paranormal phenomena, as it accumulated between 1914 and 1939. In trying to clear away the debris of misconceptions and misinterpretations I have found it difficult not to slip into the role of counsel for the defence, and for that reason my own interpretation must be treated with reserve; but the records are there, for anybody who cares to check on them. And they are far more extensive; there are scores of further well-attested cases in the publications and the archives of psychical research societies the world over.

Some sceptics are prepared to concede that the quantity of evidence is impressive; but this, they claim, is irrelevant because there is no single totally convincing case. Where Barrett argued that the evidence had acquired the strength of a 'faggot' (on the analogy of individually weak twigs acquiring strength when bound together: the image Mussolini used to promote fascism), they insist that a thousand leaky buckets hold water no better than one: they await one which is cast-iron, copper-bottomed.

In no other branch of human life is such a demand considered reasonable. The evidence for love at first sight is anecdotal; it has never been replicated under test conditions, with controls; and in its nature is apt to be reported in ways calculated to exaggerate its impact; yet nobody in his right mind would seriously deny that it happens.

Why, then, the reluctance to accept the much stronger evidence for ESP, or PK? The disturbing fact is that the academic world is still in the grip of the materialist faith which Tyndall preached, in spite of the way in which the quantum physicists have undermined its foundations. 'A well-established theory,' James B. Conant, President of Harvard, observed in his perceptive *On Understanding Science* in 1947, 'may prove a barrier to acceptance of a new one.' The barrier is all the more effective because the new one has yet to present a satisfying alternative. Quantum physics has con-

Postscript

tinued to provide evidence of paranormal-type phenomena, translocation and action-at-a-distance, at the micro level, and Bergson, Geley and others made a start in explaining why and how the phenomena take the form they do at the macro level; but there is still no acceptable new paradigm, of the kind Thomas Kuhn postulates as essential, before the old one can be discarded.

The main problem here is that whereas the new physics could replace the old without disturbing anybody except physicists, to accept the reality of paranormal phenomena would mean making nonsense of much that is still being taken for granted, and taught, in many other disciplines: in biology, psychology, anthropology, medicine and even history; most of all, perhaps, in philosophy.

This in itself would be sufficient to breed resistance to the admission of 'psi', the blanket term which has come into use to cover the phenomena and the forces involved. But the real obstacle is that psi cannot be pinned down. The phenomena occur spontaneously, often without rhyme or reason; and they can take unpalatable forms – Thomas Mann called them 'preposterous'; Maeterlinck 'vain and puerile'.

At no time have they taken more preposterous and puerile forms than in the 1914–45 period. In the reports, they sound bogus; in photographs, they look bogus. And yet, paradoxically, this is a powerful argument in favour of their being genuine. Psychical researchers of the calibre of Richet or Schrenck-Notzing were not spiritualists, 'longing to believe' in the existence of discarnate entities capable of materialising. They were *materialists*, anxious to find an explanation for telepathy and telekinesis within the framework of orthodox physics, with the help of the discovery of some force analogous to magnetism. The last thing they wanted to find was two-dimensional ectoplasmic forms looking as if they were made out of crumpled chiffon.

By extension, this helps to exonerate mediums such as 'Eva C.' I repeat: if she were a supremely gifted conjuror, capable of baffling even Houdini, why waste her talent on psychical researchers who would much rather have had her produce simple, straightforward telekinetic effects, and who submitted her, week after week, to indignities that she would not have had to suffer in the halls? But in any case, a study of the hundreds of transcripts of her sittings make it clear that conjuring – except in the original, biblical sense of the term – cannot account for the phenomena observed and reported. If there was fraud, there must have been collusion; not just with Mme Bisson, but with Richet, Schrenck, Geley, and others. And the notion that they were all involved in a demonic conspiracy is too grotesquely implausible to take seriously.

In any embryonic discipline, admittedly, which is seeking recognition there is bound to be a temptation to rig or fudge the evidence. Parallel with the development of psychical research, for example, the neo-Darwinians were trying to provide the missing links which would prove their case; and what with Ernst Haeckel faking his illustrations to make the human embryo look more like a rabbit's, his pupil Eugene Dubois concealing specimens which would cast doubt on his 'Java Man's' authenticity, and the Piltdown fraud, their record is unattractive. But the psychical researchers did not have quite the same motive. Citing the deceptions of the neo-Darwinians in his *The Neck of the Giraffe*, Francis Hitching quotes Stephen Gould's comment about the temptations facing academic scientists: 'I suspect that unconscious or dimly-perceived finagling, doctoring and massaging are rampant, endemic and unavoidable in a profession that awards status and power for clean and unambiguous discovery.' But such awards go only to those who provide clean and unambiguous discoveries *which fit the prevailing dogmas.* If academic advancement were what a researcher was seeking, he was far more likely in this period to obtain it by eschewing any connection with psychical research, or by following the example of Muensterberg, Jastrow and Coover, and denouncing it.

Men like Richet, Lodge and Schrenck knew that what they did could only damage their reputations in orthodox scientific circles; they were certainly not concerned to advance their careers – or, for that matter, their financial prospects. It is no coincidence that the only well-known psychical researcher about whom fraud is proven in this period was Harry Price, the only one who actively sought fame and fortune. Later, when the work at Duke began to hold out the prospect of academic recognition for ESP, at least, the temptation to doctor and massage results inevitably increased; it was eventually to trap Soal.

'All records of experiments must depend ultimately on the probity and intelligence of the persons recording them, and it is impossible for us, or any other investigators, to demonstrate to persons who do not know us that we are not idiotically careless or consciously mendacious,' Sidgwick had observed in 1883. 'We can only hope that within the limited circle in which we are known, either alternative will be regarded as highly improbable.' Insofar as I have been able to enter that limited circle, retrospectively, I have

Postscript

found it to be composed mainly of individuals of exceptional integrity, dedication and courage: men of the calibre of Barrett, Lodge, Richet, Geley, Schrenck, Ochorowicz, Gardner Murphy and Rhine.

Ironically, where their standards slipped was almost always when they were trying, not to establish, let alone popularise, psychic phenomena, but to weed out what they took to be spurious elements. In this they were often unwittingly giving aid and comfort to their opponents. The most grievous harm to psychical research in the years between the wars was done not by sceptics, but by psychical researchers. Initially the damage was done by those who, like McDougall, could not bring themselves to accept the physical phenomena of mediumship; and, worse, by those who followed the Podmore trail, and were willing to impute fraud to anybody who reported successful results with physical mediums. Inevitably, to convince sceptical academics that psychical research was 'clean' the researchers had to introduce controls of a rigour which no other academic discipline was asked to accept: controls designed to ensure not simply that subjects could not cheat, but also that the investigators themselves could not cheat.

It proved a futile enterprise. People in strait-jackets are taken to be crazy, however lucid they may sound: if parapsychologists' results were confirmed by the witnesses employed to control them, suspicion simply fell on the witnesses, on the 'who is to guard the guards' principle. As Lodge realised, psychical research had taken a wrong turning, in seeking academic recognition, if it meant losing contact with the general public; an understandable but disastrous error of strategy which vitiated much of the valuable research undertaken between the wars, and unfairly destroyed the reputations of some of the most dedicated researchers. If I have done nothing else, I hope I have done something to rehabilitate them, at least in the eyes of their successors.

Acknowledgments

My thanks to Anita Gregory and Bernard Levin for wrestling with the typescript, and offering pungent comments and criticisms; to Dr Alan Gauld for reading the proofs; to Eleanor O'Keeffe and Nick Clark-Lowes at the Society for Psychical Research, A. D. Wesencraft at the Harry Price Library, and C. D. W. Shepherd at the Brotherton Library, Leeds University; to Dr Eric Dingwall, for unravelling some mysteries; to Marian L. Nester for information about 'Margery'; to Seymour H. Mauskopf and Michael R. McVaugh, as the timely publication of *The Elusive Science* spared me a great deal of time in connection with J. B. Rhine's contribution, and the repercussions (on both sides of the Atlantic); and to Ruth West for her invaluable help at all stages.

Sources

Although I trust I have covered the ground sufficiently to justify the book's subtitle, I must emphasise that between 1914 and 1939, psychical research was being conducted in many parts of the world and reported in many languages; I have been able to use only those works which were published in, or translated into, English or French. I have not dealt with the research of L. L. Vasiliev and others in Russia, because evaluation of material from the Soviet presents problems which are best treated separately – as also, though for different reasons, is the evidence for psychic healing, for shamanist phenomena, and for ESP in the animal world.

Commentaries by latter-day sceptics are included only if the case they present for a fresh interpretation of the evidence merits serious attention. Professor Ian Stevenson once remarked that, in this context, he felt 'a little like an early settler in the American West': if the settler concentrated on fighting the Indians he would not get his crops planted, but if he concentrated on his crops they, and his homestead, might be burnt down. Tempting though it has been to expose the distortions and evasions of some of today's critics of parapsychology,* I have kept this for another occasion – not a difficult decision, as none has surveyed the evidence for the

---

* A typical example of the tactics which sceptics feel justified in employing occurs in Professor C. E. M. Hansel's *ESP and Parapsychology*, in which he accuses me of having 'cast a blind eye at the report in *Science*, in which Eusapia was finally exposed'. The report, published on 20 May 1910, described how a committee set up to test Eusapia had come to the conclusion that the phenomena which she had produced could be accounted for by trickery, though it had not actually caught her. But as one of its members, Walter Pitkin, pointed out, the report was not to be trusted, omitting as it did 'all those details about methods and results which are properly considered indispensable to any such statement made by scientists to scientists'. Another member, R. W. Wood, who had stationed himself so that he could observe what went on behind Eusapia's back, described how he had seen 'a black object' reaching out to move a table: 'those who believe in Eusapia's supernormal powers will say that this was the third arm' – in other words, a pseudopod. Eusapia was not 'exposed' by the committee: the committee itself was exposed as incompetent to conduct the investigation.

Science and Parascience

1914–1939 period systematically, and the offerings of those who have picked upon individual aspects of it have rarely been worth the labour of demolition.

The edition cited is the one I have consulted: the date of the first edition, if it is earlier, follows in brackets.

1. Books and Articles

Abramowski, Edouard, *Le Subconscient Normal*, Paris, 1914.
'A.E.', *The Candle of Vision*, London, 1918.
Agee, Doris, *Edgar Cayce on ESP*, New York, 1969.
Allen, Gay Wilson, *William James*, London and New York, 1967.
Anspacher, Louis, *Challenge of the Unknown*, London, 1952.
Ashby, Robert, *Guidebook for the Study of Psychical Research*, London, 1972.
Balfour, Jean (Countess of Balfour), 'Palm Sunday', *Proc.s SPR*, 1960, lii, 79–265.
Barnard, G. C., *The Supernatural*, London, 1933.
Barrett, Sir William, *On the Threshold of the Unseen*, London, 1920 (1908).
Barrett, Sir William, 'Reminiscences of Fifty Years', *Proc.s SPR*, 1924, xxxiv, 275–97.
Barrett, Sir William, *Death-bed Visions*, London, 1926.
Barrett, Sir William, and Theodore Besterman, *The Divining Rod*, London, 1926.
Beadnell, C. Marsh, *The Reality or Unreality of Spiritualistic Phenomena*, London, 1920.
Bennett, Sir Ernest, *Apparitions and Haunted Houses*, London, 1939.
Bergson, Henri, *Creative Evolution*. London, 1964 (Paris, 1911).
Bergson, Henri, SPR Presidential Address, *Proc.s SPR*, 1913, xxvi, 462–79 (in French); *Proc.s SPR*, 1914–15, xxvii, 157–75 (in English).
Besterman, Theodore, *Crystal-gazing*, London, 1924.
Besterman, Theodore, *Some Modern Mediums*, London, 1930.
Besterman, Theodore, *Inquiry into the Unknown*, London, 1934.
Bevan, Edwyn, *Seers and Sybils*, London, 1928.
Bird, Christopher, *The Divining Hand*, New York, 1979.
Bird, J. Malcolm, *My Psychic Adventures*, London, 1923.
Bird, J. Malcolm, *'Margery' the Medium*, Boston, 1925.
Bisson, Juliette, *Les Phénomènes de Matérialisation*, Paris, 1914.
Blatchford, Robert, *More Things in Heaven and Earth*, London, 1925.
Boirac, Emile, *The Psychology of the Future*, London, 1919 (1917).
Boring, Edwin G., 'A Paradox of Psychical Research', *Atlantic Monthly*, January 1926, 81–7.
Boston Society for Psychical Research, *Walter Franklin Prince*, Boston, 1935.

Sources

Bozzano, Ernesto, *Les Phénomènes de Hantise*, Paris, 1929.
Bozzano, Ernesto, *Animism and Spiritism*, London, 1932.
Bozzano, Ernesto, *Discarnate Influences on Human Life*, London, 1938.
Bozzano, Ernesto, *Polyglot Mediumship (Xenoglossy)*, London 1932.
Bradley, H. Dennis, *Towards the Stars*, London, 1924.
Bradley, H. Dennis, *An Indictment of the Present Administration of the SPR*, London, 1931.
Bradley, H. Dennis, '... *And After*', London, 1931.
Bramwell, J. Milne, *Hypnotism*, New York 1956 (1903).
Brandon, Ruth, *The Spiritualists*, London, 1983.
Brath, Stanley de, *Psychical Research, Science and Religion*, London, 1925.
Broad, Charlie D., 'The Philosophical Implications of Foreknowledge' (1937), in *Ludwig*, 1978, 287.
Broad, Charlie D., *Religion, Philosophy and Psychical Research*, London, 1953.
Broad, Charlie D., *Lectures on Psychical Research*, London, 1965.
Brown, Michael H., *PK*, New York, 1976.
Brown, Slater, *The Heyday of Spiritualism*, New York, 1970.
Brown, William, *Science and Personality*, Oxford, 1929.
Brunton, Paul, *A Search in Secret Egypt*, London, 1935.
Burt, Cyril, *Psychology and Psychical Research*, London, 1968.
Burt, Cyril, *ESP and Psychology*, New York, 1975.
Bush, Edward, *Spirit Photography Exposed*, Wakefield, 1920.
Carrel, Alexis, *Man the Unknown*, London, 1961 (1935).
Carrington, Hereward, *The Physical Phenomena of Spiritualism*. New York 1920 (1907).
Carrington, Hereward, *Psychical Phenomena and the War*, New York, 1918.
Carrington, Hereward, *A Primer of Psychical Research*, London, 1932.
Carrington, Hereward, *The American Seances with Eusapia Palladino*, New York, 1954.
Carrington, Hereward, and Nandor Fodor, *The Story of the Poltergeist down the Ages*, London, 1953.
Christopher, Milbourne, *Houdini: the Untold Story*, London and New York, 1969.
Coates, James, *Photographing the Invisible*, London, 1922.
Conant, James B., *On Understanding Science*, Oxford, 1947.
Coover, J. E., *Experiments in Psychical Research*, Stanford, 1917.
Cornillier, P. E., *The Prediction of the Future*, London, 1935 (1926).
Crawford, William J., *The Reality of Psychic Phenomena*, London, 1916.
Crawford, William J., *Experiments in Psychic Science*, London, 1919.
Crawford, William J., *Psychic Structures of the Goligher Circle*, London, 1921.
Cudden, Eric, *Hypnosis*, London, 1938.
Cumberland, Stuart, *Spiritualism: the Inside Truth*, London, 1919.

Curnow, Leslie, *The Physical Phenomena of Mediumship*, Manchester, 1925.
Dingwall, Eric J., 'A Report on a Series of Sittings with Mr Willy Schneider', *Proc.s SPR*, 1926–8, xxxvi, 1–33.
Dingwall, Eric. J., 'A Report on a Series of Sittings with the medium "Margery"', *Proc.s SPR*, 1926–8, xxxvi, 79–155.
Dingwall, Eric J. 'An Amazing Case: the Mediumship of Carlos Mirabelli', *JASPR*, 1930, xxxv, 296–306.
Dingwall, Eric J., *Very Peculiar People*, London, 1950.
Dodds, E. R., 'Why I do not Believe in Survival', *Proc.s SPR*, 1934, xlii. 147–72.
Douglas, Alfred, *Extra-sensory Powers*, London, 1976.
Doyle, Arthur Conan, *The New Revelation*, London, 1925 (1918).
Doyle, Arthur Conan, *The Vital Message*, London, 1925 (1919).
Doyle, Arthur Conan, *The Case for Spirit Photography*, London, 1922.
Doyle, Arthur Conan, *The Coming of the Fairies*, London, 1922.
Doyle, Arthur Conan, *The Edge of the Unknown*, London, 1930.
Driesch, Hans, *The History and Theory of Vitalism*, London, 1914.
Driesch, Hans, *The Crisis in Psychology*, Princeton, 1925.
Driesch, Hans, *Mind and Body*, London, 1927 (1916).
Driesch, Hans, *Psychical Research*, London, 1933.
Duchatel, E. and René Warcollier, *Les Miracles de la Volonté*, Paris, 1914.
Dunne, J. W., *An Experiment with Time*, London, 1934 (1927).
Eddington, Arthur S., *The Nature of the Physical World*, Cambridge, 1929.
Ellis, K., *Science and the Supernatural*, London, 1974.
Ernst, Bernard, and Hereward Carrington, *Houdini and Conan Doyle*, London, 1938.
Erskine, Alexander, *A Hypnotist's Case-book*, London, 1932.
Estabrooks, G. H., 'A Contribution to Experimental Telepathy', *Boston SPR Bulletin*, v, 5–27.
Feilding, Everard, *Sitting with Eusapia Palladino*, New York, 1963.
Fitzsimons, Raymund, *Death and the Magician*, London, 1980.
Flammarion, Camille, *Death and its Mystery* (3 vols), London, 1922 (1920).
Flournoy, Theodor, *Spiritism and Psychology*, New York, 1911.
Fodor, Nandor, *Encyclopedia of Psychic Science*, London, 1934.
Fournier d'Albe, E. E., *The Goligher Circle*, London, 1922.
Fort, Charles, *The Book of the Damned*, New York, 1919.
Fort, Charles, *Lo!*, London, 1931.
de France, Vicomte Henri, *The Modern Dowser*, London, 1930.
Freud, Sigmund, 'A note on the Unconscious in Psycho-analysis', *Proc.s SPR*, 1912–13, 312–18.
Freud, Sigmund, 'Psycho-analysis and Telepathy' (1921), Van Over, 1972, 109–26.

Sources

Fukurai, T., *Clairvoyance and Thoughtography*, London, 1931.
Fuller, John G., *The Airmen who would not Die*, London, 1979 (New York, 1979).
Gardner, Edward L., *Fairies*, London, 1966 (1921).
Gardner, Martin, *Fads and Fallacies*, New York, 1957 (1952).
Garrett, Eileen, *Telepathy*, New York, 1941.
Garrett, Eileen, *Adventures in the Supernormal*, New York, 1949.
Gauld, Alan, *The Founders of Psychical Research*, London, 1968.
Gauld, Alan, *Mediumship and Survival*, London, 1982.
Geley, Gustave, *From the Unconscious to the Conscious*, London, 1920 (1919).
Geley, Gustave, *Clairvoyance and Materialisation*, London, 1927 (1924).
Goddard, Sir Victor, *Flight Towards Reality*, London, 1975.
Grattan-Guinness, Ivor (ed.), *Psychical Research*, London, 1982.
Gregory, Anita, 'Anatomy of a Fraud', *Annals of Science*, Sept. 1977, xxxiv, 449–549.
Grumbine, J. C. F., *Telepathy*, London, 1915.
Hack, Gwendolyn, *Modern Psychic Mysteries*, London, 1930.
Hack, Gwendolyn, *Venetian Voices*, London, 1937.
Halifax, Lord, *Ghost Book* (2 vols) London, 1936, 1937.
Hall, Radclyffe Marguerite and Una, Lady Troubridge, 'On a Series of Sittings with Mrs Osborne Leonard', *Proc.s SPR*, 1919, xxx, 339–554.
Hall, Trevor, *The Spiritualists*, London, 1962.
Hall, Trevor, *New Light on Old Ghosts*, London, 1965.
Hall, Trevor, *The Search for Harry Price*, London, 1978.
Hankey, Muriel, *James Hewat McKenzie*, London, 1963.
Hansel, C. E. M., *ESP: a Scientific Evaluation*, New York, 1966.
Hansel, C. E. M., *ESP and Parapsychology: a critical re-evaluation*, New York, 1980.
Hardy, Sir Alister, Robert Harvie and Arthur Koestler, *The Challenge of Chance*, London, 1972.
Harper, George Mills (ed.), *Yeats and the Occult*, London, 1976 (New York, 1975).
Hettinger, J., *The Ultra-perceptive Faculty*, London, 1938.
Hettinger, J., *Exploring the Ultra-perceptive Faculty*, London, 1941.
Heywood, Rosalind, *The Sixth Sense*, London, 1959.
Hill, J. Arthur, *Letters from Sir Oliver Lodge*, London, 1932.
Hoagland, Hudson, 'Science and the Medium: the Climax of a Famous Investigation', *Atlantic*, Nov. 1925, 666–81.
Hodson, Geoffrey, *Fairies at Work and at Play*, London, 1925.
Holms, Campbell, *The Facts of Psychic Science*, London, 1925.
Hope, Lord Charles, 'Report of a Series of Sittings with Rudi Schneider', *Proc.s SPR*, 1932–3, xli, 255–330.
Houdini, Harry, *The Unmasking of Robert-Houdin*, London, 1909.
Houdini, Harry, *A Magician among the Spirits*, New York, 1924.
Houdini, Harry, *'Margery' the Medium Exposed*, New York, 1924.

Hyslop, James H., *Contact with the Other World*, London and New York, 1919.
Inge, W. R., *Outspoken Essays*, London, 1919.
Jacks, L. P., *Confessions of an Octogenarian*, London, 1940.
Janet, Pierre, *Principles of Psychotherapy*, London, 1926.
Jeans, James, *The Mysterious Universe*, London, 1931.
Jephson, Ina, 'Evidence for Clairvoyance in card-guessing', *Proc.s SPR*, 1928-9, xxxviii, 38-223.
Joad, C. E. M., 'Adventures in Psychical Research', *Harpers*, June 1938.
Johnson, George L., *The Great Problem and the Evidence for its Solution*, London, 1928.
Johnson, Raynor C., *The Imprisoned Splendour*, London, 1953.
Joire, Paul, *Psychical and Supernormal Phenomena*, London, 1936 (1909).
Jolly, W. P., *Sir Oliver Lodge*, London, 1974.
Jung, Carl, 'The Psychological Foundation of Belief in Spirits', *Proc.s SPR*, 1920 xxi, 75-93.
Jung, Carl, *Modern Man in Search of a Soul*, London, 1934.
Jung, Carl, *Memories, Dreams, Reflections*, London, 1975.
Kennedy, David, *A Venture in Immortality*, Gerrards Cross, 1973.
Kingsford, S. M., *Psychical Research for the Plain Man*, London, 1920.
Koestler, Arthur, *The Roots of Coincidence*, London, 1972.
Koestler, Arthur, *Janus*, London, 1978.
Leeds, Morton, and Gardner Murphy, *The Paranormal and the Normal*, Metuchen, N. J., 1980.
Leonard, Gladys Osborne, *My Life in Two Worlds*, London, 1931.
Leroy, Olivier, *La Raison Primitive*, Paris, 1927.
Leroy, Oliver, *Levitation*, London, 1928.
Litvag, I., *Singer in the Shadows: the Strange Case of Patience Worth*, New York, 1972.
Lodge, Sir Oliver, *Survival of Man*, London, 1909.
Lodge, Sir Oliver, *Raymond*, London, 1916.
Lodge, Sir Oliver, *Raymond Revised*, London, 1922.
Lodge, Sir Oliver, *Past Years*, London, 1931.
Lodge, Sir Oliver, *My Philosophy*, London, 1933.
Ludwig, Ernst, *Philosophy and Parapsychology*, London, 1978.
Lyttelton, Edith, *Our Superconscious Minds*, London, 1931.
Lyttelton, Edith, SPR Presidential Address, *Proc.s SPR* 1932-3, xli, 331-44.
Lyttelton, Edith, *Some Cases of Prediction*, London, 1937.
McCabe, Joseph, *Is Spiritualism Based on Fraud?*, London, 1920.
McCreery, Charles, *Science, Philosophy and ESP*, London, 1967.
McDougall, William, *Body and Mind*, London, 1911.
McDougall, William, SPR Presidential Address, *Proc.s SPR*, 1921, xxxi, 105-23.
McDougall, William, *The Riddle of Life*, London, 1938.

Sources

MacKenzie, Andrew, *Hauntings and Apparitions*, London, 1982.
McKenzie, James Hewat, *Spirit Intercourse*, New York, 1917.
Maeterlinck, Maurice, *The Unknown Guest*, London and New York, 1914.
Mann, Thomas, 'An Experience in the Occult', *Three Essays*, London, 1932.
Mann, Thomas, 'An Evening with the Occult', *Encounter*, April, 1976.
Marais, Eugene, *The Soul of the White Ant*, London, 1937.
Mauskopf, Seymour H. and Michael R. McVaugh, *The Elusive Science*, Baltimore, 1980.
Mercier, Charles A., *Spiritualism and Sir Oliver Lodge*, London, 1917.
Mitchell, T. W., *Medical Psychology and Psychical Research*, London, 1922.
Moore, R. Lawrence, *In Search of White Crows*, London, 1977.
Mowbray, C. H., *Transition*, London, 1936.
Muldoon, Sylvan and Hereward Carrington, *The Projection of the Astral Body*, London, 1929.
Murchison, Carl (ed.), *The Case For and Against Psychical Belief*, Clark University, 1927.
Murphy, Gardner, *The Challenge of Psychical Research*, New York, 1961.
Murphy, Gardner, and Robert Ballou, *William James on Psychical Research*, London, 1961 (New York 1960).
Oesterreich, T. K., *Occultism and Modern Science*, London, 1923 (Dresden, 1921).
Olliver, C. W., *An Analysis of Magic and Witchcraft*, London, 1928.
Olliver, C. W., *The Extension of Consciousness*, London, 1932.
Ostrander, Sheila and Lynn Schroeder, *Psi: Psychic Discoveries Behind the Iron Curtain*, London, 1973 (1970).
Osty, Eugène, *Supernormal Faculties in Man*, London, 1923.
Osty, Eugène, *Une Faculté de Connaissance Supranormale: Pascal Forthuny*, Paris, 1926.
Osty, Eugène, *Les Pouvoirs Inconnus de l'Esprit sur la Matière*, Paris, 1932.
Osty, Eugène, *Supernormal Aspects of Energy and Matter* (SPR, Myers Lecture), London, 1933.
Owen, A. R. G., *Can We Explain the Poltergeist?*, New York, 1974.
Palmer, E. Clephan, *The Riddle of Spiritualism*, London, 1927.
Palmstierna, Erik, *Horizons of Immortality*, London, 1937.
Pauwels, Louis, and Jacques Bergier, *The Morning of the Magicians*, New York, 1968 (1960).
Piper, Alta, *The Life and Work of Mrs Piper*, London, 1929.
Playfair, Guy Lyon, *The Flying Cow*, London, 1975.
Podmore, Frank, *The Newer Spiritualism*, London, 1910.
Pratt, J. Gaither, *Parapsychology*, London, 1964.
Price, Harry, '*Stella C.*', London, 1928.

Price, Harry, *Rudi Schneider*, London, 1930.
Price, Harry, *Fifty Years of Psychical Research*, London, 1939.
Price, Henry Habberley, *Perception*, London, 1932.
Priestley, J. B., *Man and Time*, London, 1964.
Prince, Morton, *The Dissociation of a Personality*, Oxford, 1978 (1905).
Prince, Walter Franklin, *The Case of Patience Worth*, Boston, 1926.
Prince, Walter Franklin, *Noted Witnesses for Psychical Occurrences*, Boston, 1928.
Prince, Walter Franklin, *The Enchanted Boundary*, Boston, 1930.
Ramakrishna Rao, K. (ed.), *J. B. Rhine: on the Frontiers of Science*, Jefferson, N. C., 1982.
Randall, John, *Parapsychology and the Nature of Life*, London, 1975.
Randall, John, *Psychokinesis*, London, 1982.
Rayleigh, Lord, SPR Presidential Address, *Proc.s SPR*, 1938–9, xlv, 1–18.
Rayleigh, Lord, *Sir J. J. Thomson*, Cambridge, 1942.
Reuter, Florizel von, *Psychical Experiences of a Musician*, London, 1928.
Rhine, Louisa E., *Hidden Channels of the Mind*, London, 1962 (New York, 1961).
Rhine, Louisa E., *ESP in Life and Lab*, New York, 1967.
Rhine, Louisa E., *Mind over Matter*, New York, 1970.
Rhine, J. B., *Extra-sensory Perception*, Boston, 1934.
Rhine, J. B., *New Frontiers of the Mind*, London, 1938 (New York, 1937).
Rhine, J. B., et al., *Extra-sensory Perception After Sixty Years*, New York, 1940.
Rhine, J. B., et al., *Parapsychology from Duke to FRNM*, Durham, N.C., 1965.
Richardson, Mark W., et al., *Margery-Harvard-Veritas*, Boston, 1925.
Richet, Charles, *Thirty Years of Psychical Research*, London, 1923.
Richet, Charles, *Our Sixth Sense*, London, 1930 (Paris, 1927).
Richet, Charles, *L'Avenir et la Prémonition*, Paris, 1931.
Rinn, Joseph, *Searchlight on Psychical Research*, New York, 1954.
Rogo, D. Scott, *Parapsychology: a Century of Inquiry*, New York, 1975.
Roll, W. G., *The Poltergeist*, New York, 1972.
Romains, Jules, *Eyeless Sight*, London and New York, 1924 (1921).
Roberts, Bechofer, *The Truth about Spiritualism*, London, 1932.
Russell, Eric, *Ghosts*, London, 1970.
Sabine, W. H. W., *Second Sight in Daily Life*, London and New York, 1951.
Salter, W. H., *Ghosts and Apparitions*, London, 1938.
Salter, W. H., *Zoar*, London, 1961.
Salter, Helen, *Evidence for Telepathy*, London, 1934.
Saltmarsh, H. F., *Evidence of Personal Survival from Cross-correspondences*, London, 1938.
Saltmarsh, H. F., *Foreknowledge*, London, 1938.

Sources

Sardina, Maurice, *Where Houdini was Wrong*, London, 1950 (1947).
Scatcherd, F. R., *Ectoplasm as associated with Survival*, New York, 1924.
Schiller, F. C. S., *Must Philosophers Disagree?*, London, 1934.
Schmeidler, Gertrude (ed.), *Extra-sensory Perception*, New York, 1967.
Schrenck-Notzing, Baron von, *Phenomena of Materialisation*, London, 1920 (Munich, 1913).
Sidgwick, Eleanor, 'An Examination of Book Tests', *Proc.s SPR*, 1921, xxxi, 242–397.
Sidgwick, Eleanor, 'Phantasms of the Living' *Proc.s SPR*, 1923, xxxiii, 23–429.
Sidgwick, Eleanor, SPR Presidential Address, *Proc.s SPR*, 1932–3, xli, 1–26.
Sidgwick, Ethel, *Mrs Henry Sidgwick*, London, 1938.
Sinclair, Upton, *Mental Radio*, New York, 1930.
Sinel, Joseph, *The Sixth Sense*, London, 1927.
Sitwell, Sacheverell, *Poltergeists*, London, 1940.
Smith, Hester Travers, *Voices from the Void*, London, 1919.
Smith, Susy, *The Mediumship of Mrs Leonard*, New York, 1964.
Smythies, J. R., (ed.), *Science and ESP*, London, 1967.
Soal, S. G., 'A Report on some Communications Received through Mrs Blanche Cooper', *Proc.s SPR* 1926, xxxv, 471–589.
Soal, S. G., and F. Bateman, *Modern Experiments in Telepathy*, London, 1954.
Spray, Arthur, *The Mysterious Cobbler*, London, 1935.
Stobart, Mrs St Clair, *Ancient Lights*, London, 1926.
Sudre, René, *Introduction à la Métapsychique Humaine*, Paris, 1926.
Sudre, René, *Treatise on Parapsychology*, London, 1960 (Paris, 1956).
Symns, Ann M., *Dreams that Come True*, London, 1933.
Tabori, Paul, *Harry Price*, London, 1950.
Tabori, Paul, *Companions of the Unseen*, London, 1968.
Tenhaeff, W. H. C., *Telepathy and Clairvoyance*, Springfield, Ill., 1972 (1965).
Thalbourne, Michael A., *A Glossary of Terms used in Parapsychology*, London, 1982.
Thomas, C. Drayton, *Some New Evidence for Human Survival*, London, 1922.
Thomas, C. Drayton, *Life Beyond Death*, London, 1928.
Thomas, C. Drayton, *An Amazing Experiment*, London, 1936.
Thomas, John F., *Beyond Normal Cognition*, Boston, 1937.
Thomson, J. Arthur, *The Outline of Science* (2 vols), London, 1921–2.
Thomson, J. Arthur, *Science and Religion*, London, 1925.
Thomson, Sir J. J., *Recollections and Reflections*, London, 1936.
Thouless, Robert H., *Experimental Psychical Research*, London, 1963.
Thouless, Robert H., *From Anecdote to Experiment in Psychical Research*, London, 1972.
Thurston, Fr Herbert, *Modern Spiritualism*, London, 1938.

Thurston, Fr Herbert, *The Physical Phenomena of Mysticism*, London, 1952.
Tietze, Thomas R., *Margery*, New York, 1973.
Tischner, Rudolf, *Telepathy and Clairvoyance*, London and New York, 1925 (Munich 1921).
Troland, Leonard Thompson, *A Technique for the Experimental Study of Telepathy*, London, 1926 (Albany, 1925).
Troland, Leonard S., *The Mystery of Mind*, London 1926 (1917).
Troubridge, Una, Lady, *The Life and Death of Radclyffe Hall*, London, 1961.
Turner, James (ed.), *'Stella C.'*, London, 1973.
Tyrrell, G. N. M., *Science and Psychical Phenomena*, London, 1938.
Tyrrell, G. N. M., *Apparitions*, London, 1942.
Tyrrell, G. N. M., *The Personality of Man*, London, 1946.
Tyrrell, G. N. M., *Homo Faber*, London, 1951.
Underhill, Evelyn, *Man and the Supernatural*, London, 1934 (1927).
Van Over, Raymond (ed.), *Psychology and Extra-sensory Perception*, New York, 1972.
de Vesme, César, *Experimental Spiritualism*, (2 vols), London, 1931 (1928).
Vyvyan, John, *A Case against Jones*, London, 1966.
Walker, Benjamin, *Beyond the Body*, London, 1974.
Walker, Nea, *The Bridge: a Case for Survival*, London, 1927.
Walker, Nea, *Through a Stranger's Hands*, London, 1935.
Warcollier, René, *Experiments in Telepathy* (ed. Gardner Murphy), London, 1939.
Warrick, F. W., *Experiments in Psychic Photography*, London, 1938.
West, D. J., *Psychical Research Today*, London, 1962 (1954).
White, Rhea and Laura Dale, *Parapsychology: Sources of Information*, Metuchen, N.J., 1973.
Whitehead, A. N., *Science and the Modern World*, London, 1975 (1925).
Whitehead, A. N., *Nature and Life*, Cambridge, 1934.
Wiesinger, Alois, *Occult Phenomena in the Light of Theology*, London, 1957.
Wilson, Colin, *The Occult*, London, 1973.
Wolman, B. B. (ed.), *Handbook of Parapsychology*, New York, 1977.
Wundt, Wilhelm, *Lectures on Human and Animal Psychology*, London, 1894.
Yeats, W. B., 'Seances at Mme Bissons' (unpublished: in SPR archives).
Yost, Casper S., *Patience Worth*, New York, 1916.
Zohar, Danah, *Through The Time Barrier*, London, 1932.

Sources

2. Periodicals
American Society for Psychical Research: *Journal and Proceedings*.
Annales des Sciences Psychiques.
Annals of Psychical Science.
Bedrock.
Boston Society for Psychical Research: *Bulletins*.
British College of Psychic Science: *Quarterly Transactions*.
Institute of Parapsychology: *Journal*.
Institut Métapsychique International: *Revue Métapsychique*.
Light.
National Laboratory of Psychical Research: *Proceedings*.
Nature.
Science.
Scientific American.
University of London Council for Psychical Investigation: *Bulletins*.

3. Conference Reports

Le Compte Rendu Officiel du Premier Congrès International des Recherches Psychiques, Copenhagen, 1922.

L'Etat Actuel des Recherches Psychiques: Deuxième Congrès International tenu à Varsovie, Paris, 1923.

Résumé des Rapports Presentés au Troisième Congrès International des Recherches Psychiques, Paris, 1927.

Transactions of the Fourth International Congress for Psychical Research (Athens, 1930), ed. T. Besterman, London, 1931.

Source References

The words in brackets refer to the subject matter to be found on the page in the text: the source itself is identified by the author's name and the date of the book (or article), which will be found in the Sources.

CHAPTER 1: THE FORERUNNERS

As this covers the same ground as *Natural and Supernatural*, I have given sources only for fresh or amplified material.

Page
- 19 (D. D. Home) An admirably balanced biography, *The Shadow and the Light*, by Elizabeth Jenkins, was published in 1982, winning the respect even of Dr E. J. Dingwall, whose earlier commentary on Home's life and career was decidedly more critical.
- 25 (William James on Eusapia) Gardner Murphy and Robert Ballou, *William James on Psychical Research*, 1961, 90–2; G. W. Allen, *William James*, 1967, 472.
- 26–7 (The American investigations of Eusapia) Muensterberg, *Metropolitan Magazine*, February 1910; Jastrow, *Colliers*, 14 May 1910; *Review of Reviews*, July 1910; *Science*, 20 May 1910, 726–8; Carrington, *American Seances*, 1954, 209; Hyslop, *JASPR*, 1910, 169–85, 337–42, 401–24; 1919, 350–1. Flournoy, 1911, 285–6. (Eusapia's career post-1910) Carlos Alvarado, *SPR Jnl.*, June 1982, 308–9. (Willis's career) Holms, 1925, 383.
- 27–34 'Eva C.'. (Richet investigations) *Annals Psychic Science*, Oct., Nov., 1905, April, 1906; Richet, 1923, 523; *Les Nouveaux Horizons*, November 1906; *Proc.s SPR*, 1914–15, xxvii, 336–43. (Schrenck-Bisson investigations) Schrenck-Notzing 1914, 1920, *passim*; Bisson, 1914, *passim*. (Mathilde von Kemnitz) James Webb, *The Occult Establishment*, 1976, 305–7. (Yeats and 'Eva C.') unpublished typescript; SPR archives.
- 34–6 (Tomczyk/Ochorowicz) *Annales P. S.* 1909, viii, 271–84, 333–99, 516–33; 1910, xx, 37, 208; Flournoy, 1911, 288–90; *JASPR*, 1921, xv, 207; Richet, 1923, 428, 438; Feilding, *SPR Jnl.*, February 1915, 24–31; Dingwall, *Proc.s SPR*, 1926–8, xxxvi, 336–7; Sudre, 1960, 248.
- 36–8 (Balfour) *Proc.s SPR*, 1893, x, 7; (Bergson) *Procs. SPR*, 1914–15, xxvii, 157–75.

Source References

Page
40 (Van Helmholtz) Barrett, *Prosc. SPR*, 1903–4, xviii, 323–50. (Schiller) Murchison, 1927, 215–18.
42 (Harvard and Stanford) Mauskopf/McVaugh, 1980, 44–6.
44–5 (Mgr de Lanyi) Richet, 1923, 386.

CHAPTER 2: THE FIRST WORLD WAR

The Cross-correspondences
46 (Lodge), Hill, 1932, 25.
47–8 Sidgwick, 1917, 258–9; Salter, 1961, 169–207; Heywood, 1959, 69–91.

'Raymond'
49 (Dewar) Jolly 1974, 180.
49 (Lodge) Hill, 1932, 15, 49.
50–3 (Raymond) Lodge, 1916, *passim*.

Mrs Osborne Leonard
53 Sidgwick, 1917, 258–9.
55–6 (Mrs Hugh Talbot) *Proc.s SPR*, 1921, xxxi, 253–60.
56 (SPR post) *SPR Jnl.*, Jan. 1919, 19.
56–7 ('A.V.B.') Susie Smith, 1964, 57–8.

A 'traveller' in Dublin
58–62 (Trials) Barrett, 1917, 178–9, 238–45; 1920, 176–89; *Proc.s SPR*, 1920, xxx, 230–50; Travers-Smith, 1919, 11–16; Dodds, 1978, 103–4.
60 Travers-Smith (castle), 1919, 48–9; (calendar) 1919, 13–15.
61 (Pearl tie-pin) Barrett, 1917, 184–7; Travers-Smith, 1919, 29–30.
62 Travers-Smith (evidence ephemeral) 1919, 24.

The Goligher Circle
62–6 (General) Crawford, 1916, *passim*.
63 (Bogoraz) Mircea Eliade, *Shamanism*, 1964, 255; Crawford, 1919, 184.
63 (Rods) Crawford, 1916, 25ff.
64 Barrett (on PK), *Proc.s SPR*, 1886–7, iv, 39–40.
64 Barrett (on Palladino), 1920, 67.
64–5 Barrett (on Goligher Circle), *Proc.s SPR*, 1920 xxx, 334–7.
66 Sidgwick, *SPR Jnl.*, Feb. 1917, 29–31.
67 *Light*, 3 March 1917, *et seq*.

CHAPTER 3: POST-WAR BRITAIN

Page
67 (Rayleigh) *Proc.s SPR*, 1920, xxx, 276–80.
68–9 (Crookes) Medhurst/Goldney, *Proc.s SPR*, 1964, liv, 123–7; Scatcherd, 1924, 127–9.
69 (Galton) *Proc.s SPR*, 1964, liv, 41.
69 (Russell) cited Langdon-Davies, 1960, 11.
70 (Inge) Blatchford, 1925, 21; Bevan, 1928, 31.

'Feda'
70–3 Mrs Leonard (Troubridge) *Proc.s SPR*, 1922, 344–78; (Drayton Thomas) *SPR Jnl.*, May 1921, 89–107; Thomas, 1921, 15; (Glenconner) Smith, 1964, 130–1; Sidgwick, 1921, 375–8.

Phantasms Revisited
73–5 Sidgwick, 1923, 23–429; (Dickinson) 107–9; (Larkin) 151–60; *SPR Jnl.*, 1919, 77–83.

Goligher Circle revisited
76–8 Whately Smith, *Proc.s SPR*, 1920, xxx, 306–33; Crawford, 1921, *passim*; *Light*, 11 Sept. 1920; (Lodge review) *Proc.s SPR*, 1924, xxxiv, 317.
79–83 Fournier d'Albe, 1922, *passim*; SPR Jnl., Nov. 1927, 141; (*Westminster Gazette*) cited *Light*, March and April 1917.

Psychic Photography
83–5 (Traill Taylor) *British Jnl. Photography*, 17 March 1893.
85 (Case histories) Holms, 1925, 207–20.
85 (Hyslop/Cook) *JASPR*, 1916, x, 1–114.
85–6 Goddard, 1975, 91–2.
86–7 (Crookes/Hope) *Proc.s SPR*, 1964, liv, 125.
87–8 Conan Doyle, 1925, 15–50.

The Cottingley Fairies
88–92 (General) Gardner, 1966, *passim*.
88 *Strand*, Dec. 1920, March 1921; *News*, 21 Jan. 1921.
88–91 Conan Doyle, 1922, *passim*.
92 (Lodge) *SPR Jnl.*, March 1921, 63–70.

The Advent of Harry Price
92–3 (Marriott) *SPR Jnl.*, Feb. 1922, 219–23; April 1922, 259–66.
93–4 (Price) *SPR Jnl.*, May 1922, 270–1.

Source References

CHAPTER 4: THE CONTINENTAL MEDIUMS

Page

'Eva'; Geley's investigations
95– (General) Geley, 1920, *passim;* (Vitalism) 1920, 51–62; (materialisation) 1920, 260–82.

'Eva': the SPR trials
98 (Hyslop/Verrall) *JASPR*, Jan. 1915, 333; *SPR Jnl.* June 1915, 82–4.
99 (Verrall review) *Proc.s SPR*, 1914–15, xxxii, 336–43
99 (Schiller) *Proc.s SPR*, 1921–2, xxxii, 44–6.
100–105 (investigation) *Proc.s SPR*, 1921–2, xxxii, 209–343; (Houdini) Doyle, 1930, 60–1; (Dingwall) *Proc.s SPR*, xxxii, 309–30; (Tomczyk) Oesterreich, 1923, 123–5; Yeats, *Letters*, 1977, ii, 553–4; (verdict) *Proc.s* 332–40; Richet, 1923, 544–5.

Willy Schneider
105–9 (Dingwall investigation) *SPR Jnl.* Oct. 1922, 359–72; *Revue Métapsychique*, 1923, iii, 19–26 *et seq*. (Price's library) *SPR Jnl*, May 1922, 270–1.
109–12 (Thomas Mann) *Encounter*, April 1976; *Three Essays*.
112–13 (Dingwall review) *Proc.s SPR*, 1924, xxxiv, 324–32.

The 1921 Congress
114–15 (Sauerbrey) *SPR Jnl.*, Jan. 1922, 199–207; Conference Report; Gauld/Cornell, 1979, 76–9.
115 ('Mme B.') *Revue Métapsychique,* 1921–2, i, 3–17; Geley, 1927, 97–138.
116–17 Tischner, 1925, *passim*.
117–18 (Brugmans) Conference report. (Consensus) Richet, 1930; Rhine, 1934; Heywood, 1959; Murphy, 1961.

Madame Przybylska
118–19 (predictions) *Revue Métapsychique*, Sept., Oct. 1921; Geley, 1927, 166–72; Osty, 1933, 40–4.

Franek Kluski
119–22 (general) *Revue Métapsychique*, 1920–1, i, 117–26 *et seq.*; Geley, 1927, 7, 198–271; Sudre, 1960, 274–5, 281; Rinn, 1954, 278–9; *Scientific American*, Nov. 1923, 316–17, 273–4.

Stefan Ossowiecki
122–5 Richet, 1931, 145; Geley, 1927, 42–65; *Revue Métapsychique*, 1920–1, i, 275–7 *et seq*.

Page
Flammarion and Richet
125–6 Flammarion (Presidential Address) *Proc.s SPR*, 1924, xxxiv, 1–27.
126–8 Richet (Academy address) *SPR Jnl.*, April 1922, 255–6. (telekinesis) Richet, 1923, 607; Lodge, *Proc.s SPR*, 1924, 34, 75; (precognition) Richet, 1923, 344; (poltergeists) 1923, 591–2 (telekinesis, importance of) 1923, 435; (conjurors) 1923, 39–40; (materialisations) 1923, 468.
128–9 (sceptics) *L'Année psychologique*, 1922, 602; *Revue Philosophique*, 1922, 5–32; 1923, 466–7.
129 'Eva C', *L'Opinion* 8 July 1922 *et seq.*; *SPR Jnl.* Dec. 1922, 402–3; July 1923, 122; Geley, 1927, 380–95.

Jean Guzik
129–32 Geley, 1927, 272–337, 386–8; Osty, *Revue Métapsychique*, Nov., Dec., 1926, vi, 445–80.

Eugene Osty
132–5 Osty, 1923, *passim*
135 Schiller, *Proc.s SPR*, 1924, xxxiv, 333–5; Gauld, 1982, 133–4.

The Death of Geley
135–7 Dingwall, *SPR Jnl.*, May 1924, 259–63.
137 Sudre, *JASPR*, 1925, xix, 30–40.
137–8 Lodge, *Proc.s SPR*, 1924, xxxiv, 34, 207–11.
138–9 Geley, 1927, intro.
139 Geley, 1927, vii.
139 (Collective experiments) Geley, 1927, 3–5.

CHAPTER 5: THE USA

Patience Worth:
142 (Schiller) *Proc.s SPR*, 1926–8, xxxvi, 574–5.
142 (Telka) Prince, 1926, 240; Litvag, 1972, 68–71.
143 (Morton Prince) Litvag, 1972, 75–83.
143–4 Hyslop, *JASPR*, 1916, x, 189–94.
144 Prince (on Hyslop) 1926, 420
144 Hyslop (on Jost) *JASPR*, July 1917, 361; Litvag, 1972, 14.
145–6 (Reviews) Prince, 1926, 72–7.

The Sceptics
146 Schiller, *Proc.s SPR*, 1921, xxxi, 223.
147 (Troland) Hyslop, *JASPR*, July 1919, 355–60; Mauskopf/McVaugh, 1980, 55–7.
147–8 Hyslop, 1919, 1–11, 477–88.

Source References

Page

Walter Franklin Prince
148 (Early career) Moore, 1977, 171.
148 (Dream of accident) *JASPR*, 1923, xvii, 86–9.
148 ('Doris Fischer') *Proc.s JASPR*, 1915–17, ix–xi, *passim*.
148–9 (Dream of 'head') *JASPR*, 1923, xvii, 89–101.
150–2 ('Senora de Z') *Proc.s ASPR*, 1921, xv, 189–314; 1922, xvi, 1–136; Murchison, 1927, 196. (Later commentaries) Tyrrell, 1946, 186–7; Roll, *JASPR*, 1967, lxvi, 219–46.

William McDougall
152–3 (Wells) McDougall, *Proc.s SPR*, 1907, 410–31.
153 (Telepathy) McDougall, 1911, 349–54.
154 (Presidential Address) McDougall, *Proc.s SPR*, 1920, xxxi, 105–23.
155–6 Jastrow, *Fact and Fable in Psychology*, 1901, 42–3.
156 (Resignation) Mauskopf/McVaugh, 1980, 16–21.

'Margery'
156–60 (Early career) Dingwall, *Proc.s SPR*, 1926–8, xxxvi, 80; Tietze, 1973, 2–18; Bird, 1925, 33ff; (Griscom) Tietze, 1973, intro.

The First Harvard Investigation
160–1 Bird, 1925, 57ff; Tietze, 1973, 27–31.

The Scientific American investigation
161–3 Bird, 1925, 149ff; Richardson, 1925, 8ff; Tietze, 1972, 32ff.

Houdini
163–4 (Houdini) Sardina, 1950, 16ff.
164 (Houdini's breathing exercise) Christopher, 1969, 232.
164–5 Conan Doyle, 1930, 1–3, 56.
165 Christopher, 1969, 159.
165 Crawford letter is in *Psychic News* archives.
165–6 (*A Magician among the Spirits*) Houdini, 1924, *passim*; *SPR Jnl.*, Nov. 1924, 332; Prince, 1930 148–50; Medhurst, 1964, 102.
166 (Valiantine) Christopher, 1969, 178–9.
166 (*Scientific American*) Houdini, 1924, 5.
166–8 ('Cabinet') Conan Doyle, *Boston Herald*, 26 Jan. 1925; 1930, 9–13; Houdini, 1924, 5–19; Tietze, 1973, 48–55.
168 (Collins) Tietze, 1973, 53; Christopher, 1969, 193–4.

Dingwall's Investigation
169–76 Dingwall, *Proc.s SPR*, 1926–8, xxxvi, 79–155.
171 (Schrenck) *Revue Métapsychique*, Feb, 1925; Murchison, 1927, 80.
175 (McDougall) *JASPR*, June 1925, 301.
176 ('Nut') *Proc.s SPR*, 1926–8, xxxvi, 156–8.

Page

The Second Harvard investigation
176–7 (Outcome of Scientific American investigation); McDougall, *New York Times*, 21 Feb. 1925; Richardson, 1925, 9–21; Bird, 1925, 438–9.
177–82 (Hoagland and Code) Richardson, 1925, 38–82; Tietze, 1973, 74–89.

Margery Harvard Veritas
182 Richardson, 1925, *passim*; Bird 1925, 442–3; Tietze, 1973, 62.
183–4 Boring, *Atlantic*, Jan. 1926, 81–7.
184–5 Feilding, *Proc.s SPR*, 1926–8, xxxvi, 159–70; *Proc.s SPR*, 1926–8, xxxvi, 414–32.
186–7 (Uterus) Tietze, 1972, 117.

The McComas Enquiry
187 (Mina's oath) *Proc.s SPR*, 1926–8, xxxvi, 515–16.
187–8 (McComas report) Tietze, 1973, 90–100.
188–9 (Houdini) Christopher, 1969, 235–6.
190 McDougall, *Psyche*, 1926, 25.

The Clark University symposium
190 Hall, *American Jnl of Psychology*, 1888, i, 128–46.
192 Sigerist, 1932, 52.
192–3 Driesch, 1925, 229–42.

CHAPTER 6: THE SPR IN DECLINE

'Feda'
197 (Mrs Leonard) Blatchford, 1925, 69ff.
197–9 (Mrs Dawson-Smith) *Proc.s SPR*, 1926–8, xxxvi, 299–310.

The Death of Barrett
200 (Reminiscences) Barrett, 1924, 284–5.
200 Haynes, 1982, 166–7.
201 (Dowsing) Barrett, *Proc.s SPR*, 1911, xxv, 390–404.
201 (Psychic photographs) Barrett, 1924, 289.
201 ('Thought transfusion') Barrett, 1924, 294.
202 Kastenbaum (unpublished typescript).

Gilbert Murray
202–4 *Proc.s SPR*, 1918, xxix, 46–63; Verrall, 64–110.
204–5 Sidgwick, *Proc.s SPR*, 1924, xxxiv, 212ff; 336ff.
205 *Times*, 13 Dec. 1924.

Source References

Page
207 Conan Doyle, 1930, 34.
207 (Houdini) Fitzsimons, 1980, 146.

The Black Box
208–12 Lancet, 24 Jan. 1925, 177–81.

The Chaffin Will
212–14 *Proc.s SPR*, 1925, xxxvi, 517–24; *SPR Jnl.*, Sept. 1963, 157–69.

The Easing-out of Dingwall
214 (Mrs Leonard) *Proc.s SPR*, 1926–8, xxvi, 194–6.
215 Piddington, *Proc.s SPR*, 1924, xxxiv, 145–6.
215–7 Dingwall, *Proc.s SPR*, 1926–8, xxxvi, 1–33.
217 (Schrenck) Dingwall, *Proc.s SPR*, 1926–8, xxxvi, 387–92.
218 (Price) Dingwall; Hall, 1978, intro; Mauskopf/McVaugh, 1980, 26.
218–19 Tillyard, *Nature*, 31 July, 1926, 147–9; Tabori, 1968, 103–19, 164–84.
219 (BBC) *Proc.s SPR*, 1928–9, xxxviii, 1–9.
220 (Woolley) *SPR Jnl.*, May 1928, 257.
220 (Dingwall) *SPR Jnl.*, Oct. 1927, 114; (Price) *SPR Jnl.*, March 1928, 214; (Hack) *SPR Jnl.*, Jan. 1930.
220 (Conan Doyle) Price, 1939, 53.
221 Lodge, *Proc.s SPR*, 1932–3, xli, 71–2.
221 Conan Doyle ('Eva') 1930, 222–3.

Carlos Mirabelli
222 Salter, *SPR Jnl.*, Oct. 1927, 127; Perovsky, *SPR Jnl.* Nov. 1927, 144.
223–6 Dingwall, *JASPR*, 1930, xxxiv, 296–306.
226 Driesch, *JASPR*, Nov. 1930, 486–7.
221–7 (General) Playfair, 1975, 78–110.

An Experiment with Time
227 Podmore, 1897, 337–9.
228 (Tarde) Sudre, 1960, 375.
227–31 Dunne, 1934, *passim*; Priestley, 1964, 244–61.

Dame Edith Lyttelton
231–5 Lyttelton, 1931, *passim*.
232 ('Patience Worth') Lyttelton, 1931, 245–52.
233 (verses) Lyttelton, 1931, 253.
235 Richet, 1931, *passim*.
235 Lodge, *Proc.s SPR*, 1932–3, xli, 73–4.
235–6 Besterman, *Proc.s SPR*, 1932–3, xli, 186–204.

Science and Parascience

CHAPTER 7: MIND OVER MATTER

Page

237–59 Rudi Schneider (General): Price, 1930, *passim*; Gregory, 1977, *passim*.

238 (Prince) *Boston Socy Bulletin*, Jan. 1928, vii, 5–70.

The Besterman Rumpus

239–40 (Dingwall/de Brath) *Proc.s SPR*, 1926–8, xxxvi, 387–92; Geley, 1927, vi.

240–2 ('Eva') Lambert, *SPR Jnl.*, Nov. 1954, 380–6; Perovsky, *SPR Jnl.*, Oct. 1928, 344; Richet, 1923, 460–72; Besterman, 1930, 98; (Schrenck) Oesterreich, 1923, 127.

The SPR indicted

243 (de Brath) Bradley, 1931, 206–7; (Besterman) Bradley, 1931, 9, 204–5; (SPR) Bradley, 1931, 198; (Membership) Price, 1939, 54.

244–5 Osty, *Proc.s SPR*, 1931–2, xl, 428–36.

The 1932 Trials

246 (Sidgwick) Gregory, 1977, 480–1.

246–7 (Hope) Gergory, 1977, 501–2.

247 (British Association) *SPR Jnl.* Oct. 1927, 113–14; (Telepathy) Brown, 1929, 217–18.

248–9 (Price, Brown and Fraser-Harris) Gregory, 1977, 502–12.

The Hope/Rayleigh series

249 (Price/Osty) Gregory, 1977, 512–15; *Nature*, April–May 1933.

249–50 (Rudi: the Hope Rayleigh investigation) *Proc.s SPR*, 1932–3, xli, 255–330.

250–1 (Price's 'exposure') Gregory, 1977, 518–24.

251 Hope, *Proc.s SPR*, 1931–2, xli, 287–8.

252 (Goldney/Beenham) Gregory, 1977, 518; (Photography) Gregory, 1977, 524–38.

253–4 Brown, *Proc.s SPR*, 1932–3, xli, 84; Lodge, *Proc.s SPR*, 1932–3, xli, 86–7.

The SPR's Jubilee

255 Sidgwick, *Proc.s SPR*, 1932–3, xli, 1–26.

255–6 Lodge, 1931, 347–8.

256 Hill, 1932, 254.

256 (Conan Doyle) Lodge, *Proc.s SPR*, 1932–3, xli, 71–2.

Thoughtography

256–7 Fukurai, 1930, *passim*.

256 Coates, 1922, 16–23.

257 de Brath, 1925, 114–18.

257–9 (Hope) *SPR Jnl.* 1968, xliv, 362–9; Proc.s SPR, 1932–3, xli,

Source References

Page
  121–38; Sudre, 1960, 286; Copenhagen conference report, 343–5.
259 Coates, 1922, 16–23.
259 Hill, 1932, 231.

CHAPTER 8: EXTRA-SENSORY PERCEPTION

Page
260 Mauskopf/McVaugh, 1980, intro.; (Coover) Rhine, 1934, 21–2.

The Experimenters
261 Murphy, *JASPR*, Jan. 1980, 26–31.
262 (Broadcast) Murchison, 1927, 273.
261–3 (Experiments) *Revue Métapsychique*, July/Aug. 1926, vi, 272–87; Warcollier, 1939, 26, 56–7; Murphy, 1961, 52–5; Sudre, 1960, 139–48; Mauskopf/McVaugh, 1980, 29–32.
263–4 (Clark) Murchison, 1927, 266–77.
264 Estabrooks, 1927, 24; Soal/Bateman, 1954, 18–19; Sidgwick, *SPR Jnl.*, Oct. 1928, 329–31.

The Jephson trials
265–6 Jephson, *Proc.s SPR*, 1928, xxxviii, 223–71; Tyrrell, 1946, 109; Mauskopf/McVaugh, 1980, 107.

J. B. Rhine
266–8 (Early career) Rhine, 1938, 18–20; Moore, 1977, 185–96; Mauskopf/McVaugh, 1980, 71–4.
266–7 ('Margery'), *Jnl. Abnormal Psychology*, 1927, xxi, 401–21.
267 (Duke) Mauskopf/McVaugh, 1980, 69–84.
267–8 (Lundholm) Rhine, 1937, 55–6.

Mental Radio
268–71 Sinclair, 1930, *passim*.

The Zener Cards
271–3 Rhine, 1937, 57–112; Mauskopf/McVaugh, 1980, 108ff.

The Monograph
273–5 ('Not sensory') Rhine, 1934, 2; (not perception) Sudre, 1960, 123ff; Heywood, 1964, 27.

Repercussions
275–6 (The Media) Mauskopf/McVaugh, 1980, 151ff; Rhine, 1937, 157–72.

Science and Parascience

Page
276–7 (Garrett) Mauskopf/McVaugh, 1980, 137ff, Palmer, 1927, 116; Garrett, 1949, 155–8; ('Uvani') Fuller, 1979, *passim*.
278–9 Thouless, *Proc.s SPR*, 1935, xliv, 24–37; Rhine (reply) *Proc.s SPR*, 1935, xliii, 542–4.

S. G. Soal
279 (Mrs Cooper) Soal, 1926, 471–589; Bradley, *SPR Jnl.*, March 1926, 32–8; West, 1952, 102–7; Vyvyan, 1966, 73–89; Gauld, 1982, 137–8.
280 (Crawford) Soal, *SPR Jnl.*, Oct. 1931, 130–5.
280–1 (Warcollier) Soal, *SPR Jnl.*, Oct. 1931, 135–6.
281 (Jephson) *Proc.s SPR*, 1930–1, xxxix, 375–414.
281–2 (Rhine) Mauskopf/McVaugh, 1980, 121ff.
282 (Garrett) Soal/Bateman, 1954, 106–8.

G. M. N. Tyrrell
282 Tyrrell, (first report) *SPR Jnl.*, June 1922, 294–327.
282–5 Heywood, 1959, 148–9; Tyrrell (second report) *Proc.s SPR*, 1937, xliv, 99–168.

Research on the Continent
285 (Bender) Mauskopf/McVaugh, 1980, 175–7.
285–7 (Ossowiecki) *Proc.s SPR*, 1932–3, xli, 345–51.
287–8 (Forthuny) Osty, 1926, *passim*; *SPR Jnl.* March 1927, 47–8; Richet, *JASPR*, Sept. 1935, 241–54; Sudre, 1960, 168–70.
288–9 (Berger) Krippner, 1977, 1; Burt, 1975, 75.
289 Carrell, 1961, 102–6.

CHAPTER 9: BACKLASH

290 *Journal of Parapsychology*, 1937, i, 260–3; 1939, iii, 79–88.
291 (Statistics) *Journal of Parapsychology*, 1937, i, 305.
291 (*Science News Letter*) Mauskopf/McVaugh, 1980, 262–4.
292 Dingwall, *SPR Jnl.*, Dec. 1937, 141.

The Fatal Thumbprint
292 ('Margery') Tietze, 1973, 142–3.
292–3 (Dudley) Tietze, 1973, 152–7; *Bulletin*, xviii, (October); *Proc.s SPR*, 1935, xliii, 15–23; Sidgwick, *Proc.s SPR*, 1931–2, xli, 115–19; Besterman, 1930, 154–5.
294 (Rings) Randall, 1982, 131–2; Yeats, *Letters*, ii, 549.
295 Hack, 1930, 6.
295 (Prince) Tietze, 1973, 164.
295 (Comstock) *JASPR*, 1925, 674.
295–6 (Prince's verdict) Tietze, 173, 164.
296 Tietze, *JASPR*, 1976, 1–34.

Source References

Page
Mirabelli revisited
297 Walker, *JASPR*, 1934, 74–8.
297–8 Besterman, *SPR Jnl.*, 1935–6, 25, 141–53.
298 Herbert, *SPR Jnl.*, Nov. 1936, xxix, 286.
298 Rhine, 1970, 27.

The Demise of Physical Mediumship
299–300 Rayleigh, *Proc.s SPR*, 1938–9, xlv, 1–18.

CHAPTER 10: BALANCE SHEET

302 (Richet) Lodge, *Proc.s SPR*, 1936–7, 1924, xxxiv, 99ff; 1936–7, xliv, 1–4; Hill, 1932, 181.
302–3 (Feilding) Bennett, *Proc.s SPR*, 1936–7, xliv, 5–6.
304 (Sidgwick) Haynes, 1982, 191; Sidgwick, 1938, 178.
304 McDougall, *Psyche*, Oct. 1926, 18–31.
304–5 (Oesterreich), Mauskopf/McVaugh, 1980, 15; Tabori, 1950, 173.
305 Ostrander/Schroeder, 1970, 412.

Hypnosis and Multiple Personality
306–7 Price, *Proc.s SPR*, 1900–1, xv, 466–83; Moore, 1977, 153–5.
308 Bramwell, 1956, 141–3.
308–9 Alrutz, *Proc.s SPR*, 1921, xxxii, 151–78. Boirac, 1920, 168–71.
309 Price, *Proc.s* 1938–9, xlv, 316–17.

Parapsychology
310 Flournoy, 1911, vii.
311 Jones, *Freud*, iii, 402–36.
311–12 Jung, 1975, 126, 178–9.
312 (Jastrow) Tyrrell, 1938, 154.
312–13 Lodge, 1933, 267–75.
313 Troland, 1926, 2–4.
313 (Boring), Mauskopf/McVaugh, 1980, 265–9.
314 (Lashley) Mauskopf/McVaugh, 1980, 268–71.
314 (Coover) Mauskopf/McVaugh, 1980, 273–4.
314 (James) Flournoy, 1911, 21.
314 *Nature*, 20 Nov. 1926, 721–3.
315 Gregory, 1977, 494.
315 (Carington) Mauskopf/McVaugh, 1980, 120.

Paraphysics
316 Flammarion, 1921, i, 57.
316 Eddington, 1929, 276.
316 Whitehead, 1928, 21.
316 Hill, 1932, 224.

Science and Parascience

Page
316–17 Lodge, *Proc.s SPR*, 1928–9, xxxviii, 481–516.
317 Jeans, 1931, 137; *SPR Jnl.*, Oct. 1931, 135–6.
317 Brown, 1929, 17.
317 Besterman, *SPR Jnl.*, Feb 1938, 33.
317 Whitehead, 1934, 13–19.
317 Eddington, 1929, 275.
317–18 (Einstein) *Science*, 30 Sept., 4 Nov. 1977.
318–19 Romains, 1924, 21, 39; Pauwels/Bergier, 1968, 315–16.

The Demolition Squad
319 Fisk, *Proc.s SPR* 1936, xliv, 153–7; Tyrrell, *Proc.s SPR*, 1936–7, xliv, 157–9; *SPR Jnl.*, May 1938, 223–5.
320 Dingwall, *SPR Jnl.*, July 1936, xxix, 107–8.
321 Rhine, 1938, 273–8.

The University Council
322 (Soal) Mauskopf/McVaugh, 1980, 234–6.
322–3 Joad, *Harpers*, June 1938; Salter, *Proc.s SPR* 1938–9, xlv, 217–22.
323 Hall, 1978, intro.
323 (Dingwall) Hankey, 1963, 139.
324 (Thomas) Mauskopf/McVaugh, 1980, 79–86 *et seq*.
324 (Garrett) Hankey, 1963, 135.

Spontaneous phenomena
324 Lodge, 1933, 270–3.
324 Schiller, *SPR Jnl.*, 1936, 249.
325–6 Bennett, 1939, 62–75; MacKenzie, 1982, 171–5.
326 (Viré) Richet, 1923, 231; Bird, 1979.
326 de France, *Revue Métapsychique*, July/Aug. 1931; *SPR Jnl.*, July 1931, 143–54.
327 Thomson, 1936, 158–9.

Mediumship
328 (Richet/Lodge) *Proc.s SPR*, 1936–7, xliv, 1–4; Bozzano, 1938, 6–11, 267–74; *Psychic News*, 2 Dec. 1976.
329 Carington, *Proc.s SPR*, 1934–9, *passim*.
329 ('Palm Sunday') Balfour, *Proc.s SPR*, 1935, xliii, 43–318; Haynes, 1982, 73.
329 Murphy, *JASPR*, Jan. 1980, 29.
330 Heywood, 1959, 69–106.
330–1 Saltmarsh, *Proc.s SPR*, 1929, xxxix, 47ff.
331 (Mrs Leonard) Smith, 1964, 22; Heywood, 1959, 112.

Survival?
332 Thomson, 1936, 158.
332 Jacks, 1940, 234.

Source References

Page
332–3 (Mrs Leonard) Dodds, 1934, 147–72.
333–5 Palmstierna, 1937, 351–65; *SPR Jnl.*, Nov. 1937, 132–6.
335–6 Tyrrell, 1938, 361–71.
336–7 Gauld, 1982, 88–9.
337 (Bernhard) Tenhaeff, *SPR Jnl.*, 1939–40, xxx, 2–6.

Postscript
338 ('Faggot') Tyrrell, 1938, 10.
338 Conant, 1947, 102–3.
340 Sidgwick, *Proc.s SPR*, 1883, i, 250.

INDEX

A. E. (George Russell), 58
'A.V.B.', 56–7
Abrams, Albert, 208–9
Academia de Estudos Psychicos, Santos, 223
Academy of Sciences, France, 18
Advisory Scientific Council, Boston, Mass., 155
Alexander II, Tsar, 20
Alrutz, Sydney, 309
American Journal of Psychology, 195
American Magazine, The, 25
American Society for Psychical Research (ASPR): founded, 22; and Eusapia Palladino, 25; and McDougall, 154–6; split in, 156, 158; and Rhine, 278; and Crandons, 292–3; Bird dismissed from, 293; *Journal*, 85, 143, 155, 223, 226, 266, 293; *Proceedings*, 155
Animism, 153
Annales des Sciences Psychiques, 34
Annals of Science, 246
'apports', 219, 227, 254, 297
Aranyi, Jelly d', 333–5
Arsonval, Jacques Arsène d', 24
Atlantic Monthly, 181, 183–5
automatic writing, 46–7
'automatism', 46, 53, 147, 329–30
Axham, Frederick, 208

B., Madame (medium), 115
B., Miss von (medium), 116
Baggally, Wortley, 24, 101
Balfour, Arthur J., 1st Earl, 22, 37, 48, 205, 329
Balfour, Gerald, 2nd Earl, 22, 43, 49, 255, 325
Barker, Sir Herbert, 208
Barlow, Fred, 258
Barrett, Sir William: founds SPR, 21–2, 200; von Helmholtz and, 40; in Ireland, 58–9, 61–2, 64–5, 69, 76, 78, 82–3; and investigations, 71, 200–1, 302; and Cottingley fairies, 92; and William Hope, 94; at Warsaw Conference, 135; death, 200; and Murray's 'hyperesthesia', 205; portrait of, 303; and dowsing, 326; on accumulated evidence, 338; integrity, 341; *Death-bed Visions*, 201–2; *The Divining Rod* (with Besterman), 220; *Psychical Research*, 261
Baruch, Bernard, 207
'Beauchamp, Sally', 143, 152, 306, 309
Bedrock (journal), 41
Beenham, Ethel, 252
Bender, Hans, 285
Bennett, Sir Ernest Nathaniel, 302; *Apparitions and Haunted Houses*, 325
Béraud, Marthe ('Eva C'): background and mediumistic activities, 27–34, 36, 38; ectoplasm and pseudopods, 28, 97–8, 113, 174; Crawford and, 62; and Geley, 95–8, 129, 138, 240–2; SPR investigates, 98–105, 215; Houdini and, 102, 163, 165, 339; Paris tests on, 129; Doyle on, 221; Besterman on, 240–1; suffers tests, 339
Berger, Hans, 288–9
Bergson, Henri, 24, 36–8, 95, 127, 153, 192, 266, 328
Bernard, Claude, 195
Bernhard, Prince of the Netherlands, 337
Besterman, Theodore: at SPR, 220; and Dunne, 235–6; denounces 'Eva C', 240–1; and Osty's tests, 245; and Soal, 281; and Ossowiecki,

Besterman, Theodore – *cont.*
285–7; and 'Walter' thumbprint, 294; transatlantic tour, 297–8; resigns as SPR research officer, 298; on Heisenberg's indeterminacy, 317; *Some Modern Mediums*, 239, 242–3
Bevan, Edwyn: *Seers and Sybils*, 70
Bird, James Malcolm, 161–3, 166, 177, 182–4, 196, 238, 292–3
Bisson, Juliette: and 'Eva C', 29, 32–4, 95, 99, 102, 174, 240–2, 339; at Copenhagen Congress, 114; at Warsaw Congress, 135
'black box, the', 208–12
Blackwelder, 212–13
Blatchford, Robert, 197
Bogoraz, Waldemar, 63
Bohr, Nils, 316–17
Bolton, Francis, 276–7
'book tests', 72–3
Boring, Edwin G., 179, 183, 295, 313
Borley rectory, 246, 325
Boston Society for Psychic Research, 274, 281, 293
Boutlerow, Alexander von, 20
Boyd, W. E., 209–11
Boyd-Carpenter, William, Bishop of Ripon, 70
Bozzano, Ernesto, 220, 328
Bradley, H. Dennis, 243, 280
Braid, James, 205, 306
'brain-waves', 288–9
Bramwell, J. Milne, 155, 308
Brath, Stanley de *see* de Brath, Stanley
breathing: rapidity of, 254
British Association for the Advancement of Science, 21, 200, 205, 308
British Broadcasting Corporation, 219, 322
British College of Psychic Science, 93, 323–4
Broad, Charlie Dunbar, 300, 305
Broca, Paul, 139
Brocken mountain, 246, 248
Brookes-Smith, Colin, 252
Brown, William, 247–8, 253–4, 317
Browning, Elizabeth Barrett, 20

Brugmans, H. I., 117–18, 135, 261
Bryce, James, Viscount, 48
Bull, Samuel, 325–6
Bush, Edward, 92

'C, Eva' *see* Béraud, Marthe
'C, Stella', 237
Callahan, Philip, 67
Calmette, Albert, 97
Carington, Whately (*formerly* Smith), 77–8, 83, 100, 209–10, 305, 315, 329
Carpenter, C. R., 276
Carpenter, W. B., 205
Carrel, Alexis, 289
Carrington, Hereward: and Eusapia Palladino, 24–5; at Copenhagen Congress, 114; and 'Margery', 162–3, 166, 177; and William Hope, 258; and Freud, 311; *The Physical Phenomena of Spiritualism*, 25
Carroll, Lewis (C. L. Dodgson), 22
Cayce, Edgar, 326
Chaffin, James L. (and family), 212–14
Chamberlain, Joseph, 48
Charcot, Jean-Paul, 25, 306
Christopher, Milbourne: *Houdini, the Untold Story*, 165, 168, 188
Church of England, 53, 69–70
Clark University (USA), 190–1, 263, 316
Coates, James, 257–9
Cochet, Georges *see* Forthuny, Pascal
Code, Grant H., 179–87, 267, 296
College of Psychic Science, 218
Collins, James, 166–8
'communicators', 22, 54, 72, 330–1
Comstock, Daniel, 162, 167–8, 177, 295
Conant, James B., 338
'controls', 22, 329; *see also* individual controls
Cook, Rev. Charles Hall, 85
Cook, Florence, 20, 69
Coombe-Tennant, Winifred ('Mrs Willett'), 48
Cooper, Blanche, 279
Cooper, Joe, 90
Coover, John E.: at Stanford, 42, 115, 141; on ASPR council, 155; at Clark

Index

University symposium, 190, 194; Rhine and, 260–1; scepticism, 264; Thouless and, 278; retirement, 314; and recognition, 340; *Experiments in Psychical Research*, 146–7
Copenhagen *see* International Congress for Psychical Research, 1st
Cottingley fairies, 89–92
Coué, Emile, 193
Courtier, Jules, 24, 33, 97
Crandon, LeRoi Goddard: and 'Margery's' activities, 157, 159–62, 166, 168–70, 172–83, 185–7, 189; at Clark University symposium, 190, 195; and Prince, 194
Crandon, Mina ('Margery'): career and activities, 156–63; Houdini and, 163–4, 166–9, 177, 187–9, 295–6; Dingwall and, 169–76; second Harvard investigation, 176–83, 262; *Margery Harvard Veritas*, 182–7, 196; McComas investigates, 187–8; and Clark University symposium, 195; and W. Prince, 238, 295–6; Rhine and, 266–7; Upton Sinclair and, 268; Bird and, 292–3; and 'Walter' thumbprint, 293–4; discredited, 294–6
Cranshaw, Stella, 218
Crawford, William J: investigates Golighers, 62–6, 75–83, 158–9, 179; death, 81; and Kluski, 121; and Houdini, 165; Barrett and, 201; Soal on, 280; Rayleigh on, 299–300; portrait of, 303; *Experiments in Psychic Science*, 76; *The Psychic Structures of the Goligher Circle*, 81; *The Reality of Psychic Phenomena*, 65, 76
Crookes, William: and Home, 20, 312; and SPR, 22, 58; and 'full-form' materialisation, 28, 96, 126; reputation, 40–1, 87, 301; Rayleigh and, 67; death, 68; psychical beliefs, 68–9; Fournier d'Albe and, 81; and William Hope, 86–7; Richet and, 126–7; Order of Merit, 200

cross-correspondences, 47–8, 52–3, 153, 329–30
cryptesthesia, 127, 274
cryptomnesia, 232
Cuddon, Eric: *Hypnosis*, 309
Cumberland, Stuart, 202
'Cumberlandism' *see* hyperacuity
Curie, Marie and Pierre, 24
Curran, Mrs Pearl (*later* Rogers), 141–6, 232, 309

'D., Fräulein', 285
Dam, A. van, 117–18
Damon, S. Foster, 177, 179
Darwin, Charles, 69
Davis, Gordon, 279–80
Dawson-Smith, Mrs, 197–9
Dawson-Smith, Frank, 198–9
death-bed visions, 201
de Brath, Stanley, 115, 243, 257
de la Mare, Richard, 228
Derrygonyelly, 201
Dewar, Sir James, 49
Dexter, Douglas, 216
Dickinson, Goldsworthy Lowes, 42, 73
Dickinson, Janet, 73–4
Dingwall, Eric J.: and Stanislawa Tomczyk, 35–6; on Crawford's methods, 81; as SPR research officer, 94, 202, 214–15, 218, 220; and 'Eva C', 101–4, 106, 129; and Schneider, 106–9, 112–13, 215–17; and Tischner, 117; on Paris investigations, 129; at Warsaw Congress, 135–6; tests Ossowiecki, 135–6, 285, 287; tests 'Margery', 169–76; and 'black box', 210; split with SPR, 218, 220; on Mirabelli, 223, 226, 297; on decline of SPR, 239; on US experiments, 292; on Feilding, 304; attacks Tyrrell, 320; scepticism, 322; on Price, 323
divining rod *see* dowsing
Dodds, Eric, 59, 332–3
Donkin, Sir Horatio Bryan, 40, 42, 205–6, 218
Douglas, James, 92–3
Dowden, Edward, 58
dowsing, 201, 220, 308, 326–7

373

Doyle, Sir Arthur Conan: and supernatural pictures, 87; and Cottingley fairies, 88–9, 91–2; and Houdini, 102, 164–6, 207; tours USA, 158; and Mina Crandon, 161, 166; and Clark University symposium, 190–1; and College of Psychic Science, 218; and SPR, 220, 243; death and tributes, 221, 256; and Price, 246; attempted communication from, 277; and Gordon Davis, 280; *History of Spiritualism*, 218

Doyle, Jean, Lady, 164

dreams, 227–31, 234–6, 337

Driesch, Hans, 190, 192–3, 227, 316

Dubois, Eugene, 340

Dudley, E. E., 293–4

Dufferin and Ava, Frederick Temple-Blackwood, 1st Marquess of, 126

Duke University (USA), 267, 272–9, 282, 290, 304–5, 313, 319–21, 340

Dunlap, Knight, 187

Dunne, J. W.: *An Experiment with Time*, 227–31, 234–6, 321, 337

ectoplasm: 'Eva C' and, 28, 97–8, 174; Kathleen Goligher and, 78–80, 82, 174; Kluski and, 119–21; Richet on, 128; McDougall on, 156, 304; 'Margery' and, 170–5; Doyle on, 191; Rayleigh on, 300; *see also* pseudopods; teleplasm

Eddington, Sir Arthur, 316–17

Edmonds, Judge J. W., 87

Edwards, Rev. Frederick, 156

Ehrenwald, Jan, 318

Einstein, Albert, 248, 316–18

Elliott, Mrs Warren, 330

emanometer, 210–11

Emmanuel (church) movement, 170

Empire News (newspaper), 251

Encounter (magazine), 109

endosmosis, 37–8

entelechy, 192–3

'Erwin' (Willy Schneider's control), 110

Estabrooks, George, 264–6

Eusapia *see* Palladino, Eusapia

Evening Telegraph, 149

extra-sensory perception (ESP), 274, 310; *see also* parapsychology; Rhine, J. B.; 'super-ESP'

fairies, 88–92

Faraday, Michael, 18, 49, 181–2, 206, 276, 316

'Feda' (Mrs Leonard's control), 72–3, 114, 198–200, 234, 329; *see also* Leonard, Gladys Osborne

Feilding, Everard, 24, 35–6, 92–3, 100, 103–4, 184–7, 302, 304

Feilding, Stanislawa *see* Tomczyk, Stanislawa

Few, William Preston, 267

'Fischer, Doris', 143, 148

Fisher, R. A., 278, 331

Fisk, G. W., 319–20

Flammarion, Camille, 87, 119, 125–6, 131, 316; portrait of, 304

Fleming, Alice (*née* Kipling; Mrs Holland), 47

Flournoy, Theodor, 307, 310

Fontenay, Guillaume de, 97

Forthuny, Pascal (Georges Cochet), 287–8

Fournier d'Albe, E. E., 81–3, 102–4, 299–300

France, Henri de, Vicomte, 326

Fraser-Harris, D., 248–50

Fraya, Madame, 134

Frazer, Sir James: *The Golden Bough*, 310

Frederick Myers Lectures, 244

Free, E. E., 275

Freud, Sigmund, 229, 307, 310–12

Fukurai, T.: *Clairvoyance and Thoughtography*, 256–8, 301

Fuller, John G., 277

'full-form' materialisations, 20, 28, 80, 96, 300

Galton, Francis, 20, 69

Gardner, Edward L., 88–91

Gardner, Leslie, 88

Garrett, Eileen, 276–7, 282, 324

Gauld, Alan, 135, 280, 336

Geley, Gustave: and 'Eva C', 95–8, 100–2, 129, 138, 174, 240–2, 339;

Index

and 'ideoplasty', 100; at Copenhagen Congress, 114, 119; and Madame B., 115; and Kluski, 119–21; and Ossowiecki, 123–4, 136; and Guzik, 129–32; at Warsaw Congress, 135; killed, 137–8, 215, 240; and testing, 139, 318; Crandon on, 176; Besterman disparages, 239, 242; integrity, 341; *Clairvoyance and Materialism*, 138
Geller, Uri, 301
General Medical Council, 208–9
'Ghost Club', 322
Gifford Lecture, 1927, 316
Gladstone, William Ewart, 22
Glenconner, Edward P. Tennant, 1st Baron, 72
Glenconner, Pamela, Lady, 72
Goddard, Air Vice-Marshal Sir Victor: *Flight Towards Reality*, 85
Golden Dawn, 58
Goldney, Mrs K. M., 252
Goldston, Will, 238
Goligher, Kathleen and family, 62–6, 75–83, 159, 165, 174, 179, 201, 280, 299
Gould, Stephen, 340
Gow, David, 66, 81–3
Gramont, Count de, 130
gravity, 18
Greene, Willard P., 168
Gregory, Anita, 237–8, 251–3, 315; 'Anatomy of a Fraud', 246, 251–2
Gregory, C. C. L., 245, 248–9, 251
Gresham, Lindsay, 168
Griffin, Donald, 314
Griscom, Stewart, 158
Gulat-Wellenburg, Walter von, 33, 99, 217, 240
Gurney, Edmund, 21, 43, 47, 125–6, 325
Guzik, Jean, 129–32, 138

Hack, Gwendolyn: *Modern Psychic Mysteries*, 220, 295
Haeckel, Ernst, 340
Haldane, J. B. S., 205–6
Halifax, Charles Lindley Wood, 2nd Viscount, 325
Halifax, Edward Frederick Lindley Wood, 1st Earl of, 325
Hall, Radclyffe, 56–7
Hall, Stanley: Fund, 190
Hall, Trevor, 323
Hand, Sarah A., 149
Harcourt, Vernon, 308
Hardie, Keir, 48
Harper's (magazine), 322
Hart, M. D., 209
Harvard University, 42, 147, 304, 314; *see also* Crandon, Mina
hauntings, 127–8
Haynes, Renée, 43, 200, 304, 329
Heald, C. B., 209–11
Heisenberg, Werner Carl, 194, 316–17
Helmholtz, Hermann L. F. von, 40
Helson, Harry, 160–1
Henze, Paul, 129
Herbert, C. V. C. *see* Powis, C. V. C. Herbert, 6th Earl of
Heywood, Rosalind: *The Sixth Sense*, 274, 282, 285, 301, 330–1
Hicks, Rev. E. Savell, 58–60
'higher phenomena', 18, 21, 201, 308
Hill, Elsie (*née* Wright), 89–90, 92
Hill, J. Arthur, 49, 52, 256, 259, 316
Hinchliffe, Capt. Walter, 277
Hitching, Francis, 340
Hitler, Adolf, 106, 304
Hoagland, Hudson, 177, 179–86, 296
Hodgson, Richard, 24, 26, 148
Hodgson Memorial Fund (Harvard University), 147, 155, 262, 264, 304, 313–14
Holms, Campbell: *The Facts of Psychic Science*, 217
Home, Daniel Dunglas, 19–20, 23, 35, 67, 123, 160, 173, 312
Hope, Lord Charles, 246–53, 286–7
Hope, William, 86–7, 92–4, 257–9
Horace: *Carmen Saeculare*, 50
Horder, Thomas, 1st Baron, 209–11
Houdini, Harry: and 'Eva C', 102, 163, 165, 339; reproduces Kluski phenomena, 121; and 'Margery', 162–4, 166–9, 177, 187–9, 295; and spiritualism, 164–6, 207; death, 189; and Clark University symposium, 190; and Murray, 207–8

375

Huggins, William, 200
Hume, David, 17–18
Huxley, T. H., 53
hyperacuity (hyperesthesia; 'Cumberlandism'), 116, 118, 202–7
hyperesthesia *see* hyperacuity
hypnosis, 205, 306–10
Hyslop, James Hervey, 25, 27, 85, 143–4, 155; death, 148; *Contact with the other World*, 147
'hysterical fugue', 307

'I-principle', 336
'identifying paramnesia', 230
'ideoplasty', 100
Inge, W. R., Dean of St Paul's, 70
Institut Métapsychique International, 95, 120, 240, 243, 245, 251, 304
International Congress for Psychical Research: 1st, Copenhagen, 1921, 114, 117, 155, 197; 2nd, Warsaw, 1923, 135; 4th, Athens, 1930, 304; 5th, Oslo, 1935, 304
Irving, Rev. W. S., 214
Irwin, Flight-Lieut. H. Carmichael, 277

Jacks, L. P., 332
Jackson, Freddy, 85–6
James, Henry (novelist), 26
James, Henry (son of William), 314
James, William, 22, 25–6, 40–1, 43, 153, 310, 314
Janet, Pierre, 128, 150, 155, 308
Jastrow, Joseph, 26, 141, 155, 190, 194, 290, 312–14, 340
'Java Man', 340
Jeans, Sir James, 317
Jephson, Ina, 265–6, 281
Joad, C. E. M., 249, 321–3
Jodl, Alfred, 40
Johnson, Alice, 43, 47, 330
Johnson, Gertrude, 283–5, 319–20
Johnson, J. M., 212–13
Jolly, W. P., 305
Jones, Ernest, 311
Journal of Abnormal (and Social) Psychology, 267, 309
Journal of Parapsychology, 277, 290
Jung, Carl Gustav, 44, 311–12, 318

Kaempffert, Waldemar, 275
Kardec, Alain, 125
Kastenbaum, Robert, 202
Kellogg, Chester E., 290, 322
Kelvin, William Thomson, Baron, 316
Kemnitz, Mathilde von (*later* Ludendorff), 33, 99
'King, Katie', 28
'King, John' (Eusapia's control), 22–3, 160, 335
Kluski, Franek, 119–22, 138
Krebs, Stanley L., 26–7
Kuhn, Thomas, 339

Lady (horse), 267
Lafayette (magician), 165
Lambert, Rudolf, 240–1
Lancet (journal), 211
Lane, Sir Hugh, 60, 62, 302
Lang, Andrew, 88, 310
Lankester, Ray, 41–2
Lanyi, Joseph de, Bishop of Grosswardin, 45, 337
Laplace, 227
Larkin, James, 74–5
Lashley, K. S., 314
Lecky, W. E. H., 39
Leclainche, E., 130
Lee, Margarite du Pont, 85
Lee, Wallace, 273
Lefroy, Major H., 209
Leonard, Frederick, 54
Leonard, Gladys Osborne: and Lodges and Raymond, 50–2, 305; mediumship, 54–7, 67, 118, 331–3; and Radclyffe Hall, 56–7; SPR and, 70–1, 202, 214–15, 326–7; and Blatchford, 197; Brown and, 247; portrait of, 303; *see also* 'Feda'
Lewis, Mrs Wilfred, 332–3
Light (journal), 66, 68, 75, 83, 251
Lindemann, Frederick A. (*later* 1st Viscount Cherwell), 248
Linzmayer, A. J., 272–3
Lippman, Walter, 207
Litvag, Irving: *Singer in the Shadows*, 145–6
Lodge, Mary, Lady, 50–1
Lodge, Sir Oliver: and SPR, 22, 255–6; and Leonora Piper, 22; on

Index

Tyndall, 40; on automatic writing, 46; and survival, 48–50, 58, 69; and 'Raymond', 50–2; and Crawford, 66; and experiences, 74; on Fournier d'Albe, 81; and Hope's pictures, 86–7; and Cottingley fairies, 90, 92; and Guzik, 131; tribute to Geley, 137–8; influence on Crandon, 157; at Clark University, 190–1; and Eusapia Palladino, 194, 305; and Mrs Dawson-Smith, 198–9; on Haldane and Murray, 205; on temperature changes, 218; and BBC telepathy investigations, 219; on Doyle, 221, 256; on precognition, 235; on Brown, 247; on scientific scepticism, 254, 312, 341; autobiography, 255; and Hope, 259; and 'Walter's' wooden rings, 294; on Richet, 302, 328; portrait of, 303; death and tributes, 305; and new physics, 316; and spontaneous phenomena, 324; reputation, 340; *My Philosophy*, 312, 324; *Raymond*, 52–3, 55, 67; *The Survival of Man*, 49
Lodge, Raymond, 50, 52
Lombroso, Cesare, 328
London, Jack, 268
London University: Council for Psychical Investigation, 321–3
Lowell, A. Lawrence, 189
Lüder, Lina, 116
Lumière, Auguste, 139
Lundholm, Helge, 267
Lusitania, SS, 60–1, 231, 302
Lyttelton, Dame Edith, 231–4, 320
Lyttelton, Mary, 329
Lytton, Edward George Bulwer, 1st Baron, 20

Macaulay, F. W., 332
McComas, Henry Clay, 187–9
McConnell, David, 74–5
McCullough, 247
McDougall, William: vitalism, 95, 192; dualism, 127; career and writings, 152–6; Presidential Address to SPR, 154; and 'Margery', 156, 160–2, 170, 174–5, 177, 182, 189, 191, 262, 268, 295, 304; and Houdini, 189–90; at Clark University, 190–1; and Murphy, 262; Rhine and, 267, 274, 277, 324; and Sinclairs, 270–1; and physical phenomena, 296, 304, 341; death, 304
Mackenzie, Andrew: *Hauntings and Apparitions*, 326
McKenzie, James Hewat, 93, 323–4
Maeterlinck, Maurice, 228, 339; *The Unknown Guest*, 38
Magic Circle, 216
Mängl, Mitzi, 245, 249
Mann, Thomas, 109–11, 179, 339
Marais, Eugene: *Soul of the White Ant*, 38
'Margery' *see* Crandon, Mina
Margery Harvard Veritas, 182–7, 196
Marriott, William, 92–3
Martinique, 229–30
materialisation, 127–8, 193, 224–6; *see also* 'full-form' materialisations
Matin, Le (newspaper), 32
Mauskopf, Seymour H. and McVaugh, Michael R.: *The Elusive Science*, 260, 274, 276
Mayo, Herbert, 307–8
mediumship, 326, 327–31, 335–6; *see also* individual mediums and controls
Mercier, Charles A., 52
Mermet, Abbé A., 326
Mesmer, Franz Anton, 18
'metagnomy', 274
meteorites, 18
Metropolitan Magazine, 26
Meyer, Jean, 95
Meyer, Robert, 117
'Mina' (Willy Schneider's control), 110
Mirabelli, Carlos, 221–7, 297–8
miracles, 17
Miroir, Le (journal), 32
Mont Pelée, Martinique, 229–30
Moody, Raymond: *Life after Life*, 201
More, Adelyne ('A.M.'), 205–7
Morel, Madame, 132–4
Morselli, Enrico, 328
Moses, Stainton: *Spirit Teachings*, 47

377

Muensterberg, Hugo, 26–7, 141, 147, 154, 340
multiple personality, 152, 306–10
Munn, Orson, 161
Murchison, Carl, 190, 194–5
Murphy, Gardner, 160, 190, 228, 261–4, 301, 329, 341
Murray, Gilbert, 202–8, 270–1, 288, 322, 332
Myers, Eveleen (*née* Tennant; Mrs Frederick Myers), 27
Myers, Frederick: and SPR, 21–2, 43, 232; and cross-correspondences, 47–8, 50, 330; Richet and, 127, 194; vitalism, 247; anti-materialism, 310; and spontaneous phenomena, 325; *Human Personality*, 87, 214, 266; *see also* Frederick Myers Lectures

Napoleon III, Emperor of the French, 20
National Laboratory for Psychical Research, 218–19, 237, 243, 248–9, 252; *Bulletin*, 250
Nature (journal), 218–19, 228, 314–15
New Scientist (journal), 69
Newton, Sir Isaac, 18
New York Herald Tribune, 275
New York Times, 177, 181, 275
Nichols, Beverley, 211

'O., Mrs', 337
Ochorowicz, Julian, 34–6, 118, 194, 341; *Mental Suggestion*, 36
Oesterreich, Traugott, 135, 217, 237, 304–5
'Olga' (Rudi Schneider's control), 250
Olliver, C. W., 282
Ossowiecki, Stefan, 122–5, 135–6, 217, 285–7; death, 305
Ostrander, Sheila and Schroeder, Lynn: *Psi: Psychic Discoveries behind the Iron Curtain*, 305
Osty, Eugène: and Madame Przybylska, 119; career and methods, 132–3; and Madame Morel, 132–5; and Perovsky, 222; and 'Eva C' photographs, 240–2; and Rudi Schneider, 243–5, 252–3; photographic apparatus, 244, 250;

300; and Price, 245–6, 249, 252–3; and 'metagnomy', 274; on Forthuny, 287–8; death, 304; *Supernormal Faculties in Man*, 132, 135
Osty, Marcel, 244
ouija board, 46–7
Ousterhout, Dr, 180

Pagenstecher, Gustav, 150–2
Palladino, Eusapia: mediumship and powers, 23–7, 35, 173; scientific experiments on, 24, 26, 28, 63, 131; 'cheating' in trance, 26, 99–100, 120, 255; SPR report on, 24–5, 113; Richet and, 28, 127, 194; Bergson and, 36; Barrett and, 64; pseudopods, 78, 112; Jastrow and, 194; Lodge and, 305; death, 328
Palmer, E. Clephan, 276
Palmstierna, Erik, Baron, 333–5
'Palm-Sunday' case, 329
paraphysics, 315–19
parapsychology, 310–15
Pauli, Wolfgang, 318
Pearce, Hubert, 273, 275–6
Pennsylvania, University of, 42
Perovsky, Count, 222, 240, 255
Perrin, Jean-Baptiste, 24
Peters, Vout, 51
Phantasms of the Living, 73
'Phinuit, Dr' (Mrs Piper's control), 22
photography: investigation of, 83–92; Osty's apparatus, 244; affected by clairvoyants, 256–9
physics *see* paraphysics
Piddington, J. G., 43, 215, 325
Pieron, Henri, 128
Pilsudski, Marshal Josef, 123
Piltdown fraud, 340
Piper, Leonora, 22, 38, 42, 47, 50, 54, 261
planchette, 47–8
Podmore, Frank, 44, 101, 127, 194, 201, 217, 227, 341
poetry, trance, 233
Poincaré, Henri, 316
Poland, 118–25
Pollard, A. F. C., 250
poltergeists, 35–6, 114–15, 127, 201, 221

Index

Powis, C. V. C. Herbert, 6th Earl of, 245, 252, 298
Pratt, Gaither, 273
precognition (prevision), 227–31, 234–6, 300, 320–1, 337
Prévost, Marcel, 130
Price, Harry: investigates Hope, 93–4, 252, 258; and Willy Schneider, 106; library, 106, 220, 321, 323; and SPR, 106, 218, 220, 237, 239, 243, 255, 321–2; sets up National Laboratory for Psychical Research, 218–19, 245; and Rudi Schneider, 237–9, 245–54, 315, 321; publicity, 246, 248–9, 253, 322; suspicions over, 246–7, 340; and Brocken (Walpurgisnacht) legend, 248–9, 255; and University of London, 321–3; and Soal, 322; and popular interest, 325; and dowsing, 327
Price, Henry Habberley, 305, 307, 309–10
Priestley, J. B., 230, 236
Prince, Morton, 143, 150, 152, 155, 267, 306–7, 309
Prince, Walter Franklin: at Copenhagen Congress, 114, 155; and 'Doris Fischer', 143, 148, 306; and 'Patience Worth', 144–5; and ASPR, 148, 155–6, 194; career and experiences, 148–9; and Senora de Zierold, 150–2; and McDougall, 155; and 'Margery', 162, 167–8, 177, 186, 195–6; and Houdini, 165–6, 168; resigns over Bird, 182; at Clark University, 190, 194–5; and Crandons, 194–5, 238, 295–6; and Mirabelli reports, 226; and Rudi Schneider, 238; and Rhine, 274, 281, 296, 315; and telepathy tests, 275; death, 281, 296; and Bird's dismissal, 293; *The Enchanted Boundary*, 165, 296
Przybylska, Madame, 118–19
pseudopods, 27, 78, 82, 112–13, 120, 163, 166, 174, 179, 295; *see also* ectoplasm; teleplasm
Psyche (journal), 205
Psychische Studien, 44

psychokinesis (PK), 83, 298
psychology, 308–9
psychometry, 150–2
Pulitzer, Ralph, 207

quantum physics, 318, 338–9

R., Madame, 132–3
R 101 (airship), 277
radionics, 211
Rampling-Rose, Major W., 258
Ramsbury (Wiltshire), 325
Rayleigh, John William Strutt, 3rd Baron, 22, 24, 67–8, 154, 200, 206
Rayleigh, Robert John Strutt, 4th Baron, 246, 249, 251, 253–4, 299–300, 305, 332
Renan, Ernest, 48
Revelations of a Spirit Medium, 171
Revue Métapsychique, 95, 119
Rhine, Joseph Banks: career and methods, 266–7, 276–8, 290–1, 323; and Zener cards, 271–4, 277, 290–2; SPR and, 278–9, 319; Soal and, 281–2; and Tyrrell, 283, 285; criticisms of, 290–1; and psychokinesis, 298; Boring and, 313; and precognition, 321; Soal attacks, 322; integrity, 341; *Extra-sensory Perception*, 118, 260, 274–6, 278, 290, 294, 296, 315, 320, 324; *New Frontiers of the Mind*, 290, 321
Rhine, Louisa (née Weckesser), 266–7, 298, 301, 321
Richet, Charles: and 'Eva C', 27–9, 32–3, 98–9, 101, 104, 240–2, 339; and Eusapia Palladino, 28, 127, 194; and Sarajevo precognition, 44; and Institut Métapsychique International, 95; and 'full-form' materialisation, 96; and Kluski, 119–21; and Ossowiecki, 123–4; career and writings, 126–9, 158; and Guzik, 131; Crandon on, 176; and death-bed visions, 201; tests, 218, 267; on precognition, 235; Besterman disparages, 239, 242; Nobel Prize, 289, 301, 302; reputation, 301, 340–1; death, 302;

379

Richet, Charles – *cont.*
 materialism, 328, 339; and
 Bozzano, 328–9; *Thirty Years of
 Psychical Research*, 328
Riess, Bernard, 290
Rinn, Joseph, 121–2
Rivers, W. H. R., 152, 305
Robinson, Lennox, 58–60
Rogers, Edmund Dawson, 21
Rogers, Mrs Edmund Dawson *see*
 Curran, Mrs Pearl, 232
Romains, Jules, 318–19
'Rooney, Peter' (Mrs Travers Smith's control), 59–60
Royal Society of Medicine, 210
Ruskin, John, 20, 22
Russell, Bertrand, 69
Russell, George *see* A.E.

Salter, Helen (*née* Verrall): and 'Eva C', 99–100; at Copenhagen Congress, 114; and 'Feda', 198, 214; and Mrs Dawson-Smith, 200; and Irving, 214; Besterman succeeds, 220; and Mirabelli, 222; and Eleanor Sidgwick, 304
Salter, W. H., 246, 322–3
Saltmarsh, H. F., 320–1, 330
Santoliquido, Rocco, 130
Sarajevo, 45, 337
Sauerbrey, Ernst (and family), 114–15
Scatcherd, F. R.: *Survival*, 68
Schiller, F. C. S.: and scientific scepticism, 40; reviews Schrenck, 99; on Osty's case histories, 135; on 'Patience' and Mrs Curran, 142; on Coover, 146–7; on Hodgson Memorial Fund, 155, 278; at Clark University, 190–2; on spontaneous phenomena, 324–5; death, 324
Schneider, Rudi, 237–9, 243–6, 248–54, 298, 315, 321; breathing speed, 254
Schneider, Willy, 105–13, 119, 179, 215–16, 237
Schrenck-Notzing, Albert von, Baron: and 'Eva C', 29, 32–4, 97–9, 101–4, 106, 113, 174, 240–2, 339; and Stanislawa Tomczyk, 35, 98; Crawford and, 82; and Willy

Schneider, 105–13; at Copenhagen Congress, 114; at Warsaw Congress, 135–6; and 'Margery', 171; Crandon on, 176; and sceptics, 217–18; and Mirabelli, 222; death, 237, 304; and Rudi Schneider, 237–8; Besterman disparages, 239, 242; materialism, 328, 339; reputation, 340–1
Schumann, Robert A., 334–5
Science News Letter, 291–2
Science Service, 291–2
Scientific American (journal), 161, 163, 166, 169, 177, 182, 188, 275
Selborne, William W. Palmer, 2nd Earl of, 325
'serialism', 231, 236
Seybert report, 294
Shapley, Harlow, 178, 180
Shaw, George Bernard, 48
Sheldrake, Rupert, 192
'shell-shock', 307
Sidgwick, Eleanor: and SPR, 24–5, 43, 98; on cross-correspondence, 47, 53–4; belief in survival, 49, 53–4; and Mrs Leonard, 55; and Ireland, 58; criticises Crawford, 66, 76, 80, 299; on results of tests, 72–3; and individual cases, 75; historical analysis, 125–6; at Warsaw Congress, 135; and Mrs Dawson-Smith, 200; and Barrett, 201; and Gilbert Murray, 204–5; and Price, 246; made SPR 'President of Honour', 255; and telepathy experiments, 264; and 'Walter' thumbprint, 294; on Richet, 302; portrait of, 303; death and tributes, 304
Sidgwick, Henry: and SPR, 21, 43–4; and fraud, 23–5, 253, 315, 340; death, 24, 43; reputation, 40, 42; automatic writing, 47
Sinclair, Mary Craig, 268–71
Sinclair, Upton, 268–71, 317
Skinner, B. F., 291, 314
Slade, Henry, 41, 294
Smith, Susy, 331
Smith, Mrs Travers (*née* Dowden), 58–62

Index

Smith, Whately *see* Carington, Whately
Smith-Battles Fund, 190
Soal, S. G., 235, 279–82, 299, 319, 321–2, 326, 340
Société Astronomique, 125
Society for Psychical Research: founded, 21–2, 200; Presidential Addresses, 37, 67, 154, 202–3, 207, 215, 254, 299–300, 307, 309; scepticism in, 42–4; scientist members, 69; and William Hope photographs, 93–4; and 'Eva C', 98–105; and Harry Price, 106, 218, 220, 237, 239, 243, 255, 321–2; and Willy Schneider, 106; and Flammarion, 126; and Ossowiecki, 135–6; and 'Margery', 175–6; and 'Feda', 197–8, 214, 331; Barrett and, 200–2; inter-war investigations, 202–15, 324–7; dissensions in, 215, 226, 243, 249, 292; and BBC telepathy experiments, 219–20, 322; Besterman and, 220, 243, 297; and Dunne, 235–6; and Rudi Schneider, 249, 251; and trickery, 255; and Rhine, 278–9, 319; Jung and, 311; negativism, 319–20; and dowsing, 326–7; *Journal*, 66, 71, 73, 115, 212, 214, 222, 252, 258, 335, 337; *Proceedings*, 41, 53, 73, 75, 77–8, 169, 176, 198, 201, 212–14, 250, 285
Society for the Study of Supernormal Pictures, 83, 87
Sophie, Queen of the Netherlands, 20
spontaneous phenomena, 324–7, 339
Spray, Arthur, 326
Stanford University, 42, 146–7
Stanley, Dorothy (*née* Tennant; wife of H. M. Stanley), 27
Stephens, James, 58
Stewart, Balfour, 22
Stobart, Mrs St Clair, 70
Strand (magazine), 88
Sudre, René: on Kluski, 120; and Ossowiecki, 124–5; at Warsaw Congress, 135; on Geley, 137; on Jephson trials, 266; and 'metagnomy', 274; and Forthuny, 287–8; on Osty, 304
Sunday Dispatch (newspaper), 250, 252
superconscious mind, 231–4
'super-ESP', 328, 332, 336
survival, 329–30, 331–7
Swaffer, Hannen, 294

table-turning (and moving), 18–19, 65, 76–7, 82, 181–2, 206, 253–4
Talbot, Mrs Hugh, 55–6
Tarde, Gabriel, 228
Taylor, H. Dennis, 105
Taylor, J. Traill, 84–5, 105
telekinesis: Home practises, 20; as natural phenomenon, 38; Podmore discredits, 44; Barrett accepts, 64; and ectoplasm, 80; Richet on, 127–8; Mirabelli and, 223, 297; Rudi Schneider and, 253–4
'telepathic leakage', 59–60, 335
telepathy: scientific resistance to, 38, 40, 314; and 'Feda', 73; tests and experiments on, 115–18; and Murray's 'hyperesthesia', 205–7; BBC experiments on, 219, 322; Warcollier on, 261–2, 281; Murphy and, 263; Estabrooks and, 264–5; *Scientific American* tests, 275; Berger on, 288–9; *see also* Zener, K. F.
teleplasm, 111–13, 170–2, 178, 187
Tenhaeff, W. H. C., 337
Tennant, Edward Wyndham ('Bim'), 72
Tennyson, Alfred, Lord, 22
Thackeray, William Makepeace, 20
Thomas, Rev. C. Drayton, 71–2, 114, 232, 331–3
Thomas, John F., 324
Thomson, Sir Joseph John, 22, 24, 327; *Recollections and Reflections*, 332
thought transference, 201
'thoughtography', 257–8, 301
Thouless, R. H., 241, 278–9, 320, 329
Tietze, Thomas R., 157, 186–7, 293, 295–6
Tillyard, E. J., 218–19, 322–3

381

Times, The (newspaper), 71, 126, 205, 247–8
Tischner, Rudolf, 116–17, 217, 237, 272, 304
Tomczyk, Stanislawa *later* Feilding, 34–6, 38, 98, 104, 113, 118
Tovey, Sir Donald, 334
Toynbee, Rosalind (*née* Murray), 203–4
Troland, Leonard Thompson, 147, 155, 262, 313
Trollope, Thomas Augustus, 20
Troubridge, Una, Lady, 56–7, 70–1
Tubby, Gertrude, 149
Tyndall, John, 40–1, 49, 316, 338
Tyrrell, G. M. N., 282–3, 300, 319–20, 335–6

Utrecht, University of, 337
'Uvani' (Eileen Garrett's control), 276–7

Valée, Professor, 130
Valentine, George, 166
van de Water, Marjorie, 291
Verrall, Mrs A. W., 43, 47–8, 50, 203–5
Verrall, Helen *see* Salter, Helen
Vesme, César de, 310
Viré, Armand, 326
Vitalism, 95, 97, 153, 192

W., Dr, 65
Walker, Mary S., 297
Wallace, Alfred Russel, 20, 22, 44, 87, 200

'Walter' (Mina Crandon's control), 157, 160, 162–3, 167–73, 175, 177–80, 182, 184–5, 196, 292–6
Warcollier, René, 261–2, 264, 280–1
Warsaw *see* International Congress for Psychical Research, 2nd
Watson, J. B., 207, 314
Way, Frances (*née* Griffiths), 89–90, 92
Webb, Sidney and Beatrice, 48
Wells, H. G., 153, 228
Westminster Gazette, 66
Weygand, General Max, 119
Whitehead, Alfred North, 316–17
Wilberforce, Samuel, Bishop of Oxford, 53
'Willett, Mrs' *see* Coombe-Tennant, Winifred
Wood, R. W., 187
Woolley, V. J., 100, 219, 220
Worcester, Elwood, 155, 170, 172–4
'Worth, Patience' (Pearl Curran's control), 141–4, 232
Wright, Mrs, 89
Wundt, Wilhelm, 40

Yeats, W. B., 33–4, 58, 104, 294
Yost, Casper, 142–4

Zener, K. F.: cards, 271, 275, 277–8, 290–2
zenoglossy, 328
Zierold, Senora Maria Reyes de ('Senora de Z') 150–2
Zöllner, Johann, 294
Zugun, Eleanore, 218, 322–3

www.ingramcontent.com/pod-product-compliance
Lightning Source LLC
Chambersburg PA
CBHW020322170426
43200CB00006B/241